M000315184

SURVIVAL OF SPECIES

SOL ROTHMAN

A 1940's Bronx tenement kid survives a childhood of dyslexic
confusion and cruel, alcoholic abuse to test his crazy
wit and talent in Will Eisner's art bullpen.

Survival of Species
A 1940's Bronx tenement kid survives a childhood of dyslexic confusion and cruel,
alcoholic abuse to test his crazy wit and talent in Will Eisner's art bullpen.
All Rights Reserved.
Copyright © 2017 Sol Rothman
v3.0

ISBN: 978-1-7351002-0-3

Library of Congress Control Number: 2020909938

Survival of Species contains mature content and may not be suitable for all readers. This book is a
personal memoir and many of the names have been changed to protect the privacy of individuals I
have known.

Cover Photo © 2020 Sol Rothman. All rights reserved - used with permission.

Cover design: Sol Rothman, Sharon Rothman
Cover graphics and production: Claudine Calabrese Joyce
Production Edit: Sharon Rothman; Kimberly Hayes

First Edition 2020
Croes Fly Media, Publisher
9 4th Street,
Bergenfield, NJ 07621
www.croesflymedia.com

*The flying crow logo is a trademark of Croes Fly Media, a symbol of creative freedom and progressive
ethics in publishing.*

Visit the author's website at: www.solrothman.com/book-blog;
www.facebook.com/SolRothmanAuthor

PRINTED IN THE UNITED STATES OF AMERICA

This book is for my Mom.
I love her completely, but never really understood her
until now

ACKNOWLEDGEMENTS

MY FEELINGS FOR my sister, Millie, my only witness, go deep. She alone shared the secret hell we went through at the hands of our step-father, Harold. Reliving it through writing my story has helped us both come to some kind of terms with the fact of Harold's abuse.

But this book would still be on my desk if it weren't for Sharon, my beloved friend and wife of 56 years. She shares my sideways sense of humor, and loves exploring cosmic concepts with me. Through the years, Sharon has been my greatest supporter, and keeps my inspiration alive; she has listened to my stories a thousand times over, and is skilled at untwisting my dyslexic delivery. Her unwavering belief in me helps me believe in myself.

I love that my son, Evan Laurence, and I are linked together intuitively, and can share our improvisational humor every day. I greatly appreciate his contributions in laying the foundation for my author bio, and his expertise in editing suggestions for the front matter of this book.

My sincere thanks go to Kimberly Hayes for her valuable insights in shepherding my manuscript through the maze of perfect punctuation and grammar, not easy when dealing with my Bronx vernacular. Kim understands what I'm trying to say from her own experience, and her respect for my writing has meant a lot to me.

My long friendship with Claudine Calabrese Joyce and Stephen Joyce is built on hours of hysterical laughing and creative collaboration. With Steve's passing, I lost a tender friend who identified with my craziness, and shared his love of music with me. His dear wife, Claudine, a true graphic design talent, has translated my rough design into a powerful cover for this book. I am grateful for her creative flexibility, type savvy, and impeccable design eye.

Thanks to Cecily Moore, www.thepapercurator.com, for her graphic design skills in formatting my art website and book blog: www.solrothman.com.

My creative vision found a home at Croes Fly Media and I'm grateful for their respect, patient guidance, and support throughout the publishing process. Many thanks to Outskirts Press for their attention to quality in the printing of this book.

TABLE OF CONTENTS

Part Two
Bronx: Survival of Species

Part Three
The Little House on 32nd Street

INTRODUCTION

GOOD OR BAD, the people I grew up with in my neighborhood were part of my life. They were just human beings trying to exist the best way they knew how, coping with their pain and hopes in an imperfect world.

I've been both blessed and cursed with a good memory of my childhood growing up in the South Bronx. Everyone who knows me has heard me tell about my crazy adventures – but for this telling, I remembered deeper than I thought I ever could, reliving the brutality and fear, the crushing erosion of self, and the shame I kept hidden inside for a long lifetime.

And though my experience is from a different time and place in history, it gives voice to generations of defenseless children, abused in countless ways, whose pain still lives inside them, spilling out into their adult lives, as it did in mine. I want them to know they can survive and live a creative life.

PART ONE
BRONX: ORIGIN OF SPECIES

HARD TIMES

IT WAS JANUARY 13, 1936, a cold, snowy Monday afternoon, when I burst into this new world.

Sounds and voices filter through in floating dreams of my first recollections of childhood – many little islands of unconnected memories, incomplete pictures that fade in and out of my consciousness. As soon as I remember one, it's gone and another takes its place. In between my brief recollections are stories told to me so many times that some of them have become part of my own memories.

I was two years old in 1938. These were the hard times of the Great Depression, and the WPA was at its peak. My father, Manny, dug ditches during the day, and at night, he worked in the garment district making buttonholes on garments. Still, it wasn't enough to feed a family of five, and when they couldn't use him digging ditches, we had to live on Welfare.

We were living then on Croes Avenue in the South Bronx. One morning my mom was cooking beef neck-bones in a large jar she had placed in a pot of water, simmering it very slowly over a low flame to extract the juices from the bones. The rich smell warmed our kitchen.

Without knocking, a thin woman with her face flushed almost beet red, walked into our apartment. She was a Welfare worker. She never said a word, and as if my mother wasn't there, investigated our apartment like she owned it and owned my mom.

"What are you cooking there?" Not giving my mom a chance to answer, "Is that beef I smell? How can you afford meat?" She said it as if my mom had committed a crime.

"I didn't pay a dime for dem neck-bones. The butcher gave it to me for nuttin'."

In those days you didn't have to pay for beef bones, the neighborhood butcher would give them for free. The Welfare worker didn't believe my mom and talked down to her, scolding her like she was a child.

"It's people like you ignorant foreigners who come to this country and take advantage of the good people. You should be ashamed of yourself!"

"I don't have to take dis crap!"

Even if it meant not being able to collect Welfare, Mom took hold of the woman's coat collar and threw her out of our apartment.

She went back to the stove where she was rendering chicken fat with onions. When she finished, she poured the chicken fat into a few jars, leaving the greasy-crisp pieces of chicken skin and onions in the frying pan – what my mother called 'greavelach,' and I later called a heart attack. But my sister, Millie, and I craved those little, greasy missiles that detonated in our stomachs. It was a losing battle in our childhood of indigestion -- what we thought was a natural condition.

After the Welfare worker abruptly left, my oldest brother, Harry, interrupted Mom's cooking with tears in his eyes.

"Vhat's da matter? Vhat's da matter, bubbala?"

"Alex took my ball."

"So, you're a big boy – get it back."

"I did, but his mother screamed at me to let him have my ball."

Mom took Harry's hand and, swishing her apron off into the air behind her, "We'll see about dat."

Outside, Harry and Mom found Alex and took back Harry's ball. From one of the apartment windows, Alex's mother, Mrs. Viola, screamed out at my mom, "You fuckin' bastard! Don't you touch my son!"

"What are you talkin'? I ain't touchin' him. I'm just takin' the ball that belongs to my Harry."

"It's okay, Alex. Give it back. I don't want you to catch anything from that filthy, stinkin' Jew boy."

"Vhat did you say?"

"You heard me, a filthy Jew boy. All you Jew bastards are filthy, dirty, diseased people."

"Come down here and say dat!"

"Okay, I will!"

Mrs. Viola's window slammed shut and a minute later she was facing my mom. Her face was as hard as her body. Trying to look mean and dangerous, she spoke out from the turned down corners of her mouth, "Okay, you Jew bitch, here I am, and your son is still a slimy little Jew bastard!"

"Are you going to take dat back?"

Mrs. Viola gave a quick flip of her fingertips from under her chin, "Up your ass!"

Before she knew what was happening, Mrs. Viola was on her back with Mom on top of her, swinging her fists across Viola's face, playing her like a drum.

"Get offa me! Get offa me, you asshole... get the fuck offa me!"

A crowd gathered and cheered Mom on. Even Mr. Viola cheered for Mom, "That's it, Molly! Give it to her. The old witch is always asking for it. Give it to her! Teach her a lesson!"

A cop pushed his way through the crowd, "What's going on here?" As soon as he saw who it was, "That's it, Molly, give her hell!"

Our neighbors had built strong resentments toward Mrs. Viola but never stood up to her. Now all of their frustrations were being released through my mom's punches.

Sobbing, her voice shaking, gulping air, "Okay... okay... I'm sorry."

"And you'll never say those things to my son? Say it, say it."

"Yes, yes... Never again!"

My mother let her go. Crying, she ran back into her building, "Fuck you, Molly! Fuck you! Fuck you and your fuckin' kids!"

After that day Mrs. Viola made sure she avoided my mom and Mom never had any trouble with her again. After that day, Mr. Viola was a very happy man.

A year later, Mom's uncle, Moishe, got her a full time job in a sweatshop working on furs. He was in the garment industry and knew a lot of people. It didn't pay much, but it was work. Sometimes Mom would come home with cardboard boxes filled with fur collars. She spent nights sewing the furs by hand in the living room. It was called piecework. The fur smelled up the house like wet dogs. She had to be careful because piecework was illegal for union workers. For Mom it was easy work because of her experience with furs on her father's farm in Bessarabia, before she came to America.

My brother, Walter, came home from his after school job at a grocery store on Watson Avenue just in time for one of Mom and Manny's screaming bouts, which were always about money. Every week Manny played the numbers and this time he won $180. That was a lot of money. Today that would have been about three thousand dollars. With that money, Manny wanted to start his own business, a vending cart selling frankfurters. Mom thought he was nuts and argued against it, "A cart! Vhat are you crazy? Vhat da hell are you talkin' about? We have bills. We need food, clothes and utta things... we need the money now! Such a mashugana."

"But it will be my own business. I'll have a permanent job. And I'll be making money!"

"You don't know dat."

"You're a stupid woman."

Mom looked up from her piecework, "Manny, you don't know vhat it is to be a man."

Manny said, "And who the hell are you? I want to do something right. You're killing me!"

"So die! Why don't you die?"

It got worse and more words were spoken that could never be taken back. It ended in bitter resentment toward each other. Mom won the argument and the money was gone in a few weeks, paying off the bills that were owing. And we were broke again.

THE TURKEY
COMMITS SUICIDE

FROM THE OTHER room I could hear the music, *Elmer's Tune*. At first I couldn't separate it from the background noises, but eventually it became part of the memory unfolding in front of me. I was four years old and lying on my Mom's bed watching her decorate herself like a Christmas tree. A soft belt was cinched around her waist, with black straps dangling down both sides of her thighs. She snapped the buckled ends of the straps to a pair of silk stockings that hugged the shape of her calves and thighs, and left naked skin peeking between the garter belt and stockings.

Mom turned slightly, arched her back and, like a ballerina, stood on her toes and lifted one of her legs. Reaching down, she felt the smooth, full curves of her leg, following the dark seam line of her stocking up to her thigh. She slipped on a silky, blue dress with a sparkly-white, sequined feather traveling diagonally across the front of its form-fitting torso, caressing her shapely body.

Around her neck she draped several rows of marble-sized white beads, each painted with tiny red flowers. Every once in awhile she would step back, puff on a cigarette, and take a long look at herself, admiring her creative efforts. Noticing me watching her reflection in the mirror, she smiled as she applied the finishing touches – lipstick, rouge, and little red mobiles that dangled from her ears. They jingled every time she moved her head, announcing, "Here I am, look at me!"

Manny was a good-hearted man with a sense of humor, but he didn't joke around too often. These were desperate times and there was not much to laugh about. But this was a special night, and I could hear Mom and Manny laughing from the other room as they prepared. They were going out to a party given by the garment workers union.

Impatient with Manny, Mom asked, "Did you call Sondra?"

"Of course I did."

"Vel, vhere is she?"

"Stop worrying... it's still oily."

"You talk like a mockey."

"And you talk so good?"

As soon as the babysitter, Sondra, walked in, Manny and Mom left the apartment, and I began to cry. Sondra calmed me down enough to tell me a story.

"Did you ever hear about the Sandman?"

I stared at her face as she told me the story. I loved Sondra.

Her skin was creamy and smooth like chocolate milk.

"Well, the Sandman lives in the walls, always watching, and he has these hungry wild wolves as pets, living in a dark pit right here under our feet. If you listen very carefully you can hear them growling, with spit bubbling from their mouths and around their sharp white teeth, waiting to eat little boys that cry and won't go to sleep.

"The Sandman searches at night for these little bad boys and, when he finds them, he takes them away and throws them into the dark pit where no one will ever hear from them again. It's so dark down there that you can only see the red eyes and white, sharp teeth of the growling wolves. Then the hungry wolves will tear you to pieces. First, they'll eat your eyes out, then your arms and legs until there's nothing left of you."

That did it. She didn't have to say another word. I closed my eyes and pretended to be asleep. I spent half the night listening to the creaking sounds in the walls. I knew it was the Sandman coming for me to carry me away behind the walls and into his black pit with the hungry wolves.

Sondra was on the couch in the living room, which was also my bedroom, and during the night, half asleep, I heard whispered moans that I thought were part of my dreams. Then out of the night, loud laughing voices, mingled with a screeching wild animal sound, crashed into the living room from the front door. Sondra jumped to her feet, pulled away from her boyfriend and straightened her dress.

In the doorway behind Mom, Manny was struggling with a live turkey in his arms, almost as big as he was. The turkey's head was poking rapidly in and out of Manny's armpits as he tried to hold onto its twisting legs.

During all the commotion, the boyfriend slipped out the front door, leaving Sondra to face the music alone.

"Vhat's dis? Vhat's going on here?" Mom was surprised, "Sondra! Vhat's wrong mit you? You're not like dis..."

Sondra was embarrassed and ashamed, especially for being caught by my mom, who had done so much for her. "I'm so sorry, Molly. I'm truly sorry."

Manny shoved the turkey into the hall closet, "I'm sorry, Sondra, but this is the last time you'll be takin' care of da kids."

"Manny, don't be so mean. So she made a mistake... give her another chance. She's a good person."

"No, she's gotta go!"

Millie heard everything. She attached herself to Sondra and began to cry. In between gulps of air, "Take me with you! Please, take me with you! You can do that! You could be my mother... I love you."

When Manny pulled one of Millie's arms away from Sondra, the other arm snapped back like a rubber band. Sondra gently pulled Millie away and she reluctantly let go.

Sondra bent down to Millie, "Sweetheart, I love you, too. But you can't come with me."

Mom paid Sondra, "I'm so sorry to lose you. You're such a good person and I like you very much." She pointed to Manny, "I've tried, but he won't change his mind."

We all woke up the next morning in a *Tarzan* movie, with jungle sounds like growling beasts and screaming birds. Our dog Rusty was sniffing and growling at the closet door and the poor turkey was screaming for its life. Mom opened the closet door a crack, Rusty stuck his muzzle in and the turkey nipped at his nose. He ran behind Mom and bravely barked back from between her legs.

Walter was in the hall giggling, "Where did you get a turkey? Why a live turkey?"

Manny quickly slammed the closet door shut, "I von him at da party."

Mom was annoyed, "And vhat are you going to do vit it? Have it for supper? Is dat vhat you think? And I ask you, who's going to kill it? I'm not going to do dat! It's your turkey… you do it! Vhy don't you answer me?"

Manny frustrated, "I can't. I can't kill it."

"Sooo… vhat are you going to do? Tell the turkey to kill itself?"

"Dat's it! Heschel, go to my room. You'll find in my closet some rope. Bring it to me."

Feathers were flying in every direction as Manny and the turkey wrestled each other to the floor. Everyone was screaming and laughing, the dog was barking, all trying to get out of Manny and the turkey's way. Finally, Manny got the turkey's legs tied together. Harry, Walter, Millie and I followed Manny and the turkey out the front door, down the stairs and outside to the back of our apartment house. A building had been demolished back there, and all that was left of it were sharp, jagged pieces of concrete.

Manny placed the turkey in the middle of the rubble and let it go. The turkey desperately tried to escape and threw itself against the jagged concrete, opening bloody wounds all over its body. Exhausted, the turkey succumbed to its own suicide. That night we had turkey for dinner, and so did Rusty.

Mom's deep voice drew me to the kitchen. Our neighbor, Connie, was sitting with my mom, laughing through her dimples, "That's right, he paid me five dollars to let him suck my nipples." Connie giggled, "Molly, you've got to promise me you won't tell anybody."

"You know me, I won't say a word... so what happened?"

"He told me that his doctor told him he was a very sick man and needed human milk for his health."

Mom asked, "Was he at least good lookin'?"

"He was very good looking." They both giggled.

Mom turned around and saw me standing at the kitchen doorway, listening.

"Mine Sollinue, vhy don't you go out and play? Go ahead, totala, go and play."

Our block on Croes Avenue was an authentic Bronx village, with rows and rows of two-story, look alike buildings. At the back of each building was a small, square, fenced-in yard and between each building was a narrow alley. One of these alleys was a secret passageway to Connie's backyard, where you weren't in the Bronx anymore, but in a secret garden filled with beautiful colors you can eat – fruits, vegetables, tomatoes, and figs on trees. Covering part of her yard was a trellis with crawling vines of grapes that Connie and her husband Anthony made into wine. This is where they held their parties. How could they fit all those people into such a small yard already crowded with plants? Yet they found a way.

I left Connie's house and the street was empty of kids. I walked to the empty lot at the corner of Watson and Croes, across the street from the grocery store where Walter worked. I stopped by a large boulder the older kids called the Camel Rock. There was a plank of wood jutting out over a hole full of junk. I thought I'd try to walk the plank, like in the movies. I lost my balance, fell into the pit, and hit my head hard. I didn't think anything of it until I got up and felt something warm and wet dripping down my chest. A nail was sticking through a thin block of wood, right between my eyes.

Crying more from fear than pain, I walked home with the nail and wood block still hanging from my face. By the time I got home, I could hardly see through the blood. My white T-shirt was deep red with the blood gushing down from my head.

When Mom saw me she screamed, "Oy gevalt! My totala!" And that was the last thing I remember. She took me to the hospital and when I opened my eyes, strangers were putting me back to sleep. *Floating shadows stood over me... they were busy building a wooden model airplane on my nose.*

Mom's cures for any problem or pain always involved either eating out or going to a movie, or both. After the hell we'd been through, Mom wanted the cure to be extra special and, a few days later, she took Millie and me on the trolley to the Grand Concourse – the living quarters of the rich – and to the Paradise movie theater.

The Paradise stood alone, upstaging the surrounding buildings with its majestic bas-relief detailing. A large clock was inserted into a cavity at the top of the building's facade, and underneath it a sun rose with raised letters reading, "Lowe's Paradise Theatre."

All the movie houses I knew had marquees reaching out toward the edge of the sidewalk, but the Paradise marquee was neatly pushed back flush against the building. With its overbearing arrogance the theater had no need for a protruding marquee, you knew where you were – among the rich.

We walked through one of the golden doors and into the lobby, and I breathed in the warm, soft air of the movie theatre's perfume.

I was standing in an eighteenth century palace! At any moment, at the top of the winding, carpeted stairs to the balcony, I expected to see Errol Flynn standing there with sword in hand.

Golden panels circled the walls of the huge hall, repeating the designs on the banisters. My eyes lifted higher and higher, looking up at the painted ceiling of people in floating robes, until I got so dizzy I almost fell over backwards. In the center of the lobby was a huge, sparkling, jeweled chandelier above my head, holding the whole room together.

To my right against a wall, water was flowing out of an open sea-shell, held on each side by a naked woman. Water cascaded down from the top of the shell and into a pool. Every once in awhile the water would ripple. There was something alive in there. Inching my-self closer to the edge, I saw six long, plump goldfish with sheer, silky fins swirling in a dance around the pool. I forgot we were in a movie theatre until a door opened from the orchestra seats and a man stepped out into the lobby in an usher's uniform. Behind him, I caught a glimpse of brilliant colors screaming at me from out of the dark. A cartoon boy danced across the screen over a pulsating back-ground of buildings. The orchestra door slowly closed on a cushion of air, cutting me off from the thrill of seeing more. But now I knew what was in store for me.

Mom took Millie and me by the hand and walked up to the bal-cony. Our steps were muffled on the thick rug, sounding as if I was listening underwater. Inside, around the walls of the balcony, were sculptured golden gardens built for the ancient Greek gods supported by ornamental columns set into the walls. Above my head, clouds floated and stars twinkled against a dark blue night sky. My eyes were in shock as they breathed in the scene around me. Who the hell could watch the movie below?

In those days, every time we went to the movies, we expected to see a black and white picture. So when a color film appeared on the screen, it was unusual and something very special. The thrill of a Looney Tunes cartoon flashing its bright colors on the screen pulled me in. Even the grownups screamed with joy. A travelogue was next with its washed out colors, followed by a newsreel about the black and white war in Europe, then a movie, *Dr. Cyclops*, and finally the main attraction, *Pinocchio*.

Mom went to the movies so often it became her second home. She'd bring all the essentials you might need if you were stranded on an uncharted island – sandwiches, soda drinks, and lots of her favorite treat, polly seeds... and of course, her knitting. Mom carried her knitting everywhere. She could watch a whole movie or hold a conversation on the train without dropping a stitch.

While camping out in the Paradise, Mom cracked open her polly seeds, dropping the empty shells on the floor in front of her. The pile of shells grew into a large, living mound that spoke back to us every time anyone plowed through on the way to their seat.... sounding like the crunching of roaches.

By the time we got home, the song, *Wish Upon a Star*, was haunting me, replaying over and over in my head. And after we ate supper, *Dr. Cyclops* became a foggy memory.

From the radio a voice threatened, *"Lights out everybody. Itt... iss... laterr... thaann... youuuu... think."* A gong vibrates, turning into a whistling wind – a warning of evil to come. *"This is the hour when dogs howl and thunder is let loose on a sleeping world. Sit in the dark now and listen to... Lights Out."*

Our older brother, Walter, jumped into the room with a ghoulish laugh... "Whoooaaa-ha-ha!" and turned out the lights leaving us in complete darkness and scaring the shit out of Millie and me.

The last thing I took to sleep with me was Mom's voice, as she walked by my room, singing and humming, *You Are My Sunshine*. Her voice slid me into sleep.

"Oy yoy, yoy, yoy, yoy..." Mr. Zausner, was rubbing a half lemon on his forehead, "Oy gutanue, it's so hot." He sighed again, a big boned, bald man sitting in his kitchen with his belly stretching his white tank top.

Mom left me at the Zausner's while she was at home with her

friends, getting another Italian cooking lesson for tomato sauce. This time, they were teaching her how to cook from scratch, and the aroma filled our apartment while it simmered slowly for almost two days.

That morning the whole Zausner family was in their kitchen – Mrs. Zausner, daughter Rosalyn, and two teenaged sons, Harvey and stuttering Arthur. I was always welcome there, because Mr. Zausner was my godfather. Sitting on the kitchen floor were cardboard boxes, bigger than I was, tightly wrapped around with cord. Both Harvey and Arthur tried to lift them, but they were too heavy for them to handle and they ended up pushing them to the front door.

Mr. Zausner was an ox of a man and when he got up, each of his steps shook the room around him. When he lifted the boxes the cords pinched his fingers. He kissed his wife goodbye and walked out of the front door. He spent his days on Manhattan street corners selling men's underwear from his boxes and wouldn't be back until the boxes were empty at the end of the day. This is one of those incomplete memories that won't let go of me.

It was the summer of 1941, and I was five years old. The block was filled with kids playing street games. A couple of boys were on the sidewalk, playing hit-the-penny. Others were playing stoopball off the steps of a building. The connection to almost every game was the cheap, reliable, high-bouncing Spaldeen, the only piece of equipment we needed. We weren't taught to play the street games, we just knew how. It was part of being from The Bronx.

I ran into Millie, who was standing in an alley with a strange man. "I was looking for you, Millie."

"And who is this?" asked the man.

"That's my kid brother."

"Your sister and I were going to play hide and seek. Would you like to play?"

"Yeah."

"And what's your name?"

"Solly."

"Well, Solly, since you just joined the game, you'll have to be 'it.' Now, close your eyes and count to fifty... and no peeking."

Counting to fifty was too much for me, and I searched for them at nine. I found Millie and the man in the basement doorway. He was pulling down Millie's panties. Millie screamed at him to stop it. I knew something was wrong. The man tried to chase me away, and I ran to Mom. I told her what I saw and showed her where they were. Then, all hell broke loose. Mom attacked the guy and kept slapping him across the face. He ran for his life, but she chased after him to his apartment. She called the cops, and they arrested the guy, but he showed up on the street a week later.

To get us away from the whole ugly thing, Mom moved us to Noble Avenue, to the second floor of a two-story building exactly like the one on Croes Avenue.

ALL WE GOT WAS STATIC

ONE COLD SUNDAY afternoon on Noble Avenue, frozen water filled an entire section of the concrete park, surrounded by a high mesh, metal fence. Harry and Walter were ice skating. I was five years old and dressed so thickly in layers that I waddled around the park like a penguin. Millie and I went sliding across the ice until we were soaking wet.

Mom called out from the window, "Solly! Come upstairs, now!"

She peeled off my layers of clothes and put them on the radiator to dry. Warm and content, I stared out the front window watching our dog Rusty trying to catch up to Harry and Walter. Rusty lost his footing and slid across the ice, scrambling to hold onto something solid. He lost control and slammed into the fence.

The music on the radio, *Elmer's Tune*, was suddenly cut off by a stunned voice, *"We interrupt this program to bring you a special news bulletin: the Japanese have attacked Pearl Harbor by air. President Roosevelt has just announced that Hawaii has been bombed. We take you now to Washington…"*

Danger and fear took over the mood in the apartment. Even the radio was in shock… all we got was static.

Mom's voice, an extension of the radio's immediacy, screamed out from the window, "Heschel! Velvul! Millinue! Come upstairs!"

Walter answered, "Yeah Mom, in a couple of minutes."

"No! You come up right now!"

They heard the desperation in her voice and rushed upstairs.

"What's wrong? What happened?"

"Da Japanese bombed us."

Harry, "Where?"

"I don't know."

The radio static cleared, and the announcer repeated the news. Harry and Walter looked at each other, knowing that soon they would be the right age for the draft. All I wanted to do was go out and play. I nagged Mom until she got me into my dry layers, and I took off like a shot.

The street was empty and the quiet was so thick, I could walk on its stillness. Afraid of being alone, I started back to my building. People began to fill the street, walking with empty eyes, like a piece of them was missing. Their shock rubbed off onto the street, from storefronts to lampposts.

For the next couple of months, Mom wasn't working. Her furrier's job was off-season, and Manny had just lost his job at the WPA. We couldn't pay our rent. After one of their never-ending fights, Mom went out and found us an apartment on Fteley Avenue, where they were giving three weeks of free rent. It was north of where we lived, across Westchester Avenue, just past the El.

During the move, we lost our dog, Rusty. My world was so upside down that I didn't have time to grieve for him. About a week later, Connie gave Mom a party for moving. The Italians would give a party for anything, even for Rusty being lost. In a way I was glad Rusty was gone; who knows how long Mom would have kept him? She loved dogs when they were puppies, but as soon as they reached a certain age, well… we never saw them again. We had dogs in our lives like a revolving door, enter here and exit there.

While Walter was shooting his B-B gun from the front window at the garbage-scavenging rats in an empty lot, Manny was fighting with Mom in his Russian-Yiddish accent, "I vant ya to be very nice to him."

"I vill not."

"You're always complainink about money... now's our chance to get some."

"If I do this ting, I'll never let you touch me again. And you think I don't know vhat those pimples on your head is? Syphilis, that's what it is! You think I don't know you're fooling around? That's where you got it. I'll never let you touch me again."

"Vhat da hell are you talking? I don't have syphilis."

"It doesn't matter vat you say. I'll never touch you again."

Manny insisted, "So I vant you should be nice to Johnny, and I could be having my own cab and making some money."

Manny had befriended this Irish goyim, Johnny, who wasn't too bad looking until he smiled with a mouthful of rotten teeth. He told Manny he had important connections in the government, and there was a good chance he could help him to get a job driving a cab... and maybe get him a medallion of his own.

Johnny came to our house the day before my sixth birthday and brought a present with him, a wooden popgun. I caught my Mom hiding it on top of the tall, glass-front cabinet in the hall. I became obsessed with wanting that popgun. I climbed the cabinet after my prey. A few inches from the top I reached out for my prize, but the weight of my body tipped the cabinet off-balance and it came crashing down on top of me.

"Sollinue! Vhere are you?"

Johnny crawled under one end of the cabinet, and Mom crawled under the other. But I had already escaped and Mom found me sitting against a wall, bleeding from the top of my head. The cuts weren't deep, just enough to make an enormous amount of blood. In those days, I always seemed to be bleeding.

Mom gently removed the glass, and Johnny helped her bandage me. She put me on her bed and Millie read joke books to me while

Mom was in the other room being nice to Johnny. About half an hour later, Mom and Johnny came back to the living room. She couldn't look at him and tried to get him out of the apartment. He wouldn't leave, so she just pushed him out the front door, and that was the end of Johnny.

Mom put the radio on and the Andrew Sisters were singing, *Oh Johnny, Oh Johnny, Oh.*

PACK UP WE'RE MOVING

WHILE MANNY WAS in the process of getting his cab job, we still couldn't afford the rent. In those days, we never stayed in one place long enough to unpack. That way, we could quietly move out late at night without anyone being the wiser. But even though we were moving like gypsies from place to place, Mom always made sure we had enough to eat. However this time, Mom moved from Fteley Avenue earlier than she had planned. One night, a rat as large as a cat squeezed up through the kitchen drain – We were gone!

Next stop, Boynton Avenue, and two weeks of free rent. From there we moved to Simpson Street for three weeks of free rent in a half-rounded building across the street from the 41st Precinct. The furrier season had begun, and during our whole stay there, I was very sick with a high fever. A colored couple took care of me while Mom and Manny were back at work. I got better just as the three weeks of free rent was up, and this time, even though we had enough money for the rent, we moved to Aldus Street near P.S. 75.

It was early one morning on Aldus Street, after driving his cab all night, I watched Manny sigh deeply and sit down at the kitchen table. He was wearing his tweed newsboy cap low over his eyes. He sighed again as he watched the morning sun flash into the kitchen and flicker off his silver coin changer. He started to write on his clipboard, adding up the bills from his cigar box. Without looking, he hit different levers on the silver coin changer and different coins, from quarters to nickels, jingled out into his hand. Manny recorded the totals for the night's work, took his cap off, sighed once more, got up and went to bed.

My first day of school, I was so proud walking to P.S. 75 all by myself, feeling grown up, wearing my first tie ever. The wind was blowing, and I watched from the sides of my eyes as my tie whipped across my chest and over my shoulder. When I got to school my little fantasy disappeared. It was a week after the term had started, and the kids made fun of me, teasing me mercilessly, to the point where my emotions became raw. Someone pushed me hard. I turned around and attacked, swinging my arms like pistons, and knocked the kid to the ground. After that morning, no one ever bothered me again.

This was my first class, and the teacher had some sort of system in place for seating. She assigned each student a letter of the alphabet and I was given the seat with the letter 'Y' – but I didn't know what the alphabet was. It was as meaningless to me as the Hebrew letters on the butcher's windows. Everyone in the class already knew their alphabet, and most knew how to read at least a little.

When the teacher called my letter, I didn't know who the hell she was talking to. I was so ashamed I stood there sweating, too afraid to ask and too afraid to hear my own voice. This all happened in a few seconds, standing there with everyone's eyes on me. Swallowing a lump of tears, I never let any of them see me cry. By the end of the school day, I had learned what a 'Y' looked like.

My teachers at P.S. 75 spoke to me in a jumble of words I couldn't straighten out in my head. I could see their lips moving, but I didn't know what they were saying. I didn't realize at the time that I was dyslexic; nobody knew what that was then. If I had enough time, I might have been able to change their words to my way of hearing them. But no matter how much I tried to make myself understood, they weren't listening. Everyday I was living a riddle that I had to solve to survive. To everyone else, I was just stupid... even my family.

Mom couldn't help me learn to read. She was too ashamed that she couldn't read English. My brothers and sister were too busy with their own lives to bother with me, and Manny was always too tired. No one read stories to Millie and me; the radio was our storyteller.

So I had to daydream myself out of the confusion around me.

On Aldus Street, I became friends with a kid named Shugie who was two years older than me. He was so black that at certain angles he'd glow with blue highlights on his satin skin. Standing next to him I felt naked of color. Shugie was between Millie's and my age. They were always holding hands, and I guess Millie was his girlfriend.

On a warm spring day, Shugie and I crossed Whitlock Avenue to the Creek, just past the swimming pool. We were hidden by tall, dry weeds and thought it would be fun to build a campfire. But then a spark flew from the fire and, in seconds, all the weeds around us burst into flames. We tried to stomp it out, but it was out of control. Billowing smoke blocked out the sun.

The fire raced through the Hunt's Point Swimming Pool and we heard the fire engines coming from all directions. Shugie and I were scared shitless and ran for our lives. It was our secret and we made a pact never to tell anyone as long as we lived. Walking home, we were two of the most innocent looking kids in The Bronx.

My adventures with fire didn't stop there. It was late morning, and while Manny was sleeping, I found a box of matches and hid in his closet where no one could see me. A smoldering match ignited one of Manny's shirts. This time I was able to put the fire out, but the smoke filled the bedroom. I ran into the bathroom and hid into the smallest crevice between the tub and the wall. I thought no one would ever look for me there, because no human being, even as small as I was, could fit in that space.

Manny woke up choking from the smoke and knew who was responsible. He called Walter and Harry, and they came running into the smoke-filled room.

"What happened?"

"Solly started a fire, and I can't find him. He must have run out of da house. Do me a favor and find him."

Manny walked into the bathroom, never suspecting I was there, crunched between the tub legs. I was as still as I could be, didn't even move a finger for fear he might hear my joints crack. So I was forced to listen to Manny's farting and endure the smell of him shitting. Maybe this was my punishment.

They searched for hours but found no sign of me and began to get worried. They even recruited little Millie.

Walter suggested, "Maybe we should call the police?"

"You tink so? Maybe you're right."

When I heard "police," I gave myself up. Everybody was so glad to see me alive, they forgot all about the fire. When Mom came home and found out what happened, of course, she fought with Manny about it. Those last few weeks on Aldus Street got so bad that every time either one of them just opened their mouths, they'd fight.

Mom never told us that Manny was going to leave her, or that she was going to leave him. We woke up one morning, and he was gone. We just lived our lives as if nothing had happened. We moved to East 165th Street, between Hoe Avenue and Faille Street, and settled down there for the next ten years.

It was Friday morning on Aldus Street the day we moved. Mom was wearing a dark blue and red checkered dress, partially covered by an apron she had folded down around her waist. Millie was sitting at the kitchen table, while Mom stood behind her trying to brush through Millie's thick, curly hair.

"Ow! Ow! That hurts."

"Stop that! Stop chewing your finger! You'll lose a finger dat way.

"Now listen to me, both of you. Vhile you're at school, we're going to move to East 165th Street. Listen goot! After school, come to 928 East 165th Street, Apartment Three-Eight. You got it? Say it back to me."

My inner world was made up of infinite compartments of fear and this one was my fear of moving, because I had to memorize and learn to spell a new address.

Mom saw the blank look in my eyes, "Oy, gutenue! Listen hard and repeat it after me, Nine-Two-Eight."

"Nine-Two-Eight. Jeez, Mom, I've got it... I've got it!"

"East 165th Street, apartment Three-Eight."

"Yeah, I've got it – apartment Three-Eight."

It was three o'clock and the end of the school day. I walked up one block on Faille Street and turned left onto East 165th Street, to the building numbered 928. But I couldn't find apartment 38. Maybe if I went through the whole building again... but it still wasn't there. Maybe I've got the wrong street. What if I went the wrong way? I went back to school and started over.

I followed Mom's directions and went back to 928 East 165th Street. It was twilight and the halls were getting dark. I slowly took a closer look at each door. Four times I went up and down the building and still no 38.

I became frantic and wanted to hide in my heart. Mom could still be on Aldus Street, packing. I ran back, but our old apartment was as empty as I felt inside. Desperate, I returned to East 165th Street.

Sitting on the stoop, I thought about how Mom loved dogs, but so easily got tired of them, and as easily got rid of them. Mom also loved me... did she get tired of me, too? Is she getting rid of me?

I didn't know what to do. I sat there holding in my tears until they built into uncontrollable shaking. I couldn't hold it in any longer and every inch of me cried. I lost my Mom.

Mom came out of the building, "Sollinue, I vas getting worried. Vhy are you sitting dere crying? Vhat's wrong? Vhy didn't you come upstairs?"

Feeling stupid, I stuttered, "I... I... I... I couldn't find you. There's no apartment 38."

"Oh Solly, vhat am I going to do vit you? It's so easy, apartment Three-Eight!"

I stood up and leaned my head against her thigh and she wiped my face on her apron.

"Come. I'll show you."

She took me upstairs and showed me the door to our new apartment. And in big bold letters it said, **3-A**. "You see, it's Three-Eight!"

"But Mom, it says 3-A."

She insisted, "Vhat's the matter vit you? Dat's vhat I said."

We didn't only get a new apartment we also got a special Cracker Jack prize – a stranger who was there to greet us. Not exactly to greet us... he was just there. He came with the apartment. The man's name was Harold.

Inside the front door, I walked into a long hall covered with dark paisley linoleum. Off to the right side was a small bedroom that Harry and Walter would share. Millie had a small bedroom at the end of the hall, and there was a large, almost empty living room where I was going to sleep on a canvas army cot. Off the living room were French doors that opened into a large bedroom where Mom and Harold lived.

Harold was quiet and kept to himself. Walter and Harry accepted him without question. They knew they'd be joining the Armed Forces soon, and with Harold there, they wouldn't have to worry about Mom. Harry and Walter were rarely home. Mom was working full time as a furrier and needed someone to take care of Millie and me.

"Momala, take Solly to the corner of Southern Boulevard and Westchester Avenue and ask a woman to take care of you and Solly. Make sure she's colored, and someone you like."

Millie never blinked, it was just a fact of life. She took my hand and we stood on the corner like little orphans. Within an hour she found someone whose warm smile made us feel at home.

"My mom wants to know if you'd like to take care of us. She would pay you for it. Can you come talk with my mother?"

"Don't you want to know my name?"

"Yes, yes I do."

"It's Nyomi."

Nyomi looked down at Millie and took her hand, "You're a very sweet young girl. And what's your name?"

"Millie. And this is Solly."

We didn't get to know her too well though, because she wasn't with us that long.

Harry had just turned eighteen and was eligible for the draft. One of the last times I saw him before he went into the service, he was on his way to a dance with a blind date, looking cool in his zoot suit. I thought he looked really weird.

Just before Harry left for the Army, he had a fight with Walter. It was the same old theme – Walter taking Harry's stuff without him knowing. One time Walter sold Harry's trumpet for a hot date. When Harry found out he screamed, "You've got your balls! That trumpet was mine."

Walter looked up at Harry, "What are you complaining about! You stink at it anyway."

Harry was dumbfounded. He was six foot, three and Walter was five foot, six and they looked like Mutt and Jeff from the comics. The next time they fought it was over a stupid tie.

"That's my tie! How dare you take my tie!"

"My God, I only borrowed it."

"You little prick! Next time you ask me!"

Walter screamed up at Harry, making sure his voice would carry up that high, "Here, keep your fuckin' tie."

That was their last fight before they left for the service. Harry was working as a draftsman for an architect in Manhattan, and his boss advised him to join up before he got drafted. This way he could pick the specialty he wanted. After only a month of living at East 165th

Street, Harry left for the Army. It was very unusual for the Army to give a recruit what he asked for, but Harry was very lucky and was placed in a non-combatant engineer outfit... exactly what he wanted.

Walter passionately wanted to be in the Navy, but he was just a little bit too young to join on his own. He needed Mom's permission and signature. Mom fought harder to keep Walter out of military service than she had for Harry. After all Walter was her favorite. Walter begged Mom everyday until he convinced her that by joining before he was drafted, he'd get the same deal Harry got.

Walter joined the Navy, and for the first time, I had my own room. The German measles moved in with me. Being sick in my own room was easier to take than being sick in the living room, with people walking through all the time.

Now that my brothers were gone, Mom lost the money they contributed toward the household. She couldn't afford Nyomi anymore or Millie's dance lessons at the Hunt's Point Palace. The dance teachers pleaded with Mom to let Millie continue her lessons. "You've got to let Millie stay! She is a very talented girl, with great promise."

But once Mom made up her mind, there was no way she'd change it. That was the end of it.

THE MONSTER
COMES ALIVE

HAROLD OWNED A garage down at the end of The Three Hills, on the corner of East 165th Street and Whitlock Avenue. That's where Mom met him. Mom was warned to stay away from him by one of his mechanics who said he was a mean son of a bitch. But all she saw was a gentle, white Christian, an educated man with a college degree who had his own business. And this intelligent man was interested in her.

At the beginning, Mom made me deliver lunch to Harold at his garage. I tried to please him, but for the first couple of months he never talked to me. He was very quiet, especially when Harry and Walter were still living with us. When they left for the military, Harold started to drink heavily and often.

The first words that came out of his educated mouth at me were, "Get the fuck away from me, you half wit."

He said to my mother, "Keep those little Jews away from me."

He looked back at me like I was a cockroach that should be stepped on. That's the day it all began, Harold's first lesson in teaching me who and what I am, and who and what he was. I had lost my father – he had been replaced with a monster.

Harold spent most of his time in his bedroom, but on this Saturday afternoon he was in the kitchen with Mom. At times I was so concentrated on the moment that I didn't notice where Harold was. His arm shot out like an iron rod from the kitchen doorway, and grabbed my hair. He brought me to a sudden stop, jerking my head back, and for a few seconds the rest of my body continued to run without my head. I looked up into his face.

"What are you gawking at, you moron?"

He pounded his stone-like fist on my head. If he had hit me any harder, my head would have cracked open like an egg. The violence and pain took me by surprise. The only thing that helped was to cry.

"What did I do?"

"Shut up."

Mom looked up from doing the dishes, "Vhat are you doing? Vhat did the boy do?"

While he was talking to my Mom, Harold swung out his arm and slapped my face, knocking me off my feet. But I was more in shock than in pain from his unexpected violence. He said, "You deserve it, you little prick. Where are you going, you retard? I didn't say you could leave."

"Sollinue, maybe you and Millie should stay in your room right now."

That's it? That's all the protection I get?

Mom brought Harold into the living room, "I'll tell the little cock suckers when and where they can go."

"Harold, vhy are you like dis?"

Harold exploded, "This is my home now. I'm making the rules, not you. Remember that!"

Harold carried his anger into his bedroom, and I prayed he would keep it there. Putting my ear close to my wooden radio, I tried to close Harold out of my room.

"*Up, up and away!*" Swoosh! Superman flies out of my radio in his bright red and blue costume. All four inches of him flies around my room searching for a mysterious uncharted island in the Pacific and, in the middle of the vast unending ocean, an island appears at the foot of my bed.

"*Down...Down...*" Superman gracefully glides down with his

cape flowing behind him, and gently lands on the island.

Still shaking from Harold's outburst, I wanted my radio closer to me to drown out his angry voice, still threatening from his room. I didn't realize the electric cord wasn't long enough and pulled the radio off the table. It fell on the floor, sparks jumped everywhere, smoke filled the room, and the radio smashed to pieces.

Harold charged into my room. He broke through the smoke, and stood over me. "You damn fucking idiot! That's it! You've had it... no more radios for you!"

Mom was behind him, "Of course you're getting a radio, my totala."

"We can't afford another radio. Your stupid little Jew bastard would only break it."

Mom trying to soothe him, "Harold, I'll take care of it. Go, I'll clean it up."

With the brain of a dull-witted bull, Harold quickly lost interest and lumbered back to his bedroom. From that day on, Millie and I stayed in our rooms, never eating together again. But we didn't eat alone. We had friends on the radio to keep us company.

One day Mom brought home a puppy to ease the sting of living with Harold. She was a round, tiny, soft powder-puff – mostly white, with reddish brown spots and a pink nose. Naturally we named her Spotty.

Harold had a son from his first marriage whose name was also Harold. To distinguish them from each other, we nicknamed him, Little Harold. He was about my brother Harry's age, and unlike his father, he was a very thin and modest man. We very rarely saw him, but when we did, he was very gentle with us. It was hard to believe he was Harold's son.

Little Harold absolutely loved Mom and confided his personal problems to her. He lived alone and Mom felt sorry for him, and she thought it would be a good idea for him to have a companion. And just like that, she gave Spotty to Little Harold to keep him company. For a brief moment we had a dog, and then we didn't... so much for soothing our fears from Harold's violence.

Of course, the usual cure for Mom's guilt was to take us to the movies. As we walked into the balcony, the darkness shook with a booming roar. An angry gorilla, as big as our apartment building, filled the entire screen. His furry fists hammered away at giant wood doors held closed by a tree-sized beam of wood. With a thunderous crash, the doors broke wide open and smashed into splinters.

A primal roar pushed me back into my seat. I couldn't catch my breath. The ape pounded his chest, sounding like a hollow drum. He grinned and stared into the audience. I knew he was looking at me, because in that moment, it was the same look of hate that Harold gave me.

Throughout the picture there were huge dinosaurs running around menacingly, looking like plucked chickens. After seeing a giant gorilla burst onto the screen, those impossible images were still fresh in my mind and I didn't care if I saw any of the shorts that followed on the theater bill. We had missed the beginning of *King Kong* and in order to stay and see the first part, we had to sit through the second feature. It was an adventure movie called *Gunga Din*. I thought it was just another British film about India, but it turned out to be a comic adventure story that unexpectedly thrilled me as much as *King Kong*.

After *Gunga Din*, a color cartoon burst onto the screen, a character called Goofy. I never figured out what kind of animal he was. Then *The Adventures of Captain Marvel* flashed on the screen, CHAPTER TWO - *THE GUILLOTINE*. An actual man, not a cartoon, jumped off a huge boulder, flew across the screen and straight out of the pages of my comic books. I didn't know such things were possible.

When Billy Batson, cub reporter, speaks the name, '*Shazam,*' a thunderclap and a cloud of smoke changes the boy into a tall, muscled, super hero in tights. At the end of the chapter, an electrical bolt knocks him out and he falls onto a conveyer belt that carries him under a guillotine. The guillotine is released and speeds down to its victim. *NEXT WEEK: CHAPTER THREE - TIME BOMB*

Yetta Melnick lived one flight below us and seemed to have known Mom before we moved here. Mom was sitting at Yetta's kitchen table drinking coffee, kibbitzing about the people living in our building. Yetta started by filling Mom in about Mrs. Levine, the landlady.

"Mr. and Mrs. Levine had three children, two boys and one girl. After they had bought this building, on the first day they moved in, one of their boys, the youngest, about sixteen years old, took his bike out for a ride, and on the corner of Hoe Avenue, a car jumped the curb and killed him. Soon after that, Mr. Levine died."

Mom said, "Tsk, tsk, tsk... dat's terrible."

Yetta noticed me, "Ahhh, dis must be Solly. Solly I have a son, Melvin. Wait, I'll get him."

She shouts his name, "Melvin! Melvin! Come, I want you to meet Solly."

Melvin was a little younger than me. He had olive skin and plastered-down, straight black hair.

"Go, go out and play, my little Arab. Maybe you can show Solly the block."

It had only been a week since we moved just one block away from Aldus Street, but it might as well have been another planet. Only a block away, and I never saw Shugie again.

As soon as we hit the street, Melvin became my guide. He took me all around the block, pointing out the different stores, and we ended up on the corner of the next block at the Hilltop Cleaners, just before the three steep hills that sloped all the way down to Harold's garage at Whitlock Avenue.

Walking up The Three Hills toward us was a boy with black, curly hair and dark eyes set into a bony face. He was my age, and like me, he was very short and skinny. Melvin started acting like a wise guy. The kid tried to pass by, and I stepped aside, but Melvin started to bully him. The kid knocked Melvin on his ass. His name was Sergie Garcia, and like me, he had just moved on the block into the building next to mine. And now there were three of us. I didn't know it then, but Sergie and I were to become the best of friends.

For a long time, Harold's business had suffered, because the war had created a shortage of car owners. The people who did own one could never use it. That's the way things were. During that summer, Harold sold his garage and got a job working as a mechanic in a shipyard on City Island. He left early everyday and came home late. This gave us some breathing room from his unexpected visits during the day.

It turned out that Little Harold developed tuberculosis. The doctors told him he couldn't keep Spotty because of her constant shedding, so Mom offered to take Spotty back. Little Harold loved Spotty, and when he dropped her off at our apartment, Mom tried to make him feel better.

"Harold, darlink, at least you'll know where the dog is. It couldn't hurt if you visit her once in awhile. Spotty vill always be here for you."

But that wouldn't happen for a long while. Little Harold had to spend the next year and a half quarantined in a hospital on Randall's Island on the East River.

At first Spotty was a stranger, not that tiny, fluffy ball that I remembered. She had grown into a medium size dog, but still had her pink nose and the reddish brown spots on her white coat of fur. It could be Spotty... I wasn't sure. I didn't know how to react to her until she greeted us like she had never left and smoothly slipped back into the family.

A CHRISTMAS
GONE WRONG

PISSING ON THE hot steam pipe hissed into the hall, creating the acrid odor any kid who grew up in the tenements would never forget. It gave me a feeling of power. It was my way to stink up their lives as they did mine.

Never looking back, I tear-assed down the worn marble steps, intently trying to hear if anyone was behind me. I escaped through the twisted, black wrought iron and glass doors and out into the street, only to be stopped by a wall of rushing snow that filled the air in every direction. My eyes touched the round mounds of softness all at the same time. Not a footprint, not a mark of any kind, and it was all mine.

It was The Bronx of 1942, a winter twilight, just before the early rush of workers on their way home from the Simpson Street train station. The streets were not the streets I knew. Their hard, concrete angles had begun to melt away, softened by the rolling snow. The world around me didn't exist anymore, only the intimate closeness of the untouched snow. I can still feel my child's feet crunching into the snow as I plowed through its deepening thickness on my way to the Boulevard. The streets were empty of traffic. What little there was, had been silenced by the white fluff, except for the occasional muffled clanging of an invisible trolley.

A flutter of animated colors on the snow drew my attention. The reflecting colors were coming from a toy store window, filled haphazardly with Christmas decorations. Clumps of snow were still clinging to the tips of my galoshes when I stepped out of the snow and into a slushy, marble-like vestibule between the store windows.

Inside one of the windows was a mechanical Santa Claus, worn and faded. One of Santa's eyes winked as his head dropped spasmodically to his chest. The silent Santa, separated from the sound of his laughter, beckoned me to the window. It was filled with toys that my sister and I never ever dreamed of having.

In our home, we never celebrated Christmas, Chanukah, or birthdays. The only time we ever got a present was when either of us was sick, and then it would be just a coloring book or a joke book.

When I stepped back onto the street, I looked up and saw the thick, rushing flakes falling from the sky. The wind brushed the snow across my face and the streetlights carried the white specks to the ground as I continued my trek to the train station. I wore my scarf like a mask wrapped around my face, showing only my eyes and part of my nose.

Breathing and re-breathing my hot, wet breath sharpened the smell of each store as I passed by – the barbershop with its perfumed tonics and the deli's knishes, kishka and spicy, garlicky salami, frankfurters, pastrami and corned beef. Then came the bakery, where the cakes and breads were all freshly baked behind the swinging doors that led to the back of the store. I could taste the air with its warm fragrances, playing with my senses.

Strung across the streets along Southern Boulevard from Westchester Avenue to Hunt's Point Palace, were crispy clear red, green and white lights shaped like stars, dangling above my head. They went way into the distance, getting brighter as they got smaller and closer together. The Boulevard wore them like a promise, a promise that something special was going to happen.

The falling snow had shut out the sky with a gray-white, glowing haze that surrounded the streets and touched the rooftops. It felt like this small section of the city had chunked away from the rest of the world and was the only place that existed. Every store was dressed with Christmas lights blinking into the streets. Their vivid brilliance bounced off the snowflakes flickering down onto the streets and sparkled on the snowdrifts like shadows of color. Flakes landed on the tip of my nose and melted away. The air smelled fresh and bright. The streets were alive and breathing. Everything tickled my heart.

It was dark by the time I reached the train station, and I was beginning to feel the cold. I stood leaning against a steel post at the bottom of the El, with my gloved hands buried deep into my mackinaw pockets, waiting to surprise my mom. After awhile, I wandered over to the Brighton Cafeteria, right next to the station.

The Cafeteria had two entrances that we kids used from time to time as a short cut from Southern Boulevard to the Westchester Avenue side. The busboys in the Cafeteria didn't care much for us cutting through and chased us when we tried. I suspected they enjoyed the chase. Eventually, it became a game between them and us.

Standing outside the Cafeteria windows, I lost myself in the reflections of people and automobiles passing by. When the image of a car came to the wide curve at the corner of the window, it bunched up into a little stubby car and abruptly slowed down to a crawl until it reached the other side of the window curve, where it pulled away onto the flat window, and looking larger than it was, took off like a shot from a rubber band.

Inside the Cafeteria there were old men with gray beards who spent hours sitting at tables over their glass of tea. I swear I saw one of those men sitting at the same table for days at a time, reading his Yiddish newspaper. Why would any of them want to stay in a lonely place like this and never go home... were they being held captive?

The Cafeteria doors opened, releasing one of the prisoners. Also escaping was the overwhelming aroma of a soup kitchen. In those few seconds before the doors closed, I could hear the hollow echoes of shuffling trays, clanking spoons, forks and glasses – an operetta of sounds vibrating off the tile floors and high ceilings.

Pressing my head against the window gave me a better view of the Cafeteria. The walls were painted with touches of pastel-like reds and yellows, but it was mostly dark green and blue that controlled the mood and muted all the other colors. The long walls were divided into large rectangular panels outlined in thin molding. Within each panel was a painted mural. The one in front of me was of a huge, floating, naked man with round, bulging lumps for muscles and black hair screaming out into space. His body was wrapped around a twisted horn that hid his genitals. His wide-open eyes stared wildly down at the cornucopia watching fruit zooming out from its center into space.

Around the edges of the naked man, a halo of light began to glow and throb, as if he was about to pull away from the wall. He knew I was watching him and his wild eyes turned in my direction, staring back into mine. I tried to turn away, but I could feel him looking at me, forcing me to watch him climb down off the wall. He was coming for me. I jumped away from the window. The cold heat of blood rushed back into my forehead, and I ran back to the station, as far away as I could from the painting's control.

At the bottom of the station stairs I heard the growing rumble of an approaching train. Its massive armored cars screeched to a stop and pulled at the wood and steel of the platform, causing it to lurch forward. The entire station moved under my feet. It was moving on its own. The train was like an insect that had crawled on the station's back and awakened the giant out of its sleep.

The wooden platform above me filled with a herd of shuffling feet, rushing to the exits. A flood of people overflowed onto the metal steps. All the men wore hats, but not just hats – they wore fedoras. My eyes squinted and strained, searching for my mom between all the bobbing hats that swayed from side to side, bouncing down the steps.

The trains were coming faster now. As soon as one pulled out, another was right behind it. After about the eighth train and still no Mom in sight, I began to worry that I missed her. Maybe somehow she had passed me in the crowd and at this very moment was on her way home without me. What if I left now and she was on the next train? I stood there frozen in my indecision, waiting for just one more train, then another and another. They came and went and not a sign of her anywhere.

Not knowing what to do, I became desperate and thought I had lost her forever. Again, people emptied onto the stairs, but this time I caught a glimpse of her face peeking in and out of the crowd. My mom's bangs were sticking out from under her red paisley kerchief, sweeping across her forehead. My whole world lit up.

"Sollinue, vhat are you doing here?"

My mom hugged me with joy and when she held my hand with her firm grip, I became permanently attached to her – she owned me.

"Come, I've got to pick up a few tings."

What we called the Triangle, was a group of food stores and out-door produce stands that were positioned to form a triangle near the Simpson Street Station. Hunt's Point was my neighborhood. It was the focal point of food imported from across the USA, from the East Coast to the West Coast, and from all nations around the world -- from the everyday to the exotic. People came from all over The Bronx just to buy their food. Each store was an adventure in shopping, and shopping was a social contact sport, a daily ritual hunt for fresh food.

There was an Italian store that specialized in noodles, nothing but noodles everywhere, any shape or any size I could think of, each in its own open wooden bin. The fish store had huge, weird looking fish, real live fish swimming right before my eyes in a big white bathtub of water.

It was a different kind of life in the 40s, when business was done on a personal basis with people we knew, not with strangers who could care less if you shopped there or not. The stores were human size. Everything then wasn't bigger than us, or beyond us. It was a time when your credit was always good and uncomplicated – the shopkeepers just put it on your tab. And if my mom was late in pay-ing, she was never penalized with interest charges. It was a time when shopkeepers catered to our individual needs, like being able to buy only one stick of butter or one egg at a time.

No matter how often I had been in these stores, when I was with my mother, they were all new again. Each time she brought her full-ness of life with her and renewed their vitality. It was like being in the market place for the first time.

My mom and I stepped into the midst of bickering voices and pressing bodies. Everyone was cueing up to the vegetable stand, afraid to be left with second best. Mom leaned against the produce stand, searching through the tomatoes.

"Uh-uh, don't touch the tomados."

"Vhat ya talking about, I'm not touching."

I pressed close to my mother's rough cloth coat, my cheek snug-gled against her firm thigh. I could feel her concentrated energy and warmth radiating and spilling over me. The vegetable man wore a long, white apron that flared out from under his short, tightly but-toned wool jacket. On his head was a stocking cap, flimsily cocked to one side. His words puffed out in little white clouds of smoke that slowly rose and, for a few seconds, twisted and turned above his head like delicate ghosts, then dissipated into the night air.

"How many tomados do you want?"

"A pound. And make sure there are no rotten ones."

"Hey, I don't sell rotten tomados." He plopped the tomatoes on a squeaking metal scale.

My mom shouted… "You be careful vit dat! I'm paying good money for dat!"

The vegetable man shuffled from one foot to the other and banged his hands together trying to keep warm. He crossed his arms and put his hands under his armpits.

"Dat's nineteen cents."

My mom was a little surprised and half-jokingly she teased him, "So much? Veigh it again. Dis time, do me a favor, take your thumb off da scale."

"What thumb? Come on, Molly, I've got other customers."

"But, nineteen cents. Please darlink, I can't afford dat much dis veek. Be a sveetheart and do me a favor."

The vegetable man sighed, "Okay, okay, Molly. What did I charge you last week?"

"Ten cents for a pound."

We crossed to the other side of Westchester Avenue, to the Jewish butcher. The store had Hebrew letters crawling around its window, more like abstract designs than letters. I stayed as close as I could to my mom, trying to hide myself from a chance meeting with my friends. I didn't want them to see me going into the Jewish butcher. My friends were black, Spanish and Irish Catholics who saw Hassidic Jews as freaks – as I did – strange people with curly ringlets hanging out from under their black fedoras.

We walked out of the freezing cold and into the stifling heat of the butcher shop, and I began to percolate under my many layers of clothes. While Mom was giving her order to the butcher, my attention wandered to an open door leading to a back room.

The floor was covered with sawdust and a man in a long white smock sat on a chair in the middle of the room, holding a dead chicken. The limp chicken would jerk and jump up from his lap as the man yanked, tugged and twisted at the bird's feathers. The feathers flew into the air in all directions and slowly floated down, resting in a soft pile covering his feet. The few remaining hollow shafts were put under a steady stream of fire shooting up from a narrow, vertical pipe. A column of smoke spiraled around and through itself, escaping into the room where I was standing and filled it with the acrid odor of burning hair.

The butcher threw a slab of Romanian steak onto the butcher's block and, with his knife hovering over the steak, moved it from one end to the other, measuring an imaginary line.

"How much? Here? Here?"

"There! Dat's a good piece."

The butcher's long, finely honed knife, worn thin from thousands of sharpenings, lightly touched the steak and effortlessly slid through. He then ripped off a thin layer of the meat's tissue and made quick crisscross slices with his knife, cutting through the sinews of the steak.

Across the way at another table, a third man rolled square pieces of brown wax paper into cone shapes. With a small wooden spoon he scooped dark, golden mustard out of an open, wood barrel, filled the paper cones and then pinched the tops closed. The whole process was done in a continuous motion, filling one cone after the other exactly like the one before. Firmly, but gently, he felt the roundness of each plump cone as he lined them up neatly into a cardboard box. If only I could have one of those cones so I, too, could touch its roundness the way he did.

My mother opened her pocketbook to pay the butcher and it exhaled the aroma of Juicy Fruit gum. When she fumbled through her paper money, it smelled of her perfume. For the longest time, I thought money was supposed to smell like that. The heat of the store became unbearable; my pulse throbbed and pounded against my skin. It seemed like we were going to be there all night. I felt my brain would burst if we didn't get out of this place and back into the cold air again.

On our way home, we passed by Loft's candy store and stood on the corner of Southern Boulevard and Westchester Avenue, right by the wood clubhouse where newspapers were sold. As we waited for the traffic light, I felt safe and warm standing by my mom. She put her shopping bags down and held my hand in her cold, intense grip.

That night the Boulevard was more crowded than usual because of the last-minute Christmas shoppers and their mad rush for the last Christmas trees. Christmas started later then, which made it more immediate and exciting. All the stores along the Boulevard were only window dressing for the movie theatres. The Spooner, the Boulevard and Star proudly strutted their marquees out toward the street. Flashing lights ran around the movie titles, announcing that they knew they were the main reason for the existence of the busy Boulevard.

My eyes made a full circle around the street and back to my mom. She was carrying two heavy shopping bags with twine handles that pressed deep into the flesh of her fingers. The creases in her hand turned purple, with white streaks squeezing out from her strained grasp. Looking up to her face, I saw no signs of pain and there were no groans or sighs, not a word of complaint. I remember thinking how strong my mom must be.

Her kerchief framed her flushed, red cheeks, and I followed the lines of her high cheekbones to her nose. It was shaped like a sharp arrow that gracefully pointed to her deep red, thin lips. My God, she was a handsome woman! She was drenched with a natural sexuality that drew men to her like lust-crazed dogs after a bitch in heat. My mom was a tough woman, yet she had a child-like innocence reflected through her luminous, soft blue eyes. And there in her eyes, I saw a sadness that pulled me in and melted my heart.

About halfway to our block, at the shoe repair shop, we met my sister walking toward us.

"Millinue? Vhat is dis?! Everybody's meeting me?"

Millie looked up into my mom's face and wrapped her arms around her waist. Mom put the packages down and caressed Millie's hair, straightened her hat, and we were on our way home again. On the Hoe Avenue corner of our block, in front of the Chester Drug Store, there was a man standing by a pushcart. The cart itself was a metal stove with two doors at its front, one on top of the other. Four wooden spoke wheels were connected to the side of the metal stove and, on top at the far end, was a smoking chimney.

Millie asked, "Mom, can I have a sweet potato... Please?"

"You'll be too full for supper."

"I promise I'll eat all of my supper. Please?"

"Okay... Vhy not, it's oily yet. You, too, Solinue? You vant?"

My eyes widened and I nodded, "U-huh!"

We approached the cart and watched the sweet potato man taking a handful of broken crate pieces out of the box attached to the side of his cart. He snapped a piece of wood over his knee and used it to open the lever on the bottom door. The door swung open and a few lazy sparks trickled out. The sweet potato man gingerly placed the wood pieces on the red-hot embers in the oven. As he fed the fire, the hungry flames reached out for his hands. He pulled back and waited for the flames to subside. Again, he placed splinters of wood on the fire and, once more, the flames ignited.

My mom asked, "Two sweet potatoes, please?"

The man wore cotton gloves with the fingertips cut off and his bare fingers stuck out of the holes. From his pocket he whipped out two pieces of thin glassine paper. With his other hand, he grabbed the handle of the top compartment, which was tightly wrapped in rags, and opened the oven. This time the sparks escaped in a fury, shooting out like excited fireflies that danced above our heads. The snow sucked at the burning stars that fluttered around us, putting out their fiery glow.

The sweet potato man took two hot sweet potatoes from the oven and put them each into a glassine paper.

"Here, I picked out the best ones just for you."

The sweet potatoes warmed our hands and the cold air carried their sweet smell, teasing our taste buds. Millie and I bit into the steaming sweetness and the potato's crispy, burnt skin crumpled in and around our mouths.

"It's still oily yet, I vant yous to go upstairs and vait for me dere. I von't be long. I'm going to Abie's for a few more tings."

Abe and Moe's was a small grocery store on the corner of our block and Faille Street.

My mother handed one of the packages to Millie, "Sveetheart, dese are very heavy. You tink you and Solly can carry dem up for me?"

Millie, wanting to please her, "Sure, Mommy."

We struggled up three flights of stairs to our apartment, one step at a time. Spotty, greeted us at the door. She acted as if we had left her alone forever, and she would never see us again. She exploded with joy and, in a wild spurt, jumped into the air and fell to the ground, groveling and slithering on her stomach, peeing little puddles. Springing up from the floor, she dashed away from us to the other end of the long hall, paused briefly, and turned her head in our direction. We could see the energy building in her eyes as she accelerated for another attack of love.

Just as Millie and I started to wonder what had happened to Mom, the front door opened and in she came, bringing the cold air in with her. She touched my face with her crisp, cold hands. The brown paper bags crackled on the kitchen table and, as she emptied their contents, her talking hands unconsciously molded the air around her into deliciously thick, rounded shapes that I loved touching with my eyes.

Millie asked, "Where were you? You were gone for such a long time."

Mom's hand swatted at the air in disgust, trivializing her tardiness. "Ehhh, I met Yetta and we got talkin' for a few minutes."

She glanced up to the square, green electric clock on the kitchen wall, "Oy gutenue, look at the time! Harold's going to be home any minute. I vant yous to go to your rooms and be very quiet. I don't vant any trouble."

BACK INTO THE SNOW

WAY AT THE other end of the hall was Millie's room, which faced the street. The fire escape outside her window was a balcony seat to the outside life that filled her room. At night the streetlights were the projector of my imagination, and Millie's room was the magic room of shadows chasing shadows, up the walls and across the ceiling.

All the other rooms in our apartment were off to one side of the long hall, except for Harold and Mom's room, which shared a wall with Millie's room facing the front street. After Millie's room came the living room, then the kitchen, and the bathroom. The last room, by the front door, faced the back alley – what my sister referred to as "the dungeon." It was my room.

During the night in my dungeon, I would hear cats sounding like human babies being tormented and was forced to listen to their hollow mournful cries of intense agony. Even with these eerie sounds of the night, my dark dungeon was my sanctuary. There, I was alone and didn't have to pretend or work so hard, so incredibly hard, to protect myself from the wolves with sharp teeth.

As I walked to my room, I saw something looming in the dark shadows of the hall, blocking my way. The closer I got, the clearer the shadowy form became. I recognized the red squares on the back of a monster, the monster named Harold. He was swaying in slow motion, like treading under water, making a great effort to think and decide where he was. I stopped about five feet away and could see him clearly now in his red checkered, mackinaw jacket that he wore like a second skin.

Struggling to keep his balance, Harold grabbed me with his large, beefy hands to steady himself. The longer he leaned on me, the more I could feel his crushing weight. My legs began to shake and buckle and just as I was about to cave-in, Harold shoved me against the wall – I hit it like a limp wet rag.

Harold's alcohol-spit sprayed across my face, "Get the fuck out of my way you little stupid, Jew bastard!" His hand felt like a hammer. One blow would have crushed my thin bones, and he could have killed me so easily, either by accident or intention. That was the first time in my life I truly believed I could die.

Everything in me wanted my mom, but I was too afraid to scream for help. An outburst from my scrawny, insignificant self might be taken by Harold as a personal attack. So I swallowed the lump of fear that was stuck in my throat. It gathered into a hard ball of desperation that pressed against my chest and drew tears from my heart. I didn't make a sound or move a muscle – like you'd react to a mad dog.

Some people, like my mom, thought Harold was a good-looking man, but Millie and I didn't think so. Harold had a square-shaped head with short, tight, wavy hair. He was large-boned, thick and muscular and carried his strength quietly, like an unexploded bomb that at any time could activate and violently explode. We never knew if a word, a gesture, or us just being there, would turn him into the monster he was.

Harold bent forward to lift a couple of paper bags from the floor and tripped over his own drunkenness. His arms thrust out against the hall wall for balance. Taking a deep breath, he lifted one of the packages and grabbed me with his other hand. Looking at the other bag still on the floor he said, "Bring that bag into the kitchen. You hear me? Yes? No? ...What!?"

Afraid to hear my own voice, I inaudibly whispered, "Uh-huh."

Harold banged and probed the top of my head with his steel-like fingertips "Hellooo? Anybody there?" In pain, desperate and confused, I answer with a nod.

"Don't you shake your head at me." His yellow-stained hands forced my head around. "Look at me when I'm talking to you!"

The tears were swelling in my eyes. I tried to answer but nothing came out. I was choking on my fear.

"What's the use – why am I even talking to this fucking idiot?" Harold stumbled into the kitchen.

I picked up the bag from the floor and it began to pulsate in my arms, then popped and snapped against my chest. A hand with teeth broke through the bag. I screamed and dropped the bag on the kitchen floor and watched as another toothed hand broke through, and another, until the entire bag ripped open. Creatures with hard oval bodies sounding like ivory dice clanking together, spilled out all over the floor and scattered in all directions.

"You fuckin' stupid, stupid, stupid! Look at what you did! Can't you do anything right? You'll always be a stupid, asshole Jew!"

Harold rushed to his crabs. Their snapping claws clamped onto one of his fingers, but he was too numb to feel it. Spotty barked and started to herd the crabs. One of them stood its ground, ready to defend itself from this undignified harassment. Spotty walked up to the bold crab and cautiously sniffed around it. The crab snapped at her nose, and she jumped back to a safe distance, bravely barking from where she stood.

Harold corralled all the crabs onto the kitchen table and, one by one, dropped them into a pot of boiling water. The remaining crabs on the table started to panic, as if they had heard the tortured cries of the others being boiled alive. The pot was full of squirming crabs tearing at each other, ripping off their claws. When they turned a bright red, nothing moved, except for the bubbling water that found its way to the surface, filtering through, around and between the crabs.

Harold switched his attention to the other bag and pulled out two towering bottles of Rheingold beer. They stood there above my head, a threat of what to expect for the rest of the night. Harold turned and saw me looking at him. From behind his thin, gold-rimmed glasses, he gave me a loathing stare and started toward me.

"Who the hell are you looking at?!"

Before he reached me, my mother walked into the kitchen and asked... "Harold, vhy don't you trim da tree? Go on, I'll take care of the crabs. Sollinue, go in the living room and help."

I didn't understand, I thought she came into the kitchen to save me and now she was sending me into the living room to be alone with him.

For Millie and me, the living room was a no-man's land, a buffer zone between Harold's room and ours. It was very large and sparsely furnished. The largest piece of furniture was a dark maroon, paisley velvet couch. Across the room was a matching chair. Their heavy, dead weight pressed hard against the floral linoleum floor. The room had two windows facing the back alley and, almost lost on the walls, were two very small cheap prints of windjammer ships on a calm sea. That's all there was. I almost forgot about the tall floor lamp standing erect like a sentry over the maroon chair, looking like a place used for reading. But it was only a prop, because no one ever read in our house.

My sister Millie and I watched as Harold set up the nativity scene under the Christmas tree. Each piece was individually wrapped in colored tissue paper, packed neatly in little square cardboard compartments. He handled them very delicately, as if they were so fragile that by just touching them, he would break them.

My mom came into the room as Harold started to trim the tree. "Harold, vhy don't you let da kids help trim da tree?"

He sharply turned to my mother, "I'm not going to let a couple of cocksucking Jew brats go near my tree!"

"Harold, shush, don't have such a mouth."

"This is *my* tree. It's *my* Christmas, and I'm not going to have a couple of filthy, Jew bastards infect my tree by touching it."

Millie and I knew Mom was pushing Harold a little too far and that at any moment he was going to ignite. If she wanted peace in the house, why didn't she leave him alone and let us go to our rooms?

But she continued, "Harold, you're right. It is your Christmas and the children have no presents. Vhy don't you get them presents?"

Millie and I were relieved when Harold said nothing and continued to decorate his Christmas tree.

"Da kids never get presents."

Why, on this particular night, did she care about presents when she never did before?

"Come, Harold, it's Christmas. Christmas is for kids. Get dem something."

To my surprise, Harold reluctantly agreed. And then, from out of nowhere, Mom said..."Millie, Solly, go with him and pick out something nice."

Without hesitating, Millie refused. No matter how insistent my mother was, Millie couldn't be budged. I had great respect for her courage and, even if I was two and a half years younger, I tried to imitate Millie and refused to go. But there was nothing I could say or do to change my mother's mind. I couldn't bear her not loving me for any reason, so I couldn't refuse her. She still had that power over me. It was her love and joy of life that kept me alive. All she had to do was insist and I was lost. I was forced to go with Harold. What had I done to make her punish me like this?

It was after rush hour, and there was no one in the street. No movement, nothing. The neighborhood was at a standstill. The wind glanced off my ears, whistling a warning. Each snowflake thundered down, landing like a soft cat's paw. It fell so heavily it dissolved all traces of concrete in soft undulating waves. The glowing circus of lights was now trapped between the thick mountains of snow.

From time to time I saw a few stragglers with last minute presents held tightly under their arms, walking home in the opposite direction. When they passed us by, they puzzled at the sight of a little boy and a drunken man fighting their way out into the blizzard and back toward the Boulevard. I couldn't accept the idea that I was alone with

Harold. All I could think of was how much I wanted to be home. But this nightmare had to be played out.

My eyelashes were heavy with frozen flakes of snow, and I could hardly see as I fought back my tears. Harold stared down at the snow in front of his feet, never saying a word to me, never looking back to see if I was still with him. All the way to the toy store, the wind carried Harold's resentment back into my face.

The clatter of dangling bells over the door made my skin jump as it announced our entry into the toy store.

"I'm sorry but I'm closing up."

"Sir, this won't take long just a couple of minutes of your time," Harold said in his best polite manner.

"Ok, but make it fast. I'd like to get home before it gets any worse out there."

"Don't worry, Sir, I assure you we'll be gone in a few moments."

Harold was always the perfect gentleman with strangers and especially with the police. They never suspected he was a cruel bastard. Realizing we were standing too close together, Harold stepped away in disgust, distancing himself from me. He didn't want anyone thinking I belonged to him in any way.

"Well Stupid, don't just stand there, hurry up and get something."

It was almost impossible to imagine that I... me, Solly, was in a toy store able to pick any toy I wanted. Toys I'd always seen in store windows but could never own. And here was my once in a lifetime chance, a child's lifetime – in this child's lifetime. But because of Harold's all encompassing hatred of me and my deep fear of him, I'd have given up all these toys in exchange for being home alone in my warm room. I took two small steps into the store and my mind froze. All the toys blended together in a blur.

"Don't you understand English! I said get something! We don't have all day. Move it!"

I grabbed what was closest to me, a basketball – a game I didn't like and never played, or ever wanted to play. The games I loved were the street games my friends and I played. But there I was, trekking back home in the storm with a drunken mass of hate, carrying a ball a third my size.

By this time of night all the stores were closed, leaving a desert of snow in ominous blue shadows. I was lost in this dark and strange place where there wasn't a single person to be seen – alone with a monster, never to find my way home.

It had gotten very cold while we were in the store, and the freezing cold was another insult to my soul. A hat whipped around the corner of Hoe Avenue and into the empty street, breaking the monotony of the white and gray night. The hat was followed by the silhouette of a man dressed in an overcoat. The stranger's arms and overcoat were flapping in all directions, his twists and turns dictated by the deep snow. Desperately he screamed out, "Stop my hat! Please help me!"

"Vhat's dis?" said my mother, looking at the basketball. "Is dat vhat you pick? My Sollinue, vhat are you going to do vit dat? Its snowing. Look... look out da window. It's the middle of winter. Vhere are you going to use it? Vhere's your brains? Vhat am I going to do vit you?"

Mom shook her head, sighed and, with her lips puckered, made quick rhythmical sounds with her tongue like water dripping from a leaky faucet.

"Vell anyway, vhy don't you and Millie wait in the living room, I'll finish mit supper."

Since Harold, Mom had spent most of the time keeping us kids away from him and now, once again, she was sending us into the living room to be with him. Why was she doing this?

My sister and I sat quietly on the couch cringing, hoping, and praying that Christmas Eve would end. Harold walked by, ignoring us, and disappeared behind the French doors leading to his bedroom. He was gone. Millie and I were alone. We looked at each other, sighed, and began to breathe again.

Then from Harold's room, we heard him rummaging through dresser drawers, heard doors opening and closing. It all stopped abruptly, as if someone breathed in and forgot to breathe out.

Suddenly and with a lively gait, Harold proudly burst into the living room holding a long, black leather case with a big bump at one end. He opened the case and a golden light glistened into the room.

It was a trombone with engraved curlicues spiraling up and down and around the instrument. A real trombone – not just a picture of one or something I saw in the movies. It was real and right in front of me. Looking closer, I noticed that it was in pieces. Each piece was snuggled in its own dark purple-blue velvet bed. All the pieces smoothly slid together, gently clicking in place.

Harold caressed the slide with soft hands, pushing the paper clip-like shape back and forth in long and quick short strokes. This controlled the deep, bellowing, fart-like sounds vibrating out of the bell shape at its end. After he tuned-up, Harold began to play excerpts of music he knew. And in between these abbreviated tunes, he stopped to reminisce about his illustrious career as a musician.

"I played with the big ones. I played with the best of them, the best of the bands. I never had to have an audition, they all heard of me."

His eyes glazed over and almost mumbling to himself, Harold's mind walked through swollen thoughts.

"I had a distinguished reputation. Yeah… a brilliant future… I was respected then." Harold throbs out of his numb stupor. "Vaudeville! Yes! I played for the big names, like Jack Benny. That's right, Jack Benny, and others just as great. My best friend was a songwriter, and I was there when he thought of the song, a classic, *Yes, We Have No Bananas*. He was my best friend."

Like his trombone, Harold slid into a different tune. "I'm an educated man, a college graduate. Brilliant... yes, brilliant. I could have been anything I wanted to be, do you understand? They respected me. They all respected me. I could have been anything, anything... anything."

Harold stared off to the side, almost crying.

He switched gears again and played another tune. Looking straight at me, he said, "Books, wonderful books of great men, Ralph Waldo Emerson, Thoreau's *Walden Pond*. *"If a man does not keep pace with his companions, it is because he hears a different drummer!"*

Harold asked me, "Do you know what that means?"

The quote and the strange names meant nothing to me. I was only listening to my fear. All I knew was that they were just sounds coming from his face, with sticky white gook at the corners of his eyes and spit that bubbled and pulled from his lips, leaving a thick rim of white coating the edges of his mouth.

Then Harold asked me the question he always asked me, over and over again, "How old are you?"

It was his subtle way of telling me I was very dumb for my age. By this time I knew it was a rhetorical question, so I didn't answer and turned away. Wrong move.

"You little prick, look at me when I'm talking to you. Look at me!"

His arm shot out like a steam shovel and shoved me deep into the couch, leaving a lingering hurt in my chest. I tried, but I couldn't bear to look into Harold's hating eyes. Instead, I concentrated on his forehead.

"That's better."

Harold put his angry face inches away from mine.

"Do you know what I do with my life now? I break my balls in a freezing cold shipyard, lifting as much as two to three hundred pounds everyday. Everyday! For what? A Jew whore and her little bastards? You don't understand a word I'm saying, do you? Do you?"

It was a jumble of words I couldn't straighten out in my head. I was desperate. I didn't understand a word he was saying. I was trying to unravel his words, but I couldn't make them fit into my world of understanding... it wasn't working. I was in a desperate dilemma. If I kept silent it would anger him, and if I gave the wrong answer he'd kill me.

"Answer me, you stupid little cocksucker!"

My decision was made for me, because I had nothing to say. This infuriated him and he came at me like an angry bull. Harold grabbed me and his knuckles pressed against my bony chest, pulling at both sides of my shirt and scrunching my shoulders together. "You brainless shit."

In the middle of Harold's tirade, my attention focused on the cigarette that never left his lips. It had burned down almost to his mouth leaving a long trail of ash still attached, replacing the cigarette that was once there. Throughout his violent attacks, the ash never fell off. What kept it there? Why didn't it fall off?

Harold didn't know what to do with me. My silence frustrated him into a rage, and he threw me to the floor. My situation was hopeless. There was no fight left in me. Harold grabbed an open bottle of beer next to him and poured it over my head. It flowed down my face and into my eyes. I couldn't blink fast enough to stop the burning pain. Rubbing my eyes just made it worse. Who could ever have known that a simple thing like beer could hurt so much.

Harold stood Millie and me up against a blank wall in the living room. Millie smartly realized that this was not the time to rebel.

"Hitler, I love that man – a wonderfully brilliant man. He knows the truth. He knows what you really are. You little Jews are filthy animals... slimy, crawling little roaches. You're not human. America just doesn't understand. He doesn't want our country, all he wants is to help the world rid itself of you fucking maggots, once and for all. He's brilliant, but I don't think its being done fast enough. I'm afraid the war might end before he finishes the job."

I couldn't understand what he meant about the Jews. I didn't know what Jewish was. All I knew was that I was Jewish. It wasn't my fault. I had nothing to do with it. It was just a word to me. It could have been just another part of my anatomy, like the arm, the liver, the lung, the Jew. But Harold was an educated man, and he seemed to know what a Jew was... what I was. So, it must be so.

"Vhat's going on in dere?"

Mom rushed in from the kitchen. "Supper is finished and if you vant to eat, you leave the children alone.

After having worked up a good appetite, Harold walked calmly into the kitchen. Millie and I started for our rooms. This is what we had done every night since Harold came to live with us, eat alone in our rooms.

"Vhere are you two going? Come, we're all going to eat together." She said it like she was doing us a favor. I sank down into the chair, lost behind the white rectangle of the enamel kitchen table. The silence was heavy and full of tension. Millie and I could practically touch each other's thoughts. We could hear them screaming out for someone to save us. Harold began to pontificate again about his great intelligence, spouting excerpts of books he had read, and once more repeated the quote from *Walden*.

"If a man does not keep pace with his companions, perhaps it is because he hears a different drummer. Let him step to the music..."

While Harold droned on I thought to myself, Here is a man who talks about books, but I've never seen him read one. In fact, there wasn't a single book in our apartment. Not one. And here is a man who tells us that he is a great musician, but never listens to music.

"Sit up! Don't slouch. And get your elbows off the table."

"Harold, let the boy eat."

"Eat? He'll eat the way I tell him to eat. This is my house and it's my money that's paying for his food."

My mother retorted, "I also work hard to pay for dat food."

Harold conveniently ignored what she said and changed the subject back to me. "The little retard eats like a pig. You don't just eat one thing at a time. You go around your plate like this -- Harold demonstrated – and you eat a little of everything."

Harold might have been right, but his seething hate turned my stomach. I didn't even want to look at the food. But food meant everything to my mom. She begged me, "Please, Solly. Eat."

The phone rang from their bedroom. My mom went to answer, leaving us alone again with Harold. He looked at me with contempt, his lips pressed tightly together into two thin lines holding back his hatred. In a low, seething voice that sucked back his anger he said,

"Eat... your... supper."

"I can't. I don't feel good."

"You think I'm a fool? I know what you're trying to do. When I say you eat, you eat!"

Harold got up and stood over me. He scooped up a handful of large boiled potato pieces from my plate and ground them into my face, trying to force them down my throat. His yellowed fingers smelled of tobacco and alcohol, mingled with his sweaty hands. He grabbed another handful and mashed them up into my nose and mouth. The potatoes overflowed from my mouth and squeezed through his fingers, crumbling down to the kitchen floor. Whatever he could not get into me, he smashed on my face until I couldn't catch my breath. I was suffocating and he wouldn't stop.

My mother ran into the room. "Harold, vhat are you doing? You son of a bitch, he's choking!"

I coughed up most of the potatoes except for a small lump that lodged between my nose and throat. Tears ran down my face. My mother held a handkerchief to my nose, "Blow hard! Quick, blow!" I blew hard and it cleared my passageway. I clung to my mom like a vise while I took in trembling gulps of air.

"You could of killed the boy! He's only six – a baby. Vhat's wrong vit you? How could you do such tings to a small child? Vhat kind of man are you? Your hands should only fall off!"

"Your little prick is not so innocent. He knows what he did. He's just trying to get away with it."

"Vhat are you talking? Get away vit what?"

"Listen, Bitch, this is my house and he's going to live by my rules."

"Noooo! You're just drunk, and you're going to leave him alone. Solly, Millie, go to your rooms."

Thank God – at last! Harold pushed Mom aside and put his face into mine, "Listen, and listen good. If I hear so much as a peep from your room, I'll kill you. That you understand, don't you? Now you little moron, get to your room like your mother said."

Who was this man? Why did he despise me so? Maybe it was true.

Maybe I was mentally retarded. Maybe I was horrible, contemptible and ugly. After all, Harold should know... he was an intelligent man.

Behind my closed door, I could hear Harold's deep, guttural whiskey-phlegm, wrenching up his evil self. At that very moment, I felt an irritation in my throat. Breathing in created a tickle that triggered a cough. I tried to smother it with my blanket, but it was no use, my muffled cough escaped my room. Harold's reaction was swift. He must have been waiting and listening for any excuse to punish me for whatever he thought I had done to him. He ran down the hall, and each of his steps was like a hard blow to my head.

The monster broke into my room... "You mother-fuckin' Jew bastard! Make fun of me, will you!"

Mom was right behind him and stepped between us..."Leave him alone! Don't you touch him!"

Harold warned her, "Get out of my way."

She didn't move. "Christmas, Chrustmas! It's all bullshit isn't it? You phony! All this love and peace means nothing to you... Harold, if you love me, don't do this."

"You Jewess whore! Get out of my way."

"Harold!"

Harold's eyes narrowed and leered at my mom... "Last night I kissed and licked your Jewish cunt. Love you? Isn't that enough love for you? Next time you can suck my Christian dick."

"Harold! Harold, please... the children."

Since Harold moved in with us, I had developed a system to escape listening to all the garbage that spewed from his educated Christian mouth. I learned to create a distorted clogging sound in my ears, like the middle of a yawn. I became very proficient at it and, in time, I was able to prolong the pulsating effect that vibrated over and over into my brain. Not only could I dull my hearing, I could lose all connection to anything outside myself. I couldn't hear or think of anything else but the erratic vibrations in my head.

But it didn't work this time. There was no escaping Harold. He broke through my defenses when he tore my mother's dress into shreds.

"You're nothing to me! You and your little fuckin' retard... Nothing!" He hit me on the head with his concrete knuckles. "The very sight of you makes me sick."

"Harold, enough already! I beg of you."

Harold was out of control, and my mom tried to run. He grabbed her hair, turned her around and, with his bulging fist, punched her in the stomach, sending her crumbling to the floor.

Mom's voice was weak and low, "Please Harold, you're going to kill me. Please."

Harold looked down at her and answered with a grunt, turned and walked away exhausted. I was too young to hate as much as I hated Harold.

A dead, meaty thud shook the apartment. It was Harold passing out onto the living room floor next to his nativity scene. This was the time of the weekly collection, Mom's religious ritual. Every Friday, and on holidays, Harold would pass out and my mom would take up the collection by searching Harold's pants pockets for his pay envelope. If she didn't, she'd never see that money again.

Harold lay unconscious on the floor, outlined by a puddle of urine and wallowing in his own shit. I closed my door to separate me from the smell of his filth seeping into my room.

I wore my room like the clothes on my back. The dresser, chair, bed, walls, and ceiling were all saturated with my energy. Everything carried my scent. It was my room and now was my time. When the lights were on, it was a safe place where I could daydream my own reality, and the rest of this night belonged to me. But later, when the lights were out, the blackness came down over my face, engulfing me in endless nothing. Opening my eyes as wide as I could, I would strain and stare into the thick darkness, but see only the black night flooding back through my eyes and into every corner of my thoughts.

There was an uneasy truce between me and the ominous silence of the pitch black room. After a while, I could sense a presence. There was someone or something in my room with me. I could hear it stirring — it was watching me. Slowly it materialized into fuzzy, agitated dots that connected and formed into distorted, threatening phantoms.

The dark shadows would begin to bend and waver in and out of the black ink. Their changing contours swelled to enormous proportions and hovered above me. Every night they made an appearance and every night they got closer, devouring anything in their path. I would feel their groping hunger pulling me toward them. And every night there was a moment when they were about to reveal themselves to me. And if they did, I knew I would be lost in their power.

I had only one way to escape and that was under my blanket, my magic shield. With my blanket over my head, I didn't exist. I became invisible to their world. In the crisp smell of clean sheets, my dark brown Bakelite radio and I cuddled together under my blanket tent. We created our own world, safe from their invading eyes. I wondered if those beings were really out there, or did they need me to live? I had this sinking feeling that I belonged to them and they were out there in limbo waiting for me to breathe life into them.

I turned on my radio and watched the pin-pointed lights of the tubes grow brighter and brighter until their warm, golden glow and the odor of the hot tubes heating the plastic shell filled my tent. I peeped out from a tiny crack at the corner of my blanket and the radio's light streamed out into the room, sending the phantoms back to their world of conditions – back to their fragile sleep, waiting to wake again, always waiting. I closed the breach in my blanket, and I was back, safe in my fortification against evil.

Looking through the transparent plastic bubble of the radio's face, I fell into a trance, staring at its musical Emerson trade mark, illuminated dial and the gold parallel lines that ran like tracks around the edges of the rectangle holding the station numbers together. To the left of the dial was a woven fabric that spoke to me in sounds that fired my imagination.

"Crackle... squeak... crackle..." Sensitive to my touch, the radio complained when I turned its dial ever so gently between the static until I found the show I was searching for. This is how I spent the rest of Christmas Eve -- with my surrogate family, Jack Benny, Edgar

Bergen and Charlie McCarthy. I didn't always understand their jokes, but just hearing their voices, grown people laughing and doing fun things together... felt like family.

I had other favorites like *The Shadow, The Lone Ranger, The Green Hornet, Superman,* and *Tom Mix.* Each show had its own theme music, and I didn't know it at the time, but they were mostly excerpts from classical music. The music meant more to me than the show itself and thrilled me with great expectations of things to come. It became an integral part of me – as if a nail had been hammered into a young tree, and when the tree grew, it grew around the nail and over the years the nail became part of the tree, fused together forever. And that's what the theme music did – became a part of me, fused together forever. By chance, when I hear the same music today, I become that child again, thrilled with the same expectations.

Every Christmas at the end of each program, the actors would step out from their characters and wish me a Merry Christmas and each time they gave me a warm, special Christmas of my own.

"My Sollinue, are you asleep?" My mom's soft, low, rich voice invaded the room. I was angry at her for what she put me through with Harold, so I ignored her and pretended to be asleep. Mom sensed that I was faking it. She stroked me with her infectious laugh then gently kissed my forehead. Her warmth penetrated my tense wall of protection, melting it all away and everything was right again.

After all the pain Harold inflicted on me that night, I was still alive. Eventually from living with it day after day, year after year, Harold's violence and my fear became part of me. It never got easier, but just like any other habit, I got used to it.

At night, Spotty's nails tapped an uneven rhythm on the linoleum floor. She would stroll through the long hall between Millie's room and mine, sharing her love by sleeping with each of us for part of the night. Late at night it was Spotty's apartment, and we belonged to her. And when all of her possessions were quietly gathered together in the same place, this was when she patrolled the apartment to protect what was hers.

STUFF HAPPENS

CLANKING METAL, A sudden booming… the radiator was getting even with me for pissing on the steam pipes in the hall. And now it was pissing steam into my room. Listening to the uneven clanking, I could've sworn someone was trapped in the walls, sending me messages for help.

"Millinue! Do me a favor, go get the mail."

Ever since Walter and Harry were in the service, Mom couldn't wait for their letters.

"I already got the mail. It's a letter from Harry!"

"Goot, goot. Read it to me."

"Hold on, hold on… I've got to open it first."

Mom sat on Millie's bed and Millie sat beside her and began to read the V-Mail.

Dear Mom, Millie and Solly,

I know I've promised to write more often, but they're really keeping us busy here. I'll try to write more often.

It's really crazy down here. These people live in their own world, separate from the rest of the country. One morning I caught my barracks buddies giving my head a real going over. I asked, "What the hell are you looking for?" Most of these guys are from the South and are convinced that Jews have horns. They were searching for mine! This is all new to me!

Until next time, love you and the kids,
Harry

Since Mom couldn't read or write, she dictated a return letter to Millie. Millie wrote it down exactly the way Mom said it.

My Heschel,
  Please write some more. I enjoy them. It makes me very happy. Everything's fine here.
  Love you, my boychickal,
  Mom

It was another day in the third grade, and my main job was to work very hard at hiding myself from the teacher. I prayed that there would be no written tests. This was not my lucky day. Mrs. Davidson announced, "This afternoon after lunch, we are going to have an arithmetic test. So be prepared. Remember, if I catch you using a fountain pen or cheating with the times table from your composition book, you'll not only fail, but your parents will be called in to see the Vice Principal."

The lunch bell rang and we all marched in an orderly line, two by two, down the caged stairway to the lunchroom. Lunch was free for students who couldn't afford it. That included Millie and me. The lunchroom had rows of long wooden tables, with long wooden benches, set up like a prison in the movies.

At the front of the room was a plain brick wall, and along the length of the whole wall was a rectangular hole where a stocky woman, wearing an apron, served hot soup out of tall metal vats. There were no choices. Everyone ate the same thing. Each soup was served with a piece of dark brown bread with peanut butter wiped across it. The bread was stale, dry and chewy. Today we were having a mystery soup. It was tasteless, like dishwater. Ahhh! To be home eating a delicious salami sandwich with lots of mustard, and a cream soda.

After lunch I knew what was waiting for me, the arithmetic test. Maybe I'll get sick and walk out of the school and go home. That's what I'll do, right after lunch… go home. While playing with my food, I saw a heavy figure walking in my direction. It was Manny!

"Solly! Come. You're going with me. Vait here vhile I get Millie."

Manny took Millie out of her classroom and we walked to the Simpson Street El and took the downtown train. What a great present – I got out of taking that damn test.

Manny had rescued us once before when he took us to a rodeo starring Gene Autry. There they were in person, right out of the movies – Gene Autry sitting on his horse Champion. When Champion reared up on his hind legs, kicking at the air, his saddle and harness lit up with sparkling gold, encrusted with jewels, outshining Madison Square Garden. At that moment, I definitely knew that Gene Autry was the King of the Cowboys.

We got out of the train at Times Square and stood on a concrete island next to the military recruiting station, across from the Times building, waiting for the light to change.

"If you're thinking vhere we are going? It's the circus." Manny didn't talk much except for a few words here and there. "Stay close." He held my hand and pointed, "Look at dat."

Behind us was a huge sign that stretched across two buildings, a man smoking a Camel cigarette and puffing real smoke circles out into the street, floating above our heads. It was starting to get dark and all Broadway was on fire with lights. Millie and I were standing in the midst of a magical kingdom of castles with moving lights, dressed in bright blinking colors.

In front of us on the roof of a two-story building, was a movie screen on a billboard, showing three animated characters in a commercial for Ajax cleanser – three little elves in one-piece pajamas, with pointed hats that flopped to one side. There was a fat one, a tall thin one, and a short one, singing their radio jingle as they foamed down the drain.

We walked past the Paramount Theatre, to between 49th and 50th street, right across from the Mayfair movie theater. Manny took us to the futuristic Horn & Hardart Automat. We entered through revolving doors and our footsteps echoed on marble floors. Everything was marble. All my radio and movie fantasies didn't compare to the real magic inside – two walls of small compartments, each with it's own window, lined up in four rows, one on top of the other, evenly placed like a honey comb. Behind each glass door was a different kind of food, from chicken potpie, to sandwiches, cakes, and fruit pies.

First, Manny showed Millie and me how to do some window shopping and let us pick out what we wanted. He went to the glass change booth, where a grumpy woman made change for his dollar bills. She hit the cash register lever and coins swirled down a chute, swishing into and around a smooth hollow in the marble slab. Manny gave us some change and showed us how it all worked.

No waiters, no waitresses. There was just me and the glass doors filled with prizes waiting for me. All I needed to open the magic doors were everyday coins, like nickels or quarters. I put them into a slot and, "Open, O Sesame!" the enchanted glass doors opened and there was the prize of my own choice: a ham sandwich. I didn't like what I got, but I didn't care. I just wanted to put more coins in the slots and watch the doors pop open.

After my chocolate doughnut dessert, we stepped out into waves of people rushing home from work. Just before we got to Madison Square Garden, we stopped at a corner store and Manny bought us a couple of toy whips made of braided cloth. They were soon to fall apart, but they meant a lot to Millie and me. A crowd was gathering at the ticket booths. We didn't have to wait, because Manny already had tickets from his union, and we walked past the long lines into the Garden.

The halls smelled like elephants. It could have been their shit we were smelling, but it was definitely elephants. Before the main show started, they entertained us with a sideshow. We could get up close to several elephants, feed them peanuts, and pet their leathery, armored trunks.

At the far end of the open landing was a small stage. On it, one of my nightmares had come to life. When I was much younger, Mom took Millie and me to a movie called, *Freaks*. In it were small people with pointed heads, who made a normal woman into a freak like them by chopping off her limbs, one at a time. And now on the stage in front of me, were those same pointed-head freaks! Each one held a rubber ball tightly in their hands, and the barker told us that if they didn't hold onto it, they would die. I almost vomited up my special food from the Automat. The horror of this moment was too real and gave me many nights of waking up in a cold sweat.

We climbed a mountain of steps to our seats in the balcony, until our legs got heavy and tired. Once in a while Manny had to stop to catch his breath. When we got as far as we could go, the doorway led us into the balcony, and then we had to walk back down the steps to our seats. They were so steep I thought at any moment I would tumble down off the balcony. I needed to feel safe and held onto Manny so tightly I felt I was a part of him. He never said a word.

Our seats were in the first row of the balcony, right at the railing, with nothing in front of us but empty space. I pushed myself back into my chair to keep from falling. When we settled into our seats, I relaxed enough to soak in the sparkling brass of the band instruments that reflected the crackling colors of the circus. I was surrounded by sharp animal smells and the circus sounds of clowns honking their horns when they bumped into each other.

We were so far up from the three rings that it was difficult to see any of the circus performances below. The only act I could see clearly was the high wire act at my eye level. There must have been twenty, long-legged women dangling from ropes around the perimeter of the stadium. They greeted the crowd with twists and turns on their ropes, wearing scant, shimmering tights, with their asses fighting to be free. The main acrobats performed in the center.

With whips and cotton candy in our hands, we watched them fly though the air in a synchronized, aerial dance, jumping from one trapeze to another.

"Oooo-ooo... Ahhhh!" The audience cooed with each dangerous leap. But not Manny. His only reactions were sympathetic, "Tsk, tsk, tsk... "

All I can remember of Manny was that he was shorter than Mom and heavy, with a full, round face and dark skin. He spoke with a strong, soft accent. I do remember our ride home on the subway. Millie and I smothered ourselves into his pillow-like hug and slept all the way home.

Mom paced the floor till we got home from the circus. She had received a letter from Walter and couldn't wait for Millie to read it.

"I'm so glad you're home! Here, here... a letter from Velvul. Read it, momala, read it." We all sat in the kitchen while Millie read.

Dear Mom,

I'm writing to tell you that I wasn't shipped out with my buddies like I was supposed to. I came down with the measles. Right now I'm in the hospital in Brooklyn and my ship took off without me. It never made it to the ocean. A German U-boat sank it. I think, I'm not sure... I think no one made it. Those poor guys, I guess I'm very lucky.

Don't worry about me Mom. Soon as I get well, I'll be coming home for a three-day leave. I told you nothing's going to happen to me.

Love, Your Walter

"My Velvul could have died!"

"But he didn't, Mom, he didn't."

"Vhy did I let him go? If anything happens to him... It's all my fault."

"But Mom, he's alright."

"Yes, momala, you're right. He's alright."

RUNTS IN TIMES SQUARE

SPRING – WHEN everything is new again, including the Super, Mr. Frick, who moved into the cellar apartment. I didn't even know there was an apartment in the cellar or that anyone ever lived down there. To me it looked like a torture chamber with dank, rough stone walls. But there was a real apartment door between those stone walls that didn't belong there. That's where Mr. Frick lived with his family: his wife, two girls, Katharine and Betty, and one boy, Bobby.

Bobby was my age and his sisters were more like Millie's age. He looked like Roy Rogers but acted like an Irish tough. There were no introductions. Bobby was just there and blended in with the rest of us guys – and now there were four of us.

There is an unwritten contract that's part of a boy's make up: after a fight, no matter who wins, the combatants become close friends. This windy spring Saturday morning wasn't any different. A kid we'd never seen before appeared on the block flying a kite. He was taller than the rest of us, and his name was Johnny Sheen. By accident, I stepped on the string of his kite, and when he saw me standing on it, his face turned red.

"Get offa my string!"

I didn't like the way he was talking to me, and I didn't like being ordered around. I refused to move.

"If you don't, I'll kill you!"

"Ehhh, in your dreams."

With a wild look in his eyes, he knocked me to the ground. Now we were five. I don't know what the block was like before we moved in, but the five of us seemed to breathe life into it. With new kids moving onto our block everyday, we now had an unending source of games we could play.

Sergie and I went through all of the garbage cans on our block and found lots of empty soda and milk deposit bottles. We cashed them in and ended up with fifty cents apiece. We were seven years old and, with our newfound riches burning a hole in our pockets, we took the subway to the City.

On the top of the turnstile post was a magnifying glass eye. When I deposited a nickel into the coin slot, it magnified it about ten times its normal size. I guess it was to keep us from putting in slugs. Anyway, Sergie and I were so small that just by bending our heads slightly, we could've walked under the turnstiles without being noticed.

The Simpson Street El was almost empty. Only one woman, besides us, was waiting for the train. There were two trains that came through the station, the Lexington and the Seventh Avenue Express. We didn't care which one we took and got on the first train that stopped, which happened to be the Seventh Avenue.

Standing in the first car, we watched the train hug the tracks as it cut through the apartment buildings. First stop, Intervale, then Prospect, and Jackson stations. From Jackson, down we went into a black hole below the street and onto the Third Avenue Station. We were riding in the belly of an iron snake, wiggling as it weaved through the twists and turns, its metal shell screamed painfully at every turn. When I pushed my head against the front window of the car, I could make the train disappear and see only my speeding body flying through the tunnels.

We got off at 42nd Street and climbed up the stairs and out onto the street. Sergie and I found ourselves across from the same military recruiting station where Manny, Millie and I had stood when we went to the circus. Sergie's older brother, Frankie, had taken him downtown many times before, so Sergie knew where we were and what places to go. We walked past the Freak Show and Jack Demsey's, heading straight for the Penny Arcade.

There were so many people walking along Broadway that nobody cared about two small kids on their own. So much was going on, it was hard to take it in all at once. It wasn't only the lights on the huge signs dancing around the buildings that gave me the feeling I was living in a cartoon world; it was being plugged into all that electricity that was turning me on.

Inside the Arcade, we could hardly see over the top of the pinball machines that filled the whole right side of the wall, from baseball games to war games. The center of the floor had telling-your-fortune and measuring-your-strength machines and at the back wall was a shooting gallery, where we spent all of our money. Time to go home.

Before we took the uptown subway home, Sergie wanted to show me one last thing, the Laugh Movies on 42nd Street. The Laugh Movie house showed 15-minute comedy shorts, one after the other, like Laurel and Hardy – we kids called them Fat and Skinny – and the Charlie Chaplin shorts. There was a never ending supply of films with the usual cast of character actors who had their own specialties and nick names, like the Slow-burn, the Drunk, the Sneezer.

Behind the ticket booth, facing the sidewalk were six doors with funhouse mirrors. Even if we couldn't go in, we had a great time watching ourselves being distorted in the mirrors. We stayed a few minutes longer to watch passersby being turned into mutants. It was later than we thought, and we ran, dodging the crowds of people, back down into the dark hole where the trains tunneled under the streets above.

Back in The Bronx, the train pulled at the El's wooden platform as it stopped at the Simpson Street Station.

"Solly? Solly! Is that you?" It was Walter looking handsome in his navy blue sailor uniform. He was getting off the same train.

"Where's Mom?"

I didn't answer. I couldn't think fast enough... but my face and body betrayed my guilt.

"What the hell do you think you're doing alone on the train?"

"I'm not alone. Sergie's with me."

"Don't wise-ass me. Does Mom know?"

"No."

"I'm not going to tell Mom. But if you ever try a stupid stunt like that again, I'll..." Walter held back his frustration, "I'll... well, just don't you ever do it again, you hear me?"

"Ah-huh"

"Promise!"

"Yes, I promise."

I lied. Within a month, Sergie and I did it again, then again and again.

Mom wasn't home, but Walter knew exactly where she would be. When she was working steady and it was payday, we all ate out at the Chink's. We sat in our usual booth and ordered the same food every week: chicken chow mein, fried rice, and a free ice cream. It was enough for all of us for only $1.75. She really didn't need to order; they already knew what she wanted.

Mom first asked for a pot of tea, and without thinking, went through her weekly routine, automatically adding five big teaspoons of sugar to the teapot and stirring it in. Then she served the usual enormous amount of chow mein and fried rice equally on our plates. As always, she said, "Don't use the soy sauce. It might be pigeon blood, and it will make you sick." For herself, Mom ordered a dish of roast pork, lean and steaming in its own bubbling juices. She wouldn't let us go near it. It was hers and hers alone.

Mom jumped out of her booth when she saw Walter, "Velvul! Mine boychickal! Look at you, my handsome Navy boy."

She noticed me standing next to Walter, "Vhere were you? We were worried! Millie and I looked all over for you."

"I was with Walter."

Walter looked at me, but he didn't give me away.

"Next time you first tell me. I was sick with worry."

Whenever Walter was home, Harold crept into his sarcophagus, waiting for Walter to leave, so he could return from the sleeping dead.

So that night, without any complaints from Harold, Walter took Mom dancing to a servicemen's club. She didn't want anyone to know she was his mother, so for the rest of the evening Walter called her Myrtle. Every one was convinced she was his date. While dancing a fast lindy with Mom, Walter spun her out and missed grabbing her hand. She flew across the dance floor toward the bandstand and crashed though the large drum. Walter pried her out of the drum and they escaped from the pissed-off band and took the first train home. They got off at Simpson Street and for two and a half blocks, they held hands laughing and skipping all the way home.

The very next day, Walter's furlough was canceled, and he was told to report to the Brooklyn Navy Yard. He was assigned to a new ship, a tanker called the Esso Paterson. Sergie told me that just one bullet in the right place and it would blow up the whole ship. It seemed that Walter wanted to find the most dangerous duty he could. He even tried to get on a submarine, but couldn't make the grade.

The Paterson took Walter to the West Coast where he volunteered for the Armed Guard on a Liberty Ship. The guys in the regular Navy called the sailors on the Liberty ships, "shark bait," because about eighty percent of them died during the war. The name of his new ship was the Edgar W. Nye, and he manned an anti-aircraft gun. Mom never knew how dangerous it was. In his letters to her, he made it seem like he was on a holiday.

COME, WE'LL GO
TO THE MOVIES

MILLIE AND I took a trip to the Public Library, a few blocks south of the Hunt's Point Palace. There was absolutely no reason for me to go to the library, because I couldn't read. But I loved it anyway.

We went around the corner to the children's entrance of the library. There were books everywhere – walls filled with books, books with answers about the world, answers I could never know. Here there were unending stories, more than I could dream of in my imagination. The pictures in the books were the closest I could get to reading. I took out as many books as I was allowed, and it was all for free. And I did it all by myself. Without even reading them, I could feel the knowledge in my hands.

At the checkout desk I was mesmerized by the way the Librarian did her job. Everything she touched came alive. Her pencil had a small rectangular stamp attached to the top of it with a due date on it. She effortlessly dabbed it on an inkpad, pressed it down on a card, and slipped the card into a pocket in the back of each book. She made the whole process look so deliciously important, and she was doing all this just for me. I wanted that pencil and inkpad. I wanted to feel what she was feeling.

"Here you are. Now remember to return the books on time."

We just about made it to our block carrying the heavy books and had to stop to put them down before the last push up the three flights

74

of stairs to our apartment. In front of our building, we watched a man unfolding a wooden tripod with a camera on it. He draped a heavy black cloth over the camera until it hung halfway down the crutch-like legs. When he finished setting up, he announced to the pass-ersby, "Only pennies for your picture. No waiting! Right here, right now!" Watching him work was like watching a sideshow performer.

Mom appeared at the doorway of our building and decided to have our pictures taken. The photographer worked quickly, told us to smile, and snapped our picture. His hands disappeared under the black tent. Millie and I heard the swishing of water, and in about one minute, out came his hands holding our photograph. It was like a small miracle. A couple of weeks went by and our photograph started to turn brown, then black – and all for "only pennies a picture."

That afternoon it got oppressively hot. To cool off, Mom took Millie and me to P.S. 75 where they had free outdoor showers in the schoolyard facing Bruckner Boulevard. I was having fun jump-ing under the shower and screaming with the rest of the kids until I stepped on a piece of broken glass. It stuck deep into the heel of my foot. I hopped to my mother and she carried me all the way to Chester Drugs. One of the Chester Drug brothers took the glass out and stopped the bleeding. "Molly, it's not a minor cut. I think you should get a doctor to look at it."

Mom said "yes," but we never did go. We very rarely went to doc-tors, and then only for serious problems. We didn't have the money to make those kinds of decisions. Our local drug store handled all the small emergencies, like splinters or something in your eye. They were the in-between angels we could always count on.

It was a dark and stormy afternoon when the monster awakened and emerged from his crypt, well-preserved with alcohol. I was so concentrated on hopping around on my painful foot that I didn't no-tice Harold behind me in the hall.

He grabbed me by my hair and said menacingly, "You little prick. You might be fooling your mother but you're not fooling me! You're not hurt, you're just a fuckin', sniveling Jew coward. Just stop it, you hear me? Just stop it or I'll give you some real pain."

I didn't know who Harold hated most, the Jews or me. But he always hung over me like a heavy iron anvil, held by a worn piece of rope about to unravel and come crashing down on me.

"Now, walk on that foot. Do you hear me? Walk on that fuckin' foot!" He pulled me by my shoulder, digging his fingers into me. "Moron! The only thing that's damaged is your brain." Harold hit me on the top of my head with his knuckles. It was like being hit with a rock.

Mom rushed out of the kitchen and pulled me away from Harold, "Vhat are you doing to the boy?"

Millie and I ate our suppers alone in our own rooms again, our normal routine. Harold always ate first in the kitchen before we got our supper. I never saw my mom sit and eat a meal at home. She just tasted as she cooked.

Invisible swords swished and clanked as Sergie and I jumped off and onto the fenders of parked cars, fighting our way home, reliving the movie we just saw about pirates called, *Frenchman's Creek*. We fought our way toward Hoe Avenue to the barbershop. I stopped and watched the red and white stripes chasing each other around the candy cane pole. I turned and smashed into a pair of long legs in Army khaki. I looked up and saw a soldier's uniform and then up into my brother Harry's face.

Harry laughed, "Whoa, easy does it! This is my kid brother, Solly."

Standing beside him was a woman beautiful enough to be a movie star. She was wearing a short fur coat and matching hat. Her smiling eyes looked down on me.

"Hello, Solly, my name is Sylvia. Harry, you didn't tell me he was so cute."

When Sergie saw my brother with this beautiful woman, it made me feel proud. I followed them home, and Sylvia asked me if I liked school. Most kids knew that grown-ups wanted you to say, "Yes," so I didn't disappoint her. She was trying to be friendly and get me to like her, which I did already. She began asking me to spell a few simple words. And my fears came flooding back. This wonderful moment became a nightmare. The more Sylvia tried to help me with some spelling hints, the more my mind became blank, and the more terrified I became that she would find out how stupid I was. And then this pretty woman wouldn't like me anymore.

Harry announced to Mom that he and Sylvia were engaged and would be married soon, before he shipped out. This was all new to Mom, but she accepted Sylvia without question.

Sleeping buildings, sleeping streets, even the El tried to muffle its screeching sounds so as not to wake this noiseless Sunday morning. It seemed the world had ended, and Sergie, Bobby Frick, and I were the only ones alive. Our voices and footsteps left a trail of echoes in the empty streets.

We heard the clacking of high heels on the sidewalk. A woman was walking toward us from the direction of the train station. She wore a black, lacy gown and hat, shiny red shoes, and sequined purse.

Sergie asked, "Late night?"

She stopped in front of us, "Hello, boys," she spoke with a man's voice. "What are you doing up so early on a Sunday?"

I asked, "Are you a man?" It was really hard to tell.

"Yes, my little dears. I'm a man, dressed like a woman."

"Why?" Sergie asked.

"Because it's fun. Well, it's nice talking to you, but I've got to be going." Then he or she slithered away.

I was eight years old, and my friends and I thought that it was really cool that you can change yourself with make up and clothes and no one would know who you were... you could have a secret identity. That Halloween we all dressed up as women.

THE SHADOW KNOWS

MOM SENT ME to Manny's to collect the weekly ten dollars. On my way, I stopped at the cigar store at the corner of 167th Street and Southern Boulevard, just past the church. Inside, they had moving picture machines. A few pennies would unlock a handle on the side of what looked like a small mailbox. Attached to the top was a pair of binocular viewers. I pressed my eyes against the rubber lining that hugged the viewer and saw a deck of cards with pictures of silent comedy stars like Charlie Chaplin. When I turned the handle for a few seconds, the cards flipped creating the illusion of movement as Chaplin got hit in the face with a pie.

Across Southern Boulevard near the Art movie theater, was a mountain of granite cropping up between two apartment buildings. It looked like it should have been in the Bronx Park. It reached from the Boulevard over to Simpson Street, where Manny lived.

Manny's front door opened into his kitchen. I could hear him snoring in the bedroom. Mom said he slept all the time because he was lazy, but I figured out it was because he worked at night.

On top of his refrigerator there was a picture of Manny when he was a young man with a full head of black hair, looking down at me, watching me search his kitchen. To the right of the front door against the wall, was a tall, white cabinet. Paint was peeling off the edges and under the peelings, I could count about eight layers in different colors of paint. In one of the drawers, I found a jackknife. It was brand new and stood out in a bed of junk. I hesitated, listened for Manny's snoring, then took the knife.

Every few weeks, Manny would replace the missing jackknife with other little prizes, or another knife. And every time he would put them in the same place for me to find. This led me to believe he knew I was taking them. It was a game between us, and for that brief moment, I felt he loved me in the only way he knew how.

I sat on the edge of Manny's bed, and he pretended he was sleeping. I rubbed his sandpaper beard to see what it felt like. Suddenly, he snapped at my hand and we laughed. Manny got dressed and took me with him to the garage to pick up his cab. We walked side by side, not saying a word to each other, past the Freeman movies to the garage. To get to Manny's cab, we walked though a cool wind tunnel, blowing with the smell of gas and grease.

Manny sat me in front with him on the passenger side of the cab. There was no car seat, so I sat on a wooden crate while he drove me home. Staring up out the window, I watched the rooftops following us. I felt they were coming after me, but we traveled a little bit faster and left them behind.

When I got home, all our furniture was collected in the center of the living room. Two house painters wearing splattered white paint overalls were covering the floors and furniture with heavy canvases.

"Sollinue, I'm glad you're home. I'm taking you and Millie to the movies vile the painters paint. Come, I made some salami sandwiches. We'll eat at the movies."

Harold spent his day bar hopping. He went everywhere, but never to Harry's Bar just across the street. That would have been so much easier than traveling all around The Bronx, but he didn't want to end up lying dead drunk in the gutter in his own neighborhood.

Spotty stayed home alone, locked up in Millie's room having a show of her own at Millie's open windowsill by the fire escape, watching the streets below.

At the Boulevard movies, we saw the second feature first, *The Curse Of The Cat People*. It gave me nightmares... nothing new to me. During the movie *Meet Me In St. Louis*, I was fixed on the way the actors on the screen savored each bite of food they ate. They made it look so good I could almost taste it. Whatever they were eating, I wanted it. By the time the movie ended, I was starving. Hungry gurgles raced around in my stomach, "Let there be food."

By the time we got home, the house painters were finished, and with paint-spotted faces, they folded the canvases and took down their ladders. Spotty was busting a gut. She pulled at the cuff of my pants, and dragged me to the front door. We both raced down the stairs, Spotty beating me to the curb as always. After she peed, we raced back up the stairs, and I dashed into my room. It was five o'clock – time for *The Shadow*.

"*Who knows what evil lurks in the hearts of men, The Shadow knows...*" The show ended with an echoing, evil laugh.

Mom started to make supper, and the smell of paint cooking together with her food burned my eyes and dulled my appetite.

A loud, heavy growl came from the kitchen. "Why don't you let the little Jew brat get his own food? Let me give that little piece of shit his food."

"Vhat are you talking? I'll give it to him."

"Next time I'll show that little prick what's what."

When *The Jack Benny Show* was over, Millie came to my room to see if I had any new joke books she could borrow. She noticed the new jackknife on the night table by my radio.

"Where did you get that?"

"Manny gave it to me."

"No he didn't. I can tell you're lying. You stole it, didn't you?"

"No, he gave it to me."

"Liar. You stole it. If you don't tell me the truth, I'll ask Manny if he gave it to you."

"Okay, okay, I took it."

"I knew it. I'm gonna tell Mom."

"You bastard!"

"Call me what you want. I'm telling her anyway."

I punched her on the arm, "You fuckin' bastard."

With her sharp, cat-like claws, Millie scratched my arm, leaving two trails of blood. Harold was in the bathroom next to my room, "What the hell is going on in there? If you two don't shut the fuck up... you'll be sorry if you make me come in there!"

Millie and I went to our neutral corners. She was alone in her room, and I was alone in mine, feeling hurt and betrayed. I wanted revenge. I thought of Millie's expensive doll carriage that Manny had given her. He gave me shit: a box of leather gun holsters that someone left in his cab. I mean for chrissakes, what the hell am I going to do with all those empty holsters? They didn't even have belts!

I snuck out of the front door and down to the basement, found Millie's doll carriage, and with my stolen jackknife, cut the hood to shreds. I threw my knife away into a garbage pail, and unseen, went back upstairs. No one ever knew I had left my room. I was back in time to hear the *Edgar Bergen and Charlie McCarthy Show*.

It was the night before school, and my weekend was ending. I tried to slow down every minute of every radio show to make those minutes last a little longer and hold onto my freedom. A warm, glowing light from the radio tubes chased away any lingering monsters of the night. My radio and I went to bed together under the protective cover of my blanket.

It was hard to enjoy the Bergen and McCarthy show, because *The Shadow* was haunting me. I kept hearing the ending of the show:

"The weed of crime bears bitter fruit. Crime does not pay. The Shadow knows. Crime does not pay... The Shadow knows... The Shadow knows."

MILLIE OVERPLAYS HER HAND

I STOOD THERE in front of the class, the only kid in the school – no, the whole neighborhood – who still wore knickers. Harold forced me to wear the fuckin' things.

"Mr. Rothman. You will begin by reading the first two pages."

Several weeks before, Mrs. Davidson had assigned each of us a page from a children's book to read to the class. The problem was, I didn't know how to read. Mom had given Millie the job of teaching me. Millie felt it was an impossible task, so she took a short cut and made me memorize the two pages assigned to me.

Book in hand and my knickers bulging at the knees, I stared at the book, pretending I was reading the first lines.

"Wait! Wait, I'm sorry Mr. Rothman. I gave those two pages to someone else. You'll have to read a different page."

A groan slipped from my mouth, "Now? You mean now?"

"This is a very easy book. I know you can do this."

They say you can only die once, but they're wrong. I died many times in that moment. But lucky for me, Mom was playing match-maker for Mrs. Davidson, matching her up with the gym teacher Mr. Mackay, so Mrs. Davidson let me off lightly.

It was almost lunch when an unexpected rainstorm pelted the school windows. Millie and I were told to meet our mother in the ground floor gym. What was Mom doing here? She was supposed to be working. As soon as I saw her waiting in the gym, I didn't care about why. She was my home and wherever she went, she brought it with her.

"Here, I brought galoshes and umbrella. Millinue, later I want you to vait for Solly and come home together. Look vhat I got for you. I went to the deli and bought pastrami sandwiches on club... also a bottle of Pepsi. Okay, I've got to go now."

"Mommy," Millie winced with pain.

"Vhat is it?"

"I have this terrible pain inside. It's hard for me to walk."

"Where? Show me."

"Right here." Pointing to her right side.

"I can't go back to school, it hurts too much."

"You're coming home with me."

When Millie looked at me, I knew she was lying. What a great way to get out of school. It worked so well, she complained for two more days and stayed out of school.

After the third day, "Dis is not good... I'm calling the doctor."

"Doctor? Why the doctor?"

"I'm not taking chances."

Doctor Parato pressed the right side of Millie's belly, "Does this hurt?" It was too late to stop now, and Millie continued the charade. She groaned as if she was in pain. Dr. Parato pressed again and Millie forgot to react. He knew she was faking it and pressed harder. Millie doubled up in make-believe pain. Dr. Parato decided to teach her a lesson.

"This girl needs to have her appendix removed right away. She's in a very serious condition."

I think Millie had overplayed her hand. They left immediately for the hospital in his car. She tried to tell the truth – but no one would believe her. This had gone too far, and she begged to go home, screaming all the way to the operating room.

Dr. Parato took out Millie's healthy appendix to teach her a lesson. But the lesson never took. There were many times after her appendix incident when Millie still pretended to be sick to get out of school. I guess staying out of school was worth losing her appendix.

The day Mom was bringing her home from the hospital, Sergie and I found a chair in the hall at the bottom of the steps of my building. It sat there empty for a long time and didn't seem to belong to anyone. It was a toy just waiting to be played with, but by the time we were through playing, its back legs were broken off. When we learned from Bobby Frick that the chair was there for Millie to rest on before her big trip up the three flights of steps, we quickly balanced the back legs under the chair and ran from the scene of our crime.

Harold came downstairs, carried Millie into the hall and sat her down to rest. The legs of the chair gave way underneath her, and she fell backwards onto the floor. Harold tripped over Millie and what was left of the chair and, with a groan, picked Millie up and carried her upstairs, cursing all the way. They never found out who was responsible for this heinous act.

"Stop complaining!"
"I'm tellin' ya, it was in the box!"
"Bullshit."
"What the fuck are you tallkin' about? It *was* in the box."
"No, it wasn't!"
"Ah, come on! I want a do-over."
The morning was warm and soft, and while we were waiting for the rest of the guys, Sergie and I played box baseball. It was a game of quick reactions and control, played with a Spaldeen, within the grooved outline of three sidewalk boxes.

When the guys showed up, we all walked to the Boulevard movies. A long line of noisy kids filled with excited expectations were waiting for the box office to open, holding ten cents for admission in their hot little hands. Every one carried crinkling brown bags filled with their lunches.

It was the Saturday Matinee, which included three cartoons, a serial, a comedy short, a travelogue, a newsreel and two feature films. In front of the theater facing the street was a huge, colorfully painted poster of Charles Laughton as *The Canterville Ghost* surrounded by action scenes to entice us. The second feature was a B-movie, *Cobra Woman,* with Maria Montez, Jon Hall, and Sabu.

Some weird acting kid on line in front of me wearing a flyers' cap with goggles was swinging his arms wildly and hit me right on the nose. The blood gushed out of my nose, but I stopped it with my handkerchief. No bloody nose was going to keep me from the Saturday Matinee.

When I got home late that afternoon, a horse and wagon was parked in front of my building selling fruits and vegetables. Sergie, Bobby Frick and I walked over to the horse, "Hey! You kids! Get away from my horse."

Hand-painted prices on brown paper bags hung over wooden sticks for each vegetable and fruit. There was a whole different sound to the block: a squeaking metal scale, paper bags being snapped open and a gathering crowd around the wagon.

"Solly!" Mom called me from her window "Stay dare. I want you to get me a couple of onions and four apples. Here!" She threw down some change, wrapped in a piece of newspaper.

"Bring dem right up!"

Mom shouted down to the vegetable man what she wanted and told him I'd pay for it.

"Alright, Lady, you got it."

"Now don't you give me any rotten apples, d'ya hear?"

"Lady, I only have the best."

Harold wasn't home yet, so we were in the kitchen with Mom as she was cooking. Millie sat in a chair reading a letter from Harry. The letter came a couple of months after D-Day, the Normandy Invasion.

Dear Mom,

    I'm somewhere in France, but I can't say where.

The next line in the letter was blacked out. It wasn't till later we learned he was in the special service, the 361st regiment, non-combatant engineers.

My job is to guard the German Prisoners. They are so arrogant, I feel like I'm their prisoner. I'm glad they don't know I'm Jewish. They think I'm German, because my name is Schnell.

They made me a staff sergeant in charge of our section. Everyday the troops are further inland and deeper into France. We are constantly on the move. My friends and I confiscated a railroad car and changed it into our own private living quarters. Now every time we have to move inland, our barracks moves with us.

I'm stopping now. I only have a little time left to write Sylvia. She told me she found us an apartment. Have you seen it?

Let me know what's happening at home.

Miss you and the kids,

Love, Harry

"Sollinue, do me a favor. Supper ain't ready yet. Here, I owe Yetta five dollars. Here, go give it to her and come right back."

On my way out, I grabbed an apple and while walking downstairs to Yetta's, I was replaying the movie, *The Canterville Ghost,* over and over in my mind. Lost in my daydream, I knocked on Yetta's door. Just as I was about to take a bite of the apple, the door opened and, to my surprise it wasn't Yetta, it was Mr. Gamson who lived directly below us. The Gamson's stayed pretty much to themselves and didn't have a particular liking for us. They must be able to hear Harold's ugly, violent episodes right above them.

"Well, what do you want?"

I was confused and couldn't answer.

He said, "What the hell are you doing here knocking on my door?"

I was frozen to the spot, wondering how did I get here? To me, his voice sounded thick and slow.

"You little bastard, I caught you, didn't I? Play tricks on me will ya!" He hauled off and slapped me hard across the face, knocking the apple out of my hand.

The shock of it held me there for a moment. Then I ran up the stairs into my room and cried. Not because it hurt so much, but because it felt like such an insult. And I was ashamed of doing another stupid thing.

"Solly, vhy are you crying?" I handed the five dollars back to my mom.

"So what happened?"

I told her everything, "… and Mr. Gamson believed I did it on purpose. I didn't, I swear to you I didn't. And he slapped me."

Harold came in the front door and stood by my doorway, listening.

Mom turned to Harold, "Harold, do something."

She must have been kidding… I mean, Harold was going to stand up for me when he would have liked to be the one who slapped me?

"The little prick probably deserved it." Harold says these things and Mom acts like she doesn't hear them.

"If you won't, I will."

When Mom left the room, Harold walked over to me, "I'm curious, how did he slap you? Did he do it like this?" He swung his hand like a bat and slapped me across the face, almost knocking me across the room. He made me feel I was less than human. He was just about to hit me again, when Mom walked in.

"They won't answer their door. That's all right, they'll have to come out sometime and I'll catch them."

"Don't waste your time. The boy is a lying little prick." With that he walked away.

"How do you feel, my totala? Oy, look at the side of your face. It's all red. That bastard had no right to hit my little boy."

Mom didn't know the bruise wasn't from Mr. Gamson.

"Does it hurt?"

"I'm okay."

"I'll bring a delicious hot supper to you. Okay, mine boychick?"

THE FBI IN WAR
AND PEACE

BOBBY, JOHNNY AND Sergie were outside chalking a triangle on the street that reached from gutter to gutter. At each corner of the triangle they drew a base – first, second, and home. In the center of the triangle, they chalked a circle for the pitcher's mound. The finishing touch was a scoreboard of nine innings, labeled, "Them" and "Us"... looking more like the skeleton of a dead fish.

Sergie and I chose up sides by declaring, "odds or evens." With our fists closed, we shouted out, "Once, Twice, Three – Shoot!" And sliced our fingers through the air, pointing our choice of fingers into the empty space between us. The winner got first pick for his team.

Halfway through the game, Bobby hit the ball so hard it bounced off the front window of Mr. Lee's Chinese Laundry, almost breaking it. Mr. Lee came out screaming in Chinese, waving a meat cleaver in his hand. He just wanted to scare us, and he did a very good job of it. We took off in all directions. Poor Melvin wasn't fast enough, and Mr. Lee grabbed him by the shirt collar and picked him up off the ground. Pleading for his life, Melvin pissed in his pants. Mr. Lee smiled when he saw the puddle on the sidewalk.

Sergie and I ended up hiding in the abandoned fish store, soon to become the Pan Am Bar, at the corner of Faille and 165th Street. We played there until the heat was off. When we crawled out, I saw Manny standing across the street in front of our building, holding

Millie's hand, "Come. I talked to your mom, and I'm taking you to the movies."

We entered the subway in daylight and exited from a Manhattan kiosk into a dark night. In front of us, one block away, the night became daylight in a halo of brilliant lights radiating from the Roxy Theatre, fanning out and touching the sky. The buildings around the theatre disappeared in the shadows. There were American flags on each side of a picture of the actor Alexander Knox as President Wilson, and American flags crossing above his head. Flags were everywhere, and with buntings along the edges of the marquee.

A crowd of bobbing heads with mumbling voices, saying nothing, gathered around the lights like fluttering moths. Millie and I didn't know anything about Manny, the way he thought about politics or religion, or his feelings of everyday life. By taking us to see the movie *Wilson*, maybe he was telling us something about himself in his own way.

It was the week of the presidential election of 1944, between President Franklin Delano Roosevelt and Thomas E. Dewey. People were everywhere, joining in block parties all over the neighborhood with live bands on little truck stages, stopping on each block and playing music as people danced and listened to political speeches. Everyone was part of the excitement in the air.

Millie was ten and belonged to a volunteer group for the war effort. Her group was on the Boulevard receiving awards for their outstanding collection of newspapers. One of the awards was having a group picture taken and put into the Daily News. Millie appeared right in the front row with her Shirley Temple smile.

Sergie and I got a job handing out flyers for FDR. They paid us a quarter apiece up front, and that was a lot of money. But for Sergie and me, it wasn't much fun just handing out flyers; we had to make it special. We built tables out of wooden orange crates and attached flyers to the sides, advertising our product.

A couple of older kids walked over to our little store to give us a hard time. One of them, trying to imitate FDR's voice said, "I've been in war, and I've been in Eleanor, and I'll take war."

I tried to ignore them, but Sergie opened his big mouth, "What are ya, a bunch of fuckin' wise guys?"

"Careful, asshole, or I'll put you on your ass."

"Ahh come on, leave the little shmucks alone."

As they turned to leave, Sergie shouted back at them, "Ehh… kiss my ass in Macy's window."

I grabbed Sergie's arm, "Why don't you shut the fuck up."

"Hey, shit face, better listen to your friend."

Sergie was about to say something, but thought better of it. After the wise guys left, handing out flyers wasn't fun anymore. We didn't know what to do with the piles of flyers we had left, so we took them to the corner and, when the coast was clear, stuffed them down into the sewer. I felt like I had just killed someone and was hiding the murder weapon.

Rrrring… Rrrring, the race was on. Every time the phone rang, Millie and I would see who would get to the phone first. With a head start, Millie got there before me, but the sewing machine in the hall got in her way, and she caught her pinky toe on its black wrought iron leg.

She hopped around in pain, "My foot! My foot!"

I wondered do we always jump around when we get hurt? Does it make us feel better? Does it take our minds off of the pain? Or is it our brain telling us it's time to hop around, so everyone will know we've been hurt?

Millie called Mom at work, which was a no-no. We were forbidden to use the phone, because Mom had to keep the phone bill down. She rushed home and took Millie to Chester Drugs to get a free first opinion. He said that Millie's toe was broken, and she should be taken to Lincoln Hospital. At the hospital they put a cast on her foot and sent her home.

Even though my mother worked a full-time job as a furrier, she kept us clean and cooked our dinners, did the shopping, washed our clothes and kept our apartment spotless -- her normal routine. I never gave it a second thought, that's just the way it was. Mom got laid off the week that Millie broke her toe, and I got one of my super head colds. So now she was taking care of two sick kids.

Being sick was okay with me, as long as it kept me out of school. Mom fed me soft-boiled eggs with little square pieces of toast soaking up the yoke, and for supper, chicken soup. No matter how delicious it might have been, I couldn't taste a thing.

I developed a fever and was shaking with chills. Mom heated a clothes iron, wrapped it in a towel and placed it up against my feet. She pinched the corner of a tiny metal box, popped it open, and took out an aspirin, dissolved it in a spoonful of water and gave it to me. Then she wrapped a heavy comforter around me, and tightly tucked me in.

You could have filled a bathtub with all the sweating I did. In a few hours, my fever came down to normal and Mom changed my soaking clothes and sheets. The clean bed was like breathing in fresh air, and made me feel like I was going to be all right.

For the next few days, I spent my time being conscious of my stuffed up nose. One nostril would open and close again, then switching sides, the other one would open for a while. This miserable game went on for hours. We didn't have tissues then; we used hand-kerchiefs. I blew my nose so often it was hard to find a clean spot on the hanky. The dried snot hardened the handkerchief into an abstract sculpture.

Although I was weak and tired, once in awhile I'd have a short burst of energy. I found an empty shoebox in Millie's closet and took it to my room. I got some of my old joke books together and cut out the action figures and background art. I glued the different pieces into the box, one behind the other, reconfiguring them and building my own three-dimensional scene. Then I cut a hole in the short end of the box so I could look in and enjoy the action story I had invented.

While putting on some additional touches to my scene, someone knocked on our front door. It sounded official. Mom answered the door and three very tall men in dark suits, all wearing fedoras, introduced themselves as agents of the Federal Bureau of Investigation. Their voices vibrated from their chests with authority.

The First Agent saw Mom's blank look, "That means the FBI, Ma'am."

Listening from my room, I couldn't believe what I was hearing. Honest-to-goodness real G-Men were standing in our apartment. Could it be Field Agent Sheppard from *The FBI in War and Peace*?

"Mrs. Schnell?"

"That used to be my name, now it's Rothman."

First Agent: suspicious, "Are you using an alias, Ma'am?"

"Vhat does dat mean, "alias"?"

Second Agent: more sympathetic to Mom, "It means you're using a fake name."

"Vhat are you talking about?"

First Agent: "Why are you using a fake name?"

"Vhat fake? That's my name. Ooooh, I see. I was married two times. My first husband vas Schnell, and my second vas Rothman. Now darlink, vhat do you vant from me?"

Second Agent: "Is Walter Schnell your son?"

"Yes. Vhat's wrong? Did anything happen to him? My got, vhat's wrong?"

Second Agent: "We have to ask you just a few questions. Your son, Walter Schnell, has been AWOL for three weeks and, during this time, he has committed several crimes... like forging checks."

I couldn't believe they were saying that about Walter.

"No. No, my son is a good boy."

First Agent: "We are trying to locate him to get this straightened out. If you cooperate, it will make it easier for your son."

"Vhat are you saying? Walter is on his ship... I've got letters. Wait, I'll show you. Millie! Millie!" Millie hopped into the hall.

"Sveetheart, get me the last letters from Velvul."

Millie came back with the letters.

"See? Dis vas just yesterday. It's from his ship. See? Millie show them." Millie pointed out the name of his ship on the stationary.

"See, it says his ship. So, darlink, how could he be anywhere else? I'm telling you, he's a good boy."

Third Agent: "Let me see that." He looked through the letters.

"Mrs. Rothman, can my partner use your phone?"

"It's right here in da hall."

The Third Agent read the date on the letters into the phone.

Second Agent: "Mrs. Rothman, this might take awhile."

"Come, sit down, you'll have some fresh coffee."

Mom brought them into the kitchen. "Vhat are you going to do vit my Walter?"

First Agent: "I'm truly sorry Mrs. Rothman, but there is no way of getting around it, it looks pretty bad for your son."

"Vhat bad?"

"Well, if we find him and he's found guilty... and it looks that way... we could put him away for a long time."

"Put where? Vhat do you mean, a long time?"

First Agent: cold and matter of fact, "He'll be put in prison. Can't say exactly how long, that's up to the authorities. But my guess is, from 10 to 30 years."

Mom turned white, "Oy, gutenue. Not my Velvul!" She leaned against a chair. Her legs gave way and folded in half as she plopped heavily onto the chair.

The Third Agent hung up the phone and whispered to the others.

Second Agent: looking at Mom, "Good news, Mrs. Rothman, we were able to make a quick call to corroborate the information in your son's letters. You needn't worry any more. Your son, Walter Schnell, is definitely not the one we are looking for."

"See, see I told you he was a good boy."

Second Agent: "Someone is impersonating your son. It might be a close friend of his. Could you give us the names of his friends?"

"There's Eddy, and ahh... ahh... Millinue, the one vit the dimples?"

"Carl, Mom."

"Yes, yes, dat's it, Carl."

"And their last names?"

"Vell, it's Eddy Mitchell, and Carl... Carl..."

"It's Glickman, Mom."

First Agent: "Anyone else?"

"No, dat's all I can remember."

Finally the Third Agent spoke: "Sorry to have upset you, Mrs. Rothman, but everything is alright now."

"Darlink, thank you so much. Would you like another cup of coffee?"

Third Agent, "No Ma'am, we have lots to do. But, thank you."

And that was the last we heard from the G-Men. Through the entire questioning, Harold hid in his room.

I sneezed as Mom walked by my room on her way to the living room, "Gezunt und be vell! Sollinue, you need anything?"

"No."

She came in anyway and rubbed my stomach with alcohol and put some Vicks under my crusted nose, burning my sore nostrils.

The radio was playing while I was cutting out airplanes from Walter's card collection. When I was sick, I didn't really listen to the radio, but the voices kept me company.

"It's Make Believe Ballroom time, put all your cares away..." Walter and Harry's music streamed in from Millie's room, filtering through me. It wrapped around and burned into my heart. It was their music I heard, but I made it my own... all mixed up here in my chest. If their music is inside me, then where am I? Is there room for me?

Bing Crosby belched out *White Christmas, Moonlight Becomes You,* and *Don't Fence Me In* with the Andrew Sisters; Johnny Mercer sang his version of *You've Gotta Ac-cent-chu-ate the Positive* with the Pied Pipers; then the Andrew Sisters harmonized, *Shoo Shoo Baby.*

I walked into Millie's room to look out her window. Across the street, high up on a blank brick wall, was a worn out metal sign swaying in the wind. Painted on the sign was a picture of two horses pulling in two different directions at a pair of Levi's dungarees. Standing beside one of the horses was a farmer in overalls holding a whip. For some reason it always gave me comfort.

All of a sudden, frozen rain pellets hit the window, sounding like hundreds of people tap dancing on the fire escape.

Millie was annoyed, "Get the hell out of my room!"

"Okay."

"Move it. I don't want to catch your cold."

"Okay, okay… stop pushing, I'm going."

There was nothing to do… I played around with a piece of paper and folded it to look like a propeller. The rain stopped as quickly as it started. I opened my window and released my folded paper. It spun just like a propeller as it flew and floated on cushions of air and gently landed in the back alley.

Mom walked into my room whistling *You Are My Sunshine*. She carried in a clean, neatly patched white shirt, a pair of slacks, and my tie, and laid them out on top of my dresser. Now I was all prepared for going back to school on Monday after my sick vacation. I was well enough to go back on Thursday, but Mom's reasoning was to keep me in the house for a few more days to make sure I was cleansed of any possible evil germ that might be hanging on. She had no mercy for germs of any kind. Maybe it's because as a young girl she lost her mother to the 1918 Spanish Influenza pandemic. "Better to be safe than sorry…. vhy not get a fresh start on Monday?" That was okay with me!

When I got back to school, I was in for a treat – we were having a field trip. Mrs. Davidson took the whole class to Macy's department store for a marionette show.

Ding, ding… "Second floor, Men's Sportswear."

We took the elevator to the top floor and walked into a cavernous room, a storage space for rugs. Everything was big. The windows were big, the rugs were big – it felt like a giant lived here. A whole bunch of noisy kids were looking for places to sit on the rolled-up rugs scattered all around the room. Mrs. Davidson quieted us down and told us to pay attention to the small stage that was set up in an oversized box at one end of the room.

A marionette in gladiator armor appeared on the stage carrying a sword. His enemy dropped down from nowhere, swishing his sword at the empty space around him. They moved like they had a nervous disorder, swinging their swords everywhere except at each other. Two disembodied voices coming from somewhere in the box, screamed at each other, "Mph... m... flumping stat... muph... that... and that!"

The huge space muffled their voices, and it all sounded like gibberish to me. The marionettes seemed as surprised as I was when they finally made contact. The room full of kids cheered. When the strings got tangled and the gladiators looked like they were making love instead of war, we all roared with laughter.

During the entire show, this kid from my class, Julio, who was much bigger than me, took a disliking to me. He was sitting behind me and every chance he could find, he'd push me, punch me, and make fun of me. From that day on at school, there was no let up.

Mom got wind of my problem, and over my protests, invited Julio to our apartment for my birthday. My Birthday? We never celebrated my birthday before! It ended up with just Julio and me. I felt silly and out of place in this mock birthday.

Mom served us lemonade and a piece of my favorite, fluffy ricotta cheesecake. Julio took a liking to my Mom, but that didn't really mean much to me. All my friends liked her. If anyone came within ten feet of her, there was no escaping her overpowering natural warmth. Julio never bullied me again.

WHERE THE FUCK DO YOU THINK YOU'RE GOING?

THE LONGER I lived with Harold, the more new ways I learned to stay out of his way. But every so often I would make a mistake and Harold made me pay for it.

Mom was downstairs at Yetta's. Harold, I thought, was in his room. As I was returning to my room, I bumped into him in the hallway.

"Hey! Where the fuck do you think you're going? How many times must I tell you to get your fucking hands out of your pockets?"

He dragged me into the living room and sat me down on the couch. Harold was so drunk that I was getting dizzy from his whiskey breath. For no reason, he started telling me things I didn't want to know. He talked at me and didn't care if I was there or not. So I paid no attention to his babbling.

I watched Harold peel his glasses off, one ear at a time. He took out a handkerchief from his shirt pocket – he has done this so many times that his hands worked without him knowing he was doing it -- and with great care, he cleaned his glasses. They were very thin, wire-rimmed glasses, and he delicately hooked one end over his left ear, wrapped the glasses around his face, molding them to the shape of his head, and then hooked the other end over his right ear.

"What are you looking at?" Harold broke my concentration, and

I turned away from him.

"You son of a Jew bitch! Look at me when I'm talking to you!"

Look at him? How was I supposed to know what he wanted? First he says to not look at him and then he says to look at him. There were no answers to his damn riddles.

"Sit there and don't move." Harold talked like an expert, but behind his calm exterior, he was ready to tear me apart.

"I'm going to teach you a very important lesson about who you are. You, a Jew, are a different race than normal people. Did you know that? A foul cowardly race, the Jews, the slimy kind that creeps and crawls under rocks and in garbage pails. No, no! I take that back. Not a different race. I'd say you're actually another species. You Jews were put here on our earth by some evil being, and your sole purpose is to infect and destroy the good people, the Christian people."

I wasn't listening to him anymore. His voice became just background street sounds coming from Millie's room.

"As you know… as you know… Why am I talking to you like you were a normal person? You don't know shit. I'm a musician, a brilliant musician. I can play any instrument brilliantly. Yes, any instrument. I played music for vaudeville, only for the best. I played for silent movies, and when the sound movies started, work became scarce.

"A friend of mine, a good friend, he found a job in Hollywood doing musicals for Busby Berkeley. That's right, Busby Berkeley. He said there was a job for me too and lots of money. I wanted that job so badly I could taste it. My friend and I took a touring car all the way to California… mostly on dirt roads that turned into mud after a rain. It was an adventure. We finely got there, and I auditioned. And just like that, I got the job.

"When I got home, my wife Rosemary had given birth to my son, Harold. There was no reasoning with her. She refused to move to Hollywood. Her family was here and here is where she was going to stay."

Each of his words exploded in my face. Why is he telling me this stuff? It means nothing to me. All I could think about was that I was missing my radio shows.

"There was no work for me anymore, I had to give up my music." Harold sat silently for a long time, completely into himself.

"I could have had a job with Busby Berkeley... Busby Berkeley... yeah, Busby Berkeley." His voice was sleepwalking through his words and going nowhere. Harold sat there staring at nothing. A heavy growl rolled around from deep in his chest and escaped each time he exhaled. I thought he wouldn't notice me if I quietly tiptoed out of the room.

"Where the fuck do you think you're going!?" He tried to grab me by the waist. His drunken hand stumbled and missed, sending his thick fist into my stomach so hard it hit up against my spine.

"Gotcha, you little prick!"

I doubled up with a lump of pain in the pit of my stomach and was about to vomit when Mom walked in and Harold walked out, back to his cage. For the rest of the day, I shared my room with the pain of his iron fist still in my stomach, making my insides all twisted up.

When life seemed to be closing in on me, I always listened to my radio and looked at my joke books. In the quiet of my room, no one questioned me and there was no one to answer to.

It was Friday on a warm, lazy spring day. School was closed for some kind of teacher's meeting. While taking Spotty out, I saw a man on his knees bent over a square of sidewalk, filling it with wet cement. He was pouring a couple of new sidewalk squares in front of Mr. Siegel's hardware store. I rushed Spotty upstairs to our apartment and ran back to Siegel's before I missed anything. The cement man worked to the music of Bing Crosby streaming out of the hardware store, *You Belong To My Heart*.

He spread out the wet cement, took a long straight-edged stick and slid it across the surface, gently smoothing away all the rough spots until it looked like a giant mud pudding. Sergie, Bobby, and Melvin stood beside me hypnotized by the cement man's sorcery. But after a while, we lost interest and joined in for a game of stoopball.

Mrs. Garcia called out to Sergie from her third floor apartment window, "Coookie! Coookie! Come up! I've got lunch."

Sergie winced. He hated being called Cookie in front of his friends, "Alright, alright, I'm coming!"

"Why don't you bring some of your friends?"

Mrs. Garcia was a tall, very thin woman, but very forceful. We had refried beans, yellow rice and fried bananas. They called them something else, platanos, but they looked like bananas to me. It tasted like the best lunch I'd ever had.

Don't get me wrong, my mom was a great cook. Her tomato sauce with meatballs and Italian sausages was out of this world. She would cook the sauce all day long, leaving it to simmer through the night into another full day. She served it with Italian garlic bread for soaking up the thick rich gravy.

Mom always cooked for an army. She wasn't satisfied until we had at least two or three plates full, and I could feel her satisfaction and joy as she watched us enjoying her food. But it seemed like everybody else's food tasted much better. Well, that's not completely true. Everything Melvin's mother Yetta cooked – and I mean everything – tasted the same. From stuffed cabbage, to meatballs and spaghetti, it all tasted like left-over liver.

After lunch Sergie and I ran outside onto an empty street.

Sergie asked, "Hey, you got any money?"

"Yeah, why?"

"To buy a pack a cigarettes."

"I got a nickel. Whataya got?"

"I got ten cents. I'm in for more than you are so if you go buy 'em, we'll call it even. But I'm not sure we can get 'em anyway. No one's gonna sell 'em to us."

"I'm always buying cigarettes for my mom, I said, so I'll just tell Jack it's for my mother."

"Yeah, dat'll work. Your mother smokes Camels, doesn't she? I don't wanna smoke Camels, I wanna pack a Lucky Strikes."

"Well, that's too bad. We're just gonna have to smoke Camels."

"Okay, okay, take the fuckin' money! But I still think it stinks."

I calmly walked into Jack's candy store and, with my head peeping over the counter asked, "Can I have a pack of cigarettes for my mother?"

With some reservation Jack handed me a pack of Camels. Jack never thought twice before, but this time he looked at me suspiciously. I slowly walked out of the candy store, feeling that at any second, Jack was going grab me by the shoulder and pull me back into the store. Sergie and I continued on to the corner of Faille Street, and then, as if someone just turned on a switch, we ran down The Three Hills, crossed over Westchester Avenue, and went down by the bridge to the Creek.

Scattered by the Creek were large rocks with broken pieces of junk wood between them. We hid behind a mountain of gravel beside a vacant factory. Instead of having to mooch a cigarette, or scrounge for a half-smoked butt, I held a firm, full pack of cigarettes all my own. A couple of hours later we had smoked almost the whole pack, when Sergie spotted some wood planks that were tied together, about the size of a door. Sergie had an idea to take it down to the creek and use it as a raft. Sounded great to me. We found two pieces of wood perfect to use as paddles. Off we went, dragging the raft out onto the water. We tested it for leaks and found it sea-worthy -- not a leak anywhere.

There we were, a Jewish and Puerto Rican Tom Sawyer and Huck Finn from The Bronx, with cigarettes dangling from our lips, paddling to the widest part of the Creek. Suddenly my feet felt wet. I looked down and the water was already up to my ankles. The raft was sinking fast. Without a word between us, we paddled for our lives.

The raft sank to the bottom of the Creek. We jumped off and found ourselves only up to our knees in water. As we walked the rest of the way to shore, several pieces of shit floated by, and we realized that the soft, squishy muck that held onto our every step was old shit that had settled to the bottom of the Creek. On our way home, the composted shit clung to my pants. Its stench burned my eyes and forced me to breathe through my mouth. I was so glad no one was home that afternoon, so I didn't have to explain myself.

As I was filling the tub with water, I felt like a Marine who had been crawling in filthy jungle mud, fighting the Japs on some steaming hot island in the Pacific. The tub became a river that I had to cross during a rainstorm. I was in an ambush and threw myself down into the river with my clothes on.

Getting out of the river was a different story. My T-shirt was plastered to my skin and refused to let go. It took all my strength to get it up to my head but it wouldn't go any further. I was suffocating! No matter how hard I tried, it wouldn't move. I started to panic, on the verge of crying. Then I stopped everything and took a deep breath. I pulled at my shirt an inch at a time until it lost its grip on me. Mission accomplished!

I rewarded myself with a dry, cozy bed. Lying in my clean clothes, I listened to my radio, the *Lux Radio Theater* version of *The Guadalcanal Diary*… and I was back in the steaming jungle fighting the Japs again.

In every part of the year, you could tell what season it was by the way the sounds carried on the air. And today I heard the sounds of a hot day – the muffled clanging of a trolley, and the dull screeching of the train as it made the sharp turn from Westchester Avenue to Southern Boulevard. Out on the street, most of the kids in my neighborhood had disappeared, off to some summer camp for a month. Sergie, Bobby, and I were the only ones left on the block.

While listening to her soap operas, Mom was preparing lunch for Millie and me for the beach – an omelet of fried salami and eggs on a hard roll and butter. I especially liked the Clair de Lune theme of her favorite show. I stared off mesmerized by the hanging strip of curled, sticky paper filled with unsuspecting dead flies, some half-alive, buzzing their last buzz. Mom sent us off with sandwiches, towels, and carfare.

With a rolled-up towel under my armpit, held in place by the weight of my dangling arm, I waited for the local train at Whitlock Avenue Station. Under the platform was a warehouse filled with live chickens crammed into boxes to be shipped all over The Bronx. I could hear them clucking to each other as they were being packed into a truck, ready to become someone's dinner.

Millie, her friend Veronica, Sergie, Bobby, Johnny, and I got onto the train and we were on our way to Orchard Beach. Our excitement built with every passing station. The car was filled with people of all different ages, each holding towels under their armpits. A teen-ager stood over me flexing his muscles by holding onto the overhead safety strap as tightly as he could. His biceps and forearms popped out from his T-shirt and veins traveled around his arms looking like a subway map. Even his head bulged with muscles.

We got off at the end of the train line and waited downstairs for the bus to Orchard Beach. There were so many people on line, my friends and I decided to save our bus fare and took the short cut to the Beach. We trekked through the woods and bushes on a well-traveled dirt road. The air was heavy and hot, with noisy insects buzzing around our heads. The annoying little bastards chased us all the way to the beach. By the end of the walk, I wondered if saving the carfare was worth it.

Well-manicured gardens pointed the way to the main entrance of Orchard Beach. On the other side of the promenade steps, a gust of air filled my lungs with the smell of salt water and baking sand. Our favorite spot was Beach Number 13. When we got close to the water, we flipped open our towels on the sand and held the corners down from the wind with our shoes. We peeled down to our bathing suits and wrapped our brown-bagged sandwiches in our clothes to keep the sand out.

We ran across the wet smooth sand squeezing between our toes, leaving cookie cutter footprints behind us, and taking a deep breath, attacked the water. My body was a sponge, hot and dry, and absorbed the cold water. I couldn't swim, but I floated like an air-filled ball on the buoyancy of the salt water. We played simple games like taking turns holding our breath and diving under the water with eyes open, pushing ourselves between each other's legs. I stood there with the water up to my chest and began to imagine what might be under the water, crab-like creeping things with sharp claws, or strange animals touching and snapping at my feet. I had to keep moving to make sure they couldn't find me.

"Ow, ow, ow, ow..." we hopped across the hot sand quick enough not to burn our feet. At midday when the heat was too much to bear, we jumped onto the edges of other people's blankets to get to our own. We carefully unwrapped our lunches from our clothes, but no matter how hard we tried, sand would still get into our sandwiches. I was so hungry I put up with the grinding sand in each mouthful of bologna and wilted lettuce.

Mom had a standing rule, which she told Millie and me over and over again, "Remember, don't go into da water until an hour after you eat. If you go into da water before an hour, you'll drown and die."

Not wanting to die, we waited. While waiting, we played in the damp sand, building castles and chasing tiny fish in small puddles. If we got thirsty, we put on our shoes and walked to the boardwalk where, at every entrance to the beach, there was a water fountain and water to clean your feet.

We walked on the hexagon concrete boardwalk, past hot dog and hamburger stands. My mouth watered for just a bite of a hamburger, but they were too expensive. I promised myself that someday I'd buy my own hamburger at one of those stands, and when I finally did, was I disappointed – It tasted like tasteless crap, and I wished I could get my money back.

Back on the beach at the end of the day, we cleverly wrapped ourselves with our towels, took off our wet suits, and got into our dry clothes. It was a balancing act between towel and bathing suit. The trick was to keep the towel from falling off... and laughing didn't help. I wondered what was going on underneath the girls' towels. My shoes were filled with sand and my body hummed from a day of swimming. The sun had dried my skin and made it tight around me, but I could still smell the salt water on it. This time, sunburned and tired, we waited to take the bus to the train.

There were four older teenage kids putting on a performance at the bus stop. One of the guys was acting drunk and twirled around a lamppost, slowly sliding down to the ground. He was imitating a drunken man speaking with slushy words, "I'm Ray Milland in the *Lost Weekend*... "Please! Please! Give me whiskey! I want my booze!" His friends joined in, stumbling as they walked toward him, screaming, "No! No! No! Bats! Bats, everywhere!"

How did they have the balls to put on this little play, to take a chance at being jerks in front of all of these strangers? I felt embarrassed, but I loved that they didn't care what anyone thought of them. The crowd laughed at their clowning, but I didn't laugh out loud. I might laugh at the wrong places and they would see what a fool I was.

By the time I got home, the sunburn had cooked my skin to a fiery red. I felt chills when anything touched me. I knew I was going to grow a big crop of blisters. I loved the feeling of running my hand lightly over the soft bumps, which would soon dry up and begin to peel. One of my favorite things was peeling off my dead skin.

Mom filled the bathtub with vinegar and water for Millie and me to cool and help heal our sunburns. In bed I turned from side to side, trying to find a comfortable spot between my burns. Spotty wasn't any help, licking my sunburn with her sandpaper tongue. My room was stuffy and as hot as my sunburn. Everything was keeping me awake. The air was very still... no breeze to cool me off, and all I could smell was vinegar. Every time I closed my eyes, I was still treading and floating on the salt water.

Mom set up the fire escape for sleeping. She covered the open stairway hole with a wood board and a blanket. Millie and I lay there feeling the cool breeze soothe our burns and the open air swallow up the odor of vinegar. Sergie was out on his fire escape a few feet away and joined Millie and me singing, *Jeepers Creepers*. Millie and I quietly watched the sky flooding with stars. Their blinking lights soothed us to sleep.

JUST ONE OF
THOSE THINGS

A CHILL WAS in the air on this late weekend afternoon in June. It was 1945, and I was nine years old. Sergie and I were hitching rides on the back of trolley cars on Westchester Avenue, down to Whitlock and back again. During one of those trips, we found a couple of nails, and like any normal nine-year-old kid from the neighborhood, we thought it would be a great idea to lay them on the trolley tracks.

Hearing the distant clanging of a trolley, we hid behind the New Era cleaners on the corner of Hoe Avenue and East 165th Street and waited for the approaching trolley. As it glided up the tracks, its metallic appendage reached up like a fleshless arm holding onto the overhead wire. A flurry of brilliant white beads hissed and zapped from where the wires crossed, spitting out excited sparks that fizzled and sputtered off the cobblestone streets.

The trolley car groaned when it limped over the nails, flattening them into miniature half-moons, like tiny Arabian swords. Sergie and I dashed to the tracks, and for a few seconds, everything stopped. All we heard was the thumping pulse of our fear. We grabbed our jewels and stampeded from the crime scene, dodging cars and people, jumping over johnny pumps, and landing on our block.

With a piece of chalk, Melvin's older sister, Rachel, was tattooing boxes on the sidewalk for a game of potsy. No matter what the lighting was, her face always seemed to be in the shadows.

Sergie and I watched her as she stood up, swayback, to admire her creation.

"What the fuck are you two lookin' at?"

"Nuttin'. We just wanted to know if we could play," answered Sergie.

She stared at us through her hyper eyes. I looked back at her and said, "Well! Ya gonna let us play, or what?"

The only equipment we needed to play potsy was any found object. But it had to be considered for its aerodynamics and capacity to stop on a dime.

"Sollyyy!" My mother shouted from her bedroom window, "Solly!... come put on a sweater."

Shouting back in a whining voice, "Maaaa... I'm in the middle of a game."

"Come, it's gettin' chilly."

"As soon as I finish the game."

"No! Right now!"

"Okay, okay. Just one more minute."

My piece of twisted wire slid across the boxes and stopped on a chalked line, which meant I had to wait for another turn. The waiting was making me nervous, and I expected at any second my mom was going to call me. My energy built up until I exploded into a miniature tornado and flew around the johnny pump by the curb.

"Faster than a speeding bullet... more powerful than a locomotive... can leap tall buildings in a single bound."

I was indestructible... until my left knee crashed into the johnny pump. It reminded me that I was made of flesh and blood. Slumping to the curb, my whole body was in my knee. It was crackling with white fire. I grabbed my knee and tried to hold back the pain.

Harry's bar was near to where we were playing and a Shaeffer delivery truck was unloading its kegs of beer down into the open metal doors to Harry's cellar. The ruddy-faced driver rolled a keg of beer out of his truck. The barrel's weathered, finely-splintered wood seemed to crawl up the driver's hairy arms, fusing barrel and man into one fuzzy, ape-like creature. The barrel was dropped from the truck and landed with a dull thud, squishing onto a thick, brown, bristling mat. A mist of beer sweat sprayed out from the mat, smelling like sour rags.

"Hey, Solly! It's your turn."

As I limped onto the sidewalk toward the game, I felt an abrupt tug at my pants that snapped my head back and twisted me around to the gutter. It was the gnarled front fender of the beer truck, hooking onto my pants. The truck slowly rolled forward taking me with it. I reached out for the johnny pump and got only a fist full of air. I wanted to grab onto something, anything, but there was nothing to hold onto. The fender pulled me back into the gutter, and I found myself facing a black rubber giant, looming over me. The fender jerked me closer and closer toward the tire, crumpling me in two.

"Stop! Stop! Please stop!"

The driver must have heard me. The truck stopped, pinning my left foot under a wall of rubber. I didn't feel any pain at all, just a slight pinch and a heavy pressure on my foot. I thought it was only my sneaker stuck under the tire. If the driver would only back up, I could walk home and no one would ever know what happened.

"Please, get offa my foot!"

The driver, drunk and confused, just sat there stunned. I cried out again, "Get offa my foot! Get offa my foot!"

The driver couldn't see me. I was so small I was hidden by the tire. Instead of backing up, the truck began to creep forward, further and further onto my foot.

"Stop! Stop! Ya gotta stop!"

This couldn't be real... it wasn't happening to me. I found myself standing several feet from the accident looking back at myself. It wasn't me under that tire, just someone who looked like me.

Melvin's father, Aaron, appeared from nowhere, "Stop, you asshole! Stop the fuckin' truck! Back up! Damn it! Back the fuckin' thing up!"

Aaron carried me to the stoop by the Chinese Laundry and a crowd of people began to collect. Who were these people? Their faces touched my memories, but they were still strangers to me. Where was my mother?

My mom was my connection to the world. Without her I was lost. When she was talking with her friends, I'd shrink and hide in my mind, disappearing and living in my tiny heart. I was so terrified of adults, I had to develop a protective shield that made me invisible. There were times when I could sit on my stoop watching the people as they passed me by, and I could look right into their eyes and know they couldn't see me. They just looked through me as if I wasn't there.

Now, here I was with all these people swarming around me, whispering to each other with all eyes focused on me. They made me feel guilty and ashamed. I wanted to go home where my mom would take care of my foot and make it better.

My sister Millie noticed the group of people pressing against each other. She walked over to find out what the hell was going on, and overheard two women talking.

"It's probably his fault."

"Yes, these kids are always playing in the streets."

Millie moved through the crowd to get a closer look. She saw it was me who was the center of attention, and quickly moved back and mingled with the crowd, making believe she didn't know me. Millie was scared, scared that by knowing me she would somehow share in my guilt and shame.

During the war, the streets were filled with service men. One of them, a sailor, pushed his way through the crowd.

"Why don't you give the kid a break... give him some air."

He stood over me in his white, thirteen-button, bellbottom trousers, and on his sleeve, I recognized the insignia of a medic.

"Now, let's take a look at that foot."

Gently he untied the laces of my sneaker. My foot had swelled up, and the sneaker wouldn't budge.

I cried out, "Please don't! Don't touch it!"

"I promise I'm not going to hurt you. But I have to take your sneaker off, okay? What I'm going to do now is cut open the back of your sneaker. Alright?"

He kept his promise. I didn't feel a thing. His sharp pocketknife sliced through the back of the sneaker. He slid my foot out and tenderly peeled off my sock. My foot was a wonderful shade of blue.

Gruff voices... the clicking and clanking of metal... a quick flurry of movement, and I found myself in an ambulance driving off to I don't know where. We ended up at Lincoln Hospital, known in The Bronx as "the butcher hospital." The story was, that once you went in, you never came out alive, or all in one piece.

When my mom walked into the emergency room, my defenses caved in, and my foot began to throb. A fire of pain flashed up my leg and twisted my stomach.

"What's da matter, my Sollinue?"

"Mama, it hurts. My foot hurts. I think I'm going to throw up."

"Quick, give me something! My boy is going to throw up."

A heavyset nurse handed me a bed pan and turned to my mother, "What happened to him?"

"A truck went over his foot."

"The brat probably deserved it."

"Just shut up your mouth and give him something! My boy is in pain!"

The nurse's attitude changed, and she quickly gave me something that numbed my pain.

A doctor came into the room holding a pair of x-rays.

"Mrs. Rothman?"

"Yes, what is it? What's wrong with his foot?"

"A few bones in his foot have been broken..."

"Oy Gut, my poor Sollinue."

"It's okay, he's going to be alright. He just needs a cast. In a few months he'll be in one piece again and playing with his friends. So there's no need for you to be here."

"But I want to stay with my boy."

"You needn't worry, we'll take good care of him and you can pick him up tomorrow morning. That's not too long to wait, is it?"

"But my boy needs me."

"Mrs. Rothman, he's in perfectly good hands. I'm very sorry, but I'm going to have to ask you to leave."

I sucked at the swollen, hot air and smelled the mildew of the sweating stone walls. I was in a dark, high-ceilinged room listening to the hollow sounds of dripping water. Groaning old men lay all around me, farting, snoring and rolling phlegm around in their throats. I was left alone with these strangers, living in a *Frankenstein* movie.

Lights and voices barged into my black and white movie - Dr. Parato, my mother, and the resident doctor.

"What the hell is going on here?" Dr. Parato repeatedly hit an x-ray film with the back of his hand. "What do you mean, just a few broken bones? Are you all crazy? This boy's foot is crushed. What the hell is a cast going to do for him?

"Here's my paperwork. I'm transferring this boy to Morrisania Hospital and out of this damn madhouse!"

Dr. Parato felt my forehead, "This boy is burning up. Did you give him anything for his pain?"

He took a look at my foot, now a dark purple blue, and screamed to the nurse, "Give him morphine and get him out of this damn place! Right now!"

Two men in white coats roll me out to an ambulance surrounded by wood coffins. The two men are standing by the back doors, pulling and pushing the coffins into a blazing incinerator inside the ambulance. They are taking bodies out of the boxes and putting them into the incinerator while they are still alive. Now it's my turn, and I know what is waiting for me, I desperately hold onto the edges of the entrance to the fiery chamber. Three of the men in white coats calmly pull at my hands, loosen my grip, and push me into the chamber of fire. One of them says, "Don't worry kid, it's not real, it's only a movie." The door closes behind me.

I'm trapped in the roaring furnace with flames licking up

at my body. The heat is so intense it smothers the air and burns my lungs. The fire is blasting into my face and my skin starts to bubble and blister. I can't take anymore of this pain. I don't want to die. "Please not me, I can't die!"

Above me is a hazy blur of bright lights whizzing by. I think I am awake until I open my eyes and find myself sleeping in a bed. Suddenly it isn't a bed anymore, it's a car from an amusement ride gone amuck. It uncouples and careens down a narrow hall of twists and turns. I can feel it rumbling on the hard floor beneath me. I open my eyes again, and I'm back in a bed that is upside down, riding along the ceiling.

Once more I open my eyes. This time I'm not moving. I'm in a clean white room with other kids. Standing around me are fuzzy outlines, talking to each other with muffled voices.

"You are right… definitely gangrene."

"Now that you've seen it for yourself…"

"Yes, I agree. Prep him for surgery."

The morphine took hold again, separating me from my senses and back into my numb fog.

My mother was in the hall as they rolled me to the operating room, "No! No! Not my Sollinue!"

My mom had just been told I was going to have my leg amputated. She fainted on the spot. She had never fainted before, not even a dizzy spell. Later when I heard about it, I was overjoyed. My mom loved me enough to faint over me.

In the middle of the sterile white room, a lonely table was waiting for me. There were people around me dressed in white caps and masks, wearing their gowns backwards. They picked me up like a slab of meat and plopped me on the operating table, shoving me from side to side, centering me on the huge table.

There I was, lying like a little lump, waiting for the inevitable. I just wanted this damn thing to be over with. Another painful situation I had to accept… a one-time thing and it's done. Not like constantly facing Harold every day with no end to it.

Then, like one of my mom's radio soap operas, Dr. Parato burst into the operating room, screaming, "Stop! Stop everything! Thank God I'm in time!"

Just when I thought everything was settled, Dr. Parato upstaged my movie. Hearing his voice, I knew I was being rescued once again.

"I just came from an emergency meeting with the hospital board, and it was decided not to amputate. We're going to try the new penicillin serum on the boy."

"Are you sure about this? Are you willing to gamble with the boy's life?"

"Penicillin is being used very effectively in the military, and I want this boy to have the same chance. So, just get him back to his ward!"

The fever and morphine continued to create a sluggish world where voices buzzed in and out, talking in shapeless words. The first thing I became aware of was someone stabbing me in the ass with what felt like a broken ice pick. From then on I was assaulted every four hours, twenty-four hours a day. The penicillin seared through me like someone was holding a blowtorch to my ass. When they said an injection every four hours, they meant every four hours, even waking me up in the middle of the night. After awhile, I could rub my hand across my tiny ass and feel the rows and rows of fleshy welts flapping under my fingertips.

One morning I woke up, and there was a mysterious bulge over my leg, rising up under the sheet. It seemed to have grown overnight separating my foot from the rest of me and made me feel like my leg was in the bowels of a strange animal, slowly digesting my foot. It turned out to be a metal cage with a snow cone of ice inside, packed around my foot.

All day and all night, wet sheets were pasted to my raw, feverish skin. Chills erupted from the pit of my stomach, and I began to vomit until there was nothing left. Still, I felt the convulsive waves of nausea wrenching at my guts, puking myself inside out.

For months, I kept my foot motionless. I was too terrified to move it, imagining the crushed bones as sharp, tangled splinters ready to pierce my skin. I was sure that even if I moved only one single toe, the bones would slice through the skin of my foot. After awhile, I didn't know if I even had a foot anymore. But every so often, I'd feel a dim, prickly tingle that reminded me it was still there.

Every morning the nurses removed the metal cage from my leg, and a doctor peeled off the bandages. My foot was four times its normal size and completely covered with a pussy, wobbling, butterscotch pudding that oozed off with the bandages. The bottom of my foot was like a burnt, encrusted frying pan and smelled like a rancid piece of meat, dipped in shit and deep-fried. The stench and fumes burned my eyes. Using a wooden tongue depressor, the nurse scooped a white, pasty sauce out of a jar and buttered my foot. Every time they re-bandaged me, they packed it with that fuckin' ice and in a few hours, it had soaked my bed making it cold and clammy again.

On one of those hot, muggy mornings before hospitals had air conditioners, I laid in my wet bed, breathing in the residue of ether. It filtered through the thick, hot, hospital air with the sweet, sickly smell of fear.

My mom had seen how trapped I was, stuck in the shadows in a corner of the ward without a window or even a radio to listen to. Patients weren't allowed to have radios or move their beds for any reason. Mom wanted me at least to have some fresh air and a view to keep me occupied... and my mom had her ways. She could talk almost anyone into helping her and had the ability to instantly make friends with strangers. In fact, just give her five minutes on the subway, and she'd be telling her life story to someone she never met before.

The very next day, she showed up with a couple of nurses, looking pretty under their little white caps. Their young, erect breasts pressed against their freshly starched uniforms, creating crisp pleats, and pointing their way through the halls of the hospital.

Everyone loved my mother, including my friends. But this time, I don't think it was her charm and warmth that won over the nurses. All she had to do was show them a snapshot of my brother Walter, looking handsome in his Navy blues and giving off that sensual energy he had inherited from my mom. The nurses swooned when they saw the picture. It was love at first sight. Mom even promised them a date with Walter. From then on, they went out of their way to be nice to me and my mother. So it wasn't too difficult for her to talk them into moving my bed to the window.

My main entertainment was to twist my head toward the open window and watch a group of men below me tarring a row of rooftops. I couldn't see beyond the rooftops, but I did hear the hollow sounds of trolley cars and distant voices on the streets.

I wanted so badly to walk to the bathroom like all the other kids. But no, I had to shit in bed on one of those cold, porcelain pans. I was especially ashamed of shitting in front of the pretty nurses. And no matter how hard I tried to hide it, everyone knew what I was doing.

A sound of choking invaded my dreamy night. Urgent voices rushed into the ward, then a flurry of intensity and the rumbling of machines and carts. A wall of doctors and nurses surrounded the bed across the room. I couldn't see past their hunched backs, as they worked frantically on a young boy who had just had his tonsils removed. The next morning, I learned that the boy had swallowed his tongue. This was a mystery to me. How can you swallow something that's attached to you? Whatever they did, the boy still had his tongue.

But there was a bigger mystery – a whimpering that came from a private room next to our ward. All night, nurses went in and out of that room. No one would tell us who was in there, and why that kid was getting so much attention. So we created our own story of the 'whimpering room.' We imagined that it was used for evil experiments that the doctors wanted to hide from prying eyes. Instead of throwing away the pieces of the kids they had cut off while on the operating table, they saved the leftover parts, and late at night, put them into the 'whimpering room' to be kept alive with our blood. At night while we were sleeping, one of those body parts would sneak into our ward and drink our blood and eat our flesh to keep itself alive.

The other kids on the ward came and went while I was still there. When will it be my turn? Am I going to be stuck here forever? They weren't around long enough for me to remember their names; it was easier to remember them by what was wrong with them. The boy with the concussion became the Concussion Kid and there was Tonsil Kid and Appendix Kid. They all left, while I stayed in my clammy bed – the Stenchfoot Kid.

When the Concussion Kid went home, an older boy of about fifteen took his place. He had fallen off a swing in a play park and impaled his leg on the spear point of a metal fence – the Spiked Kid.

Most evenings, the night nurse would sit at her desk ignoring the moaning of bodiless voices. Eyes half closed, she'd refuse to pay attention to any of the children's calls. She was a short woman, tough and mean like her wiry hair. Even her white cap threatened to escape from that bundle of Brillo. There was nothing nice about her. She was a real bitch who took delight in throwing the syringe into me like a dart.

The days and nights were pretty routine until the Spiked Kid showed up. He constantly talked about girls.

"Man, she's a nice piece of ass," referring to one of the day nurses.

"Huba, huba, huba, I'd love to eat her pussy, wouldn't you?"

I didn't know what the fuck he was talking about. But I didn't want him to think I was an uncool little kid, so I hung onto every word. The Appendix Kid next to him began to giggle. It didn't make sense to me, but I went along and giggled too.

The night nurse shouted, "Shut up in there!"

The Spiked Kid shouted back, "Who the fuck are you!?"

"You watch your mouth."

"Yeah, you and what army is going to stop me?"

The Spiked Kid's attitude toward grown ups made me feel uncomfortable, and somehow he frightened me, but I did like how he wouldn't take any crap from the night nurse.

In between these occasional distractions from my misery, time floated heavily. Music escaped from a distant radio and found its way into the window near my bed. It was Bing Crosby singing, *Moonlight Becomes You*... then Glenn Miller's *String of Pearls*. They reminded me of home. I felt their music so strongly inside me, like listening to someone else's heart beating. As if they were here standing inside me... I wanted to go home.

The crisp, brittle sound of a glass straw clicked against my glass of ginger ale. My mom sat beside my bed. On my tray lay a gray-brown slab of what looked like meat. It smelled like liver, but then everything they served smelled like liver. I think Yetta cooked for the hospital.

I pushed the plate away from me, "Mom, I can't. I can't eat dis stuff."

My mother pleaded, "Eat, momala. It's good for you. Da hospital knows what's good."

"I can't, I'll throw up."

"Sollinue, my totala, please do it for me."

I started cutting at the peculiar brown slab. It felt like a piece of rubber under my knife. No matter how hard I tried, the meat rejected the knife. With one last concentrated effort, I stabbed at the brown slab. It jumped off the plate, bounced up off the floor, and slid across the room into the wall. Mom and I sat there, motionless, and then our eyes connected. We burst out laughing. Whenever we tried to stop, we looked at each other and cracked up.

Kids weren't allowed to visit the children's ward, but my mother found a way to sneak my sister Millie up the back stairway. Millie and I always had our little skirmishes, but seeing her there that day was like seeing a missing part of me.

My father never did visit me at the hospital. What kind of man was he? I didn't know him very well. Millie and I always called him Manny, never Dad. My mouth is still uncomfortable framing the word, 'dad.' Its sound is false and bounces back to me like a stranger speaking a stranger's name.

Mom and Millie showed up with toys that took my breath away, toys that I had only played with through the glass of the toy store windows in my neighborhood. How could my mother afford this? They must have been from Manny: a Buck Rogers disintegrator pistol, a pair of walkie-talkies, ancient Greek metal warriors with a cardboard fortress, along with a few of the usual cheap toys from the 5 & 10 Cent Store.

The fortress was too large to be assembled in the hospital, and as hard as we tried, Millie and I couldn't get the damn walkie-talkies to work. The toys were too big and complex and not being able to play with them was like not having them at all.

Mom felt my frustration, "Its okay, darlink. We'll take them home and dey vill be waiting for you."

A nurse overheard her and said, "Mrs. Rothman... I'm really sorry, but I'm afraid you can't take these toys out of the hospital."

"What do you mean, I can't take these toys home?"

"The hospital has rules. Someone should have told you."

"Vhat da hell is going on here?"

"You see, if you take them out, you'll be spreading germs from the hospital outside to innocent people. You don't want to do that, do you?"

"Germs, schmerms."

"Think of it as a contribution to the hospital for the poor children who don't have anything."

What the fuck is she talking about? I'm one of those poor kids who doesn't have anything. They're taking my new toys away from me, and giving them to somebody else?

"Darlink, please, you're taking everything away from him."

The nurse pointed to the cheap toys.

"Well... I guess it will be alright if you took a few things."

"You mean we can take home the cheap toys? Vhat? The cheap toys don't get germs?" As the nurses walked away, Mom mumbled to herself, "Dey should only drop dead!"

Somewhere inside, I knew the toys weren't really mine. Once

more I had to stuff it and let it fester in my own little hell.

Visiting hours were over, and I took it for granted I was going home with Mom and Millie. Whenever all three of us were together, we'd always leave together. Now for the first time, that unwritten law was broken. They left without me, and our strong bond seemed to pull apart, leaving me alone with an emptiness in my chest.

A few weeks later, Doctor Parato's hand firmly held my forehead. "Well Molly, it looks like your son will soon be able to go home." He looked at me, smiling, "Would you like that?" Not waiting for an answer, he turned to my mom. "He can go home, but you must promise to keep checking his temperature. If it goes up even slightly, you've got to notify me right away. Remember, this boy could have died, or lost his leg. So you must do as I say."

"Oy Gotinue! My poor Sollinue. Yes, yes, I promise."

"And, Molly, you'll have to bring him to my office once a week to change his bandages."

"Yes, yes, I will do dat."

Doctor Parato smiled, "I'd like to give him one more day, just to be sure. And if everything's okay, you can take him home tomorrow."

"Oh, thank you. Thank you so much! God bless you. Ya hear, my Sollinue? You're coming home tomorrow.

It had been over six weeks, and I was finally going home. In the hospital I was living a substitute life. Everything there felt outside of myself. Now, even though I knew I was going back to where Harold lived, I couldn't wait to be home.

GOING HOME

A THIRTY-FOOT BOTTLE of milk towered over Bruckner Boulevard. Its unseen eyes loomed down over the taxi, watching us as we passed by. We drove along the Boulevard by the Tip Top Bakery. The aroma of baking bread wafted out of the building into the street, and we drove through an invisible cloud that held onto the air. Its sweet smell gave me an irresistible urge to bite into the warm, fresh bread.

Our taxi passed by a couple of billboards. Their words were meaningless gibberish to me. But there was one I didn't have to know how to read: a caricature of a Jap soldier with sickly yellow skin, wearing round, thick wire-rimmed, glasses. His oversized buckteeth pushed against his upper lip in a self-satisfied grin as he caught a Chinese baby on the end of his bayonet.

We turned left off Faille Street and stopped in front of my building. It was difficult to keep a balance between the memories of my block and its reality. I found myself focusing on details I never noticed before. I could see every single crooked line on every brick on my building. Even worn out signs looked new to me, as if they'd been freshly painted.

The cabby helped carry me into the hall, and Mom hauled me the rest of the way up the three flights of stairs to our apartment. Where was my father? He was a cabby.

Exhausted from the climb, Mom put me down by the door to catch her breath. Standing on one leg, my head slid across her silky dress and pressed against her thigh. Her thigh pressed back against my cheek. The faint sound of a baseball game floated on the syrupy heat, telling me I was home again.

Harold greeted us at the door in his boxer shorts and undershirt. Barrel-chested, his shorts ballooned around his spindly legs and tiny ankles. He looked like he was made of two different bodies pieced together. Every once in awhile, Harold's red, vein-y balls peeped out from the slit of his trunks.

"How's the little bastard?"

"Harold, please help me out wit da boy."

"You can carry the little Jew bastard yourself."

That's one time Harold got it right. Millie and I had been born before Mom and Manny were married.

When we entered the apartment, Spotty, a fluffy blur of pure energy, galloped at us and slid across the linoleum, abruptly stopping at my crushed foot, then gingerly smelled it as if it wasn't part of me. She sniffed at my knees, to see if I was who I claimed to be – knees never lie. Satisfied, she welcomed me home with gentle kisses.

My mom double-hitched me up into her arms and with one last effort, whisked me up the hall and through the frosted glass door of Millie's room. The rooms of home absorbed me in, like a found missing part. They smelled of my mother's cooking, underlaid by a subtle dash of sour beer. Our apartment had been bombarded so often by Harold's abuse, it had seeped into the walls and lived there. And yet, it still felt good to be home.

Poor Millie was exiled to my room, the dungeon. And here I was in the front room, the magic room, where life was just outside Millie's window. Now I could see the sounds that I had barely heard in my room. That night, the picture show would start. The passing lights of cars ran around the room, chasing each other across the ceiling and disappearing into the corners of the walls.

Without warning, a loud, piercing siren from the top of the telephone building a block away, welcomed me to Millie's room. It blasted me deep into my bed and vibrated the room, scaring the shit out of me. The siren was a warning to take shelter in case of attack. When it stopped, the only thing I could hear was the screeching of the El train rounding the turn.

On my first day in Millie's room, at last I got to listen to my radio. A voice with a heavy lisp shouted from the speaker, reading the comic strip, *Dick Tracy*.

"Listen baby, there is something phony about that dough... but we're going to split it anyway, 50–50."

I thought he was imitating a character with a lisp, but his voice changed with each character – and they each had a lisp.

"Now picture this... She sneaks up behind Wetwash with a frying pan and," his voice explodes with excitement, "crashes it on his head – CRASH!!!"

At the end of the show, I found out that the lisping voice belonged to Mayor LaGuardia, acting out Dick Tracy comic strip from the Sunday papers. The people who delivered the newspapers were on strike, so the Mayor decided that us kids shouldn't be denied our Sunday comic.

The morning sun crept into Millie's room, accompanied by the sound of a shovel scraping the sidewalk, meaning only one thing to me – snow! But it was August. Snow on a hot day? I hopped over to the window. My drowsy ears had lied to me. Instead of snow, someone was shoveling coal from a coal truck.

On the underside of the truck was a round, metal cylinder connecting the cab to the dump-bed, which was filled with coal. The driver pulled down on a lever and the cylinder whirled into action, telescoping like a giant erection. It lifted the dump-bed, slanting it down toward my building. Looking down into its belly, I watched the wet, bluish-black coal as it roared like an avalanche of marbles shoving their way through a trap door, onto a chute, and down into the dark hole of a basement window. Holding a broom, the driver climbed into the dump bed, his arms glistening with beads of black coal-sweat, and swept the rest of the coal down through the trap door.

My foot started throbbing with pain like it was suddenly being pulled down – a ballooning dead weight hanging from my hip.

My mother rushed into the room, "What are you doink out of bed? Look at you, do you want to go back to da hospital? You'll hurt yourself. Now stay in bed! If you want something, ask. You've got a mouth, use it!"

Not only did my mother have me to care for, she also had to care for my baby brother, Ronnie, who was born only one month before my accident. Harold resented me for taking my mother's attention away from him and his new son. When he wasn't drunk, he pretty much kept to himself. For some odd reason since I came home, when he got in one of his drunken rages, his anger wasn't directed at me. It was as if he had called a moratorium. I guess it wasn't sporting for him to hunt down a crippled animal. He was waiting for me to heal, and then it would be open season again. Even though he left me alone, I still couldn't escape his violence. I could feel his hatred of me building day by day. Sometime soon, there will be no more room left in him and his hate will explode all over me.

For the next few days, I was glued to Millie's bed of metal bars. I lay on my back with my head hanging off the side edge and walked the ceiling with my eyes. I was transported into another world, climbing over the thresholds of doorways and walking around light fixtures. I found myself in an upside down world.

Spotty stayed at my side on the linoleum floor, sharing my boredom. The heat of the sun's rays streamed through the window and beat down on her, and she stirred from her comfortable spot. Struggling onto her legs, Spotty dragged herself to a cooler shady spot of linoleum and let her legs buckle beneath her, plopping to the floor with a dull thud.

Tired of doing nothing, I waded through the static of the radio but there was absolutely nothing on during the day. Only dumb shows like, *Don McNeill's Breakfast Club,* and some soap operas. They bored the hell out of me, but I stayed tuned, waiting for the late afternoons when I could I listen to my favorite kiddie shows. The radio filtered through my daydreams and took me out of my self and my room. During those moments, my whole world was coming from that little lit-up black box with its Emerson trademark.

Each one of the shows I loved had its own distinctive introduction that sent me into a tailspin. The sound of a plane drones in and out of a dive, flying through the deep chimes of a humongous clock. A voice dives with it in a sweeping fall, "Captaaain Midniiiiight!" The shows weren't complete without their exciting commercials. *Captain Midnight's* sponsor was Ovaltine, "*The delicious, healthy chocolate-y drink.*" I gagged on every drop of its gritty, chalky chocolate.

When I heard *Superman* leap from tall buildings in a single bound and swoosh through the air, with eyes wide open I could see his blue and red costume in the sharpest, most vivid colors.

"*The Tom Mix Ralston Straight Shooters is on the air.*" Tom Mix himself calls to his horse, "*Up Tony! Come on boy!*" and sings a little jingle to the sound of Tony's syncopated, coconut-hoof beats:

> "*Shredded Ralston for your breakfast,*
> *Starts the day all shining bright,*
> *Gets you lots of cowboy energy*
> *With a flavor that's just right.*
> *It's delicious and nutritious,*
> *Bite-size and ready to eat.*
> *Take a tip from Tom*
> *Go tell your Mom,*
> *Shredded Ralston can't be beat.*"

Most of the kiddie show sponsors sold cereals with special premiums. For a nickel or ten cents in coin, carefully taped to the box top of any cereal, you could send away for wonderful prizes. Millie helped me send away for a *Tom Mix* premium.

Every day, twice a day, for several weeks, I waited impatiently in my bed, nagging Millie to see if my prize was in the mail.

Eventually, I forgot all about it and one day Millie showed up with a little box wrapped in brown paper with a string tied around it. To me it was a stolen jewel from Ali Baba's cave of hidden treasures. I couldn't open it fast enough. It contained the *Tom Mix* spinning siren ring. Spinning was right. After blowing into the ring, my head would go into a dizzy spin from loss of oxygen. An extra surprise came with the ring, something they didn't mention in the commercials, "Hey kids, you can also watch your finger, right before your very eyes, turn greener than the Statue of Liberty!"

In a separate brown envelope, I got an 8" x 10" photo of Tom Mix, with arrows pointing to every part of his anatomy, showing where Tom had broken every bone in his body during his great heroic feats.

That night while listening to *The FBI in Peace and War*, I heard squeaking sounds coming from my mother's room. They got louder and faster, and Mom's bed began banging against Millie's wall. That monster was fucking my mother! I put my head closer to the radio, but it didn't help, I could still hear him molesting my mom. I made that vibration-yawning sound into my ears, feeding it through my brain, drowning out the bad taste in my thoughts.

During the night I was awakened by a woman's desperate screams, mingling with helpless cries. I didn't find out until the next day that a woman had fallen out of her third floor window on Westchester Avenue and impaled her leg on a black wrought iron spike.

Later that night a couple of drunks came out of the Pan Am bar, shouting curses at each other. How lucky we were to have two bars on our block, with twice as many interesting people. I hopped over to the window and saw the two drunks scuffling. They crashed through the Hilltop Cleaner's window on the corner of Faille and East 165th Street. The violent sounds from Millie's window drifted in and out of my sleep, getting mixed up with my dreams.

In the City on West 29th Street, my mother was a forelady in a furrier sweatshop, getting paid much less than the men who worked under her. It was a seasonal job, and during the months she was laid off, her boss, Mr. Shurtzer, gave her piecework to take home. One morning after picking up some work, Mom came home with a tiny loaf of bread, no bigger than her thumb.

"Solly, look, I got something for you!"

It was a baby Tip-Top bread, exactly like its parent, with the same white stars floating around on the red ends of the package -- a toy I could actually eat!

"Look at you! So bored. You've been stuck in da hot house too long. How'd you like to get out and go to da movies wit Millinue?"

She didn't have to ask me twice. I jumped right out of bed.

"Listen, my boychick, I can't carry you all da way to the movies, so I vas thinking we could use Ronnie's carriage."

"No Ma! I can't do dat! Someone will see me."

"Don't worry, darlink, no one vill see you. It vill be good. I'm going to keep da hood up. No one's seeing you, okay, totala?"

Mom helped me down the three flights of stairs. The baby's carriage was in the hall waiting for us by the front door of our building. She crunched me into the carriage, covered me with a sheet, snapped up the hood and off we went – Millie, Mom, the carriage and me.

The Boulevard movie marquee jutted out over the sidewalk. A banner hung from the bottom edge of the marquee with a drawing of blue icicles and penguins. Between the penguins, it read, *"Be Cool, Stay Cool. This Theatre Is Refrigerated."*

The movie theaters on Southern Boulevard were a second home for my mom, and wherever she went she made friends, including the matron of the Boulevard Theater. The matron had peppered gray hair tied tightly away from her face, and wore a white uniform with a dark cardigan sweater half open over her stocky body.

As planned, the matron met us outside the movie house just before the kids began to line up at the ticket booth. She led us through the front doors and into the spacious lobby. A cool gust of air with the smell of a movie lobby seduced me with images of what was waiting for me inside. A lush rug freshly steamed, muffled our voices and still held the mixed aromas of candy and popcorn.

On my left was a large picture of a Revolutionary War Minute Man, selling war bonds. It was attached to a wood and cardboard stand draped with American flag buntings. To my right, in brilliant colors, a three-dimensional cutout advertised next week's picture shows.

The matron led us into the dark theater. When my eyes became accustomed to the dim light, I could see the staircase to the balcony and loge. Directly in front of us were three sections of orchestra seats. The matron took us to the far right, the children's section, where the candy counter, rest rooms, and a water fountain were snuggled under the balcony stairwell, all neatly bunched together in their own little cozy cave.

Off to the side, my carriage parted a pair of weighty maroon curtains that led to the lower box seats. Mom lifted me from the carriage and gently put me into my seat and left Millie and me alone in our very own box. We were separate and special. I felt like I was sitting on an overstuffed throne. My leg rested upon the padded railing, and I could see down into the orchestra pit. Kids crowded into the theater below – the same kids who, all week long, had saved up for this moment, now waited impatiently for the show to begin. All their energy blew up in an orgy of noise like a string of firecrackers.

The lights grew dim, abruptly smothering the insane bedlam. Our numbed little bodies stared up, entranced by the smoky beam of light passing over our heads, and concentrated on a screen at the back of the stage. Then, squiggly numbers flashed on the blank screen. A theatre full of kids sang out in perfect harmony, counting down the receding numbers, ending with frenzied screams as soon as a *Looney Tunes* cartoon blasted onto the screen. This scene was probably being practiced in every other neighborhood theatre in The Bronx at that very same moment.

After the cartoons, we sang to a sing-along musical short, following an animated bouncing ball that danced above each word of a song. Millie stood up with her precious dimples and her blond baloney curls, belting out the words with a booming gusto that rode above everyone else's voice. With each blast of her golden tones, I sank deeper and deeper into my chair, petrified I'd be noticed.

The main feature was *Lassie Come Home,* and the second feature a B-movie called, *Bring on the Girls,* with Spike Jones and his City Slickers. In one of the musical numbers, *Chloe,* Spike hammered one of the guys in his band into the floor like he was a nail... these guys were crazy.

When the double feature was over, the matron emptied the theatre of children. Mom showed up with the carriage and scooted me out the front doors. We hit a wall of heat that almost pushed me back into the lobby. The blazing sun washed out the streets with a blinding light and the air was so dense and oppressive I couldn't breathe it, I had to gulp it.

As Mom wheeled me up Westchester Avenue, my stomach felt like an empty pit. No matter how much food or candy I brought with me to the movies, I always came out starving. We were about to cross Hoe Avenue when a strong urge came over me to get home before five o'clock. No matter where I was or what I was doing, an automatic reflex would kick in telling me to rush home to listen to *The Shadow.* Sundays were my last day of freedom before the school week started, and the time was etched in my brain, even if I wasn't going to school the next day.

From inside the carriage, I heard the passing voices of my friends. I quickly formed a make-believe wall that no one could see through and tried to make myself disappear by focusing on a single spot inside the carriage. It must have worked, because my friends passed us by without seeing me.

Suddenly, the carriage hit an uneven crack at the edge of the curb and stopped with a jolt. Mom tried to jump the open gap by giving the carriage one good shove. Over went the carriage and out went the sheet and mattress, taking me with them into the gutter. For a brief moment, Mom and Millie stood there, stunned. I lay on the street with a sheet hanging off my head, half covered by the mattress. Mom looked at me and started to laugh. Millie and I couldn't help ourselves – we couldn't stop laughing.

Lying there in the gutter, I thought to myself... is this how Harold sees the world?

WINDOW TO MY IMAGINATION

"WHAT D'YA WANT for breakfast... some pancakes?" Mom's pancakes were like earmuffs, small, thick and puffy, and more often than not, still gooey in the middle.

"No, Ma... not that."

Mom cooked me up what she called egg-in-a-hole: She took two pieces of bread with holes cut out of the middle and buttered them on both sides. Then she dropped an egg into the hole and fried it to a crunchy golden brown. All her egg meals consisted of the same ingredients – eggs, bread, butter and salt – but she had so many ways of cooking them and it was amazing how different each one tasted.

After breakfast, Mom set me up on Millie's windowsill with a couple of pillows on the fire escape to rest my foot. For hours, I sat in my favorite place in the house, the main focus of Millie's room, her front window. My accident gave me lots of time to be alone, thinking thoughts I never thought before, and seeing the world outside myself, and how I was connected to it.

Millie's windowsill was my front row seat where I watched the daily drama unfold. With Spotty at my side, we surveyed our territory from Westchester Avenue on down The Three Hills. Every apartment building as far as I could see was plugged into a telephone pole. The streets were empty, except for an occasional train screeching around the sharp turn of the El.

Living creatures stirred, leisurely walking out of their buildings one by one onto the sidewalks. The lazy streets slowly began waking up. Spotty sat at attention, watching every movement on the street. When I tried to hug her, she gave me a quick glance and snapped back to her unshakable focus.

My friends were playing in the streets wearing camphor balls dangling on strings around their necks. At that time it was believed that the camphor balls would ward off the evil spirits of polio. A group of kids from Bryant Avenue challenged my friends to a game of Johnny-on-the-Pony. They flew through the air with arms and legs flailing and crashed down on the backs of a row of bent-over bodies, shouting the Johnny-on-the-Pony mantra:

"Johnny-on-the-pony, one-two-three,
Johnny-on-the-pony, one-two-three,
Johnny-on-the-pony, one-two-three – All off!"

Later, as I watched the girls jumping rope and playing potsy, the rumbling of an ice truck took my attention away from their games. It pulled up in front of Jack's candy store just below me. The iceman was short with no neck. His baggy pants half-heartedly held onto his flannel shirt, cinched up with a belt too long for his waist. The end of the belt dangled down the side of his leg all the way to his knees.

The iceman let down the tailgate and climbed onto the back of his truck. He grabbed a large piece of thick burlap soaked with water, lying limp over the ice, held down by its own weight. It must have been almost impossible to lift, because he had to lean back on his heels and pull at the burlap using his whole body. Even from where I sat, I could see the blue veins swelling and branching out from the middle of his forehead. The iceman won out and gradually dragged the burlap to one side, uncovering rows of tombstone ice slabs.

My friends cautiously maneuvered themselves around the truck, stalking their prey, waiting for an opportunity to steal a piece of ice.

They pretended to ignore the truck and innocently started singing the kid's war hymn:

"Whistle while you work
Hitler is a jerk
Mussolini is a meany
Whistle while you work."

It was all so clear and obvious to me. I could see exactly what they were doing. Is this the way I am when I'm with my friends? Can people see through me as easily as I saw through them?

The iceman took his tools out of a worn leather pouch attached to the side of the truck, and with his ice pick, stabbed into a block of ice. The first blow caused a jagged lightning bolt racing through the ice, with thousands of small cracks flaring out from it. The iceman pecked at the ice and a large piece neatly chunked away. He unhooked a pair of metal tongs from around his neck. They bit into the ice like a pair of fangs. He flipped a protective rubber mat over his shoulder and flung the ice half on his back, half on his shoulder, and carried it into Jack's candy store.

Odd chunks of ice lay scattered on the back of the truck, just begging to be taken. Sergie, Bobby, Melvin and Johnny grabbed a few and ran from the crime scene over to the stoop by the Chinese Laundry. As I watched, I was down there with them, sucking at the ice, feeling the cool, clear, clean taste melting in my mouth, dripping down my chin and hands. Stolen ice was better than any drink I could buy at Jack's.

Dark clouds mushroomed across the sky. A flash of lightning crackled, mirroring the jagged fractures in the ice. Thunder roared, yelling at us to get the hell out of its way, chasing the people inside. Rain exploded off the empty sidewalks, pounding down on the hot steaming pavement and bouncing back up in a sea of crosses, smelling like boiled eggs.

I hopped back to Millie's bed and for awhile, I listened to the syncopated patter of rain off the fire escape and watched the connecting drops racing down the window. Lying on my back, I stared up at the ceiling and followed the random scratches, cracks and craters of peeling paint. The chaotic lines were filled with shadows that pulled together into detailed pictures of twisted faces, monsters and street scenes. I was rarely bored. I could transform anything in my room into a toy.

The only toy the hospital allowed me to take home was a box with bright color cartoons on its glossy cover. Inside was a stack of wax paper, with strips of cartoons drawn in black and white line. The idea was to place the wax paper over the drawings and rub across the wax paper with a wooden tongue depressor. Then, miraculously the cartoons appeared on the wax paper. It made me feel I was a part of creating the drawing.

But transferring the black and white cartoons wasn't enough for me. I got hold of an old Sunday *Tribune* and when I rubbed the wax paper over the color comic strips, like sorcery all the color drawings came off the newspapers and onto my blank piece of wax paper. Next I tried newspaper photos and typed headlines. But I wanted more. I needed to be closer to making these creations on my own. Without using the wax paper, I started to trace my joke books.

After awhile, I began drawing the pictures without tracing them. When I ran out of paper, I used whatever I could get my hands on, scrounging white cardboard laundry backings and brown shopping bags. Feeling something more than myself, I couldn't stop. Drawing was like a fire inside me burning out of control.

Pictures with perspective drew me in, and I found myself living in their depths, walking into the doorways of buildings, discovering rooms the artist never thought of. In the pictures, I found myself turning corners and finding streets where there were none. For hours, I was suspended from the counterfeit world outside and living my real self in a creative bubble that smothered the sounds around me.

"Jesus Christ! Why is everyone still caring about Roosevelt? The fuckin' man's been dead a long time now. What the hell's the big deal? It's just one less 'Jew'."

Screaming from the living room, Harold's senseless brutality always snuck up behind me, and without warning, tore through my protective bubble, jolting me into his reality. I managed to close him off and made his voice part of the background noise.

Looking up from my drawings, I saw Millie's room as if for the first time. The shape of the empty spaces that separated the sparse furniture was as tangible to me as the furniture itself. I desperately wanted to fill those empty spaces with artwork I could touch. During those days I realized that art was a window to my imagination. And it wasn't other people I saw through that window, but reflections of myself. Until now my imagination was only a way to escape being so afraid. Now I knew it was a place to find my power.

Art was who I was – there was no right or wrong in it. As for my family, they just didn't care about art. To them it didn't exist, and neither did I.

THE WAR ENDS

I WAS LYING on a soft table covered with a white sheet, listening to the metal instruments clicking in bubbling water. Dr. Parato took out a pair of bent scissors from the steaming water. He began to cut into my bandages in a business-like manner. How did he know where the bandages ended and my foot started? I jerked my foot away from the scissors.

Tony the doctor's nurse, bent over me. She was so close that her fiery red, wavy hair tickled my face. Tony looked at me with eyes that liked me. And when she spoke the beauty mark at the side of her mouth was swallowed up in her dimples.

"It's okay, Sweetheart, he's not going to hurt you." She held my hand. "The doctor's not going to touch your foot. You'll see, it's all going to be over very soon."

With her other hand she gently touched my forehead, it felt different than my mother's touch. My groin tingled as if I was on a swing going into a sudden dive.

The bandages came off with some yellow ooze clinging to it. "You poor baby." Tony's words melted me. I wanted to be smothered into her body.

The swelling of my foot had gone down and the burnt cracks on the sole of my foot were disappearing. Dr. Parato was happy with what he saw.

"Very good, very good. Molly, it looks like you can start changing his bandages yourself."

Going home, we stopped at the corner at a little, wooden Italian Ices shack leaning up against Dr. Parato's two-story building. After each of our visits to the doctor, Mom treated us to one of these delicious wonders, nothing like the ices we knew in our neighborhood. They were thicker and creamier, more like an icy ice cream.

On our trips to and from Dr. Parato's, Mom would have to carry me the whole way. She was strong, but carrying a nine-year-old for long distances was too much for her. I thought it would be so cool to have crutches and wondered why she wouldn't let me have them so she wouldn't have to carry me.

"Sollinue," Mom insisted, "You don't understand. You'll get so used to dem, you might never walk again." I suspected the real reason was that we simply couldn't afford them. Mom was too proud to admit it and continued to suffer with her burden... me.

Every so often, on our way home, Mom would have to put me down to rest. One time she was so exhausted, she stumbled and we both got tangled up with each other. As we were falling, she was able to catch her balance in an awkward dance and a laugh burst out. I saw us as a slapstick routine and joined in the fun. I loved those times when she changed my fear into laughter. Mom always saw the fun in it.

We got off the trolley at the corner of Southern Boulevard and Westchester Avenue and Mom stopped at the candy store near the deli to buy a pack of cigarettes. Inside a woman was talking to the owner.

"It's too bad the war is almost over. Looks like my son's going to live. Now I'll never have a chance to collect on his army pension or his life insurance."

"You son of a bitch!" My mother rushed at the woman and pinned her up against the front door. Grabbing the top of the woman's dress, Mom pulled her up until she stood on the tips of her toes. The woman was shaking from the unexpected explosion.

"How dare you say dat? What kind of mother are you? Mien gut! Dat's your son you're talking about. You should only drop dead for saying such tings! I should beat your brains out for talking like dat."

The woman's eyes went blank. Stunned, she couldn't believe what just happened.

"Ahh, you're not worth it. Pthoo–pthoo-pthoo," My mother spit three times while still holding her up against the door, "Don't you ever say dat again, or even think such a thing. You hear me? Do you hear me!?"

By now the poor woman was crying hysterically, "Yes, yes, I'm sorry. Please, I'm sorry!"

Mom let her go. "You son of a bitch. Get outta here and don't let me catch you around here again!" Like a shot, the woman disappeared from the candy store.

Holy Shit! My mom is Humphrey Bogart!

During World War II the young sons, husbands, fathers and brothers were losing their lives and limbs. And others were held prisoner and tortured, while we kids on the home front were romanticizing the war. To us it was only an extension of the movies we saw and the radio shows we listened to – just another story of the good guys vs. the bad guys.

In my mother's room, hanging from her front window, was a banner with two blue stars on it. I was so proud of those two stars. They told the people on my block that my brothers were out there fighting the Japs and Nazis. My mother felt differently. She'd rather have her two boys back home than those two stars on a piece of cloth hanging in her window.

My brother Harry served in the US Army Engineer Corp in Europe. Walter was in the Navy, in the Pacific. When Harry and Walter were home on leave, their uniforms would be lying around for me to investigate. I'd rub my fingers across the raised detailing of a golden eagle on Harry's dress hat. I'd put on Walter's Navy cap and touch the thirteen buttons on his bellbottom trousers. They were like the best radio show premiums, except they were the real thing. Harry and

Walter were my own private super heroes, flesh and blood, stepping out of my joke books and movies. They were my brothers dressed up in their alter egos.

On that August day when the Japanese surrendered, my mother, Millie, Veronica and her mother, Mrs. Weinman, fought through the frenzied crowds of people on their way to Southern Boulevard. From Whitlock to Hoe Avenue, every single person from every building had rushed out into the streets. I recognized all their faces, but I'd never seen them all together at the same time. They were out there releasing the tensions of a long war and infecting each other with the joy of relief.

I was stuck in Millie's room with my bandaged foot, and I wanted to join in. I started tearing strips of newspapers and throwing them over the fire escape, watching them float down to the street onto the heads of a wall-to-wall crowd of screaming people. They were so loud, they practically drowned out the air raid siren, blasting from the top of the Telephone Building.

I was doing something that, at any other time, would have been an unacceptable thing to do, but for these few hours, the unwritten laws of our community had changed. This new freedom exhilarated me, and I hopped around our rooms like a rabbit, finding and tearing every loose piece of paper I could get my hands on.

The paper in the streets undulated like a sea of waves as the people plowed through, heading toward the Boulevard. Sergie, Bobby Frick, Johnny, and Anthony were up to their necks in paper. Their heads bobbed up and down as they pushed their way to the steps of the Chinese Laundry, trying to get there before they drowned in the debris.

The Chinese Laundry man had made a life-size dummy of Hirohito and hung it by its neck from the lamppost near his store. Someone in the crowd set it on fire and the mob of people gave out with a deafening roar as the flames engulfed the dummy. During this whole insanity, Harold stayed in his room. It was as if he was hiding. He was so quiet, I forgot he was in the house... Not a good day for Harold.

BACK ON THE BLOCK

ON MY FIRST day out, I could feel the electricity on the block. My mother went across the street and set up a chair for me in front of Mr. Jacobs' Laundry. Jacobs was our own evil Dr. Sivana from *Captain Marvel's Whiz Comics*, bent over, bald, and toothless. He hated children, women, dogs, and cats – anything that breathed. We hardly noticed him as he slithered through the streets, blending into the background of our lives.

While I waited for my mom, I leaned against our building and watched my sister Millie and her friend Debra. Between Harry's bar and the New Era Cleaners was a brick wall where they were playing handball with a couple of boys, asses-up. That's when the loser bends over facing the wall, and the winner has the pleasure of throwing a Spaldeen at their ass. We didn't need adults to punish us; we found ways of doing it ourselves.

Out in the street, a group of girls were playing the alphabet game. Barbara Erb was bouncing a Spaldeen under one leg. The ball bounced up and briefly snuggled in her hand, and she softly caressed its roundness. Then with a twist of her wrist, she guided it back down to the sidewalk, bouncing the ball as she went through each letter of the alphabet.

> *"A my name is Alice, and my husband's name is Al.*
> *We come from Alabama, and we sell Apples.*
> *Our son's name is Arthur, and daughter's name is Anne.*
> *B my name is Betty..."*

Melvin, Sergie, and Bobby Frick were playing a game of stickball called, flys-up. A voice screamed out, "Heads up!" a warning from Sergie that a foul ball was flying over the heads of the unsuspecting people on the sidewalk.

There was no way I was going to let my mom carry me across the street like a baby in front of my friends. I made up my mind to walk to the chair by myself. I touched my foot gingerly to the sidewalk. The more I leaned down on the concrete, the more painful it was. So, I quickly compromised and hopped the rest of the way to the chair. My mom sat nearby with her friend Yetta Melnick.

My friends ignored me as if I wasn't there. I felt like a stranger. But the girls took care of me as if they were nurses, and I was their patient. They pampered me with cool drinks and soft pillows, and I loved it.

I noticed a new girl on the block, a tensely wired little girl named Hannah, with black baloney curls and large black eyes that stared right through me. She didn't speak English very well and kept to herself. The family Hannah lived with wanted her to mix with the other kids. I watched her stand among them as they played, and then, little by little, she lagged behind until she disappeared into the background. There was another odd thing I noticed about Hannah, she had a permanent smudge on her arm. When I had a chance for a closer look, I discovered that what I thought was dirt was a strange row of numbers tattooed on her arm. I had never heard of any kid having a real tattoo.

Tinkling bells announced the arrival of the Good Humor truck. It pulled up to the curb with its little shingled bungalow in the back. The kids dropped whatever they were doing and scattered, hollering to the open windows of their buildings. Heads popped out from windows and mothers threw down coins wrapped in paper.

Hannah didn't know what all this sudden commotion was about. As the kids ran screaming to the ice cream bungalow, lumps of tears bubbled at the corners of her eyes. Her mouth twisted open in a silent scream as she ran away in terror, disappearing into her building.

The Good Humor man stood beside his miniature house, looking official in his white uniform and white peaked cap. A brown leather strap crossed over his shoulder, connecting to a belt that carried his metal coin changer. He opened the thick vault on the side of the little house, and it was as if there was someone living in there, breathing out a smoky vapor. The white mist gathered into clouds that puffed out over the clamoring kids, smelling like cold metal, and evaporating in the hot summer air.

The vault contained so many different kinds and flavors of ice cream that it was difficult to make a choice, but there were pictures on the side of the truck to make it easier. It was cheaper and more fun to get ice cream from the Good Humor truck, but I couldn't get my favorite, the greatest ice cream of all, the Mello-Roll. Jack's candy store was the only place we could get Mello-Roll, a cylinder of ice cream lying on its side in a rectangular sugar wafer cone, fashioned to fit the roll perfectly. Jack used to dip it in sprinkles. It was true to what it was, ice cream with an emphasis on creamy – the real stuff.

Millie got me a Dixie Cup, half vanilla-half chocolate. The taste of the thumb-shaped wooden spoon mingled in my mouth with the taste of the ice cream, becoming a Dixie Cup flavor of its own. Licking the thin layer of ice cream off the cardboard cover revealed a special treat, a picture of a famous movie star, Greer Garson, in a pale green tint.

About an hour later, the fish man showed up, selling the catch of the day off of the tailgate of his truck. Mom picked out a fish and had the fish man gut it, scale it, and wrap it in a newspaper. She rushed it up to our apartment. Noticing I was alone, Melvin and Sergie circled around me and started to poke at me with a broomstick as if I was a dead cat.

"What's da matter, Solly? Don't like it, do ya?" Sergie kept poking at me, "Ga'head... that's it, grab it. Ahh, too bad, ya almost had it. Oh, tough shit." Sergie taunted me, "Come on, come on, you can do it."

Segie got too confident and relaxed his guard, giving me a chance to grab one end of the stick. He pulled at the other and forced me off my chair. I had to let go.

They laughed, "What's the matter, Solly? You too chicken ta hold on?"

Sergie whispered into Melvin's ear and Melvin started shaking his bottle of RC Cola. He shook it so hard his hair bounced up and down on his head. Then, following his master's orders, the little runt sprayed the soda all over me.

"You fuckin' bastard!"

Melvin laughed and sprayed me again, gloating in his power over me. The sizzling midday sun quickly dried the sugary soda on my hair, face and clothes, turning them into sticky clumps of matted goo. All I could do was sit there seething, trapped in my chair.

"Go ahead and laugh, I'm not always going to be sitting here. Soon, very soon, I'll be walking again. I'm gonna come after your ass, and I'm gonna kill you! You fuckin' little prick!"

Melvin walked away, but he wasn't laughing anymore.

The end of World War II was the end of my being in Millie's room. It was back to my room and back to painting pictures in my head from the street sounds that funneled into my room.

I watched Mom preparing my bed. She whistled popular tunes as she aired out my pillows and blanket, propping them halfway out my window. Then she folded my mattress over to one end of my bed, lit a candle and waved it under the exposed springs. Little black dots fell. Bed bugs were being cremated. I swore I could hear them screaming as their burnt corpses dropped to the floor, looking like chocolate sprinkles on an ice cream cone.

Entombed once more within the brick walls of the alley, listening to distant sounds, faded and indistinct, let me know I was back in my room again, back in that fuckin' dungeon. I was tired of being an invalid tied to my bed. I was buzzing with pent-up energy with no-where to go. Something had to give. My patience had run out. I stared long and hard at my toes. I wanted to move them, but I couldn't. I was too terrified of the pain that I knew would follow. A cold, clammy fear seeped though my skin, dripping along my nose in droplets and dangling off my chin.

One of my toes moved! Did I move it, or did it move on its own? There it went again, and then all the other toes followed. And to my surprise, they were wiggling without pain. All my fears disappeared. Now I could throw my whole self into playing.

I turned a wooden chair over onto its back and squeezed myself between the legs and dowels of the chair. There I was, sitting in the cockpit of a flying tiger. It wasn't make-believe anymore. The legs of the chair became four deadly machine guns, pointing into the clouds, hunting the sky. Attacked from behind, I banked my plane into twists and turns until I had the Jap in front of me and in my sights. I watched the tracers of my bullets hit their target. The Jap Zero burst into flames and fell apart as it headed down to the earth. My mother's cooking brought me down for a landing, and I limped into the kitchen.

"Ma! Ma! Look! I'm walking."

"Very nice. Now get off your foot, you'll hurt yourself."

I hopped over to her, "Whataya makin'?"

"Spaghetti and fish."

There were two things I hated most: liver and fish.

"Eyuk! Pisgetti and fish?"

Mom laughed. The word got twisted in my mouth and I couldn't straighten it out. Being laughed at made me feel like a fool. I clung to her and leaned my head against her behind. She brushed back my hair and continued to cook.

Mom's dress rippled across my face. Peeking from the edge of her dress, I could see the sickly, green clock with its wire dangling down, breaking the boredom of the blank wall. Her dress gently shifted back and filled my eyes with its rows of white polka dots. Her hand, smelling of onions and garlic, brushed across my cheek.

What made her cooking so especially wonderful was the smell of her skin seasoning all her food. Her arms moved through the kitchen like magic wands, as if breathing life into the stove, sink and refrigerator, making them do whatever her hands asked them to do.

Harold stumbled into the kitchen, and I immediately limped back to my room, listening to his educated mouth fill our apartment with brilliant gems.

"The only reason we had a war is because of you Jew bastards. The Jews… they're not good enough to wipe the ass of a nigger. At least the niggers believe in Christ. What do you believe in, bitch? Nothing but that bullshit you call religion."

I never heard Harold laugh, I never saw him smile, but he did love to listen to the *Jack Benny Show* on the radio. I wonder if he knew Jack Benny was a Jew?

Harold treated Millie and me with every verbal cruelty his stewed brain could come up with. Why did he constantly torture us? We were two defenseless kids and not in any way a threat to him. But he did show love to our dog, Spotty, a gentle love I never thought he was capable of. And Spotty, our beloved Spotty, loved him back. How was it possible that our sweet dog could love someone so evil? Why didn't she hate him like Millie and I did?

"It was that fuckin' Jew Communist, Roosevelt, that got us into this war. Yeah, I said Jew. I know for a fact he has Jewish blood in him."

"Harold, you're crazy."

"Crazy am I. What the fuck do you know? You can't even read, you fuckin' imbecile. I'm telling you, he was a Jew. The whole war was a Jewish plot perpetrated by you fuckin' yellow Jews. You're all a bunch of blood-sucking cowards. You instigated the war and then you skulking Jew cowards got us good Americans to fight and die for you."

"Vhat the hell are you talking about? My sons are out there fighting!"

"It was your war not mine. I'm sorry they didn't kill every last one of those fuckin', spineless Jew bastards… including you and your sniveling brats!"

Harold ambled down the hall and hesitated by my door. He looked in, deciding what to do with his pent-up anger. With a sigh of disgust he turned away from my room and stomped out the front door. One of these days, whatever is keeping him from me will give way, and I'll be back on his shit list – part of the family again.

THERE IS NO SAFE PLACE

I'VE BEEN CHASED many times, usually by somebody wanting to beat my ass in. When the bastard was right at my heels, I flew like a demon with wings through the neighborhood's secret world of inter-connecting alleyways up to the rooftops, jumping from building to building, ending up at my own. Quietly I would slide into my apart-ment and bolt the front door, safe in the knowledge that no one could pass through this solid barrier between me and the chaos threatening me from the outside. This night, I learned the difference between liv-ing in a fantasy and existing in the real world.

We knew when Harold left the apartment angry he was going to come back plastered. This time my mother came up with an idea of how to stop him. She would simply lock him out of the apartment.

"You bitch! Open the door! I'm warning you, open the fucking door! You Jew cunt!"

My mother didn't answer. Harold's foot kicked at the door, test-ing its strength. Suddenly, with the full force of his mindless rage, he smashed it in. I could lock all the doors I wanted, but they wouldn't keep out the monsters of this world. There is no safe place.

Mom called the cops and while we waited, Harold spewed his venom.

"You cock sucking cunt! Lock me out, will you? You know all those fucking, gutless Jews who went into the ovens like sheep? Someday you're going to be one of them!"

Harold's outbursts were building, and like a bulldozer, he crashed through the apartment, crushing everything in his way, getting closer and closer to crushing us.

As soon as the cops walked into the apartment, Harold transformed himself into a perfect gentleman.

The first cop asked, "What's the problem, lady?"

Harold answered, "We had a slight altercation."

"Sir, I was speaking to the lady. Okay Ma'am, what happened here?"

"Look! Look at da front door. Such violence! He wanted to kill us. You've got to do something! His hands should only fall off!"

The second cop pointing to the door, "Did you do that?"

Harold calmly answered, "Yes, Officer. After all, this is my home. And she did lock me out of my own home. What else could I do?"

"I understand, but that's not the way to solve your problem. Next time just call the police station, and we'll straighten it out. Understand?"

"I'm sorry officer. You're right. I do understand, and I'll do that very thing."

Standing at the kitchen doorway, my attention focused on Harold's face. He had sores on his face, the kind that drunks always get. Where do they come from? Do they appear spontaneously when people drink too much, or do they come from stumbling into walls?

The first cop asked, "Did he hurt anyone?"

The second cop followed up, "Did you hit your wife?"

Harold was keeping his cool, "Of course not. There really isn't anything wrong here."

Seeing that the cops were believing Harold, my mother became hysterical. She screamed out of frustration, "You liar! You son of a bitch liar! This is a vild man!"

"You see what I have to contend with? As I told you, it was nothing but a slight disagreement. There really was no reason for her to lock me out. Look at her. The woman is hysterical. There's no talking to her."

The first cop moved over to my mother, "Calm down, lady."

"Officer, aren't you going to do something?"

"Look lady, there's nothing we can do. He didn't hurt anyone and after all, it *is* his home."

"Vhat are you crazy? Dhat's it?! He's a liar! He lies like a drunken sailor. When you leave he's going to kill us!"

"Sir, is that true?"

"Untrue, Officer. Let me reiterate, there's no trouble here."

"Lady, if you really believe he's mistreating you, why don't you just leave him?"

The first cop motioned to the second cop, "I think we're finished here. Lady, if he hurts you in anyway, call us, okay? And you, sir, just take a walk until things cool off."

"I understand, but I assure you there's nothing wrong."

The second cop turned to my mother, "Lady, if you'd just calm down, I'm sure everything will be alright."

After the cops left, it was pretty quiet. Mom stayed in the kitchen alone, while Harold continued drinking in the living room... until he passed out. From then on, we had frequent visits by the cops. They were there so often, they almost felt like family. Maybe instead of trying to stop Harold from drinking, we should devise a way to ram the alcohol down his throat in a constant flow until he passes out. This way we could skip the in-between stage of his sadistic violence.

That night, Mom brought my fish dinner to my room and while she was setting it down on my chair, my neck went into a spasm and twitched uncontrollably.

"Vhat's dat? What is dat your doink? Stop it! You've got to stop dat. You look like a freak."

I tried my best, but it was out of my control. There was this empty feeling in my neck, and I had to keep filling it. I couldn't stop.

"You look like a crazy person!"

She couldn't take looking at me anymore and left me alone in my room. It felt like another life inside of me, and from then on, it came out whenever it chose to.

Now there was peace and quiet again. But Harold's violence lingered on through the night. I don't know how long it will take, or in what form it will come, but someday I will have my revenge.

It was the slow season for furriers. My mom had been out of work for a long time and now we were desperately in need of money. Luckily, she was called back to work sooner than she expected. But this meant I had to go back to school sooner than I thought.

The day Mom registered me for school, I was wearing hand-me-downs, a pair of oversized corduroy pants that swished with each step and sounded like two pieces of corrugated cardboard rubbing across each other. Mom would do anything to make sure we had plenty of food, but clothes were a different story. They might have had patches and raggedy edges, but they were always clean and ironed.

To save my shoes from wearing out too quickly, Mom had the shoe repairman put metal taps on the soles and heels of my shoes. Sometimes the nails worked their way through the soles and into my feet. But that day, one of the tap nails wore off and the tap was swiveling out from the shoe. I tried to break it off, but instead ended up with a piece of twisted metal dangling from the heel of my shoe and, when I walked, I created a trail of sparks. There I was with swishing pants, tapping along with my heavy limp, shooting off sparks. A one-man band with fire works following behind, feeling like a limping circus freak.

Mom brought me to my assigned classroom and, just when I thought things couldn't get worse, I entered and all I could see was a room filled with retarded children. Something grabbed at my insides, leaving an empty shell. For a few minutes all sensation evaporated from my body. The first thing I felt was my skin becoming raw and painful to my touch. I began to shake with uncontrollable chills and, from this cutting realization, a cold sweat poured out of my open wounds. Gone was the place where I only thought I was retarded.

Now, I *knew* I was. For the first time in my short life, I didn't want to live.

Harold's constant taunting convinced me I was a retarded little bastard. He had worn me down, and I believed him. I thought I had hidden it so well, but I hadn't fooled anyone. I'd been found out and could never look anyone in the eye again. Harold had won.

The vice principal sat behind a huge mahogany desk, her symbol of authority. She was a quiet but forceful woman, with short cropped wavy hair. As soon as we walked into her office, my mother blurted out, "My son isn't going to be in with dose crazy kids! He might be a little stupid, but he's not retarded!"

I knew my mother believed I was hopelessly stupid. I had to accept this as a fact, because it came not only from my teachers and friends, but also from my family. And after all, they did love me. And if they loved me, why would they lie?

I was immediately taken out of the special class and the vice principal put me back into my regular class with my friends. Everyone was half a year ahead of me. It was the fifth grade, and I had missed the beginning of new methods in math and new rules of grammar. They had all been lost to me. The teacher was frustrated with me. She didn't want to take the time to teach me what I didn't know. So she blamed it on my stupidity. No one, not even Mom or Millie tried to help me catch up. I was on my own.

For the next two years at P.S. 75, I was stuck with a teacher who could easily have been a stand-in for the Wicked Witch of the West. Her real name was Mrs. Baras, but I called her Mrs. Bare-ass. Oh how I loved the sound of it! Mrs. Bare-ass. I would say it over and over until it became my own anthem.

Mrs. Bare-ass had thick, red-gray hair pulled back into a tight bun. Every hair was in place as if glued together. I imagined her at home chunking off her hair in one solid mass and meticulously putting it to sleep for the next day. Everyday, Mrs. Bare-ass would sneer at me with mocking eyes from her narrow, wrinkled face. Her stooped shoulders were wrapped in a long, light blue smock. Nothing ever changed, her clothes, her hair, herself. Every detail stayed the same everyday for two years.

At first sight, Mrs. Bare-ass took an immediate disliking to me. I guess I wasn't her type of student, the kind she enjoyed teaching. I was one of those children educators called a slow learner, or daydreamer.

At every opportunity, Mrs. Bare-ass took great pleasure in shaming me in front of the class. I tried hard to make myself disappear at the back of the room, but she forced me to sit at a front desk where she could use me as an example to the others. Every time she had a question for the class, she would make a point of asking me first. No matter what answer I gave, she always questioned it.

"Are you sure that is your answer? Well, Rothman, I'm waiting. Is that your answer?"

Since she was a teacher, I naturally accepted her authority. Her questioning made me doubt myself until I didn't know if I was right or wrong anymore... and so I would always change my answer. Pleased with herself, a smile would cross her craggy face, "You're wrong. Sit down! Rothman, you have a brain like a sheet of ice."

The whole class would laugh. Mrs. Bare-ass took great pleasure in ridiculing me in front of my classmates, who would then volunteer to answer the same question and give the same answer I said in the first place.

Mrs. Bare-ass would coo, "Very good. That is absolutely right."

The class knew what she was doing and went along with it. From that point on, I refused to open my mouth in answer to any of her questions. I just stood there and took her insults day after day.

Then along came the young and pretty, Miss Prescott. She was a sub for Mrs. Bare-ass for two weeks. Funny, she meant so much to me, but I can't seem to remember what she looked like. But I do remember the feeling of her. She was fresh, bright and soft. Being in the same room with her, I knew there were good things to come. During that short time, her quiet gentleness toward me erased almost all of the bad taste of school, enabling me to breathe again. It was a fast two weeks, and then she was gone.

Flush against the wall behind the stairwell of my building, were small metal compartments lined neatly in a row and filled with mail. When Mom was working, Millie and I collected the mail twice a day. Inside our letterbox there were mostly bills, and every once in a while, my brothers would send their stories from Europe and the South Pacific. I was amazed at the idea of people talking to people on a piece of paper.

On this day, I found an envelope with my name on it. I had never received a letter before in my life. Maybe it was something I didn't want to know. I ran upstairs to my room, away from Millie.

The letter was from Miss Prescott. At first I didn't know what to do with it. I sat on my bed for a long time staring at the envelope. I was baffled. Why would someone like Miss Prescott, a teacher, take the time to send me a letter? Not for my mother, but just for me? I never thought she even noticed me.

Inside the envelope was a birthday card. There was a personal note on the card.

To a young boy who is better than most people think he is.
I enjoyed having you as one of my students. I hope you have
a great birthday and a great life.
Miss Prescott

This was the first time someone recognized me as a person and sent me a birthday card. That one simple act of kindness wasn't lost on me. She gave me something to hold onto and to build on. No matter how little it was, it kindled my self-respect. And no matter how few these acts of kindness would follow in the years to come, they found their way back to Miss Prescott's original gift. And when that door needed to be opened, it released a flood of hope and the promise of a future.

As for Mrs. Bare-ass, I visited her when I was a senior in high school. After two full years of tormenting me, she didn't even remember who I was.

THE DIVINE WIND

ON A SATURDAY morning in November, I was standing at Millie's window when a roar boomed overhead. A group of eight, graceful P-38s flew over my block. With twin-engines on either side of the wings and between them a cockpit, they were flying as one, in a perfect formation. Their blue metal glowed from the sun's reflection. They looked like no other planes I'd ever seen – a plane from the future.

Millie and Mom walked into the room and broke into my wandering thoughts. Mom was ecstatic and relieved to finally receive letters from Harry and Walter. I limped over to the bed and Millie started reading Harry's letter. I pictured Harry in his uniform looking like the actor Gregory Peck.

Dear Mom,

I would have written sooner, but we were told that our letters will not get through because of our top secret mission. But I did receive all of your letters. Loved every one of them. Please keep them coming.

Now that the war has ended, I'm hoping they won't black out my letters. My outfit was the 361st Special Engineers. We were on our way to the Philippines to a staging area, preparing to invade Japan. There they changed our outfit from Construction Engineers to Combat Engineers. That meant we were going to be the first ones on the beaches of Japan to fight the Japs.

It all happened so quickly we didn't have time to think about it until we got on the ship. That's when the reality of what was going to happen hit us. My buddies and I were shitting in our pants, knowing we were dead men. We sat there, knowing that most of us would never come home – that most of us would be killed on the first wave.

"Oy gutenue, my poor Heschel."
"Mom! Its okay, the war is over. He doesn't have to fight anymore."
"Millinue, go, go, read some more."

Halfway to Japan we got the news that we had dropped a terrible weapon on Japan. They called it the Atomic Bomb. Imagine that, just one bomb destroyed a whole city. About three quarters of the way there, we heard that the Japs had surrendered.

So there's nothing to worry about, and I already told Sylvia the good news. I am now stationed in Okinawa.

Love, Harry
P.S. Give my love to the kids.

"Thank Gut, he's okay. Now read to me Velvul's letter."

Dear Mom,

Just got your letter about Solly's accident. How's he doing? Is he okay?

Mom, I'm going to tell you something scary that happened to me. I'm okay now, so I don't want you to worry about me.

It all started on the 4th of October. I was on my ship, the SS Nye, anchored in Buckner Bay. The day started with our usual duties. It was a quiet, clear day. While my friends and I were eating lunch, the radio was piping in the weather report: a typhoon named "Louise" was sighted, developing in the Caroline Islands. It was going to pass us by, traveling into the East China Sea, north of Formosa.

After lunch, when I stepped out onto the deck, the sky was dark. I felt something was wrong. The ship's speakers announced that the typhoon unexpectedly shifted course and was heading north, right for us.

I never was in a typhoon before, and I didn't know what to expect, but I felt secure on my ship. First there was a heavy breeze, and I thought to myself, this wasn't so bad. The winds began to increase, and every minute it got more intense. The sudden shift of the storm had caught us unprepared. The bay was locked in with ships, and we were unable to escape to the sea.

The rain began to come down hard. The winds picked up speed. There were gusts of wind that almost swept me off the ship. It was like a giant hand scooping up the sea and slapping me across the face with it. Between the crashing sea, the winds, and the pelting rain, we couldn't hear each other, or ourselves, no matter how hard we screamed. There was confusion everywhere.

"Stop! I can't hear anymore. My boys, my boys!"
Millie hesitated, Mom screamed, "Vhy are you stopping?"
"Because you told me to."
"Never mind dat. Go, read." Mom listened as she nervously played with her bangs, rubbing them between her thumb and index finger.

I couldn't fight the storm. It had complete control over me and did whatever it wanted to. It treated me as if I was a paper doll. It was easier to fight the Japs than this storm. With the Japs I had a chance of fighting back; with this storm I was completely helpless.

Our ship dragged its anchor as we moved with the storm.

It became so dark that I couldn't see what direction we were going. For all I knew, we could have been upside down. We rammed into two ships and lost an anchor. We almost lost the second anchor when it got fouled up with another ship's anchor.

I fell on my knees by the railing and started to pray. I never prayed before, but the storm made me a believer and I prayed for my life, 'God, if you get me out of this, I promise to be good to Solly and Millie. I'll be a good person. Please give me that chance.'

In the confusion, a wall of metal appeared out of the dark pelting rain. It was right in front of me and above me, looking down at me. This enormous ship was about to crush us like a toy.

Mom was upset, "I can't take it!" She took a deep breath, "Go on, Millinue. Vhy do you keep stopping?"

Their giant anchor chains were as thick as a trolley car, but they snapped like a tooth pick. I thought it was the end, and I closed my eyes, waiting to be crushed. We smashed into its hull. It put a hole into our ship at starboard, 24' long, and 12' wide, but two feet above the waterline. Somehow I was still alive and our ship stayed afloat.

I don't know how long the storm took, but every second felt like a day. When it finally subsided, I was still alive and in one piece, but a lot of the guys weren't as lucky. The water was filled with bodies floating by our ship.

The next day, there was a mass of wrecked ships on the beach. I learned we had been hit with 35 foot waves and winds about 92 miles an hour, with gusts over 100 miles an hour. We were also told that about 222 ships were grounded, and 36 brothers died. There are 47 of us missing and 100 badly injured.

As long as I live, I'll never forget how we are only made of flesh and blood. We think we're so powerful, but nature is stronger than any of our puny lives.

That's it Mom. I'll write again soon. And remember, I'm okay.

I love you and the kids,
Walter

On a cold Tuesday morning during Christmas break from school, Millie was taking care of Ronnie. Being only a baby, Ronnie had nothing to do with my life. He was just there. Mom was downstairs telling Yetta her fortune. When Mom told people their fortunes, she transformed into a gypsy. All her humor was gone. This was serious business.

Mom was laying out regular playing cards on Yetta's kitchen table when I walked into the kitchen and broke into her trance.

"Yetta, we'll finish this another time."

She got up, put on her red-flecked tweed coat – everything Mom wore had red in it – and tightly cinched it around her waist, hugging the curves of her body, then framed her high cheek bones with a red paisley kerchief.

"Come bubbala, come with me. I need to get a few tings."

The Boulevard was filled with soldiers and sailors. Blasting out of B&J Music store was the voice of Gene Autry, my mother's favorite cowboy, singing *Back in the Saddle Again*. It was Gene's way of welcoming the servicemen back home now that the war was over.

We made a few short stops and ended up at Woolworth's 5 & 10 Cent Store. A new machine had been installed, an automatic doughnut maker, standing just inside the front door. Doughnuts made from scratch by a machine untouched by human hands – the future was on its way.

Mom pulled at me, "Sollinue, its early. Vhy don't I make some lunch, den you and Millie could go to da movies."

It was Tuesday, old movie day at the Boulevard. The first feature starred Fred Astaire and Ginger Rogers, the second was with Donald O'Conner and Peggy Ryan, both musicals. When we got home the apartment was empty. Mom stopped off at Yetta's and Millie went upstairs to Veronica's. I was all alone and free to act out the movies I had just seen, free to be the me I would never share with anybody. I imitated the dance numbers of Astaire and O'Conner, how they flew across the screen. I felt a sudden burst of energy and threw my whole self into dancing up the walls. I jumped up on top of the couch and flung myself out into the air and floated down to the linoleum floor, feeling I could do anything if I was just left alone.

MURPHY

IT WAS THE beginning of the weekend, and I was so concentrated on getting out of the apartment that I didn't notice Harold right behind me. I felt a whack on my head.

"Hey! You! Jew boy! Where the fuck do you think you're running to?!"

Harold raised his leg, and with the power of a gorilla, stuck his foot into my back and shoved me, smashing me into the hall wall. I was the only one who could hear the deafening screams I choked down inside. My face and chest felt like they had been crushed. Harold enjoyed hating me. He hated me for existing, and I was there for his entertainment.

It's amazing how flexible a young boy's body can be. In the short time it took me to escape Harold and get out onto the street, all the pain was gone. Sergie and Johnny were already outside playing box baseball by Harry's Bar. That day Sergie and I were so wired we jumped from game to game, wanting to get as much in as we could before the end of the day. We invaded Jack's candy store and got a two-cents plain. Then Jack let us look through the pile of sticky soda caps nestled under the bottle opener attached to the big, thick, red soda cooler.

We took the undamaged bottle caps and filled them with candle wax or orange peels to weigh them down, making them easier to control. The idea of the game was that the closest cap to the crack on the sidewalk square wins the game. Flicking our index finger across our thumb, we hit the cap to its destination.

I was about to take my shot and happened to look up. Crossing Hoe Avenue and walking toward me was a handsome sailor in bell-bottom blues, carrying a duffle bag over his shoulder, looking like a recruiting poster with flags waving behind him and ship cannons pointing forward. It was my brother, Walter!

"Hi Murphy."

Ever since Walter was in the Navy, for some odd reason, he loved calling me Murphy. I was so proud of him standing there in his super-hero costume, talking only to me, "Where's Mom?"

"She's upstairs."

I followed him up the stairs to our apartment.

He turned to me and said, "I want to surprise her, so I want you to be very quiet." The door was unlocked, and we walked in.

Mom was sitting in the kitchen feeding Ronnie, "Is dat you, Sollinue?" Walter stood at the kitchen doorway.

There was no answer, and Mom could feel someone standing behind her. She turned, looked up, and almost dropped Ronnie, "Oy my Velvul, my Velvul!"

She laughed, put Ronnie down, and grabbed Walter in a hug, then pulled away to get a good look at him.

"You almost gave me a heart attack!" She pulled him back into a hug, not wanting to let him go. "Vhy didn't you tell me you were coming home?" I thought she was going to squeeze the life out of him.

"Didn't you get my letter?"

"Oy gevalt, it's really you, my Velvul. Did they let you go?"

"No, not yet. But I'll be discharged soon."

"You must be hungry. Come, lets go and have some Chinks. Solly, go find Millie. Tell her we're eating out."

Millie's friends swooned as we walked proudly at Walter's side, down to Southern Boulevard and to the Chinks by the corner bank.

After Walter was released from the Navy, he moved into my room with me. As an extra bonus, he brought home his smelly athletes foot, but I didn't mind sharing my room with Walter because he was never home. Sometimes he'd be away for days.

He was only with us for about three short months, and during that time, Harold was a very quiet drunk, afraid of the Jew boy, Walter. But Harold did have his moments of senseless hatred for me when Walter wasn't home – he needed an infusion of hate or he'd melt away.

Walter brought home lots of souvenirs from the Navy, like cannon shells, and my favorite, a real grenade that was stripped of its fuse and explosive powder. He also had a machete, which I played with when he wasn't home. I used it for clearing a path through the jungle by cutting notches into my windowsill. The machete was in a wooden sheath, open on both sides, with intricately carved designs. Once I accidentally grabbed the sheath by its open sides to withdraw the machete, and the blade sliced my hand slightly like a deep paper cut. After that, I stayed away from the machete.

The best present Walter gave me was his sailor cap. He taught me how to train it. "When you're not using it, fold it like this, to look like a crescent moon and that will pinch in the sides of the cap."

He also gave me his Navy blue thirteen-button bellbottoms. Mom altered them to fit, but they were so wide on me, they looked more like a skirt than a pair of pants. I loved them anyway, except when I had to take a leak. The unbuttoning and buttoning was a pain in the ass, and I could never get them to button evenly.

Walter also had something special that he kept hidden in his duffle bag. When he opened it, I caught a glimpse of an Army jacket with words on it. Walter loved this mystery jacket and wouldn't let me go near it. When he left us and moved to Brooklyn, he gave me his precious jacket. And from that day on, I never took it off. I wore it like a second skin.

Walter noticed that Millie and I had very little to wear. The first thing he did after he was discharged was to take us downtown to S. Klein On-The-Square, the Annex at 14th Street. Then he took us to Macy's and Bloomingdale's Basement, where the clothes were always on sale and affordable. The fun thing about Bloomingdale's Basement was that its windows looked out onto the Lexington Avenue subway platform. You could see in the store while you were in the subway.

On the way home, we stopped on the Boulevard at Thom McAn shoe store to buy me a pair of sneakers. We couldn't get them during the war because of the rubber shortage. When I wore my sneakers, I felt like I had shed off half my weight, and I floated home with each step.

Walter came home late almost every night, and he'd wake Millie up to make him a scrambled egg sandwich. She loved every minute of it and felt important that someone, especially Walter, would depend on her.

Walter had no trouble meeting girls. He had a plan that always worked. He used Millie and me as ringers, bringing us with him on his dates. It worked every time, and the girls couldn't resist him.

Walter took us on a picnic with a very pretty blonde. He parked in a deserted spot out in the country and sat Millie and me on a blanket. While we were having a delicious feast, he and the blonde were in his car having their own feast. The car rocked from side to side, back and fourth, up and down. It wasn't a mystery to me; I knew exactly what was going on in the car. Millie and I kept quiet and let Walter go about his business.

Another time, Walter had a date with a hot brunette and took us all to a radio show, *The Henry Aldrich Show*. It was the first time Millie and I had been to a radio show, but I don't remember the show because my whole attention was riveted on the special sound effects. The sound of a fireplace was really a man crunching a sheet of cellophane creating the crackling of a fire. When he squeezed a box of cornstarch, we heard the sound of someone walking in the snow. It was like magic. They could make me believe anything they wanted me to believe.

Millie and I were upset to find out our impression of Henry Aldrich was completely wrong. The voice I heard on the radio was a teenaged Henry Aldrich who was tall and thin. That guy wasn't anywhere on the stage. Instead, the voice we knew so well was coming out of a short, fat man behind the microphone. Did this mean that *everyone* I heard on the radio wasn't what I imagined?

With a little nudging from Mom, Walter began to look for a job. He walked out of our building dressed in a dark blue suit and tie and carrying an umbrella. He spotted me, "Hey Murphy! Walk with me to the train station."

It started to drizzle, and we never got past the Boulevard movies. It was Tuesday and they were playing a Marx Brothers double feature: *Duck Soup* and *Animal Crackers*.

"How'd you like to go to the movies with me? But you've got to promise not to tell Mom. Well, what do you say? Do you promise?"

"Yeah, I promise."

We sat in the balcony, a special treat in itself, watching the Marx Brothers, who never let the movie's story get in their way. They were all over the place. Nothing and nobody could stop their crazy routines. They were on the verge of being a nightmare. I loved the Marx Brothers, not because they were funny, but because of the way they tore down and poked fun at authority. They made short work of the wealthy snobs who thought they were better than everyone else, including the bullies that pushed us around.

Throughout the two movies, Walter sometimes was the only one laughing. It never embarrassed him. He didn't care what anybody thought of him. He just loved having fun.

Mom heard about the new people who moved across the street from us. The Hernandez family had three children: one girl and two boys, and one of the boys, Serafin, was my age. We called him Junior. Mom wanted to help him fit in with the rest of us kids and got permission from his parents to take him with Sergie and me to the Tuesday Vaudeville Night.

After staring at two movies in the dark for a few hours straight, when the house lights came on, their brightness shocked my eyes. From our fourth row seats, we heard distant music through the mumbling crowd. It was coming from a dark pit at the front of the stage. I saw people's heads slowly rising out of the pit as the sharp and brassy music got clearer and louder. An elevated platform filled with musicians and their sparkling instruments, rose up, and stopped just below the stage. There was a hush in the audience as they played in unison to the conductor's wand.

The lights dimed again, and a man in a suit stood at center stage. He introduced each act: a tall cowboy in buckskin chaps doing lasso tricks; next, an Indian dressed like a peacock danced with little bells on his ankles and wrists, keeping a steady rhythmic beat while he moved his arms and body like a flying bird bending from side to side. They were real people, not flat images on a movie screen.

The next day, without missing a beat, Junior was out on the street playing with the rest of us like he had always lived here. It seemed that for each of us, our lives first began when we moved to East 165th Street. I was ten years old when Junior moved onto our block and everything changed. He and Sergie eventually became inseparable. Sergie and I had always been more like brothers than friends, but we were never the same again.

Every year in the late spring, Harold sprayed the hell out of our apartment trying to make a dent in the endless roach population. The rooms would fill with a cloud of poisonous vapors, killing a few roaches, but also possibly killing us. To be on the safe side, Mom took Millie and me and baby Ronnie to the movies long enough for the poisons to dissipate.

We passed the Boulevard Theater where they were playing, *Duel in the Sun*. The movie studio had created a mystique of sexual promises that were never kept. The theatre would only let people in who were over the age of 18 and wouldn't let us kids in at all, even if we were accompanied by an adult. Now, there's one movie I desperately wanted to see.

We ended up at the Star, where your feet would stick to the floor -- just a little extra for the price of admission. There was no balcony, just one floor of seats. All the B, C, and D movies were played at the Star, three in an afternoon, and you could get your fill of cowboy movies, guaranteed.

Mom loved westerns because of the horses. They reminded her of the old country, Bessarabia, when she was a little girl and had her own horse. Today, the Star was showing Wild Bill Elliot as *Red Ryder* with William Blake playing little Beaver. Johnny Mack Brown was in the second movie, and just to mix it up a little, they threw in a detective, a *Sherlock Holmes* mystery.

On our way home, we were caught in a sudden downpour with nowhere to hide. It felt like pails of water constantly being dumped over my head. We looked at each other, drenched, looking like wet dogs, and Mom smiled. Her smile slid into a deep resonant laugh, and we laughed all the way home.

The smell of roach spray was still in the apartment and got cooked into our supper. It lingered on during the night in my room. I tried to sleep under my blanket, but I was rebreathing its smell without any air and that only made it worse. I ended up with my head in the toilet bowl, retching up every piece of food I'd eaten for the past couple of days. I vomited until there was nothing left. Tears poured out of my eyes and nose, and with quick gulps, I took in all the air I could. My mouth and nose tasted like putrid milk.

"Here momala," Mom handed me a handkerchief, "Blow your nose."

She wiped away my tears and put me into bed and felt my forehead and stomach with her lips, "Oy! My sweetheart, you've got fever." She got a bottle of rubbing alcohol from the medicine cabinet and told me to breathe it in, "Dis vill stop you from vomiting."

And it did. When my insides quieted down, she again felt my stomach and forehead with her lips, "Oy, my poor boychickal!" The only attention I got from Mom was when I was sick. It was worth the suffering. When she rubbed the alcohol on my stomach, I could feel her absorbing all the aches from my body into her hands.

"Does that feel better? I called da doctor. He'll be here soon."

Dr. Feinman lived just around the corner on Faille Street, and it didn't take him long to get to our apartment. He checked me over and declared I had the German measles. German measles? I thought we won the war.

That night the fever gave me a nightmare…

We were moving to a new place to live, and I found myself standing in front of an old Victorian house. I could feel there was evil in this house and once I stepped inside, I knew I would never escape.

I could hear the whole house breathing. Something ugly lived here, and I tried to leave, but all the doors were locked. A powerful thing was keeping me from leaving. It appeared a few feet from me, a figure in a flimsy nightgown that swayed around her. It was an old woman with long, straggly gray hair. I could see the walls through her – she is this house.

An intense light streamed from one of the rooms. I couldn't resist it. I knew if I entered, my heart would stop. With all my strength, I fought the blinding light that was pulling me apart. I knew if I died here, I would become part of the evil house.

I woke up screaming and crying. Harold had set down the law: I wasn't allowed to call my Mom in the night for any reason. So I just had to live with it.

While I was sick, I was too weak to do anything but listen to the radio. The first show in the morning was *The Breakfast Club*, just noise to keep me company. I even listened to Mom's deadly soap operas.

Sometimes they put me to sleep and sometimes, if I listened too long, I felt like committing suicide. Thank God, for my late afternoon kiddie shows. The day shows on the weekend were more like it: *Let's Pretend* was my favorite, along with *The Land of the Lost,* and *Archie Andrews,* and in the late afternoon, *Grand Central Station* was my clue that the real shows were about to begin.

For years, I had kept my old broken radio hidden in my closet so my mom wouldn't throw it out. As I slowly regained my strength, I took the radio apart and saved its guts and all its movable parts -- gears, knobs, copper-colored wires, and tubes. Lots of tubes.

I found an empty cardboard box in Millie's room... well, not quite empty. I dumped whatever she had in the box and took it to my room, poked holes in it and arranged the radio parts to look like a machine from the future. I used my creation for building a monster, then it became an instrument panel in the cockpit of a plane, then a space ship, depending on whatever mood I happened to be in.

When I was finally let loose after being cooped up for so long, I played with abandon. Sergie, Junior and I chipped in to buy a Spaldeen. But, you didn't just buy a Spaldeen; you had to test it first. We did that by holding two of the balls at the same height and releasing them exactly at the same time, looking for the high bouncer. We didn't just test it once; we had to make sure... so we tested until Jack couldn't take it any longer.

"Okay, okay kids, that's enough. Pick the ball you want and out you go."

While paying Jack for the ball, a really handsome young man walked into the candy store and bought a pack of cigarettes. His nose was bandaged, and Jack knew him by name, Bernie Schwartz. I saw him around for a while and then as suddenly as he appeared, he disappeared. The next time I saw him was in a movie, *The City Across The River,* but now his name was Tony Curtis.

On our way out of the candy store, we passed by Millie. She was holding both ends of a jump rope in front of her chest, measuring it for the right height to help in her timing before she started jumping.

A blank brick wall across the street was our handball court.

Because of the bricks, we had to be ready every second of the game... we never knew which way the ball would bounce. Handball was the only game where I could hit the ball with my left hand as well as my right. That wall helped us develop our skills, and we became the best handball players in the neighborhood, including my sister Millie.

Spotty was outside with me and joined in the game by chasing after the loose balls. She slid on the rough concrete sidewalks until her paws bled, but I didn't notice it. And even if I had, I was so thirsty to play again I couldn't let anything interrupt me.

DON'T DO IT, VELVUL!

"DON'T DO IT, Velvul! Listen to me. I'm tellin' ya, she's no good!"

"Mom! I love her. Why shouldn't I marry her?"

"Behind your back she fools around with anyone who wears pants."

"You don't know what you're talking about."

"I see how Joann flirt's with your friends. Don't do it!"

"You don't know what you're talking about."

Talking wouldn't change Walter's mind, but Mom wouldn't let it go. Not her Velvul. He's not going to suffer like she had. She plotted to open his eyes and prove to him who his future wife really was – just a tramp.

Mom talked Walter's best friend into helping her. His name was Georgie, and he looked like William Holden, but with deep dimples when he smiled. Millie had a crush on him. I guess most women would. The deal was, when Joann flirted with him, and she would, he should flirt back. I was told to stay out of my room while Georgie and Joann were in there. I hid by the bathroom and heard all kinds of sounds coming from my room.

Mom had it timed perfectly. Walter came home and opened our bedroom door, and found Joann with her skirt up to her belly button lying on the bed with Georgie. His hand was rubbing her pussy. She didn't complain but groaned with pleasure.

"What the fuck?"

Joann jumped from the bed and straightened her skirt, "Please

Walter! This isn't what it looks like."

"Really? I want the both of you to get the fuck out of my room. And I don't want to see either of you again."

Her face flushed with guilt, and she ran out of the apartment crying.

Georgie turned to Walter, "But Wally, I did it for you!"

"You didn't have to do it this way. You could have just told me what she was."

"But you wouldn't have listened."

"How do you know? You should have tried!"

Walter lost his best friend. He never saw Georgie again. After that Walter very rarely came home from his job in the garment district. He stayed out almost every night. On several occasions around 2 o'clock in the morning, he would find Mom waiting up for him, "How did you do tonight? Did you make out?" He would laugh and then tell her in detail what happened. Mom wore him down until Walter forgave her and thanked her for saving him from a disastrous mistake. Besides being mother and son, they were also close friends.

After losing his weight-lifting partner, Georgie, Walter stopped going to the gym and started working out at home. But there were some setbacks. When he tried to do pullovers at one corner of the bed, the other corner would lift up and interfere with his rhythm. So he used me for ballast on the lifting side of the bed, and I felt proud to be a useful part of his routine.

Walter knew he wouldn't be living with us much longer, and he launched a campaign to accomplish things he wanted to do with Millie and me before he left. He took us to the St. George Hotel in Brooklyn, where there was a swimming pool right in the building. I thought things like that only existed in the movies. Then there was Coney Island, where we saw a sideshow with a headless woman.

During each of our field trips, Walter very easily picked up lots of beautiful women along the way. They thought Millie and I were the cutest things, and we helped break the ice. I guess they felt safe with Millie and me being with him. Boy, were they wrong.

I'd never been to or done so many things. I was dizzy with these non–stop whirlwind adventures. Next was a night visit to the Chester Theater, where they were presenting a live horror show. We were bait for Walter's next unsuspecting date. Even at the age of ten I knew this one was very sexy. Her long, wavy blond hair was perfectly groomed, not one hair out of place, like the Breck Shampoo ads in the barbershop windows. Her body's curves were as exaggerated as a calendar girl.

The movie before the horror show was *The Body Snatchers*, with Boris Karloff and Bela Lugosi. At the end of the movie the house lights went on and the screen disappeared up into the ceiling. In its place on stage was a well-lit room in comic book colors, filled with scientific gadgets. A man in a white smock walked into the room, followed by a hunchback. It was Dr. Frankenstein and his assistant, Igor.

They started creating his green monster, whose body was stretched out on a slanted table facing the audience. Electrical sparks filled the background of the room. The monster groaned, as he got stronger and broke away from the table. With each step, his huge shoes crashed down the stairs of the stage and into the audience.

All the lights suddenly went out. I felt like I was sitting in a black hole. Everyone disappeared in the dark, except for the nervous voices all around me. The monster's growls got louder. I was sitting in an aisle seat, unprotected, cringing as his steps thundered in my direction. The whole theater shook with screams. Something was lowered from above us, touching our heads.

Someone screamed, "What is it?"

"Spiders! Giant spiders!"

I dropped to the floor and hid under my chair. If I can't see the monster, he can't see me. I made that distorting sound in my head and squeezed my eyes shut. But I couldn't take it much longer. My heart was banging hard against my chest trying to escape.

Just as I was about to have a heart attack, the lights came on again. I looked over to Walter. His girlfriend was straightening her blouse and skirt, and her hair looked like she just got out of bed. The monster had disappeared. We all nervously filed out through the exits.

Walter went on a double date with himself to Orchard Beach. His two dates were Rachel and Betty. He also took Millie and her girlfriend Veronica and me. But Millie was the important link to his plans.

To make sure his dates never bumped into each other, Rachel came with us, and Betty was to meet Walter at the other end of the beach, as far away from Rachel as possible. We walked to our favorite spot, Section 13, and as Rachel was setting up the blanket, Walter called Millie to one side. He told her his predicament and let her in on his plan.

Every hour or so, Walter would find some lame excuse to leave one of his dates to visit the other. And this is where Millie came in – her job was to travel from one date to the other and keep each of them occupied when Walter wasn't there. This game of switch went on without either Betty or Rachel getting suspicious.

As the day wore on, the heat of the cooking sand was too much for Walter, and he had to take a swimming break. By now you'd think he would be exhausted, but no, not Walter. He ran to the salt water and dove into the waves, disappearing beneath the surface for a long time. Millie and I looked at each other, "Oh my God, Solly, I think he drowned."

Way out in the distance, a little head popped out of the water, waving to us. It was Walter! Swimming under water was one of Walter's passions. He told us stories about when he was keelhauled by the crew the first time he crossed the equator in the Pacific. They made him dive over one side of the ship, and swim under its hull to the other side. He loved it so much that he would do it on his own for fun.

While Walter's merry-go-round continued, I spent most of my day in the water and on the beach chasing Horseshoe crabs. I don't know how the hell Walter did it, but Rachel and Betty never found out.

Before we left, we happened to meet two kids from our building, Selma and Sheldon, and Walter wanted to take a picture of us together. While Walter was taking the picture, we sat in a puddle of water where the ocean meets the beach. My legs were folded to one side close to Veronica. I slowly worked my foot toward her until I was touching her soft thigh, almost reaching her pussy. The water tugged at my balls each time it flowed and receded, giving me a throbbing sensation with each wave.

Walter didn't know it then, but this was the end of his dating adventures. He met Sonny, a girl from Brooklyn, and soon they were married. And he was stuck in Brooklyn forever.

When we got home, I went to my room and lay down on my bed, staring at the ceiling. My eyes closed and it all rushed back to me – the beach, the sand and water, and Veronica's soft thigh under my foot.

WALK TO NOWHERE

I WOKE UP feeling the heavy, humid air weighing down the morning. Not a sound, only a soft hush filled the stillness. A sudden breeze rattled a lonely can and scraped it along the street. Then a solitary voice shouted out in dull repetition, "I cash clothes... I cash clothes..." I didn't know what the hell he was saying, but to me, his familiar rhythm was the sound of a summer weekend.

As I was stuffing down my breakfast of buttered roll and coffee, Spotty tugged at my pants and pulled me to the front door. I was ten years old and ready to attack the new day. I raced Spotty down the worn marble steps. Her brown and white blur passed me by and erupted out of the building onto the sidewalk, jamming her legs to a sudden stop at the curb's edge. She lifted her padded paw and tentatively tested the air, and ever so gently, touched the gutter to see if it was safe.

While Spotty sniffed around the gutter to find the perfect smell to take a crap on, I stood by the cigar store window and watched a dark, balding man making cigars. He sat behind a chunky, sturdy wood table with depressions worn from constant use. The back of the table had a row of compartments filled with different shades of soft and supple tobacco, like super thin sheets of leather. The cigar man knew I was watching him and gave me a special performance.

His fingers moved with purpose as he stretched and trimmed the smooth sheet of tobacco with a sharp half moon blade, then filled it with thin strips of tobacco. Effortlessly, he rolled the tobacco leaf tightly into the shape of a cigar and placed it into the last groove of a row of wooden coffins already filled with other cigars. With a ring blade he wore on the tip of his thumb, he guillotined the rough ends of the cigars and put the coffin into a press. He took one of the already pressed cigars, wrapped it with another leaf, and spread a thin coating of clouded white paste along the tobacco's edge. Caressing the cigar in one hand, he smoothed the edge along the length of the cigar, holding all the goodies inside.

Sergie popped out of his building and dashed across the street, ignoring me.

"Hey!"

Sergie turned around, "What?"

"Where ya goin'?"

"To Junior's."

"Wait a second, I'll go wit ya."

"I'll meet ya up dere."

"Ya can't wait for one fuckin' minute?"

"Fuck you!"

He turned and continued across the street to Junior's house. Every one I knew rented apartments, except for Junior who lived in a building his father owned over a costume jewelry sweatshop. It was one of a row of connected two-story brick buildings across the street from Sergie and me.

Hanging over Junior's front door, at the top of a long flight of stairs, was a pair of real bull's ears that listened intently to my footsteps climbing up to Junior's front door. His sister, Nina, greeted me at the door with her eyelids turned inside out, exposing their wet raw underside, looking at me with a fish eye stare... a new trick she had recently discovered. Behind Nina was a huge, domed cage holding a screaming cockatoo, the Hernandez' burglar alarm system.

In the kitchen, I was warmly greeted by the aroma of Spanish spices and by the sounds of hot Latin rhythms coming from a Zenith radio. Sergie and Junior were eating breakfast at the kitchen counter while Mrs. Hernandez talked to them in Spanish. I didn't understand a word of it, but I could read her eyes as they shifted emotions supporting the tones of her voice.

While waiting for Sergie and Junior, my eyes wandered around the room. Junior's mother stood over her stove in the midst of the warm and inviting smells of her kitchen. She was a short plump woman with her hair combed in neat even lines, shining like black patent leather and pulled back tightly away from her face in a bun.

It was Saturday, and Mrs. Hernandez insisted that Junior and Sergie go to church before they started their day.

When we got outside I asked them, "Why the hell do ya have to go to church on a Saturday?"

Before answering me, Junior looked at Sergie and raised his pointy eyebrows in that, we-know-and-you-don't look. Sergie taunted me derisively, "Come to church with us, and we'll show you why."

"Forget it. I ain't going to no church."

"Okay, shitface, go ahead and stay here. What do we care."

"Alright, okay… hold up, I'm comin' wit ya."

I followed them with the slight limp I still had from my accident, which, by now, I had incorporated into my own Bronx swagger.

We walked from East 165th to the Bell Building on Hoe Avenue and north to 167th Street. St. John's Catholic Church looked out of place next to the surrounding buildings – more like a medieval castle complete with round stained glass windows. The only thing missing was a moat and a drawbridge and the evil Prince John. When we climbed the steps into the church, I thought I had walked into a movie. The huge open chamber was like something out of the dark ages, filled with twisted designs carved out of wood into heavy, depressing shapes.

"Wait here. We'll be right back." Junior and Sergie left me in the dark and went into two curtained telephone booths.

There were candles everywhere. Their lights made the whole church flicker with living silhouettes that warped and turned into weird shapes reaching out for me. Just as they were about to engulf me, they shrunk back into themselves. The church felt oppressively thick with the smell of burning wax.

The only thing that gave me some sort of comfort was the pair of glowing snake eyes on the Navy watch belt my brother Walter sent home to me from the war. His belt reminded me I was connected to another world beyond the church doors.

Even though the church was empty, I felt I wasn't alone. Something was hiding in the dark watching me. Whatever it was, I could hear it breathing and could feel it whispering my name. I tried to move, but the floor held onto my legs. I refused to look into the shadows and squeezed my eyes shut, but it was no use, I couldn't stop it.

The being in the dark shadows had cast a spell on me and forced me to turn around. There above me was a life-sized figure of a man staring down at me. He was nailed to a cross and blood was gushing out of his hands, feet, head, and side, and cascading down his body. A numb swelling of fear rushed through me, and I stepped back to keep the blood from dripping on me. I kept backing up until I hit a wall and pressed hard against it, trying to push myself through it.

Nothing else existed but the man on the cross and me, as if a spotlight had appeared, illuminating us both, separating us from the rest of the church.

What kind of people would put the body of a man contorted in pain on a cross with nails hammered through his hands and feet – and hang it up in a holy place? Was it to scare the shit out of little kids like me? If that was their purpose, it worked. It worked too well; it terrorized me, and that monstrous image found its way deep inside of me.

For a few years after that day, whenever I saw a nun or a priest, the haunting image of the bleeding man forced its way to my consciousness, and I couldn't stop myself from hating them. It made me feel ashamed and evil. I knew that if I kept feeling this way, someday I would be struck down by their god.

Before we left the church, Sergie and Junior dipped their fingers into some water on top of a pedestal and made the sign of a cross on the front of their head and chest.

"Hey Solly, where ya goin? Ya know you can't just leave a church without crossing yourself."

"Yeah, right."

Junior pointed to the bleeding man, "Yeah. You know if ya don't, Jesus will never let you leave alive."

After what I'd just been through, I was scared enough to believe anything about Jesus. Sergie took my hand and dipped it into the water. I didn't care. I just wanted to get the fuck out of there. "This is holy water that Jesus himself gave to us." Junior grabbed my arm as if it didn't belong to me and shoved it around in front of me, making the sign of a cross.

Sergie laughed and wise-assed me, "Ya know ya just made yourself into a Catholic."

"Don't hand me that shit."

Sergie got serious, "No, really, you're now a Catholic."

I walked out half believing them.

Sergie, Junior, and I walked back to the one small block in a city of millions that was our self-contained community, our little town. It was slowly coming to life. Storeowners with brooms swept the sidewalks in front of their shops, while Mrs. Katz hung out of her window inspecting her subjects. Mrs. O'Connor swayed up the street to Harry's bar. Jack, with a stub of a cigar clenched in his pit bull jaws, prepared his newsstand outside the front door of his candy store. Short, toothless Mr. Jacobs, hidden by a round bundle of laundry, looked like a dung beetle carrying a ball of shit. His bony, angular arms were spiking in and out from the sides of his bundle as he walked to his laundry store.

The warm weather brought out a few mothers who were setting up chairs in front of their buildings to sit and gossip about each other. Millie was there too, meeting her friend, Veronica Weinman, for a game of potsy.

We joined Bobby, Johnny, Melvin, and Anthony in the middle of playing a game of stoopball. After a while, Sergie, Junior, and I began to feel restless and broke away from the pack. We didn't know where we were going or what we wanted to do, but we had to be on the move. Melvin tagged along. We ended up in the park nestled between Aldus Street and Bruckner Boulevard, next to P.S. 75. It was one city block of concrete, surrounded by a tall, chain link fence, and outside the fence, a thin row of hedges.

On the far side of the playground, sitting nakedly alone, was a shed that seemed like it didn't belong to the rest of the park. Its door was open wide, and its shelves neatly filled with sports equipment.

"Hey kids, what are you doing there?" asked a uniformed park attendant.

Junior answered, "Just lookin'."

An excited Sergie said, "Hey! Do you ya see that? They have tennis rackets in there."

It meant nothing to me, "So what. I don't know how to play tennis, do you?"

Sergie was his usual confident self, "Sure, I'll show ya."

"Sorry kids, you can't have the rackets and ball unless you cough up some sort of security."

"What's dat?"

"It's something of yours that I hold on to…" The park attendant saw our mystified faces, and the need to explain further, "It's like a watch or something that's equivalent in value that you deposit in exchange for the rackets and ball. Don't worry – you'll get it back when you return the rackets."

We looked at each other, knowing none of us owned a watch. We searched our pockets, but found nothing to deposit. Then I had this brilliant thought to put Melvin up for deposit. Sergie and Junior thought it was a great idea. Before we could make the deal, Melvin took off like a shot and never stopped until he reached our block.

After losing our 'deposit,' we continued on our odyssey along the banks of the Bronx River. The other side of the creek was open land covered with weeds, punks, and boulders. None of us said a word as we walked along a well-worn path. All around us were the sounds of summer, the steady buzz of insects complaining about the intense heat.

While passing along the railroad tracks, we remembered the story of the kid who took a leak on the live third rail and how the electricity shot back up his piss and electrocuted him. The thought of it chased us back onto the street and across Westchester Avenue, and then back to the creek again, away from the tracks.

On the far side of the creek was the empty land of weeds, and on our side were rows and rows of skeleton buildings gutted of their furnishings. They reached almost to the Bronx Park, several miles from our block, leaving an eerie calm in the middle of an otherwise crowded and busy Bronx. Gone were the throngs of people who had lived here, but I could still feel the heat of their footprints burned into the streets from all those years of day-to-day lives still haunting the empty streets.

I wanted to get my ass out of there, when the smashing of a window crashed through the silence and crashed through me. Sergie and Junior were throwing rocks at the empty windows. The loud noise scared away the phantoms living in my head. Then an unseen shadowy figure emerged from a hole in a pile of rubble and stealthily maneuvered itself behind me. I turned and something like a man towered over me, dressed in greasy looking clothes, smelling like vomit. He grabbed my arm and looked down at me with eyes that wanted to tear me apart. I thought we had awakened one of the ghosts.

He glared at me, "Say goodbye to your friends, you're never going to see them again. You're comin' with me."

I pulled and tugged trying to free myself, "Please mister, I didn't do nuttin'. I'm sorry we broke the windows. I'll never do it again."

His grip grew tighter, "Stop your squirming and squawkin'. You can plead all you want to, it's not going to make a damn difference. You're still comin' with me."

Sergie and Junior started throwing rocks at him. His grip loosened, and with one good tug, I pulled myself free.

"I'll kill you for that!"

Sergie taunted him, "Yeah… you and whose mother, old man."

He chased us along the creek, but the lumbering giant was no match for our lightning-like speed. We were always just beyond his reach. Every so often, we'd gain enough distance between us to stop and taunt him again. Sergie yelled, "You really scare us, you old douche bag."

Junior goaded him, "Come on... come on, old man... come and get us. You can do it!"

His bloodshot eyes stared at us, the veins bulged out from his forehead, and he screamed back in frustrated anger, "You little fuckin' wise guys. I'll kill you for this. I'll kill you!"

I turned and answered his threat, "I'm shittin' in my pants."

Sergie added, "Yeah, you and what army? Ahh, up your asshole!"

Junior, "Ahh, you big shmuck -- go choke on yourself."

As soon as he took a step toward us, we'd take off, turn and shout a few more insults, until he eventually got tired of being played with and gave up.

We walked by the demolished Starlight swimming pool and past the Chester and Ritz movie theaters, toward the Bronx Zoo. Getting into the zoo was going to be difficult, because we didn't have five cents among us. For a long while, we searched around the perimeter of the zoo for a way in, and were finally rewarded. Along the wired fence that encircled the zoo, we found a small hole just big enough to sneak through. But once inside, we weren't sure if we had snuck into an open wooded area or into the cage of a wild animal.

I could feel wild animals with sharp fangs lurking behind every tree, bush, and boulder. When we heard the snapping of twigs behind us, we thought it was an animal stalking us, ready to pounce. Afraid to look back, Sergie, Junior, and I raced back to the hole in the fence and climbed over each other, trying to be the first one out before we were torn to shreds.

Sergie took a deep, shaky breath, "You guys wanna go home?"

I said, "Yeah, let's get the fuck outta here."

We started toward the creek... I stopped, "Hey! Wait one fuckin' minute, I'm not going back to the creek."

"Junior was as worried as I was, "Yeah... that crazy asshole will probably be waiting for us."

Sergie thought about it, "Okay, then let's take the train."

Junior interrupted, "With what?"

"Yeah," I said, "how the hell are we going to pay for it?"

Sergie answered, "You shmucks. We'll sneak on."

"Whataya talkin?"

"Come on, Solly, what the hell? We got nuttin' to lose."

"I don't know..."

"What's the matter? You too chicken?" Call anyone a chicken in The Bronx, and you can get them to do practically anything. We either had to be tough, or at least act tough to get along.

The El in front of us was the end of the Seventh Avenue line, a towering mass of metal that was cleanly amputated, leaving a vertical cliff. Its network of steel looked like an unfinished bridge built out of a giant erecter set. The streets beyond the El, the ones without a train station, weren't really a part of The Bronx – not part of the web of miles of tracks interconnecting all the neighborhoods of the city. They were out in the sticks and escaped the dark shadows of heavy metal.

Train station names were our shorthand for the neighborhoods we lived in. When someone asked where I lived in The Bronx, my answer would not be Hunt's Point section, but Simpson Street Station. For someone else it might be Jackson, Prospect, or Freeman Station.

We approached the El, hesitated, looked up the long flight of stairs, and wondered how the hell were we going to sneak onto the train. Without a plan, we climbed the steps under a crested metal canopy. We reached a small landing that bridged a second steep flight of stairs going in the opposite direction.

At the top of the steps, we bunched together trying to hide from the eyes of the man in the change booth. Off to the side, I noticed a third flight of stairs I'd never seen before. It led to the train platform above, but was closed off by a metal accordion gate. I discovered a blind spot out of view of the man in the change booth, and like a marine under fire, dropped to the floor and crawled on my belly to the gate. Sergie and Junior followed my lead.

Next we had to find a way to squeeze through one of the tight, triangle spaces at the bottom of the gate. Lying on my back, I pushed down hard against the platform, let all the air out of my body making me even thinner than I was, and managed to slip through. Once on the other side, I pulled up the bottom of the gate and let Sergie and Junior through.

We climbed to the top of the steps, but a wooden fence with a big poster on it blocked our way to the train platform. Hidden behind the poster, we discovered a loose wooden plank, and pried one end of it away from the fence. That gave us a big enough hole to crawl through to the platform. Carefully, we replaced the poster board, leaving it just the way it was before. Now we had a secret entrance to a secret passageway, like in a movie serial – and we were the only ones who knew it existed.

DEAD AND DOESN'T KNOW IT

"GOD DAMN IT! You fucking bitch! All of you – all you fuckin' women who wear bangs are all a bunch of whores!" Harold was screaming at my mom, who always wore bangs. His lovely tones of hate were coming from their bedroom, way at the other end of the apartment, yet I could still hear his violence leaking out our front door and greeting me in the hallway of our building.

I was trying to sneak into my room, when Harold came rushing down our hall, chasing my mom. She was running for her life toward my room. I tried to get out of their way, but somehow got tangled between them, dodging a charging rhino at a full gallop.

My unexpected appearance gave my mom the edge. She escaped his reach and ran out of our apartment. I sometimes wondered about Harold; if it was possible that he felt secretly relieved when we escaped his anger... but not this time!

Harold turned his full attention toward me. He grabbed me around my throat with his fat fingers and choked me, lifting me off the floor and up against the wall. But it wasn't him choking me that turned my stomach with fear. It was his face, almost touching mine, spraying me with the stink of his hate.

Harold dropped me to the floor like a leftover thought. Before going after my mother, he glanced back at me. Just the sight of me put him into a rage. He took off one of his leather shoes and threw it at me. The heel smashed into my eye, bouncing it off the back of my head. I exploded with pain, as if someone had taken a hot piece of rock and forced it into my eye. Every time I moved my eye, it felt like the rock was surrounded with grains of sand grinding against it.

My whole body jumped in twists and turns, frantically trying to throw off the sudden stabbing pain that crumpled me to the floor. The pain subsided, but my eye still felt like a throbbing lump. I eased myself up off the floor and left the apartment to find my mom. I couldn't find her anywhere, not in the hall or on our block. But I did notice a group of people rushing around the corner to Hoe Avenue, and I followed them.

A crowd had collected by Frieda's basement apartment, and I could hear my mom's voice filtering its way through the mob of people, "Don't you dare come near me!"

Frieda stood between Harold and Mom. She was screaming at Harold, "Take another step, and I'll let you have it!" Frieda was a woman my mom hired to take care of my kid brother, Ronnie, during her working season as a furrier at Shurtzer's. She was a short, heavy woman, with gray, stringy hair, always looking like she just woke up. She had a strong determined look on her face that said you wouldn't want to fool around with this woman.

"Get out of my way you little, fat bitch. I don't want any trouble with you – I just want to speak to my wife."

Mom pleaded with Frieda, "Don't do it!"

Harold reached out to Mom, and she stepped back yelling, "Your hands should only fall off!"

"Are you going to get out of my way?"

Frieda stood her ground, "Go fuck yourself. If you want her, you'll have to walk over me first." He raised his arm, about to shove Frieda aside. Frieda grabbed a broomstick and whacked Harold over the head.

The crowd roared their approval and shouted, "Hit him again!"

I was afraid Mom might see me, so I hid behind the crowd. I didn't want these people to know I had anything to do with them. Whenever I could find an opening among the jostling people, I'd catch a glimpse of the action. Harold took another step toward Frieda, and she gave it to him again, one whack after the other.

The crowd was in a frenzy cheering support for Frieda with every blow. Harold knew it was useless and gave up. He made his way through the booing crowd, limping on one shoe, and went home. Mom stayed with Frieda until she felt it was safe to go home.

Mom never told Harry or Walter the truth about what was happening at home. It was like we had two different families. They never knew the torture Harold was putting us through. It was our secret.

Back on my block, Sergie and Bobby Frick were playing box baseball, standing at opposite ends of three boxes. Out in the gutter, Melivn, Junior, Johnny, and Anthony were playing triangle baseball.

Sergie looked up at me, "What the fuck happened to you?"

"What do you mean what happened to me?"

"Your eye." I looked in the side mirror of a parked car. My eye was all red and slightly blue and swollen. There wasn't any white left in my eyeball, only tangled branches of red veins.

"Jesus, look at dat."

"Hey, Solly, I axed you a question. What happened to ya?"

"I fell down my steps."

"Yeah. Sure."

Before I could back up my lie, there was a piercing screech from the sharp turn on the El by Westchester Avenue and Southern Boulevard. We looked up at the same time and watched as the El train crashed into another train that was parked on the express tracks. The two impenetrable armored trains lifted off the tracks high up into the air, pointing to the sky. For a few long seconds they hung there, locked in an awkward embrace. Then, with nowhere to go but down, they groaned like clashing dinosaurs and collapsed into each other.

My friends and I ran past the Triangle Park and were the first to investigate the accident, even before the cops. There was a low row of store buildings alongside the El. Their roofs were almost at eye level with the tracks. We climbed up a hanging fire escape ladder by the linoleum store and onto its roof. We were standing about ten feet from the engineer, who was pinned down in his cabin by the crushed metal. The man's skin was a powdered white-blue. He looked around like he didn't know where he was, swaying his arms like they were floating in water.

A couple of cops appeared on the tracks, and we were so close we could overhear them whispering. The first cop, "My God! He's been sliced in half from his waist down. "

Second cop, "No shit!"

"Yeah, the guy is dead, and he doesn't even know it."

If that was true, and if he was already a dead man, then how the hell can he be talking to the firemen, or anyone else? I couldn't make any sense of it. When they pulled the cars apart, he saw that he was sliced in half and died.

I went home feeling queasy and empty. When I got there, Harold had forgotten what he was angry about, and as usual, had drunk himself to sleep.

Alone in my room, I remembered the live dead man, who was sliced in half. My feelings caught up to me. I couldn't stop shaking with uncontrolled chills, or keep my supper down. It stayed hot in my throat. I began to feel like I was suffocating and had to get out of the apartment. I spent the rest of the night sitting on Junior's stoop with a few of the guys playing our story-telling game. It was our way of telling our gut feelings, disguised in our imaginary stories. The story changed from one kid to the next. It went on for hours until we exhausted our story ideas, and we'd all had enough.

That night in my room, I started thinking about the train engineer. Something inside me decided to jump-start my tic – my torment of freaky spasms – that all-consuming urge to grind my head down into my neck, trying to fill the empty space that had to be filled. No matter how hard I tried, I couldn't turn it off.

The only way I could stop it was just temporary. I would tighten every muscle in my body until I couldn't hold on any longer. And it would stop for a minute or two, but then I'd be back to the torment of trying to fill that empty space. Will it ever stop? I didn't think I would ever be able to sleep again, but the next thing I knew, it was morning.

THE MELTED MAN

IT WAS A warm summer morning, and my mother's faint voice rode the waves of my fragile sleep. Squinting into the dark, I saw her tiptoe by my room and out the door... then back to the monsters that trapped me with no exits. The smell of roasted coffee beans awakened my real world with different monsters.

A heavy growl rumbled through the early morning, becoming part of the darkness and vibrating through my skin. It was Harold, coughing up my nightmares with the alcohol sludge that had cooked in his throat during the night. In the dark shadows of my room I was too afraid to make a sound. I pressed hard against my mattress, trying to keep the beating of my heart from betraying me until Harold thundered by me and out the front door.

I squeezed one eye open and a few inches above me, Spotty's brown eyes intently stared into mine, anxiously waiting for a sign. I moved and her quivering body rushed at me, assaulting me with her soft, furry muzzle and lashing tongue. I threw the blanket over my head, and Spotty darted around sniffing for an opening. She poked her head under the cover and found my ear with her cold, wet nose.

I jumped out of bed and ran down the hall and into the bathroom. Every inch of the white porcelain toilet was black with roaches. Grabbing a rolled up newspaper, I swatted at the creeping little bastards. They scurried in all directions and into invisible cracks in the walls. Some crunched under my slippers like empty peanut shells. No matter how painful my cramps, I refused to sit on the bowl until every one of them was gone. Lifting up the seat, I searched all the crevasses and under the lip of the toilet, anywhere they could hide. Even when I knew they were gone, I could still feel their crawling legs on my skin.

Above the alley between two buildings, pale sunlight from a sliver of sky began to search through the kitchen window. The kitchen gradually emerged from the shadows, warm with the aroma of coffee. When I opened the refrigerator, a cool mix of smells hit my senses -- food laced with the odor of garlic.

I reached in for a fresh bottle of milk and shook it, dissolving the island of cream at the top of the bottle. I tugged at the pleated paper bottle cap, hugging the top of the bottle like a taut drum. I could feel it pull apart in a rapid stutter. Under the cover, pressed snugly inside the thick lip of the bottle, was a flat inner cap of cardboard, with a little half-moon tab. I dug in with my fingernail, pulled the tab -- and out it came with a hollow pop.

Rich echoes of a violin interrupted my breakfast. It was just a year and a half after World War II, and standing down in the middle of the back alley was a young veteran. He was a tall, handsome man with a two-week-old beard and ropes of greasy black hair touching his shoulders. He was wearing a long, oversized khaki army coat, cinched around his waist, looking more like a Cossack dressed for a Russian winter than for a hot, Bronx summer day.

He was playing classical music. Beautiful music. Either he was a brilliant violinist, or it was the rich hollow echoing of the alley that made it sound so good, taking me out of myself and into his moment. People from surrounding buildings wrapped coins in torn pieces of paper and threw them down to him, hitting the ground with a dull jingle. Once in a while, he would nod his head in appreciation and continue to play.

There was a rumor going around about a man who lived on my floor, right next door to me. They said he was a misshapen monster and referred to him as "that disgusting freak." I never saw him – until that morning. When I stepped out into the hall, there he was, walking behind his wife, his head bent, making himself as small as possible, trying to hide from intruding eyes, eyes that reflected his own disgust in what they saw.

At first I didn't know what to do. Afraid I'd be discovered, I stood motionless, trying to be part of the hall. By the time I decided to run back to my room, it was too late. He stopped suddenly and turned in my direction. He stood beside me and began to grow, lifting his head and straightening himself into a massive overhanging cliff. His eyes were cold and unnatural, as if they were painted, unblinking, staring down into mine.

He must have once had a face; now it had become like melted wax. One eye was almost fused closed with hanging skin, and only a hole remained where his left ear should have been. The stringy scars, purple-blue, red, and pink, covered his entire face like overlapping layers of transparent maps, traveling up his forehead, past his hair-line and halfway up his scalp, with little patches of hair desperately sprouting through his scars. When he realized I was only a little boy, his hard look softened and pulled back, releasing me.

The next thing I knew, I was in my sister's room with no memory of how I got there. From her third floor window, I watched the melted man and his wife get into a cab and drive off toward the Boulevard. Once I saw the danger was gone, I grabbed my brother's army jacket, my trusty Spaldeen, and a pile of baseball cards and ran out into the hall. Holding onto the banister posts at each landing, I twirled around them like riding The Whip, running down every flight of stairs in a flow of dizzy turns and leaps and out onto the sidewalk.

When my brother Walter was in the Navy on one of his missions, he met up with a soldier and traded his Japanese sub-machine gun for the guy's army jacket. What made it special was the dragon twisting and turning on the back of the jacket, with eyes of intent, ready to strike if you came too close. Its embroidered details were in luscious, dimensional hues of red, yellow, and blue, begging to be eaten. Hand-painted on the front of the jacket were the names of every port my brother had pulled into – about half the world. The jacket came down to my knees, looking like an overcoat. No matter what the weather was, I wore that jacket everyday until it fell apart into shredded pieces.

While waiting for my friends, I kept myself busy by playing an improvised game. Leaning against the fender of a car, I threw my Spaldeen at the concrete wall at the side of my building's entrance, aiming for a protruding edge. When the ball bounced back, I caught it on the fly... that was the whole idea of the game.

To the right of the wall was the window of the Plant Lady. Inside, vines crawled up and around her window glass, covering every inch of it. Staring into the plants, I was sucked into a rainforest so dense it absorbed the morning light. You couldn't see in or out. The only thing we kids knew of the Plant Lady was that she was German, tall and on the heavy side, with a tight bun of braids on top of her head.

To the left of the entrance, Mrs. Katz, a sitting profile leaning on her windowsill, watched the street as the people on our block acted out their lives. Mrs. Katz never bothered us kids, but we felt her presence. She was our sentinel, our protector, our rock. Her plump torso was the only part of her anatomy we ever saw. I don't think I would have recognized her if I saw her on the street complete with legs. There were a few times when she would break through her window frame to ask us to do simple errands, like sending us to Jack's candy store for a newspaper, or to Abe's corner grocery for milk. Who would ever have known that this quiet woman spoke six different languages fluently.

I could smell the heat of the coming day. The tar on the street was beginning to melt with a sweet, barbecued-rubber flavor. Its vapors wrinkled the air, putting ripples in the distant buildings. A sour-smelling stream ran along the gutter from a leaking johnny pump, thickening the fresh morning air.

Sergie was the first to meet me. By now, he and I had a love-hate relationship. I knew him the longest of any of my friends. We both had that cool walk. With each step, we'd limp into the silent rhythm of the tough guy, swaying from side-to-side in The Bronx swagger. We were the same size, same age, same super-thin, with ribs like scrub boards.

Sergie was a friend who was equal to my bursts of energy. That was where the similarity ended. He had curly black hair, high bony cheeks, and looked like he was holding small marbles in the lower corners of his mouth. His innocent black eyes were always working, always planning, as payback for his own hurt.

I had wavy blond hair and cheeks that looked like two small peaches when I smiled, and wide open, blue-green eyes that were hiding my secrets. My hair had a cowlick that didn't know it belonged to me, no matter how hard I tried to paste it down. Like two positive poles of a magnet, it would shoot away from my head in confused spikes.

The rest of the gang began to filter out of their buildings wearing loose T-shirts with wide candy-colored stripes and long baggy pants. No matter how hot it got, no self-respecting kid would be caught dead in a pair of shorts. The most necessary equipment of all was our sneakers – black, high-top sneakers – the ones that had a white, rubber circle on the outside ankles, with *Keds* spelled out in its center. This told us we had the sneakers of the gods. It was badge of the god of speed and swiftness.

By the time we reached the ages of eleven and twelve years old, we had learned to survive and protect ourselves from each other by never revealing our inner secrets. We would never make the social mistake of asking a sensitive question, a sissy question. We would have acknowledged it as a weakness and used it against each other. Once in a while, someone would take that chance and open up. We'd tease the poor bastard with unmerciful insults, his penalty for crossing that line.

In some ways, we were very close, and yet we could also be cruel and distant. But we always had one thing in common, our imaginations. And our great adventures brought us together. The only way for us to communicate our tender and necessary feelings was through our story telling game, or in the heat of a street game when we could feel each other out without losing face.

Every game we played had its season. Each spring we instinctively knew which day was the beginning of the card season. It seemed as if a magic potion was released into the night air. And while we slept, it seduced us with the smells and sounds that whispered in our ears, "t-i-i-i-me to flip cards." The next day, we all showed up ready to flip our mix of cards – baseball players, chapter play cliffhanger scenes, and movie stars – bought in sheets of bubble gum and in penny vending machines.

We were gathered in front of Mr. Seigel's hardware store, where he displayed metal pots, glasses and dishes in open wooden crates, and cardboard boxes outside on the sidewalk. Music was pumping out of Mr. Seigel's doorway. Our flipped cards floated down on the soft smooth mellow tones of Nat King Cole, singing *Nature Boy*.

We played one-on-one, Sergie with Junior and Johnny was matched up with me. Johnny was a lot taller than us. His head looked like a balloon that had been squeezed at one end, and his features gathered together at the bottom of his face. Long straight, reddish hair topped his head over closely cropped sides. It was difficult to tell which was his natural skin color, the thousands of connected freckles, or the pink in-between.

I was distracted from my game with Johnny by the rustling of a window curtain. Someone was watching me from the third floor window where the melted man lived. A figure stepped back, dissolving into the dark room.

When I refocused, my friends were walking away from me and crossing the street to the blank brick wall we used for handball. By the time I got there, they were already in position to play slug. Who knows why the hell we called it slug. The older boys proclaimed it as slug, so that's what it was, a meaningless word that would always be fused to the game.

Standing in our individual boxes marked by the grooved squares of the sidewalk, the street around us disappeared, and this little piece of The Bronx became our entire world. The only sounds we heard were our own voices and the rubber Spaldeen rebounding off our hands, the brick wall, and the sidewalk in a repetitive musical beat.

I hit the ball as low as I could, down and up to the brick wall, into another kid's box, making it as hard as possible for my friends to return it. Lower and lower I went until my fingertips were scraping the sandpaper concrete, making them bleed. Not paying much attention to the blood, I stuck my fingers into my mouth, sucked on them and continued to play.

Our work was our play, and this was a bad workday. Going from one game to another, nothing satisfied us. And then the jelly apple man showed up. The kids on our block danced around the pagan idol of the golden copper vat. The shining jewel reflecting the sun, stood majestically at the far end of the wagon, filled with hot melted jelly. Next to it was a bin of fresh apples and a jar of sliced coconuts swimming in their own juices. Along both sides of the wagon were rows of deep, rectangular wood cubicles. Each cubicle held different treasures of dried fruit, visible to us through tilted glass doors. For a penny per fruit, you could choose from dried apricots, prunes, pears and peaches, as much fruit as you could afford, creating your own custom-made treat.

Total disorder erupted. Smiling, the jelly apple man's thick gray mustache spread across his face, twice its normal size.

"Ok, kids, one at a time. I can't help you if you're all going to shout at me." Pointing to his side, "I want you to line up here."

We juggled ourselves into a single line. The jelly apple man stabbed the fruit onto a pointed stick and dipped it into the belly of the copper vat. He rolled the stick between his fingers, deep into the hot jelly, twisting and scooping, as it unwillingly gave up its sweetness. When it hit the air it thickened and pulled away in warm, gooey strings, like melted glass. He wove the stick through the air, balancing and directing the jelly, and with soft hands, twisted the gooey snake around the fruit.

Melvin Melnick always had more money than the other kids on the block. He whipped out a dollar bill, a fortune to the rest of us, and begrudgingly surrendered it to the jelly man. Pulling out a wad of folded money from his trouser pocket, the jelly man neatly laid the new dollar in bed with the others and gave Melvin his change.

Sitting on the curb with our feet resting on the soft tar, we ate the fruity-warm sweet goo. The jelly apple man caught us off-guard by actually talking to us. This was unheard of. He'd never talked to us before, and it made us uneasy.

"I've got some free time today. If you guys would like, you can come home with me. Hey... I'll show you some great stuff I have."

Suspiciously Junior asked, "Yeah. Like what?"

"I've got guns like the cowboys have in the movies, except mine are real." We didn't bite, so he tried a different approach. "You like little girls?" We shrugged our shoulders. We were uncomfortable talking about our feelings for girls to an adult. He got the wrong message and sat beside me. The sound of his voice was unsafe, and there was a peculiar look in his eyes.

He put his hand on my thigh. "Well, maybe you should try something different."

Like taut springs, we leaped to a safe distance and shouted, "Fuck you! You stinkin', fuckin' faggot! Fuck you!"

He looked so hurt and scared, I felt like a bully. He went to his cart and got out of there. That summer was the last time we saw the jelly apple man. He never returned.

The combination of the heat of the sun and the sweet sugar treats produced an intense thirst, and like zombies, we were drawn to Jack's candy store to quench it with more sugar. Jack's thick Bronx accent was lost amongst our own. His thin, muscled body was wound up tightly like a rubber band ready to snap. Jack always wore long-sleeved shirts rolled up above his lumpy biceps. He buttoned the collar so tight, it pinched at his neck. Jack's ass was lost in his baggy pants, held up by a pair of suspenders. The part in his straight, black hair opened a path of pink skin down the center of his head. In his hard, bony, square jaw he held a soggy, brown, half-chewed cigar that never left his mouth.

Jack and his wife, Sally, took turns caring for the store, but today they were there together. Sally was short with round cheeks, round head and round hair. Her dark features looked like they were outlined with a soft lead pencil. An apron covered her plump figure. It seemed as if all the shopkeepers, except Jack, wore aprons... as if they all belonged to a secret Society of The Apron.

When we entered the store, the soda fountain was on our left, with swivel chairs mushrooming out of the floor. Our eyes were level with the counter, and all the open boxes filled with penny candies. There were chocolate marshmallow twists; chocolate-covered squares with firm jelly insides; chewy, half-moon slices of watermelon, sprinkled with glued-on sugar.

I loved the Holloway, a long-lasting slab of hard taffy that was more like a stone on a stick. Peeling off its fused-on paper wrapper was a pain in the ass. Then you had to soak it in your mouth to soften it, or else you'd shatter your teeth.

To my right along the wall, Jack displayed the dime novels. Their covers were splashed with smoothly molded, colorful artwork of realistic figures in action, drawing me to them. But inside, there were only words, thousands of words I couldn't read. I believed I was never going to be able to enter those mysterious worlds with different voices between their covers. But I could hear the insides of those books talking to me and longed to know what they were saying.

Joke books, rows and rows of them, took up the whole back of the store. Glossy slick covers leaned forward in their wood cradles. Their newness felt thick and smooth to the touch. Thumbing though them, I could feel their energy running across my fingertips with picture stories of super heroes created only for me.

Opposite the joke books and the phone booths, was an open space just large enough to fit three tables with chairs. At the end of the counter was the hulking, red metal coffin, pressing grooves into the wood floor. Inside it, entombed in crushed ice, were a variety of sodas, like Mission Cream, Castle Orange, Yoo-Hoo, and Pepsi Cola. When I pulled out a bottle of cream soda, the cold pieces of ice melted over my hot, sweaty hand. My hand drank in the dripping wet bottle, and I tingled impatiently for that first gulp.

Grabbing our favorite sodas, my friends and I took control of one of the tables at the back of the store. We slowly sank down into our chairs and began sounding each other out. Junior said, "Ehh, ya fadda chews on scum bags."

Sergie answered with, "Yeah, well that musta been da ones I used on ya mutha."

Melvin never joined in. He sat there in his blue cowboy shirt with white curlicue-trimmed pocket flaps. His thin, oily, black hair was plastered down on his head, looking like a wet rat. He had this habit of staring at your lips while you were talking, and silently moving his, mimicking what you were saying but slightly off-sync. It drove us crazy.

Laughing at our verbal jousts, Sergie glanced over toward Melvin and caught him in the act. Sergie grabbed him and lifted him out of his chair... "What da fuck do ya think ya doin? If ya don't cut that shit out, I'll break your fuckin' ass!" Poor Melvin tried so hard to stop, but his obsession was too much for him. He broke away from Sergie, and narrowly escaping his reach, ran out of the candy store.

Sergie turned to me as if nothing had happened and continued the game. "The only reason you were born was because the drug store was closed."

I held back my laugh, "Oh yeah? Well, the best part of you dripped down ya mutha's legs."

Without warning, someone released the mother of all farts. It thundered throughout the whole store and vibrated our table. We were at the age when passing wind was the zenith of all jokes. My sudden outburst of laughter caught me with a mouthful of soda. It burned through my nose and erupted from my mouth, spraying out on everyone.

We laughed our way out of the candy store, with Sally close behind us, "Get out! Get out! And don't come back until you know how to act like human beings!"

INTO A BLACK ABYSS

THE DREADED MRS. Levine, landlady of my building, was built solid, like a sawed-off tree stump. We watched from across the street as she walked into her building. Mrs. Levine's breasts covered her entire chest. She could have set a table for four on that monumental bosom.

Every once in a while, when my mother was paying our monthly rent, she would help Mrs. Levine by giving her an insulin shot. To me, it was like watching Japanese torture in the movies: The needle presses into her skin; her fat flesh caves in, resisting the needle until it reaches the end of its flexibility; the sharp, steel point punctures through into her arm as her skin rides back up onto the needle.

Mrs. Levine looked down at me and said to my mom, "Such a goot boy, your Solly is."

They began speaking only in Yiddish – that's whenever my mom wanted to talk about things she didn't want me to hear. Yiddish... I didn't understand a word of it, except when I heard my mother's voice. It wasn't the Yiddish she spoke that I understood; it was her resonant intonation that I knew so well, sounds that had vibrated and rolled around with me in her womb.

My attention drifted down to Mrs. Levine's hands. While talking to my mother, her hands were living a life of their own. Periodically they would shake, as if possessed by two entities in a constant struggle for control. When Mrs. Levine tried to take a sip of coffee, her hands shook so violently that the cup and saucer rattled like an earthquake tremor. My mom and I left before I ever found out who won the war.

While sitting with the guys on Junior's stoop, Bobby Frick came up with the idea of setting a trap of piled-up garbage against Mrs. Levine's door. We were all in, but Bobby had second thoughts.

Johnny said, "Hey! You can't chicken out, it was your idea."

"Hey, it's *my* father who's da Super, not yours. If she sees me, my pop will kill me."

Junior reassured him, "We're not going to get caught."

"Dat's what you say. You guys can do what you want. I'm not doin' it."

Junior warned him, "You better do it, or I'll kick your ass in."

Bobby's brown Irish eyes smiled through puffy slits, looking like Roy Rogers... "Yeah, you're really scarin' me. I'm going to bust out cryin'." He calmly turned and walked away.

Feverishly, we piled the bags of garbage, one on top of the other. The tension was high... nerves were on edge. The unstable pile of garbage bags reached the top of Mrs. Levine's door. We leaned away, Olympic runners ready to spring into action. We hesitated, looking at each other for a signal. Who was going to ring her bell? Without warning, a rush of adrenalin pressed my finger on the bell.

Before my finger even left it, we were in a full gallop, whizzing down the long tile hallway. One of Johnny's shoes had a loose sole, and I could hear the slapping of leather with each uptake of his foot. The flapping sole and the electricity of our excitement crackled through the hall, screaming in my ears. How was it possible that the whole building couldn't hear us?

We hid in the shadows of an alcove at the far end of the hall. Tension built as Mrs. Levine's door cracked open. The garbage tumbled in all around her and splattered on her walls. Mrs. Levine looked in the direction of our giggling, "You little Bastards! I hear ya!" Her short, hard body shook with anger. Spit sprayed from her mouth, "I'll getcha for dis!"

In one leap, we jumped the vestibule steps, our giggles exploding into laughing, spilling out onto the street. Mrs. Levine's screams faded as we ran down The Three Hills, fear breathing down our necks. Past

Longfellow, down toward Whitlock Avenue, Junior swung a phantom punch at Johnny. Johnny ducked and Junior punched him twice on the shoulder, "One, two for flinching."

"Screw you!" Johnny shouted, "I don't need this horse shit. I'm going home." He took off, leaving the three of us continuing on to Whitlock Avenue. Observing two well-developed girls walking by, I turn to my friends, "Wow, did you see dat? They're built like a brick shit house."

Sergie said, "Yeah, nice. Ya know, you gotta be careful."

"What da hell are you talkin' about? Careful of what?"

"You mean crabs?" Junior asked.

Sergie, always the expert, "No. My brother Tony told me that girls can lock their pussies on your cock."

"Ya kiddin' me?"

"I'm not kiddin'. You know, when you're inside her, and the girl gets spooked, you know, like scared... you know, from a sudden noise, or if like her mom catches her fucking... she'll freeze and lock onto your cock, and you can't get out. You know, like, stuck there forever."

"Gee, just like dogs," I added.

Down at the bottom of The Three Hills, we came to a wire fence. We heard a low, distant rumbling coming from the other side of the fence. Stepping up on a low concrete wall, our fingers entangled in the fence, we could see way across the creek to the neat rows of cor-rugated metal Quonset huts that had sprouted up from nowhere. Just inside the fence, I looked down into the huge cave that went under the street. Deep in the cave's blackness, two glowing pinpoints of light, like a pair of piercing eyes, grew larger and brighter as they came toward me. A hollow growl matched the blood pounding through my veins, building to a booming roar, as an enormous steel beast with fiery eyes erupted out of the depths. As the Lexington Local/Pelham Bay train climbed out of its tunnel and roared past us onto the El, the force of its power knocked us off the fence.

We walked under the El across Whitlock to an abandoned public swimming pool. Its buildings and bathhouses had been burned to the ground and lay in rubble. I was the only one who knew how it got that way. That was the time when I was six and a half and living on Aldus Street... when Shugie and I set the creek on fire and destroyed the Hunt's Point Swimming Pool in a five-alarmer.

I knew the rules of my tribe. The bigger the tale, the bigger the hero you were in the eyes of your friends. But even so, I was still too afraid to tell Junior or Sergie about the fire, too frightened that someday people would find out, and I'd be put away for the rest of my life. It was Shugie's and my sworn secret.

Rummaging through the debris of the abandoned swimming pool, we found a concrete trap door flush to the ground, hidden in the rubble. Attached to the door was a metal ring. It took the three of us pulling with all our strength to lift it open. At the top of the opening was a waffle iron step leading down into a black abyss.

"Who's got a match?" asked Sergie.

"That's no good." Junior answered. "We need a searchlight or some candles."

I said, "Miller's! Let's get the candles from Miller's."

Up the hills past Bryant Avenue was Mr. Miller's Deli, noted for his five-cent sour pickles. Mr. Miller, a heavy-set balding man, wore a shirt with sleeves rolled up to his elbows and over it a white butcher's apron. My job was to keep him busy while Sergie and Junior stole some candles.

Miller had three wooden barrels, one filled with pickled green tomatoes and the other two with cucumber pickles.

"Come on, boychick, stop vasting mien time. Pick a pickle already!" The best sour pickles were soft and thin-skinned, an almost translucent light yellow-green. "Boys... boys, vat are you two doink over dere?"

Junior, Sergie, and I tear-assed out of the store. Mr. Miller screamed out, "You come back here! I'll tell ya mothers! You should be ashamed!"

The fear that Mr. Miller would tell my mother triggered my instinct of self-preservation, allowing me to believe I was unjustly accused. I screamed back at Mr. Miller, "We didn't do nuttin'!" Thinking that would be enough to proclaim my innocence, I turned and continued to run with the pack.

"Once, Twice, Three – Shoot!" Junior and Sergie each thrust out two fingers. My one odd finger chose me to go first. There was no turning back. I had to go first or be called 'chicken'.

The candle revealed a winding stairwell that led me into a bottomless black pit filled with unknown evil, with grasping hands reaching out for my legs. My heart pounded up into my head, and the internal spark drained from my legs. They were numb and rubbery as I slid onto the first step.

The candle's flickering light made solid objects animated with the quick, jerky movements of a silent movie. Two pairs of spiral stairs appeared, one real, the other its shadow. They swayed and twisted around each other, chewing and digesting me as I descended into its throat. Sergie and Junior followed close behind. The candlelight was absorbed by the total darkness above and below us. We were drowning in a sea of blackness.

It was damp and musty at the bottom of the stairs, with a pervading odor of salty mildew. Out of the depths of the pitch-blackness, another flickering light appeared and lit up a maze of tunnels with interconnecting rooms that wouldn't stand still. The light floated toward us. Who... or what... was holding it?

We didn't wait to find out. Sergie, Junior, and I shoved at each other trying to be first to the stairway. A pair of hands pounced onto Sergie's shoulders and picked him up off the floor. The last thing Junior and I saw was Sergie dangling in mid-air in a circle of candlelight.

Junior and I flew through the rooms toward the trapdoor, creating gale winds that blew out our candles and hit a wall of impenetrable night. Frozen in our tracks, we held on to each other, desperate and not knowing which way to go. But hearing Sergie's plaintive cries erased our fears, and we slowly began to push through the thick blackness. They eventually led us to the light, casting nervous shadows along the walls of a small room.

Sergie was being held by a man not much bigger than we were. His fluttering candle turned his face into valleys and crevasses, with caves for nostrils. It pulled and bent his features in unnatural ways. His voice was garbled and sounded like he was speaking through a mouthful of cotton. "What the fuck do you want?"

Like an ominous warning, Sergie pulsated in and out of the shadows. All of our toughness evaporated, replaced with the pleadings of two scared kids.

"Nothin', Mister, nothin'. I swear to ya. We didn't know anyone was here," said Junior.

I joined in, "Yeah Mister, we didn't know anyone was here."

"Then what're ya doin' here? Why ya spyin' on me?"

I answered, "We was just havin' fun. We didn't mean nothin'."

The little man stared at us around his fat pug nose, trying to penetrate into our eyes to see the truth.

Junior begged, "Please Mister, we really didn't mean anything. We're tellin' ya da truth."

He relaxed his grip and lowered Sergie to the ground. He wasn't going to kill us after all. "Ok, I believe ya. But ya better not tell anybody about me and dis place."

As soon as Sergie's feet touched the floor, his cockiness pumped back into his body, "Sure, don't worry about a thing. We won't say a word. Whatcha doin' down here, anyway?"

"Don't be so fuckin' nosey. You'll live longer," the little man answered. He glared at Sergie, "Ok. I'll tell ya, but no more questions after this. Ya hear? No more questions. I'm down here is because I hate cops."

Sergie interrupted, "Just because you hate cops?" I wished Sergie would just shut the fuck up, and so did the little man. He grabbed Sergie by the throat, "What did I tell ya. Stop wit da questions." Sergie gurgled, "Okay, okay, okay, I promise no more axing questions."

"I'm hidin' from da cops. Da cocksuckers have been makin' my life miserable for no reason at all."

We didn't dare ask him why. Anyway, we didn't particularly care for cops ourselves. I got too close to him, and the fumes overwhelmed me. The odor was like the seasoned dirt that collects in the corner of your big toe nails on its way to ripening into the smell of shit.

"If I show my face out dere, dey'll kill me for sure. Yous guys gotta help me. I've been down here a long time and I'm starvin'."

Sergie answered for us, "We can do dat. We'll getcha' some food."

"Ya will?"

"Sure, said Sergie, it's a cinch."

"Tanks fellers. Get me as much as ya can. And remember, not a word to nobody."

When I stepped outside the hole, a brilliant burst of light attacked my eyes, like looking into a hundred flashbulbs, all flashing at the same time. I stood there in the smothering heat of the midday sun, leaning into the dense cloud of hot air. The short time we spent down in the tunnels had intensely magnified my emotions. Now the world I once knew felt unreal.

Dazed, I stood outside the hole, filling my lungs with fresh air, filling my memories with who I am and which world I belonged to. I was free from the stifling tunnels. My hair had separated into thick spaghetti clumps, and I was drenched in sweat. I took my jacket off and tied the sleeves around my waist, and we began our way home.

We walked by apartment buildings five to six stories high, butted up against each other, surrounding me with tons of bricks. The buildings sat on granite and concrete streets, busy streets, with unsuspecting people who felt safe walking on solid rock, living their everyday lives, ignorant of what existed below them.

Her long, wavy, dark brown hair folded into a pompadour on top of her bangs, held in place with a red bow. Mom's bangs cascaded over her forehead, red earrings dangled from her ears, and red marble-sized beads hung around her neck. She was wearing a dark blue, silky dress with white spots, draped over a strange man's lap. His hands disappeared up her dress. She moaned with a breathless sigh.

Seeing me startled her, and she jumped from his lap. A quick tug at her polka dot dress, and it fell back into place. Mom's flushed face and tense response was the same way I reacted when I got caught at what I thought was wrong. Within a split-second, I stuffed the hurt somewhere inside. I told myself I didn't care what my mom did. That was her business, and I had my own to attend to.

Lunch was sour cream and bananas with a mountain of sugar, and a hard roll with butter. The afternoon sun was bright, and sparrows broke across a shaft of sunlight, their shadows flickering into our kitchen. Sitting between the spears of light, I stared off in a waking sleep, watching the excited dust particles riding the streams of light.

The stranger passed by the kitchen on his way to the bathroom. When he was finished, my mom took her turn. I heard her scream from the bathroom. She flashed by the kitchen shouting, "Disgusting! You pig! You son of a bitch pig!" She discovered the man was a sloppy pisser. He'd peed over her clean toilet seat and floor.

Mom was an earthy woman, with warmth and strength like the Italian movie star, Anna Magnani. She grabbed the stranger by his lapels and pulled him so hard that his feet never touched the floor as she threw him out of the front door. "You filthy pig! Don't you ever come back here!" Then under her breath she says, "Men... feh! Filthy, dirty men. De're not worth it. I don't ever want to have anything to do vit dem."

During the commotion, I filled my army jacket with half a loaf of Wonder Bread from its spotted package and a chunk of salami and snuck out of the apartment.

On our way back to the pool, there were waves of sirens, swelling and receding as they passed us on the street. One, two, three police cars sped down to the pool. Their flashing lights lit up the heads of a crowd of people and an army of cops surrounded the trap door. The cops were dragging our pug-nosed little man out of the pit. He was screaming, cursing, and laughing at the same time. He spotted us in the crowd. His eyes were filled with hate.

Junior politely asked a woman next to him, "Excuse me, Ma'am, do you know what's goin' on?"

"You see that little man with the police? He's an escaped maniac, a killer. He killed a policeman!"

We looked at each other and, almost at the same time said, "Oh, shit!" I felt lucky we were still alive.

The cops shoved him past the crowd, and the little man's complete focus was on us. He was so close that the spit spraying from his mouth rained onto our faces. "When I escape, I'm gonna kill da little pricks who snitched. I'll cut dere fuckin' little cocks off!"

One of the cop's faces swelled up beet red, with veins popping out from his temples. He grabbed the little man by his hair, pulled his head back and growled, "Just shut the fuck up!" Both cops straightened up from a crouch, bringing the full force from their thick legs slamming him against the police car – a dull thud against crackling metal. Their nightsticks cut through the blinking lights. They hit and kicked the little man into the car like a lump of laundry. The little man peered at us out of the police car's closed window. The look in his eyes had already killed me.

Someday we'll find him in our rooms, and he'll kill us in our beds. Maybe on some hot summer night, he'll find us sleeping out on the fire escape, or get one of us alone in an alley, hall or street and cut our cocks off. We told each other these possible scenarios all the way home, scaring ourselves to death and loving every minute of it.

It was twilight and the sounds of children's thin, echoing voices bounced between and into each other; Spaldeens rebounded off brick walls and concrete sidewalks; key chains skipped across chalked potsy boxes; parents called from their windows – the roll call of their children. Each step closer to our block brought aromas of different foods from around the world, their fragrances blended one with the other. The harmony of familiar smells and sounds gave us the feeling of being home and safe again.

We were back from our odyssey – three terrified heroes back

among friends. Bobby was on the block with Johnny and Junior's sister, Nina, playing in the street. And of course Melvin – always Melvin – still desperately wanting to be accepted by us older kids. Susan and Kathleen were there... and Barbara.

Sergie and I had an incurable crush on Barbara Erb that lasted throughout our young lives. And now I can't remember her face. How could I possibly have forgotten her face – lush, straight blonde hair, blue eyes, and freckles floating around in my memory with nothing to hold them together. I've always wondered if Sergie really liked Barbara, or if he was only saying that because I did. Later on in our mid-teens, Sergie went after every girl I was interested in.

During a game of kick-the-can on the four corners of Faille and 165th Street, Barbara walked up to me, looked me in the eye and in a derisive voice said, "Don't you ever take that thing off?"

In my own defense I answered, "My brother wore this jacket in the war. See all these names? They're countries my brother's been to. He was at every one of these places. He was all over the world."

Barbara blurted out in front of our friends, "You're so full of hot air." They all laughed. I knew she was mocking me, but I didn't know what it meant. My heart cried up to my throat and stuck there.

Sergie began to taunt me, "Ya don't know what it means, do ya?"

"Yeah, I do."

"How stupid can ya get."

Melvin, Sergie's lackey, was given the nod to humiliate me, "Ya better watch it, Solle-e-e. Ya so full of hot air, yer gonna float away." It seemed everyone knew what it meant but me.

Melvin stuck his finger into my face, "Look, look, his face is turning red."

Sergie got what he wanted. Barbara saw me as a fool. Smelling a wounded animal as easy prey, the others joined in, "Why don't ya take dat stupid jacket off? It's beginning to smell like shit."

Each remark slowly beat me down, leaving me naked, revealing the secret I had worked so hard to keep – that I was really retarded... their tinny voices faded away, joining the surrounding street sounds.

Another presence tugged at my attention – away from the kids, up and over their heads to the third floor of my building. A pair of eyes stared down at me. The melted man shrank back, and the curtains billowed across his window.

Someone grabbed at my jacket, an insult that invaded my wandering thoughts, drawing me back to the hard sidewalk and my attackers. Sergie, smirking, moved up close to me and calmly said, "Ya know, Solly, you're a real asshole. Look at him. Look at da sweat dripping down his Jew nose."

At least once a week they made fun of the size of my nose. The truth was I had a small nose, not as small as theirs, but a normal nose. Their constant insults had beaten me down to the point where I really believed them. The only way to save what was left of my pride was not to give in to their taunts.

"I'd rather have a nose that looks like a nose, than those two tiny holes in ya heads that make ya all look like a bunch of pigs."

That did it. I had gone too far. Their smiles were replaced with anger. Sergie struck back, "We better not catch ya on dis side of da block. If we do, we'll kick yer ass in."

Following his leader, Junior added, "And if I catch ya on my side of the street, I'll knock the shit outta ya."

I couldn't let them bully me this way. If I did, I'd always be their constant target, so I replied, "Oh yeah! Well ya both can kiss my ass in Macy's window." I stood my ground as they bunched up into a huddle, whispering, giggling secrets. They gave each other a knowing look and scattered in different directions, laughing.

Alone and numb, I had nothing left but the wrenching betrayal of my friends. On my way upstairs I overheard Mrs. Levine talking to Mom, "Molly, the bastards put garbage into my house. The son of a bitches! They're all hoodlums, except for your Solly. He's a good boy."

FRIEND TO THOSE WHO HAVE NO FRIENDS

I WAS INVISIBLE to most adults, except for the ones who hated me. Harold never called me by my name. He had his own favorite names for me: Jew Boy, Jew Bastard, Little Cocksucker, Stupid Fuck, Retard, Hey You, You, or Just Get Over Here. When he was in a creative mood, he was able to put them together in different combinations. That day when I was passing the kitchen, Harold made a complete sentence.

"Excuse me, would you please come over here? Do you always walk like that? Get your hands out of your pockets when I'm talking to you. A gentleman never puts his hands in his pockets. It makes you look more stupid than you already are, if that's possible. You're not listening, are you?"

Harold's thick hands, not made of flesh and blood, but of cold steel, clamped around my ankle. His evil heart burned into my leg. He was treating me as a subspecies in his laboratory to experiment on as he pleased. He yanked my foot around almost to the point of breaking it, shoving my heel toward my face, showing me the bottom of my shoe. The kitchen smelled of that certain combination of soured beer and cold, greasy roast beef. Many years later, anything having that certain odor triggers the despair I suppressed so well.

Sticky paste pulled at the corners of Harold's lips, "You see? Look at this. I said look at this!" He twisted my foot another inch, almost to the point of snapping my anklebone in two. "Your heel is all worn on one side. No wonder you wear out your shoes so quickly. You don't know how to walk properly."

The stabbing pain, and my stubborn refusal to scream, backed up into my stomach. A little longer, and I would have thrown up. Thank God he decided to let go.

Harold took off one of his shoes. "See?" He stuck its sole into my face. He made me feel like a dog, rubbing my nose into his shit. "See how evenly my shoe is worn?" My eyes wobbled in unfocused circles, trying to follow the alcohol fuzz that governed the movement of his shoe.

"You just don't know how to walk properly." Harold proceeded to demonstrate. "You're supposed to walk evenly, like so." He shuffled flat on his feet. "Okay, my little stupid Jew bastard, now you try it."

I might have been stupid, but I knew something Harold didn't know. There was a secret underworld of tunnels traveling beneath our building, right under Harold's evenly worn shoes.

"Are you listening to me?" I nodded my head up and down. "Then what did I say?"

I didn't know and didn't care. There was no point in answering, because I'd always lose. What a time for my nervous tic to flare up. The tendons in my neck tensed into thin, taut, steel rods, pulling my face and neck together. I scrunched my head and ground it against and across my right shoulder, pushing out, screwing up my face and stretching my features in frenzied twitches.

At first Harold stood there, stunned, watching my spastic performance. Then he took a step back, "Look at you... a fucking crippled retard. Are you finished? Now stop that shit and do what I told you to do."

With my face in involuntary muscle spasms, I tried my best to do what he told me to do. I made my feet move in off-balanced, hesitating leaps, stumbling from one leg to the other. After a while, I was able to create some form of rhythm. But I still looked like a convulsive clown in over-sized shoes, flopping with each step.

"Are you trying to be funny?" Harold lumbered toward me with loathing and contempt in his eyes.

I turned and started for the front door. When Harold realized I had an avenue of escape, he wildly swung his foot at me, but it swooshed into space like it belonged to a drunken ballerina. He caught me on his second try with the full force of his anger, right on the tip of my coccyx.

"Ha! Gotcha, you little shit."

An electrical buzz sizzled up my spine, gathering into a knot and lodged in my chest. I doubled up in pain, and lost control of my body. My throat closed and my lungs refused to take in air as I stumbled out of the front door and into the hall of the building, down onto the cold tile floor. I desperately sucked at the air, getting only quick, rasping gasps of suffocation. Refusing to succumb to the idea that I was going to die, yet realizing that breathing in only made things worse, I began to breathe out. In return, I was rewarded with small gulps of air.

Between each flight of stairs were windows facing the alleyway. From one of these windows, a sluggish light streamed into the hall, smothered by the coming of the night. Harold stood over me in washed out tones of pasty grays, glaring with self-satisfaction. He was on the verge of kicking me again when, like a flash of lightning, two scarred arms slashed through the dark shadow, pinning Harold to a wall.

A seething storm spoke in a deep whisper, riding the thick gloom into Harold's face, "I've fought a war against people like you. Do you know what it's like to kill another human being? Face to face and with your own bare hands? No, you wouldn't, would you? Well I have. Many times. I'm not fucking with you. I'm warning you. Leave the boy alone."

The brilliant and powerful Harold, who verbally and physically attacked women and children, practically shit in his pants. He answered in a strained, barely audible voice, "I won't touch him."

"I didn't hear you."

Harold, shaking and pleading, "I promise, I won't touch him again." A dimming light reflected off a scarred hand, releasing its prisoner. The brave Harold ran back into our apartment and screamed out from behind locked doors, "You fuckin' Jew lover! If I catch that scarred freak in the streets, I'll kill that mother-fuckin' son of a bitch."

Harold had to prove he was a man, to himself and to me. And he was still someone to fear. Satisfied with his brief, tough bluff, Harold turned from the door and staggered down our long hall. With each step pounding on the linoleum floor, he disappeared into the living room in a drunken stupor. For the rest of the night Harold drowned himself into an alcoholic oblivion, passing out on the living room floor.

Still trying to breathe normally again, I sat up against the hall wall and heard the door next to ours gently closing. I never saw the melted man again. He vanished from the neighborhood and my life.

Harold's encounter with the melted man never did change him, and he continued his brutal attacks. But seeing him cower changed me. It left a germ of hope that people like Harold, a man of lies and contradictions, were just self-important bullies, who bullshit their way through life. People like Harold build themselves up by humiliating and grinding down those who are most vulnerable. This planted a seed inside me that would someday awaken and grow.

"And now... On to Dick Colmer as Boston Blackie, enemy to those who make him an enemy, friend to those who have no friends."

A flurry of organ music swelled, then trickled away.

My mom interrupted the radio show. She stood in my doorway drinking a glass of tea, holding it with her thumb on the top rim and two fingers on the thick bottom. She put a cube of sugar in her mouth, and her voice and the tea filtered through the lump of sugar, "Vat's da matter, my Sollinue? You not feelin' goodt?"

My body betrayed me with shivers from a sudden chill. Thinking I had a fever, my mom touched my forehead with the back of her hand, strong and soft. She double-checked by pulling back my T-shirt and touching my stomach with her lips. My held-in tears broke loose and seeped through and down my cheeks.

"You got no fever. Vat's wrong, totala? Hmmm, you must be

overtired from playing in dis heat." She kissed my forehead... I'm engulfed in the perfume of her skin.

When the light and the door were closed, I was left alone, but not for long. Every night until I was sixteen years old, when the lights were out I had a visitor. Most children had imaginary friends to protect them. I had an old woman with a kitchen knife standing above my bed, waiting... waiting for me to move. This would be her signal to plunge the kitchen knife, held by her thin, stringy arm, deep into my chest.

My only protection was to cover myself completely with my blanket and breathe without making a sound or moving a muscle. After a while, I would deplete the oxygen under my blanket, re-breathing and drowning in the hot, stale air. Right under the old witch's unsuspecting eyes, I slowly created a tiny opening in my blanket for my nose. A gush of fresh air swept in, and like a cool sheet of silk, brushed across my chest. The sudden rush of air put out the fire in my lungs. Still too terrified to move, I lay motionless, praying my tic would not reappear and betray me. There was no way I'd ever sleep again.

Sliding through a dense fog that begins to scatter... comes the sound of a muffled puff and fluttering roar of the gas burner. Fragmented voices from the kitchen lead me into a new day. And then it all starts again.

ROSH HASHANAH

SEPTEMBER SNUCK UP on me. It had been awhile since Walter left and Mom had come out of mourning. She decided she had to clear out his stuff from my room. The first thing she wanted to get rid of was my Jap aviator cap Walter had given to me. There goes my dream of owning a real, authentic aviator's cap with goggles, just like the kind my hero, *Spy Smasher,* wore. She had to tear it away from my hands.

"Sollinue. Look, look at it. There's dried blood in dere. Who knows how he died. Feh! It's disgusting, and it will make you sick."

Into the garbage it went. On the way to the kitchen, Harold stood in the hall blocking our way. He started cursing Mom, wildly swinging his drunken arms in the air, "Whore, you cocksucking bitch, you're just a Jew bastard." I believe he was getting into a rut.

I happened to be in his way and got accidently slapped in the face with the back of his hand. His knuckles sent me into the wall. Surprised, Harold hadn't even realized I was there. At first, it almost looked like he was going to apologize, but he thought better of it. Instead, he turned away and plowed through his fog down the hallway, living in his own alcoholic dimension, arguing with himself. By the time he got to the living room, his anger exploded. I was hoping he'd keep it there, but he remembered his favorite target.

"Get in here! I'm talking to you. Yes, you. Get in here, you little Jew retard. Get in here! Don't make me come and get you!"

Before he came after me, I escaped out the front door and down to Bobby Frick's. Out on the street, Bobby, Sergie, and I started playing tagging-up, where one of the manhole covers is home base and the other one, second base. Bobby threw the Spaldeen as I was stealing second. The ball hit my foot and bounced into the large alley on our block. Sonia and Claudette's father owned the two-story building that was set in back of the alley. There was a wooden lattice there with grapevines weaving in and out and twig ends corkscrewing in the air.

As the day wore on, one-by-one, Hasidic Jews, collected in the street near their schule. It was Rosh Hashanah, the Jewish New Year, when Jews tossed coins into the Bronx River to ask for forgiveness for the sins they committed during the past year.

After they threw the money into the river, Christian boys wearing bathing suits, with a few Jewish kids mixed in, dove into the water to retrieve the coins. The Jews knew this but didn't care. They did what they had to do, and the boys did what they wanted to do.

Sergie and I followed a Hasidic Jew who was all dressed in black, from his fedora to the heavy overcoat weighing him down, walking with an air of gloom. He wore a white towel with tassels sticking out of his suit jacket, looking like he forgot to tuck them into his pants. Long baloney curls grew out of both sides of his hat, and above his thick beard, his eyes had a single purpose – the three-story building on Faille Street.

We snuck into the building behind our gloomy friend. Inside several rooms were lit with candles. Hot spots of light shimmered with yellow and warm browns. Our friend blended in with exact copies of himself, all of them mumbling in a strange language from their bible. They were phantoms being swallowed up into the wavering shadows.

A short, fat man of self-importance appeared with a curved horn almost as big as himself. They called it a Shofar. He blew into it, and it moaned like the ghost of a dead elephant echoing through the house. He was casting a magic spell, directed at Sergie and me. He knew we were non-believers, and its haunting sound chased us back into the streets. We stood in the dark night, hearts pumping from our narrow escape.

I came home to the smell of mothballs. Mom was taking our

school clothes out of storage and airing them out on the line, trying to get rid of the strong smell of camphor. It was the night before school, and all the mothers of my classmates must have been doing the same, because that Monday morning, the whole school smelled of mothballs so strong I could hardly breathe. We were being poisoned by our mothers' love.

SOLLY RISING

CHRISTMAS WAS A spontaneous occasion for people we knew in my neighborhood, and it all took place within walking distance on Southern Boulevard. What made it extra special was the mad rush of last minute shopping for presents and Christmas trees.

I mingled with the crowds of shoppers at Woolworth's. The whole store was blinking with colored lights. The shoppers infected me with their excitement, and the lights filled me with the joy of Christmas. I was so caught up in the feeling of giving that I even felt like buying a present for Harold. What am I crazy? He'd probably use it as a weapon to whack me with.

I had saved fifteen cents to buy Mom a present, and it was burning a whole in my pocket. I started my search through the rows of glass cases filled with sparkling jewelry. That was just the thing I wanted to get for Mom, but they were too expensive. Disappointed, I wandered over to the candy counter.

At one corner of the counter, there was a piece of glass missing, about two inches wide and big enough to stick my finger into. No one noticed me tickling out the loose candy. While enjoying my candy, I spotted a glass saltshaker and decided it was something Mom could use everyday, and I could afford it. All around the outside of the clear glass shaker, in even rows, were little cut-glass bumps, looking like it was embedded with little diamonds.

Every present I had ever given Mom, she had either thrown away or given to one of her friends. To my surprise, she not only kept this present, she actually used it. When she filled the saltshaker and put it on the kitchen table, it gave me the greatest feeling of pride.

Mom wanted to give me something in return. The only thing she could think of at the moment was a movie. It was one of those special films that the theater made into an all-out promotional extravaganza. The front of the Boulevard Theater looked more like the opening day of the Circus. The movie was *Golden Earrings,* and they were giving out a pair of golden earrings to the first one hundred people. Mom was ecstatic and put them on immediately. With her bangs, and the flower in her hair, and the golden earrings, she could easily have been a gypsy herself.

During that Christmas week of 1947, just before the unexpected blizzard, I stood in the snow with my friends, Sergie and Junior. We were outside the window of the radio repair shop, down the hill between Bryant and Longfellow Avenues, staring at a wooden box with a little, round glass screen. Only a few people could afford a television.

Watching TV had its own special smells, and each program was tied up with the smell of the places where my friends and I could find a TV to watch. We would lean by the open doorway of Harry's Bar in the heat of the summer, smelling the lingering whiskey layered with stale beer. We watched the cowboys' ghostly white shadows, clopping across the TV screen against a washed-out western background, and listened to their tinny voices.

Sometimes it was the smell of the cool fresh air whipping through Charley and Vicky's fifth floor apartment window, while we watched anything that moved through the thick magnifying glass on the front of their TV. We even watched dumb shows like, *The Lucky Pup,* with Pinhead and Foodini.

Charley's thin frame gave him the appearance of being tall. He was a very distinguished looking man, with gray streaks on both sides of his straight black hair. He always dressed with a tie and suit jacket, and spoke like he moved, gently. All the older Spanish people I knew had accents, but not Charley. In perfect English, he told us to stay as long as we liked.

But on this particular winter night, we stood outside the radio repair shop, smelling the burning solder that wafted into our faces with each spurt of heat from the opening and closing door. I could hear the busy street sounds from Westchester Avenue, filtering between the flakes of floating snow. The cold, white specks spotted my face, melting into my blinking eyes. I was so bundled up with layers of clothes that I began to sweat, even though I was standing still, staring at the test pattern on the screen. It was Tuesday night, and Milton Berle appeared on the TV dressed as a fat lady, flapping around the stage on his ankles, getting swatted with an enormous powder puff.

After the show, Sergie and I joined Millie on the stoop of our apartment building, watching the snow turning everything upside down. Streets became snowy clouds and the sky turned into what looked like dark gray streets. A few feet away from us was a patch of ice that people passing by carefully avoided on their way home from work.

We decided to play a dangerous game. We dusted the ice with loose snow, camouflaging it from our unsuspecting victims, who carried packages home from shopping at the Triangle on Westchester Avenue and Southern Boulevard. We sat on the stoop, trying to think them onto our trap.

Finally, our first mark slipped and shot up into the air, falling on his ass, his packages flying in all directions. We found this very funny. And, as if we had nothing to do with it, we courteously helped our victim pick up his loose groceries from the sidewalk. He thanked us and moved on. Then, we did it all over again.

After a while, my feet got soaking wet and freezing, so I ran upstairs, and wrapped my wet socks around the steam pole in the bathroom to dry. The steaming socks smelled like they were cooking on the stove. After about ten minutes, they had stiffened from being quick fried-dried. I peeled them off the pole, and put my cold feet back into the warm socks.

My mom came in and asked, "Solly, my darlink, do me a favor.

Go upstairs to the Weinman's, and see if Millinue is up dere. If she is, tell her to come down here, I vant to talk to her. Vait a minute..."

Mom rummaged through her pocketbook, and the perfume of Juicy Fruit gum filled the room.

"After you find Millie, go downstairs to Yetta. Here... here's the ten dollars I owe her. You understand?"

"Yeah, Ma, I understand."

"Now don't you forget to pay Yetta."

"I won't."

It was unusual for pay back so early in the week. Mom would always borrow money from her friends and shopped on credit from the neighborhood stores. At the end of the week, on payday, she'd pay all her debts, and we'd be broke again before the new week started. She was always one week behind, and couldn't get out of the hole.

No one answered the door, but it was slightly ajar and I walked in. No one was there... no Millie, no Weinmans. Then Veronica came out of her room, and stood there looking at me – tall, with fair skin and blue eyes. Long, golden hair surrounded her sharp, thin features. I was eleven years old, and had a deep crush on Veronica, even though she was my sister's best friend, and two and a half years older than I was. And now, for the first time, I was alone with her.

She wasn't acting like herself, which made me feel uncomfortably out of place. Veronica maneuvered me to the kitchen doorway. Above my head dangled a plant with green leaves and white berries.

"Aha! You're standing under the mistletoe. An-n-n-d, you know what that means!"

"No, what does it mean?"

The idea that I was so naïve, gave her power over me, and excited her.

"You... you don't know what mistletoe is?"

"No," I admitted.

Veronica trembled in anticipation, "If you're caught standing under it, you have to be kissed."

She bent down, and moved her lips slowly toward mine. Her hair brushed across my face. She pulled me closer to her, and I could feel the heat of her body. Gently, she pressed her soft, warm lips against mine, and lingered there. Veronica's tongue found its way into my mouth, and I breathed in her hot, sweet breath. I could taste it with my whole body.

As soon as I closed my eyes, I felt a sudden loss of gravity. I went into a thrilling ride, like the quick drop in an elevator. There was no up or down anymore. I lost all knowledge of where I was. I throbbed with a fever that left me dazed and off balance.

The heat of Veronica's lips followed me downstairs to Yetta's. I floated down the steps, holding Mom's ten dollars in one hand, and in the other, a stick of gum. I stuck the gum in my mouth, held the wrapper tightly, and without thinking, threw away the ten dollars.

Yetta answered her door, "Solly!"

"Mrs. Melnick, here's the money my mom owes you," and handed her the gum wrapper.

"What's this, some kind of joke?"

"Oh, my God!

I ran up and down the hall steps searching for the money. By now all memory of Veronica's kiss was gone. The grown-up passion I felt disappeared, and I was a child again, frantically looking in every corner of each step. It was no use. The ten dollars was gone. I sat on the hall steps for a half hour, hoping Mom would forget about the money. At last, I walked into our apartment.

"Sollinue, did you give Yetta the ten dollars?"

"Mom... I... I don't know how it happened, but I lost it."

"You what?"

"I swear to you, I had it in my hand, and then it was gone. I looked all over! I went upstairs, downstairs – I couldn't find it anywhere."

"Somebody must have taken it. How can you lose ten dollars? What am I going to do with you?"

I felt so ashamed for being so stupid. That was my punishment.

That night Harold stumbled into the living room in a drunken stupor. He trimmed his Christmas tree, mumbling his Christmas prayer:

"Kill all those fucking bastards. Kill all those filthy, fucking Jews. I hope all those son of a bitches die, so we can have peace in this world."

As his anger toward the Jews grew, it focused onto Millie and me. From my room, I could hear him screaming, "Keep those little, fucking Jew bastards of yours out of my sight! Do you hear me? If I see or hear so much as a peep out of them, I'll kill the little pricks."

I was lying in my bed listening to the radio, interrupted by Harold's ravings, as he progressively transformed into the monster I knew so well. Soon he would be parading his mindless brutality into our rooms. But, thank God, that night he never reached our rooms, or finished decorating his tree. Instead, he staggered into his bedroom, and passed out.

While he was out, Millie and I snuck into the living room. We finished trimming the tree, smelling the shit that was ground into Harold's pants coming from the next room. We tossed the silvery tinsel up into the air, and as it came down, each strand hooked haphazardly onto the tree limbs. Like slivers of mirrors, they reflected the colored lights and sparkled off the living room walls. It was like standing inside a kaleidoscope of colors.

The clanking radiator hissed out its steam, overheating my room. I could hear the clanging of a distant trolley, resounding off the brick canyons. The raw winter winds whistled through the alley with a blinding, swirling tornado of snow. Back and forth it blew, not knowing which way it wanted to go. The storm was real, and honest, and truthful, with no hidden meanings. It was what it was. I was warm and protected in my fortress of bricks, from the intense winds furiously whipping around the alley. And since Harold was out for the night, nothing could harm me.

In the morning, the storm had stopped, and snow was pasted against my windowsill. The window glass looked like a splash of water, frozen at the moment of the splash. It was as if a skater had cut though the frozen water, fracturing it into an abstract painting of ice, blurring the outside world into broken reflections.

The front door of my building pushed into the snow, and I saw that the force of the wind had carved a Grand Canyon of snowdrifts. A bright sun glared off the snow, blinding me momentarily. Last night's blasting wind was gone, and the quiet cold made everything sound brittle. Hand shovels scraped the sidewalks, and above the voices on the street, I could hear the city trucks plowing. The cold sun cast silver blue shadows on the snowdrifts.

The newspapers were calling it the Great Blizzard of 1947. I stepped into interconnecting trenches of snow, dug by the supers and storekeepers on our block, like pictures I'd seen of WW I. I stood in the neatly carved-out tunnels, and being very short for my age, the white walls reached above my head. With my hands in my mackinaw jacket, and trusting the snow, I let go and fell backward into the soft, white wall. The snow instantly surrounded me and for a few moments, I became a part of it. It was a refuge protecting and shielding me from everyone out there.

When I had enough of my intimate experience with the snow, I tried to get up, but my hands were trapped in my pockets. Every time I tried to move, the snow grabbed at me, and pulled me back. It wouldn't let go. The more I tried to escape, the deeper I got buried, and the stronger its hold on me became. Lying on my back, the only view I had was the sky. Freedom was just a few feet away. There must be someone out there. I screamed for a long time, until I almost lost my voice. But no one answered.

What if my friends found me like this? They might just cover me up with snow and laugh, and leave me there, worse off than I was now. And what if the wall of snow caved in on me? Or a garbage truck shoveled snow on top of me? I'd be buried, and no one would ever find me. Was I going to die here, at eleven years old?

With all my strength I struggled desperately to free myself, but it was no use. The snow held onto me. There was no way out. I'll never see my mom again, or get to eat the stuffed cabbage she was cooking for dinner. No more radio, no more movies.

Then I heard a familiar yelp. Spotty jumped on my chest, and licked my face. I knew someone must be out there with her. My throat was sore, and my voice hoarse, and I cried out in a raspy whisper, "Help! Help me!"

It was Millie. She pulled me up out of the snow, saving my life. Millie and I fought over the most stupid things, but she was my sister, and she knew the crap I lived through every day. I respected how she stood up for herself against Harold and Mom. Now, at least for this moment, I loved her more than ever for saving my life.

Splat! Snow slid down my face and under my shirt collar. My skin jumped from the sudden cold, dripping down my neck and onto my hot back. All the kids on the block were in a snow fight. Spotty flung herself up toward a flying snowball and snapped at it. It hit her in the face and went up her nose, but she shook it off and sneezed the snow from her nostrils. We screamed out, "Free for all!" and bombarded each other.

While we defended our fortifications, the snowplows were busy building snow mountains at the corners of our block. After the fight, Sergie, Junior, and I filled Mr. Jacob's doorway with snow. We enjoyed every shovelful of his curses, as he dug himself out.

When the mountain of snow at our corner was completed, and the snowplows were gone, we ran to the top and played King of the Mountain, tugging and pushing at each other as we tumbled down the sides. After awhile, we carved out a slide that circled the mountain of snow. We stole the metal tops of garbage pails, broke off their handles, and carried them to the summit. Sitting on our garbage-lid sleds, we slid around the mountain, back down into the street.

Later, my friends and I dug a tunnel into the mountain of snow. We may have been very different from each other, but we could work together with a single purpose. We sat inside our snow cave, secretly hidden from prying eyes, knowing that we were really out on the street. Someone brought in a candle, and its light circled us in a warm glow. We were like little rabbits, safe and snug in our burrow. Spotty was inside with us and decided to pee yellow puddles were we sat... our igloo experience was over.

When I stepped out from the tunnel, my legs were weak and shook uncontrollably, and my throat was still sore as hell. I could hardly swallow.

Slowly I climbed the three flights of stairs to our apartment. The muscles in my legs felt weak and tired. On the last flight, blocking my way, was the huge, lumbering Harold. Just to look at him, you'd never believe he was the cruel, sadistic prick that he was. Most people saw him as a subdued, quiet gentleman. He turned around and looked down at me with gooey white bubbles at the corners of his mouth. He asked in his gentlemanly way, "What the fuck are you doing back there?" As if I'd been making fun of him.

I smiled weakly. Harold took offense at my smile and grabbed me, locking his steel fingers onto my shoulders, pinching my skin through my jacket like stabbing knives. Then he dropkicked me in the forehead. My neck jerked backwards, and I jumped around the hall with white sparks crackling in my head. I squeezed my fists tightly, crunching my fingers, trying to press them through my palms.

On the verge of crying, I screamed at the pain, "Ya fuckin' bastard! Ya fuckin' bastard! Ya fuckin' bastard! Ya fuckin' bastard!"

Harold was in such a drunken numbness, his swimming mind couldn't hear or see me anymore. I snuck past him, into the safety of my room. When I closed my door, I gave in and cried to myself.

Minutes later Mom came to my room, "Mine boychick... you're still in ya vet clothes. Come, let me help you." When she started to peel off my shirt, my skin felt raw, and I twitched and shivered as it rubbed against my aching skin.

"You're shaking." Mom felt my stomach with her lips. "Oy! You're burning up!"

Her lips absorbed my pain, and in her usual no-nonsense manner, she quickly undressed me, put me into my warm, soft pajamas, and tucked me in bed. I was still shaking under the quilt.

Mom left the room, and in minutes returned with a heated iron wrapped in a towel, and tucked it up against my feet under the quilt. "I'm making some chicken soup. It'll make you feel good."

When my mom made chicken soup, she cooked two whole, freshly plucked chickens. Once in a while, she would find a special treat inside the chicken, whole egg yolks without their shells. But now I was too sick, and was going to miss being in the kitchen, fighting with Millie over the little yellow yolks.

It was hot and stuffy in my room. My eyes and nose burned with each breath, and the smell of the cooking chicken was turning my stomach. My room was closing in on me. Mom brought me the soup, but my throat was so sore and swollen, each spoonful felt like I was swallowing a part of my throat. As soon as it went down, the chicken soup bounced back up from my stomach, and out onto the floor.

Mom got out her first-aid kit: rubbing alcohol, and made me sniff it. Everything calmed down, and it took the taste of vomit from my mouth. She helped me back to bed, and rubbed my stomach with the alcohol. I groaned, and she looked at me, "My poor boychickal." I didn't know which it was, the alcohol, or my mom's hands, all I did know is that it made me feel better.

Alone in my room, my tic returned, and I couldn't think of anything but that empty feeling in my neck. I tried to make it stop, but that insistent emptiness would not be denied. No matter how hard I concentrated, I couldn't stop it.

Then the pain took over, terrible pulsating cramps that came in waves, so unbearable I had to bang my fist against the headboard of my bed. It only worked to relieve my pain for a few seconds, but even for a few seconds, the relief was worth it.

I heard Harold talking to Mom from the kitchen, "Leave the little dimwit alone. It's not as bad as he's making it out to be. Can't you see your precious little Jew-brat is pretending? All he wants is your attention. You have my baby son to take care of. Stop wasting your time with that lying cocksucker."

Millie and Mom passed by my room while I was banging my fist in excruciating pain. I couldn't believe they were laughing at me! Did my mom really think I was pretending to be in pain? Her betrayal hurt me as much as the pain... I felt so alone.

With nothing left in me to puke up, my body tried to throw up parts of myself, and would have if they hadn't been attached. After hearing me throw up all night, Mom finally believed me, and early that morning, she sent for Dr. Feinman. After his examination, he told Mom he thought I had strep throat, and intestinal grip.

"I'll let you know for sure, Molly. But in the meantime, get some coke syrup from the drugstore, and give the boy a teaspoonful, very slowly. It will give him some strength, and keep him from vomiting."

The syrup quieted down the vomiting, and Mom stood over me, watching, smoothing her bangs between her fingers like she always did, lost in her thoughts, as I finally fell asleep.

Before she left for work, Mom went to the small candy store on Faille Street where they sold secondhand joke books for two to five cents each. She didn't know the ones I liked and came home with joke books of super heroes I'd never heard of, like *Isis* an Egyptian heroine, *Doll Man, Crack Comics*. The rest were old, beat-up first issues of my favorite super heroes, *Superman, Captain Marvel, Capt. Marvel Jr.* from *Whiz Comics, Spy Smasher and Batman*. What was this old crap she bought me? I couldn't stand looking at the really bad artwork... and when she left, I threw them away.

The pain in my stomach was still there, and with it, a few bouts of vomiting. I tried listening to some soap operas to take my mind off the burning cramps, but it didn't help. They only made me feel worse. But in one of the soaps, something – a word or a suggestion – reminded me about the time last summer when all us guys were talking about jerking off.

It happened when we made a great find at the Triangle near the train station: a box of overripe tomatoes. We took them to the roof of Sergie's building and looked over its edge for the perfect target. There he was, walking along the sidewalk toward the blank brick wall we used for handball – Mr. Jacobs. We drove him crazy with our never-ending pranks. But no matter how much of a prick he was, he didn't deserve such cruelties.

Mr. Jacobs' thin, angular body was carrying a bundle of clean wash almost as big as he was. Each of us held a tomato... holding... holding... holding... waiting for him to reach the blank wall, right where we wanted him. When he got in position, we hurled a barrage of tomato missiles at him. They splattered him and his clean wash until he looked like a walking Italian dinner.

Unexpectedly, somebody else walked into our line of fire, and we almost hit him too. It was Crazy Leo. We didn't want anything to do with that nut, and as he looked up in our direction, we quickly ducked. We didn't know if he saw us or not, but we weren't taking any chances and climbed up on top of the door. We were safe there, because no one ever looked up. Even if we told the grown-ups about the roof above the door, they wouldn't know what we were talking about, because it just didn't exist for them. Sitting behind the little wall, being very small ourselves, it hid us very well.

While we were waiting for the coast to clear, Sergie brought up the subject of jerking off. Sergie's older brother, Tony, had a girl friend who told Sergie about jerking off. She told him that it was better than any amusement ride in Coney Island, and if Sergie promised not to tell anyone, especially Tony, she'd show him how it was done. Then, she took his dick in her hand and rubbed it up and down until he came. "It was great!"

We all agreed how great it was, as if we had done it, too. But we were all lying. You could hear it in our voices.

"Yeah, it's great."

"The best."

"Cool."

So now, here I was, alone in my bed with nothing to do but feel sick. And I thought, what the hell, I'll give it a try!

The bathroom was next to my room, the safest place in our apartment since it was the only room with a good lock. I went in, locked the door, pulled down my pants, and lay down on the cold tile floor. I started to rub my cock, but nothing much was happening, until I thought of Veronica rubbing it for me. My hand became her hand. I remembered her kiss and imagined rubbing my cock against her soft skin. It got so stiff I thought it was trying to escape from my body. The more I rubbed it, the more sensitive it got.

A tingling built up in my groin and rushed to my head. The faster I rubbed it, the more I throbbed with thrilling spasms. And then there was an explosion of white, creamy liquid shooting out like a bullet, almost reaching the ceiling.

After that first time, there was no stopping me, and I jerked off all day long. I even tried pumping pillows, quilts, my bed, whatever happened to look good to me. I didn't need Veronica anymore. Tony's girlfriend was right – it was better than any carnival ride I was ever on. I thought, maybe when I get better I could ask Tony's girlfriend to show me how to do it, too.

That night I listened to one of my favorite shows, *"Return with us now to those thrilling days of yesteryear. From out of the past come the thundering hoof beats of the great horse, Silver. The Lone Ranger rides again! Come on, Silver! Let's go, Big Fella! Hi-yo, Silver! Away! Faster Big Fella, faster."*

When it was time to go to bed, I couldn't sleep. My new experience ran away with my thoughts. All the girls I knew, one after the other, popped into my head as sex partners to play with. I knew I had to keep these thoughts hidden away where no one would know them but me. I fell asleep dreaming of girls.

OH, WHAT A WONDERFUL WORLD IT WILL BE

AS HAROLD PASSED my room on his way to work, his threatening growl frightened my early morning. The holidays were over, and it was time to go back to school. The kitchen table was covered with a white tablecloth with drawings of red fruits on it. As I ate the cold cereal, I stared at the cereal box and daydreamed of owning the premium they were selling: The Lone Ranger Atom Bomb Ring.

"Only one box top and ten cents, mailed to Battle Creek, Michigan, and you too can own the Atom Bomb Ring with its secret compartment for secret messages."

My mind emptied of thoughts of school, and I saw only the sun beaming through the kitchen window. Millions of white specs were caught in the sun's rays, nervously riding the beams of light onto the linoleum floor, landing on a sleeping Spotty.

When I got home after school, there was nothing to snack on, but I found some loose change under one of the cushions of the couch. I took Harold's drunken gift and went out to buy a treat. I decided to try the small soda fountain-restaurant in the hotel building, on the corner of Hoe and Westchester Avenues. I'd never been there before. This was the first time I ever bought prepared food in a restaurant on my own, but they treated me like any other customer, not like a kid.

I only had enough for a cup of coffee, toast, and butter. The toast was cut into two triangular pieces, the first time I ever ate toast cut that way. I started at one of the points and savored each bite. Toast never tasted that good. Sitting there alone, being served by a waiter, I felt independent and grown up.

Back on the block, my friends were throwing parachutes made out of handkerchiefs. We had no tissues then, but we always had plenty of handkerchiefs. I threw mine as high as I could and watched it open up and float down to the sidewalk. It landed on top of Chester Drugs' new car, the first new car on our block since the war. Everyone who passed by had to stop and look at it, as if they'd never seen a car before. I peered into one of the windows and noticed a flurry of movement inside. On the back seat sat a large, white rat. The back door was open. Usually I would take too much time to make a decision and always get caught – but not this time. Without thinking twice, I climbed into the back seat, grabbed the rat and ran upstairs to my room. I hid it in my closet and fed it some Cheerios.

Spotty sniffed, scratched and growled at the closet door. She stationed herself outside and wouldn't move. The rat was very gentle, gentle enough so that I could take her to school with me hidden inside my shirt. I felt like Sabu, in *Jungle Book*.

Two men in suits were in our classroom, "Hello, my name is Bob."

"And my name is Chuck."

"We are here to tell you what the future holds for you."

Chuck continued, "The wizards of the past would have been burned as witches if they did what we are going to do today. Now, we want you to watch us very carefully. I'm going to take these two vials of liquid, and as you can see, the liquids are as loose as flowing water, but when I combine them…"

Bob poured both vials into what looked like a metal container and continued, "We just have to wait for a few minutes." Then he picked up the metal container and threw it in our direction. We all ducked, expecting to get wet. But instead, a hard lump popped out in the shape of the container onto Mrs. Bare-ass's desk.

Chuck took over. He knocked the lump against the desk, demonstrating its hardness. "As you can see, the liquid became as hard as a rock, yet it is as light as a piece of balsa wood. We call it – Plastic." He asked us to walk to the front of the classroom and feel the hard liquid.

Bob continued, "Just imagine that toys, even cars, will be made from plastic. It's light, but strong as steel."

Chuck added, "It will also replace glass. And everything will be cheaper. This is your future, and – Oh, what a wonderful world it will be. Bob and I can't wait!"

While the men in suits were demonstrating, I was playing with my white rat, letting it crawl down my shirtsleeve onto my hand and onto my desk. A girl sitting next to me spotted it and screamed at the top of her lungs, scaring the hell out of the rat, which jumped from desk to desk. The kids popped up and down from their desks like prairie dogs, all screaming and running and bumping into each other.

Mrs. Bare-ass lost control of her class. One of the suits, Bob, opened the classroom door and my poor frightened rat scurried out of the room. No one ever found out where it came from, or who was responsible. And I never knew what happened to it. The poor thing could have died of a heart attack.

Advertised on the back of every glossy joke book cover were enticing display ads of expensive prizes, not the cheap box top premiums, exciting as they may have been. They were things I never dreamed I could own: a Schwinn bike, cameras, watches, and the best prize of them all, a Red Ryder BB rifle. All I had to do was follow what it said in the advertisement. *"Get prizes with fast-selling American Seeds. Send no money, we trust you. Just fill out and mail this coupon today."* I knew I wasn't old enough, so I signed Millie's name to the coupon.

Near the end of the school year, I checked our mailbox, and there it was, a box of seeds – my ticket to one of those dazzling prizes. Where to sell them... Ahh! The Quonset huts! The ones they just built for the returning service men.

Off I went on my quest, down The Three Hills and over the train tracks to the creek. Stopping on the bridge, I peered down at the riverbank alive with black rats with bloodshot eyes, some as big as alley cats, crawling on top of each other. The sun was hot, and the bugs were waking up from their long winter sleep.

The Quonset huts were like empty tin cans, cut in half and sitting side-by-side in rows, on a sea of mud. Wood planks were sidewalks leading to each hut. If you accidently stepped off the planks, you'd get sucked into the bottomless mud and never be heard from again. The place had a moldy smell, laced with fresh cut wood. The rats had no trouble navigating through the mud, and every so often, one would jump up onto the wood sidewalk, cross in front of me, sit down on its tail, look at me, and plunge back into the mud. The arrogant little pricks.

Everything was gray. These people should be starving for flowers to liven things up. I started to knock on doors.

"Excuse me, Miss. I have flower seeds and..."

"Sorry, Sweetie, I can't use them... don't have time for a garden."

Every hut had the same answer. They didn't care because these homes were temporary. I just gave up and threw the seeds into the garbage... so much for owning a BB gun.

The seed company hounded Millie for the payment of the seeds. Millie wrote to them, "I never ordered anything. You can complain about it all you want to, you'll never get one thin dime from me." This went on for a few months until they finally gave up.

Millie realized I must have been the one who ordered the seeds and came to my room screaming. I had no way of protecting myself. I grabbed anything I could, which happened to be her blue metal bank, and hit her on the head with it. Millie wasn't hurt, but her head left a big dent in the bank.

She was stunned by my sudden attack, and left my room with a warning, "Don't you ever, ever do that again! Don't even think of it, or I'll scratch you into a bloody pulp." I kept the bank as a trophy and placed it proudly on my dresser.

WHY WASN'T THERE ANY BLOOD?

I WAS SITTING on my stoop on a warm, quiet summer morning, staring off into nothing, deep in uncluttered thoughts. A sudden scream echoed out from the alley of my building, startling me with an electric jolt of fear. I felt raw with an aching anger and wanted to strike out at someone.

The screaming voice pleaded, "Stop it! What are you doing? Are you crazy? Oh my God! Look what you did to me!" Some guy I never saw before leaped out from the basement stairs with a numb look in his eyes. He was looking for a way to escape and ran at me, almost knocking me over.

Hearing the desperate cries, the people on my block materialized behind me. Sergie, Junior, Bobby, and I were the first down the stairs and into the alley, past the unwashed garbage pails cooking in the heat of the morning.

A woman shouted out from one of the windows above, "What's happening down dare?"

Lying on the pavement was a teenager with a knife sticking out of his chest, but there was no blood. Why wasn't there any blood? How can a knife cut so deep and his body not bleed?

"Look at me!" he screamed not believing what he was seeing. "Look at me! Look at me! Look at what he did to me!"

Jack, the candy store man, knelt down by the boy, with his

half-chewed cigar clenched in his iron jaw. He looked up to the open windows of the surrounding buildings, and with his cigar never falling out of his mouth, called out, "Somebody call an ambulance!"

The boy started to make gurgling sounds and turned his head toward me. In a plaintive voice, "Look at what he did. The son of a bitch, look at what he did!" He stared right at me like I could save him. And then he died.

The rims of my eyes and nose burned. One second he was a breathing person, and the next second he was just a lump of meat. That could have been me. There was always the threat of violence surrounding us, and I always had to be on the alert.

The cops on the beat showed up and chased everyone away. My friends and I were shoved out into the streets, and after awhile, we chunked away from the crowd. Junior's cousins, Rudy and Carmen stuck to him like glue. No matter where we went or what we did, they were there. We started playing box baseball, and I noticed two strangers in dark suits and gray fedoras. It was hard to tell them apart. They stepped inside Mr. Jacobs' laundry store.

Curious, we pressed against the window and could hear the men say they were health inspectors. They blurred in and out of the different shades of dust, grime and dirt layering the surface of Mr. Jacobs' windows. Sometimes their bodies were confused with our own reflections.

The men ordered Jacobs from the back of the counter. He refused and gave them an argument. His slight body, like a flitting insect, darted around the room waving its long angular arms, trying to keep the men from going any further. They pushed him aside and stood behind his counter. I heard a cracking sound as the two men slowly sank, and with a loud crash and swoosh they were gone. A cloud of smoke puffed up from behind the counter, and the health inspectors disappeared into Mr. Jacobs' basement.

Jacobs saw our faces smashed up against his window, laughing. "You little bastards, get away from my window!"

I gave him our usual response, "Ahh... kiss my ass!"

Jacobs chased us up the block, swinging a broomstick, "You son of a bitches. When I getcha, I'll give you such a smack, you'll never sit down again!"

We screamed back, "Ah, fuck you!" "Kiss my ass in Macy's window!"

With Rudy and Carmen trailing behind, we ended up at Triangle Park on Westchester Avenue, and stayed there until the coast was clear. Sergie and I pretended to be pirates and the park was an uncharted island. We started digging a hole by a tree where we would bury our booty.

Junior suggested, "Let's bury some real stuff, like our radio stuff. You know, like my Tom Mix siren ring."

I chimed in, "Yeah. I've got a bunch of things... like my Captain Midnight Decoder Badge and my Lone Ranger Atom Bomb Ring."

Sergie added, "And then we can make a real treasure map. A-a-nd leave the stuff buried, and like, dig it up in a couple of months."

On our way home, Rudy and Carmen's father was standing on Junior's stoop. They rushed to their father and asked him if they could get their radio premiums and bring them back to Junior's.

He told them, "No! We're going home and you can't come back to Junior's."

"We just want to bring our radio toys, and we promise we'll go right home."

He looked at them and said gently, "How would you like to be with your Mommy in heaven? It's the most beautiful place you've ever seen. You'll love it there. Your Mommy's there, waiting for us. Don't you want to see your Mommy?"

"You mean, we can really see her?"

His father cupped Rudy's head tenderly. "Yes, we can all join her. Would you like that?"

"Yes, Poppy." They disappeared around the corner.

Sergie brought back an empty milk bottle. We filled it with our booty and buried it deep in the hole by the tree. Then we drew a treasure map, burned its edges, and browned the center to make it look like an authentic, old pirate map. We hid the map in a safe place, so safe we forgot where we hid it.

Late that afternoon, a group of red-faced men, sweating whiskey, filed out of Harry's Bar with rolled up shirtsleeves, collars and ties loosened, and suit jackets over their arms. They had a predetermined plan in mind, to play a game of craps. They held folded bills between the fingers of their closed fists, looking like broken fans, and tossed the dice up against the blank wall between the bar and Junior's stoop.

After an hour or two, my friends and I snuck up to them. We hid behind a parked car and, just for fun, yelled out, "Chickie, the cops!" The guys took off, bumping into each other like the balls in a pinball machine, leaving some of their bets on the sidewalk.

We grabbed the money and ran up to the roof of my building and split it up between us – five bucks each. That was a fortune! Junior insisted that when Rudy and Carmen came back, they should have an equal share. We agreed on that, but then I insisted, "I don't think Melvin should get a penny of it. Why should he? The little prick never shares any of his money wit us."

Melvin, outraged, "That's not fair! Why should Rudy get some of the money, and I don't? He wasn't even here."

"Go fuck yourself," I gladly answered.

Junior added, "Yeah, when did ya ever split yer money wit us?"

Melvin complained, "It's not fair!"

"Why don't ya shut yer asshole, or I'll shut it for ya."

Melvin knew better than cross Junior and kept his mouth shut.

We took our loot to Jack's and bought ice cream sundaes, malteds, egg creams and joke books... lots of joke books. Before we left the store, we took some empty soda caps from the red cooler and pried out the inside corks. We put the cork on the inside of our shirts, and the bottle cap directly over it on the outside. Then we pressed them together and wore them like rows of colorful military medals.

"Junior! Junior!" It was Mrs. Hernandez screaming up and down the street. Hearing the desperation in her voice, we all ran out of Jack's. Mrs. Hernandez' whole body shook as she grabbed Junior and crushed him against her, kissing him.

Junior got worried, "Que pasa? Que pasa, Mamma?" She answered in Spanish, her voice quivering and uncontrollably crying between her words.

Junior turned to the rest of us. He couldn't believe what was coming out from his own mouth, "They're all dead."

I asked, "Who's dead?"

"Rudy, Carmen and Uncle Carlos. They're all dead."

Sergie asked, "What are you talkin' about?"

"They're dead!"

"But we just saw them. How could they be dead?"

"My uncle killed them and himself. They're dead... they're all dead."

"What?" Sergie gasped.

"He gassed them..."

I heard what he said, but it wasn't real to me. It was nothing but words without any reality to back it up.

That night, using broomsticks as spears, we went on a safari – cat hunting, chasing any stray cat we could find, from car to car, alley to alley. We even chased one up to the top of a clothesline pole about five stories high. It slipped and fell and landed on its feet, its back humped and bristled. The cat stood there for a few seconds, and then ran away.

"What the hell was that?" From then on, I felt that cats had unnatural powers. We never did catch a cat, and I never really wanted to. The fun of it was the excitement of the chase. I wouldn't have known what to do with it if we did catch one.

But we weren't the only ones hunting cats. A group of older kids actually caught one on Faille Street. For all I knew, it could have been that same poor, unlucky cat running into its own hell. The cat fought back, scratching its tormentors. That really pissed them off.

Crazy Leo had a piece of rope. He tied one end around the cat's neck and threw the other up over a lamppost. The cat hung by its neck, its fur spiked out, looking twice its size, not like a cat anymore – more like a ferocious wild animal, fighting for its life. The kids poured gasoline over the cat. Excited voices cheered when Leo lit the gas and the cat ignited into a ball of fire. I'd never heard a cat scream like that – a mixture of pain, anger and fear – as it frantically flung itself into jumps and twists, trying to shake off the pain.

A sudden downpour of rain put the fire out. The smell of smoke and the stink of burning cat flesh lingered in the damp air. I stood there watching the dangling dead cat randomly twitch and drift, riding the cool currents of air.

I never went on a cat hunt again.

FIGHTING BACK

Two empty bulldozers are working away, doing nothing, on streets devoid of people. A black 1937 Dodge appeared from nowhere, driven by a woman dressed in black whose face is covered with a black veil. The car moves in perfect sync with the yellow and orange bulldozers in a ghostly, choreographed dance.

The car stops beside me. The woman in black feels my presence, lifts the veil from her face, and glares at me with an evil, sneering grin. She is there to steal my soul. A cold chill runs through me as if my hand had just slid across a razor's edge.

I don't belong here. I want to return to my other world, but I'm at a point of crossing over... I've stayed too long and can't get back.

The woman in black changes into my mother, and kindly smiles and says, "My Sollinue, you're eleven years old now, and you've got to start taking care of yourself." She starts to shake me, then blurs into my sister, Millie, standing over me and nudging me repeatedly...

"It's your turn. Come on get up. Its your turn."

"My turn, for what?"

"It's almost 10:30."

Still half asleep, "What the hell are you talkin' about?"

"Jesus, Solly, it's Saturday. It's your turn to go to the bakery."

"Oh, shit."

I jumped out of my pajamas and got dressed. Mom gave me a dollar to buy six hard rolls and a piece of seven-layer cake, "Make sure you get change."

I was almost in the bakery on Westchester Avenue before my front door had a chance to close. Inside the smell of the fresh, warm bread and cakes from the ovens in back of the bakery escaped with each swing of the doors. While waiting my turn, I gazed through the glass case at rows of charlotte russe, éclairs, and the cone-shaped cake with the chocolate cream topping, covered by a thin crust of chocolate. The man behind the counter took a pencil from his ear, and licking its point, added the costs on a brown paper bag.

I rushed home, gave the change to my mom, took off my shirt, pants and shoes, got back into my pajamas, and back into my bed. Millie was ready, holding the wood ruler and a knife. She measured the cake before cutting it to make sure neither of us was cheated. Now we both had exactly half a piece of cake. We turned on my radio. It squeaked and squawked until we found the right station for our special Saturday morning show, *Let's Pretend*.

The only way Millie and I got our fairytales was from radio shows like, *Let's Pretend* and *Land of the Lost*.

The opening jingle had already started:

> *"Cream of Wheat is so good to eat*
> *And we have it everyday.*
> *We sing this song, and it will make us strong*
> *And it makes us shout, Hooray!*
> *It's good for growing babies*
> *And grownups, too, to eat.*
> *For all the family's breakfast,*
> *You can't beat Cream of Wheat."*

"Today's story is *Rumplestiltskin*."

This was our Saturday ritual. Even eating the cake was a ritual. We separated each creamy layer, saving the slice with the crunchy frosting on top for last, and savored each tiny bite, making it last through the entire show.

As the show was ending, Mom walked by my room on her way out the front door, "Sollinue, do me a favor. Get the sewing needles pinned to the black paper, from my sewing things, and give them to Mrs. Weinmann."

"Okay."

"Thank you, darlink."

Everyone on our block was short compared to the Weinmann's, who towered over us all with a regal bearing – tall, thin, and blond. By the time I got the needles up to the fifth floor, Apt. 5A, Millie was already there with Veronica. I walked into the open door and saw them standing next to Mrs. Wienmann, who was ironing the vestments for the priests to wear in church.

Mrs. Weinmann, forgetting Millie was right there next to her, was talking to Veronica as she ironed, "You shouldn't feel bad about that woman, she's just a Jew – pushy, loud, and cheap."

Veronica looked over to Millie and back to her Mother, "Maaa-a-aa."

Mrs. Weinmann, embarrassed, looked at Millie, "Millie… I'm sorry, I didn't mean you. You and your mother are different from them. Do you understand?"

Millie hid her heart and lied to Mrs. Weinmann, "It's okay, Mrs. Weinmann, I understand."

My sudden entrance into the living room changed the whole uncomfortable situation, "Here's the needles you wanted, Mrs. Weinmann."

"Solly could you wait? It will only take me a few minutes to mend this garment, and then you can take the needles back to your Mother. Could you do that for me?"

"Sure, Mrs. Weinmann."

"And don't forget to thank your Mother for me. You're a good boy, Solly."

While waiting, I strolled over to the front windows. From this height, our street looked different. Everything seemed to move at a different pace. It filled me with a new way of seeing things. The people below looked like little dolls walking past toy buildings and little toy cars.

Sitting across the street on Junior's stoop, my mom was talking to Melvin's mom, Yetta Melnick, in front of the Chinese Laundry. Walking up the block toward them was my mom's old friend, Devorah. Devorah was carrying two large bundles filled with clean laundry. She stopped in front of my mom and said something to her.

Mom screamed out, "You just better shut your goddamn mouth!"

Devorah hollered back, "I know a lot about you, fooling around with other men. And if you don't want me to tell your husband…"

"I'm warning you. You better keep your mouth shut."

"Why should I?"

With that, my mom got up, grabbed a bag of laundry from Devorah and hit her hard over the head several times, knocking her to the ground. The laundry spilled all over the sidewalk.

"Are you crazy? Lookit what you've done to my clean clothes?"

Devorah got halfway up on her knees, "You bastard, I'm going to tell anyway."

Mom picked up the second laundry bag and whacked her to the floor again, but harder than before, knocking Devorah senseless. Her legs wobbled from the blow. She picked up her laundry and stuffed it back into her bags as fast as she could, while my mom stood over her shouting, "Try to blackmail me will ya? Don't you ever come on this block again! And if I ever hear dat you said anything – *anything* about me – I'll come after you! You hear me?"

Mrs. Weinman walked over to the window, "What's happening out there?"

I stood there, mouth open, not believing what I just saw. "My mom had a fight with a woman who was screaming at her.

"Who won?"

"My mother did."

"Good for Molly. If I know your mother, that woman probably deserved it."

It was strange to hear that coming from a woman who was so pious, she would never even raise her voice against anyone.

Millie, Veronica, and I went downstairs to our apartment. They went to Millie's room with a booklet of lyrics of the popular songs of the month. I could hear them singing from the kitchen where I was helping my mom roll up a skein of loose yarn into a tight ball.

The yarn was wrapped with a band of paper with the color, length, and name printed on it. Mom tore off the wrapper, and like always, I put my hands into the center of the loops of yarn, pulling them apart and holding them taut, as Mom wound the yarn into a ball. I swung my hands from side to side like rowing a kayak, flipping each hand under the yarn, feeling it in rhythmic beats.

My mom enjoyed my help and giggled under her breath, which tickled me. My eyes found their way to her hands that were spotted with dark dye stains from her furrier job. It took her days of washing constantly with gritty Lava paste to get rid of them.

Sometimes she came home from her job with tacking nails through her feet, or sewing machine needles through her fingers. One time she sliced deep into a couple of her fingers in a cutting machine. She never complained, just continued as she always did, cooking, washing our clothes and cleaning the apartment.

From the hall, a deep voice grumbled into Millie's room, "Stop that damn singing!"

"Why can't we sing?" Millie shouted back, "It's my room."

Harold looked at Veronica and very politely said, "I'm sorry, but I think you'd better leave."

"No, Veronica's staying!"

Veronica noticed that Harold was standing there in his boxer shorts and said, "I'm sorry, Millie, but I think I'd better go." And she left.

"How dare you chase my friends away!"

"Shut your mouth, or I'll shut it for you."

While Harold was giving it to Millie, I felt safe and glad it wasn't me. Millie ran into the hall with Harold right behind her, "You little Jew bitch, get back here."

Harold grabbed Millie by the arm and slapped her across her face. Millie reached out and took the phone receiver in the hall and hit Harold over the head.

Harold stepped back, "You've got guts for a little Jew. You're the only Jew who ever stood up to me."

The only Jews I ever saw him bully were women and children. Harold saw me standing by the kitchen watching the whole scene.

"What the hell are you looking at?"

He picked me up and threw me across the room. Luckily, I landed on Millie's bed.

He was now directing all his pent-up frustrated anger onto me. I was an easier target than Millie. The bastard stood over me menacingly and threatened to punch me with his thick, beefy hand. Pushing his face into mine, he made quick, grunting sounds like a lion and connected his sentences in a running wall of sound.

As he was talking, I remembered that just a moment ago, Harold had told Millie he respected her for her bravery and then left her alone. Why couldn't that work for me? So I tried to kick him away with my legs, but it was like trying to push at a brick wall. It only made him angrier. This bravery thing wasn't working for me. I slid off the bed onto the floor and escaped between his legs. I ran down the hall and out of our apartment.

Harold was right behind me screaming, "You fucking little Jew! All you Jews are going to Hell. You fucking little Jew! You fuckin' Jew bastards!"

Millie was alone now and needed to cry, but her tears wouldn't come. The pressure built up in her head. It felt like her ears would burst and the pain became unbearable. She had to release the pressure in her head, so she banged it against the wall until the tears rolled down her cheeks.

I ran out onto the street and mingled with my friends. I played handball for a while until I heard, "Coookie!" Sergie's mother was calling him in her sharp Spanish accent. "Come on up! Lunch is ready!"

At one time I used to be invited up to lunch with Sergie, but after my accident, everything changed. All that affection was transferred to Junior. I was never invited to lunch again or included in those great trips to the parks in Yonkers or Radio City Music Hall.

I didn't understand it until I was in my teens and our lawsuit against the Shaffer Beer Company for running over my foot finally came to trial. When we went into the courtroom, I was puzzled to find Sergie and his mother sitting there. My mom found out from our lawyers that Shaffer had paid them to be witnesses for their company's claim. They lied in court about what happened that day and said it was all my fault. We lost the lawsuit because of that. I finally knew the answer to the mystery of why Sergie's mom had changed toward me. I think maybe she was too ashamed to face my mom and me.

I walked in the front door, and Harold was there to greet me. He blocked the door to my room and said, "You thought I forgot, didn't you?" I didn't know what he was talking about.

"What did I do?"

He cornered me and chased me into the kitchen, "You little shit, don't ever try to push me again."

With that warning, he lifted me and threw me with such force against the kitchen cabinets, a heavy glass jar fell from the top shelf and broke on my head. The blow was so hard my mind refused to recognize the magnitude of the pain and it went straight down to my stomach.

Harold stood there but didn't come in for the kill. He seemed to be satisfied that what he had done was enough.

My mom came running in, "Vhat are you doing in here?"

She measured the situation and realized what had happened, "You monster!" She made a spitting sound three times, "You should only drop dead!" Harold left the kitchen to mope in his room.

Mom felt my head, "Oy gutenue, look vhat he did to you! Oy, my poor Sollinue, you've got a big lump on your head." She took a big fat knife from the kitchen drawer and soaked it in cold water. "Don't move, my totala." She pressed the flat of the knife's blade on the lump, and I grimaced from the pulsating pain. "Don't move, my Sollinue, dis'll take down the bump.

It seemed that Harold was in my life to give me pain, and my mother was there to take the pain away.

"You feel better, darlink?"

"A-hum."

"Okay den, how vould you like to go to the White Castle for lunch? You'd like that, bubbala?" I couldn't think of anything better.

Spotty and my baby brother stayed with Harold, as Millie and I raced each other down the stairs and hopped onto the running board of my Mom's 1937 Dodge with bulging headlights staring out from its front fenders.

The White Castle was on Bruckner Boulevard, near Croes Avenue where I was born. A waitress, wearing a little, white, army sidecap nestled in her pompadours, came to our car for our order. That was part of the thrill of eating at White Castle. You could actually stay in your car and someone would bring you your tiny, square hamburgers on a tray – right to your car.

The uniformed waitress hooked the tray onto my mom's open window. Each burger came in a cardboard box shaped like a little castle, served on real dishes. We loved those little burgers and fries, and the delicious aroma of my mom's coffee drove me crazy. Mom would sometimes let Millie and me sip some of it from the thick ceramic cup. It tasted as good as it smelled, like creamy roasted chocolate.

When we were finished, Mom blew the car horn for the waitress to pick up the tray and got angry when no one showed up.

"Ah, da hell wit dem…" and drove away with the tray of dishes, adding to her collection of White Castle crockery at home.

When we got back, she parked the car in front of our building, and instead of going right home, started a conversation with Mrs. Jackson, the super for Sergie's building next door. Mrs. Jackson was thin, but a strong woman who could lift two full garbage cans by their handles with one hand and wouldn't take shit from anyone. The only time I saw her socialize was with my mom. I stood there listening to them talk.

"Yeah, I was keeping my carriage in the basement. I thought it would be safe dere."

Mrs. Jackson, being sympathetic, "Yes, nothing is safe anymore. Do you know who stole it?"

"I think it was a couple of niggers."

The look in Mrs. Jackson's eyes froze us to the spot and all surrounding sounds stopped. No one moved. I felt like the building had crashed down behind us.

My mother's voice broke the silence, "Vhat's wrong?"

Mrs. Jackson didn't answer and turned away.

My mom suddenly realized what she had said, "Oh my Got! I didn't mean dat. I only meant dose no good thieves. Not you! Vhere are you going? Please!"

It was no use. It would be a long time before Mrs. Jackson would speak to my mother again. Either at home or outside, I had never heard my mom say a bigoted remark about anyone. In fact, it always made her mad when she heard it from someone else. Mom always defended her friends against those bigoted people.

At that moment I wished I could get into my mom's head so I could understand what was going on in there. Why would she use that word? Could it be from living with Harold for all these years and constantly hearing him use the nigger word? Could it have eventually rubbed off on her? How else could she do that? I felt ashamed of her, and I took off into the street to be with my friends.

We started to choose up sides for a game of handball:

"Eeny, meeny, miny, mo – Catch a nigger by the toe,
If he hollers let him go. Eeny, meeny, miny, mo
– Out goes Y-O-U."

It flowed from my mouth like the most natural thing to say. I never even gave it a second thought.

I'M NOT GONNA DIE

JUNIOR CAME OUT of his house wearing a suit and tie and a pair of super-polished shoes. His black hair was combed in even, neat strokes, looking like the grooves on a 78 record. He was going to the funeral parlor to see his dead uncle and cousins and pleaded for us to go with him. We followed him in our street clothes, T-shirts half-tucked into hand-me-down pants, hanging off our bony frames. We took a short cut up 163rd Street to Prospect Avenue.

The twilight streets were in the same mood as Junior, gloomy. The absence of our voices made the street sounds stand out. I was sort of scared to see dead bodies of someone I knew. I peeked into the coffins. Rudy and Carmen looked like they were waiting to come out to play with us. But they weren't breathing. And then I knew they were never going anywhere anymore. Like the dead cat, they really were dead. It didn't matter if there was a heaven or not, they were gone. They no longer existed in my world.

Some old man standing next to me said to me, "You see, you can die, too."

I answered, "I'm not gonna die."

"How old are your friends over there in the coffins? They're young aren't they? I'd say about as old as you. Aren't they dead?"

Who was this fucking guy? Why was he telling me this stuff? He was scaring the shit out of me. My friends and I huddled together for safety from invisible ghosts.

It was dark outside when we left the funeral parlor. The bright lights and sounds of a carnival had magically appeared at the corner of Prospect and Westchester Avenues, and filled what was once an empty lot. The rides were so close they were almost bumping into each other.

We breathed in the strong carnival smells: sugar cotton candy, hot dogs, and frozen custard made with real cream. The colored lights reflected off piles of sawdust that had been spread over the hard dirt and rocks, making them soft and spongy under foot. Not having a penny between us, we satisfied ourselves by enjoying everyone else's joy, by imagining ourselves on the rides we watched. I felt the thrill of the swirls and turns and the screams from the rumbling rides, rushing at me and roaring past me, into the distance and back again.

Cheap Melvin was the only one who could afford a frankfurter. He ate it slowly and spitefully in our faces, making it last a long time. We just ignored the little bastard.

Going home, we crossed Southern Boulevard, which was in full Saturday night swing. The Boulevard was the hub of our neighborhood. The blinking lights from the three movie marquees, the Boulevard, the Spooner, and the Star, were filled with their own self-importance. The store lights flickered in amongst the bobbing heads of the crowd strolling up and down Southern Boulevard.

After supper Harold caught me on my way out, "Hey, Jew Boy, I want to talk to you."

Oh shit, I thought I'd be able to finish the day without seeing him again.

"Later tonight I want you to pick up the Sunday newspapers for me."

"What newspapers?"

"What newspapers? What a fuckin' imbecile... How old are you? The papers I always get, you little shit."

I couldn't go out without knowing which ones he wanted, and I was too afraid to ask.

Harold waited for a reaction from me, "You don't know, do you? You're an idiot." He gave out with a heavy breath of frustration with hate and power over me in his eyes.

"Well, I'm waiting. Do you know or don't you?"

Why the fuck doesn't he just tell me what paper he wants? I had to stop this, or he'd go on and on forever, but I couldn't think with his face in mine.

"Okay, asshole, I've had enough of you. Get me *The Daily News*, *The Herald Tribune*, and *The World Telegram & Sun*."

Another paper popped into my head and thinking I was doing a good thing, I added, "And *The Journal American*?"

"You stupid little cocksucker, did I say *The Journal American*? If I wanted *The Journal American*, I'd say *The Journal American*. My God, you're so fucking stupid. Here's the money for the newspapers. Now get the fuck out of my sight, damn it. You make me sick."

After breaking the street light for more privacy, the guys and I spent most of that night sitting on Junior's stoop, playing our game of made-up stories. By the time we got back to Southern Boulevard, things were more somber. The marquee lights were out and stores were closing for the night. Getting the Sunday newspapers was the best part of the weekend. All the tense energy was gone, and everyone moved slower and easier.

When we got there, the papers were neatly tied and piled up in front of the Boulevard Theatre. They weren't ready to be sold yet, because the sections were still in the process of being put together.

We wasted some time walking the Boulevard with the few stragglers left on the street.

The screamer was there, a crazy lady with wiry hair hanging loose down to her mid-back. She was wearing her bathrobe and furry slippers, looking like an old raggedy doll that had been lying around in a basement for years – torn, dirty, and smelling of mildew. If she caught you looking at her, she would block your way, stare into your eyes, and give out with a loud, unearthly screech. All you had to do was ignore her, and she'd leave you alone.

The B & J Music Shop was still open and we leaned against a parked car listening to the top hits being piped out onto the street.

Jo Stafford was singing, *Autumn In New York*. Then came Vaugn Monroe's *I Wish I Didn't Love You So*, followed by Dick Haymes singing, *How Are Things In Glocca Morra*.

I watched the lights of Woolworth, Tom McAn Shoes, and Vims flicker out, but the music from B & J continued, keeping the Boulevard from falling asleep. When the newspapers were ready, I picked up *The Daily News, The Herald Tribune* and *The World Telegram & Sun*.

The next day, my friends and I got caught up in each other's projects. From the Triangle Market's garbage, we picked up a couple of nice orange crates and built our own linoleum guns. There was no shortage of ammunition for our guns. In our working class neighborhood, there was a constant flow of old linoleum being thrown away in the garbage – our supply dump.

It made a formidable weapon. Even if we aimed carefully at something, we never knew where the hell the linoleum pieces would end up. They flew wherever they wanted to go. When we got tired of it, the guys and I decided to stroll through the Boulevard and ended up at the Triangle. We had nothing planned until we found more empty crates, piled on top of each other in front of a closed vegetable stand – Scooters!

We picked out the best and cleanest crates and carried them home. With the tools and materials left over from our linoleum guns, we had a great start in building our scooters. We must have watched someone make one once, because we seemed to know what we were doing. But sometimes we had to improvise.

I pulled my skate apart, got rid of the side clamps, broke off the front wheels and re-attached it with a bent nail so the front wheels could swivel. This gave it flexibility and allowed the scooter to turn on a dime.

While I was hammering a skate to the board, I happened to look up to my building and caught Harold staring out of his window. I'd never seen him do this before. What was he thinking behind those angry eyes?

I went back to my scooter, and nailed an empty can on the front to look like a headlight, and attached whatever colorful junk I could find from our supply dump. We all stood back and admired our scooters. We pretended they were police motorcycles hiding behind parked cars, darting out to chase speeders and crooks, and ended up careening into each other.

My fun was cut short when my tic flared up. Once it started, there was no way of stopping it. I became the fucking freak that I was.

"Hey Solly! Where ya goin?"

"Just remembered something I have to do..."

I stashed my scooter in the basement and ran upstairs. If my friends ever found out about my tic, they would have destroyed me. My life on the street would have ended.

Harold stood in the hall by my room, "Was that my hammer you were using?"

"Huh?"

"Don't you "Huh" me, you fucking Jewish retard." His voice got lost in the noise I created in my head.

Harold's foot always found the end of my spine. I doubled up onto the floor. Half-heartedly, he kicked at me again, but he didn't seem to be enjoying himself. He must have been in a bad mood. Silently, he turned and walked away... and took my tic with him.

It wasn't the pain that hurt me so much. It was Harold making me feel I was nothing. When the world was closing in, I wanted to be with my closest friend, my radio. I turned it on, but my mind wandered from the stories into my own thoughts. I was listening, but not really hearing:

"And now, Mr. Keen, the old investigator, tracer of lost persons."

Spotty tugged at the cuffs of my pants, pulling me to the front door. She circled around my legs, yelping, trying to tell me that if she didn't go out soon, she'd explode.

There were times when people who lived on my block, would fill the street with their voices. Then there were other days when there were no sounds at all, only the smells of the damp gutters. I plowed through the dense, hot air with Spotty, bored with nothing to do and no one to do it with. As I was taking her upstairs, I thought of the Metropolitan Museum of Art, and I remembered when Mrs. Bare-ass took us there on a field trip. It was only a nickel for the subway and the Museum was free.

I got off of the Lexington Express, walked across the Avenues where the rich people lived. I tried to blend in by walking as close to the buildings as possible. I could feel their eyes on me saying, Who does he think he is? Arrest that boy and send him back to where he belongs.

When I got to Fifth Avenue, I was confronted by a huge row of stairs leading up to the entrance of a massive palace as big as my entire block. I was the only one on the steps, a crawling little spec, on the alert, and ready for anything.

The Museum was almost empty, and I got lost trying to find the armor room where Mrs. Bare-ass had taken us. I wanted to see the armor that King Arthur's Knights of the Roundtable wore, but I was too afraid and felt too stupid to ask for directions. I ended up taking a long stairway to the next floor where I had never been before.

Listening to my footsteps following me in dull echoes through the spacious rooms, I discovered huge, bigger-than-life paintings towering over me, with colors that attacked my senses. The paintings made me feel insignificant and followed me with their eyes, reaching out, and pulling me into their lives. What did they want from me? Even though they frightened me, I couldn't stop looking at them. I couldn't wait to see what was in the next room. But there was too much to see and I knew I'd have to come back again.

The very next day everyone was back on the block. Even the

never-seen Plant Lady briefly made an appearance, and Mrs. Katz watched the whole show from her orchestra seat, her ground floor window.

Millie was the only one conspicuously missing. She had slept over at Veronica's and spent her morning eating breakfast in bed. Mrs. Weinmann treated Veronica like a princess and almost everyday gave her breakfast in bed. Mr. Weinmann was very rarely at home. He was like a tall, thin shadow, and always the gentleman, tipped his fedora to everyone he met.

Terry, one of the neighborhood kids, was outside by Junior's building, sitting in my Mother's chair. My mom had left her chair to buy a pack of cigarettes at Jack's.

"What are you doin' in my mom's chair?"

"Why don't you mind your own business?"

"That's my mother's chair."

"Go fuck yourself."

Terry was a real asshole. She had a handful of darts, and I grabbed them from her.

"Give me back my darts!"

"You want 'em then come and get 'em."

"Solly, I'm warning you."

"Yeah? Well, then, get the fuck out of my mom's chair or I'll throw 'em at you."

"Yeah, you and who else? Give me a break."

"Don't piss me off."

"I'm shittin' in my pants. Hey Solly, why don't you just kiss my ass?"

I didn't know what to do, until she said, "Go ahead, go ahead... I dare you to."

The dart flew out of my hand and stuck deep into her leg.

"You little prick!"

Junior, Sergie, and Bobby thought it was pretty funny.

"Whataya, a bunch of fuckin' assholes!" Terry jumped from the chair, and chased us for a block with the dart flapping up and down in her leg and blood trickling in a thin stream down to her ankle.

Leaving tough Terry behind us, we walked over the bridge on Westchester Avenue and noticed the ground under the bridge was moving – rats, black ditches filled with rats. We found gravel and rocks by the railing and threw them at the rats. Some screeched and ran away, but the others didn't move. They looked right at us with their threatening eyes, waiting for us.

On our way down to the creek, we walked along the stony riverbank, where clusters of piss clams jutted out from a small dirt mound, looking like rows of cobblestone steps. I pulled a few out of the clam bed and squeezed them... and they did it! They pissed all over the place.

In a field of punks, I caught myself a toad. I found some string, tied it to the toad's back leg, and threw it into the water. I was fascinated with the graceful ease of the toad as he swam across the river. Just as he reached dry land, I pulled him back into deeper water. I didn't realize what I was doing until the poor toad sank and never came up again, drowned from exhaustion. Was I becoming Harold? No! I could never be like him... I refuse to let that happen to me.

Sergie brought a toad home with us and tied it to the trolley tracks. How cool this was going to be. We're going to have a real-life cliffhanger ending. The trolley bells clanged louder as the trolley got closer and closer to the toad. But there was no way I could save it and our hero never escaped like in the movies. It ended up not being as cool as I thought. We left the gruesome scene and quietly walked back to our block.

Later that night, out came the boxes of sparklers that we bought from Sonia's father's Penny Toy Store. When we lit the tips of the sparklers, an intense glow of light sizzled from the thin wire stick, showering sparks as we swung them through the air like fiery butterflies. The fluttering light lit up our faces peeking through the sparks.

The night wasn't done yet. We were on the search for cardboard boxes of all different sizes. Sergie and I started piling one box on top of the other in the middle of the street, looking like the skyscrapers downtown. We even cut out windows and doors. Then we crunched up newspapers and stuffed them into the boxes. Our voices were building with excitement, knowing what was coming next. Kids from Hoe and Bryant Avenues, Faille, and Longfellow Streets, joined in. They were always drawn to our block. If you wanted action, our block was the place to be.

Sergie, Junior, and I had the fun task of lighting the fire. We had to be tough and look cool, so we struck our matches on the back of our dungarees, and we ran around the boxes lighting the edges of the newspapers. In a trance, I watched the flames flow from one box to the other.

Then some invisible force seemed to suck the fire back inside the boxes. Suddenly, with an angry roar, the fire erupted from every window and door. I jumped back gasping from the sudden surge of flames. And in one final threating burst, they lit up the whole block. The cardboard buildings turned black from the crackling fire, crumbled down into the street into smoldering ashes. It was a spectacular end to my night.

I rushed up the steps of my building and bumped into an immovable wall. Standing in the dark shadows on the landing outside my apartment was Harold, looking down at me.

"You! I should have known it was you. I could smell a Jew even if I was blindfolded. Are you trying to be funny, or are you just plain stupid?"

I didn't know what he was talking about... and didn't answer. His anger grew, "You fucking little prick!"

For no reason at all, he kicked me in the head. I lost all strength and control of my arms and legs and crumbled up into a heap at the bottom of the stairs, not knowing where I was. Again, the burning white specs crackled in my head, but all the pain was throbbing in my stomach, twisting my insides. My stomach desperately wanted to throw off the pain.

Harold looked at me, "You deserve what you get." He turned, held onto the walls of the hall, and guided himself into our apartment.

One o'clock in the morning, red and white lights blinked into our windows, reflecting off the walls like a Christmas tree. A loud booming voice shouted from the street with authority: "This is an emergency. Everybody, please leave your apartments. We have everything under control, so please move out quietly and slowly. Once again, please exit slowly out of your building. Thank you for your cooperation."

Two brilliant red fire engines were on the street, towering over us with lights blinking. Firemen were running back and fourth, acting busy and important. Our block had never seen this much activity at one o'clock in the morning. Not only were the people from my building out on the street, but people I'd never seen before were milling about, wearing whatever was at hand, curious to know what was happening. My friends and I were excited. It was more like a party to us.

We didn't see any actual fire, but we did see some smoke and hear serious voices from the fourth floor window by the alleyway.

"Careful..."

"Okay."

"All together now."

"Watch it! Watch it!"

The next thing we heard from the alley was a heavy thump. It wasn't a real fire after all, just a smoking mattress from Sheldon and Selma Trotsky's apartment.

Harold wasn't in the crowd. For all I knew, he was still in the apartment, but I wasn't going to tell anyone. For all I cared he could have burned down with the fucking building.

BETRAYAL

AFTER SCHOOL, SPOTTY and I sat on Millie's windowsill by the fire escape, watching our territory. I saw Millie go into Jack's Candy Store to read joke books. Millie babysat for Jack and Sally, and they had a deal: they paid her by letting her read all the joke books she wanted, whenever she wanted.

Across the street in the house next door to Junior's lived a young couple who never left their house. We all knew they held poker games almost every night lasting till early in the morning. I saw a couple of cops knocking at their door. These same cops showed up at their door at the same time every week and were handed an envelope. Which I figured was the pay off.

From the side of my eye, a woman walking on Westchester Avenue caught my attention. She moved with a cool, smooth swagger, her body saying she knew who she was – tough, strong and very sexy. It was my Mom! I could recognize her walk anywhere. She was coming home unexpectedly early from work.

Barely touching the steps, I flew through the building and out onto the street, chasing after her. I followed her into the yarn shop on Westchester Avenue, which was snuggled between the toy store and Dr. Posner's shoes. It was as narrow and long as a subway car and filled with women learning knitting techniques.

Mom went there, because she didn't know how to read and needed someone to interpret the knitting instructions. She was very clever in the different ways she used to avoid being discovered. Wherever she went, she would play her game so no one would know she couldn't read. One time when I was with her at the Unemployment, she asked a perfect stranger to help her fill out the forms. "Darlink, could you please help me. I forgot my glasses, and I can't see a thing without them." She always asked strangers to help her, and they always did.

The women in the yarn store came here from Europe, mostly from Eastern countries. It was a place to socialize and gossip. The owner was heavy set, talked with a Yiddish accent, and treated everyone like a close friend.

On the glass counter sat a small windmill and, when I came in, my Mom was putting an open skein of yarn onto the blades, rotating it as she rolled the wool into a ball.

"Sollinue! Vhat are you doing here?"

Mom never said "I love you", she showed her affection with all her bubbalas, shaynalas, totalas and Sollinues.

"Mom, can I have two cents?"

"Two cents? Hmmm, I think I can give you two cents. Let me look."

She searched through her pocketbook's endless compartments, "Ah! Here, I found dem!"

The owner asked, "Molly, how old is your boy?"

"Eleven."

"Eleven? Oy vay, he looks like a baby."

"I know. I'm afraid he's going to be a midget like his father."

"Is he going to Hebrew School to get ready for his Bar Mitzvah?"

"Nah. He's too stupid to do regular school work, so vhy waste my money?"

Didn't Mom realize I was standing right there next to her, listening to her telling these strangers how stupid I was? Sergie and I were the same size and growing was never on my mind, until now – until Mom said I would be a midget. She implanted it in my brain, and it haunted me for many years.

No matter how much Mom loved Millie and me, she had this attitude about us because we were Manny's children. She believed he was a stupid mockey and always referred to him as, "That Schlemiel." She thought him less than a man, because he was shorter than her. She colored us with the disrespect she had for him.

It was Halloween again, and the two cents was for my costume. With it I bought a piece of cork at Mr. Siegel's Hardware, rubbed the ashes of the burnt cork on my face, and with my brother's old baggy clothes...Abracadabra! I was a bum. You'd think that, with all those buildings in our neighborhood, and all those apartments in each building, it would be a cinch to clean up with candy and money, but I got shit. Maybe a penny or two... that was it.

Harold had a stash of candy, drawers filled with Hershey bars and bags of chocolate Kisses. He wasn't home, so I took a chance and helped myself to just a few of his treasured treats so he wouldn't notice the difference. I only took five Kisses, and broke off a couple of sections from an already opened, giant Hershey bar and hid them in my room.

It was getting late and the streets were getting rough. The older kids were swinging socks filled with crushed chalk and maybe something heavier. When they whacked you with it, you felt like you were being hit with a blackjack. My friends and I tried to keep our distance, but a gang of guys noticed us and chased us around the corner to Westchester Avenue.

We hid in the shadows of a storefront synagogue's vestibule. A Hassidic Jew must have heard the commotion and opened the door for us. We rushed in, seconds before we were discovered by the tough guys chasing us. The man in the black coat and hat asked us if we would put out the candles all around the room. He said he would pay the four of us thirty-five cents – a little difficult to split four ways. It was their Sabbath, and for some reason, they weren't allowed to put out candles or touch money. So the coins had been left on a shelf, waiting for us, as if they knew we were going to be there.

By the time we finished and got outside, the older guys had formed into gangs. They were out of control and went on the warpath, one street against the other. It was getting serious out there. Sergie,

Junior, Johnny, and I split up. I ran through the streets, feeling there was someone breathing down my neck. Without looking behind me, I rushed upstairs into my room and closed the door.

The older I got, the faster and smarter I became in avoiding Harold. I heard him growling from his room, "Someone took my chocolate Kisses! I had 34 Kisses and now there's only 29 of them!"

The son of a bitch actually kept an account of his precious candy. It's funny how I could steal anything from his closet, and he'd never notice, but if I touched just one of his damn chocolate Kisses, he knew.

"I know who took them! Where is the little prick? There you are. You took my Kisses, didn't you! Didn't you!"

With my most innocent face I said, "No, I didn't take them. I swear it, I didn't take anything!"

Harold pulled me by my hair and dragged me to his room. He stuck my face into the open drawer with his Hershey bars and Kisses, "You ate my chocolate, didn't you!"

"No! Please, I didn't do it!"

He almost pulled all the hair out of my head and threw me into the living room, onto the linoleum floor.

"You moron!" He hit me on my head with his knuckles, "Nothing! There's nothing there!"

Enough! I can't take much more of this. My gut reaction was to cry, but I stopped crying a long time ago.

Mom appeared by my side, "Harold! Leave the boy alone! You're hurting him!"

"He's too stupid to feel it."

"Just leave him alone, I'm begging you."

"Okay, but keep your little brat away from me." Harold looked down at me, "And you! Get the fuck out of my sight, you lying Jew bastard. And if I ever find anything else is missing, I'll kill you!"

Finally I was able to get to my room. Spotty came in to check up on me and get some love. I paid her back by pulling her tail until she squealed from the pain. "I'm sorry, Spotty, I didn't mean to hurt you."

But I did... and then I pushed her into my closet. She was shaking with fear as I closed the closet door. How could I hurt her when I loved her so?

She licked my face for letting her out. I cried with dry tears, not for her, but for myself. What kind of beast am I for doing these things to somebody I love? I reached out to pet her, and she growled at me. I didn't understand. Spotty left my room and left me feeling angry and betrayed by the only living thing that loved me and didn't judge me. But maybe, maybe she'll love me another day. In the middle of the night, Harold went to the bathroom. I knew it was him because he serenaded me with his signature farts.

The next day we had to cope with another eruption from Harold, but this time he sent Mom to the hospital. We didn't know what happened to her. When she got home she was unsteady on her legs, but there wasn't a mark on her, so Millie and I ignored it as if nothing had happened. It was just another day living with Harold. We thought that the way we lived was normal, and that everyone lived like this. Without skipping a beat, the first thing Mom did was cook supper. And the very next day she went to work, and Millie and I went to school.

Sergie warned me that we were in for a spelling test. For some unknown reason, a burning energy to do well in the test took control of me. I searched for all my past spelling tests that I had saved from Bare-ass' classes. I worked for hours, and then days, without listening to my radio shows. I could hear my friends playing outside, but I refused to pay attention to their voices. I worked harder than I ever had before. I broke my ass for that test, and I was determined to pass it.

The day after the test Mrs. Bare-ass made me stay after school. I knew something was wrong when she didn't give me back my test paper with the rest of the kids.

"Mr. Rothman, I've got your test right here, but before I give you your grade, do you have anything to say to me? No? Do you know what your test results were? Of course you do, because you cheated."

She shoved the test paper into my face. Holy shit! I got 100! I got 100! I spelled every word right.

"Mr. Rothman, you've failed every spelling test all year long. Tell me how, all of a sudden, you got a perfect paper? I'm not a fool, you cheated!"

With a red pencil, she pressed down hard on the test paper, as if she was angry at it. She wrote FAIL across my 100% grade with such force, her pencil broke in half in her hand.

"If you ever cheat again, I'll have to call your mother to school and take both of you to the Vice Principle's office. And you won't graduate with your classmates... do you understand?"

"But Mrs. Baras, I didn't cheat. I swear to you, I didn't cheat."

"That's it. Not only did you cheat, but you're also a liar. There's nothing I hate more than a liar, and I've decided not to promote you. I'll make sure you're going to be in my class again."

I thought I would finally be rid of her and have a fresh start in Junior High. Why me? There were other students she disliked, why didn't she pick on them? When my friends find out I've been left back, they'll treat me like shit.

I told my Mom what happened, and she believed me. She had to take off from her job, which we couldn't afford, but she did and went to my school to see the Vice Principle, Mrs. Bloom. Mrs. Bare-ass was also there.

Mom was angry, "My Solly worked hard every day for a week for the test. He wouldn't stop till he got it right." Mom lied for me. She didn't know what the hell I was doing that week.

She stood up and confronted Mrs. Bare-ass, "Did you see him cheat? If you did, how did he cheat?"

Mrs. Bare-ass smirked at my Mom, "Your boy is a lower than average student. He has failed every one of his spelling tests. He can hardly read."

"So you don't know if he cheated, do you? You're guessing. And dis is how you teach? Vhat kind of school is dis?"

Mrs. Bloom was sympathetic, "I see here on your son's records that he is an excellent artist. I also see here that Solomon has created murals for Mrs. Baras' class. I believe he deserves credit for his effort."

"And vhat does dat mean?"

"It means he earned enough credit to give him a passing grade, and he will be promoted." She looked at Mrs. Baras pointedly, "I'm sure Mrs. Baras will agree with me."

"Darlink, you're a good person. Tank you so much."

Mom looked at her watch, turned around, and rushed out of the office to get back to work, leaving Mrs. Bare-ass standing there with her mouth open, seething. She just couldn't believe I did so well in the spelling test. And even if I did try again, it wouldn't make any difference, anyway. So I just stopped trying.

That night, I gave myself up to my radio.

"Ladies and gentlemen, *It Pays To Be Ignorant*." The theme song of the comedy show blasted from the radio:

> *"It Pays To Be Ignorant,*
> *To be dumb, to be dense,*
> *To be ignorant – just like me."*

"If you brush Spotty every day, maybe we can keep her. But you've got to brush her every day, otherwise your baby brother will put the fur in his mouth, and it will make him very sick."

Millie and I promised Mom and we kept our promise, which was unusual for us to do. Every day after school I sat on the basement steps and brushed away. Millie brushed her on the weekends, and we both felt secure in keeping Spotty.

Mrs. Levine had a habit of climbing up and down the fire escape, knocking on windows to collect rent from the tenants who tried to avoid her. I was home for lunch when I saw her on our fire escape. I thought she was making her rounds, but she was squeezing through Millie's window, holding a metal cage.

Spotty never liked Mrs. Levine, and Mrs. Levine never liked Spotty. When she saw Mrs. Levine, she ran under the kitchen table and barked at her. Our Spotty knew something was up. Levine reached for her legs and Spotty showed her teeth, growling and snapping at Levine's hands.

I screamed, "What are you doing? Leave her alone!"

Mom held me back and Mrs. Levine finally got Spotty into the cage. Mom stood there and let the old bastard take Spotty away. I could hear her whimpering all the way down the hall steps. It hurt too much to follow her downstairs. I stayed in the apartment and cried, hearing Spotty's mournful howls getting fainter. It hurt me more than Harold ever could.

Millie came home from school to an empty house. There was no Spotty to greet her. We had kept our promise and brushed her every day, but Mom betrayed us. She lied to us and took our Spotty away. Spotty, who was our anchor of saneness in this insane house.

"You've got to understand. The doctor told me it was very dangerous for your brother. When Ronnie crawls on the floor, when he puts the fur in his mouth, it could make him very, very sick."

She saw that her explanation didn't make any difference to us and added, "He could even die. You don't want your baby brother to die?"

Millie cried, "You lied to us! You knew all the time you were going to get rid of her. You lied!"

"But Millienue, you know I loved her, too."

"You liar! How could you get rid of her?"

Mom's betrayal was too cruel, and those were the last words either of us said to her for over a month. No matter how hard Mom tried, we didn't say a word to her.

It was after school when I walked into our empty apartment. It had been over a month with no Spotty to greet us. At the end of our long narrow hall was Millie's room. The afternoon sunlight blasted through her window, flooding the hall, and for a minute, everything blurred together. All I could see was the blinding light.

There was movement by Millie's doorway. A shapeless form raised itself, and outlined by the blinding light, grew into a huge unearthly hulk. It ran down the hall at me, pounding the floor with its heavy weight. The closer it got, the bigger it grew. I had nowhere to go. My back was up against the front door. I closed my eyes as the beast jumped up and pinned me against the door. A wet dripping tongue wiped across my entire face and could have swallowed me in one gulp. The beast took the form of a giant dog, a Great Dane larger than Millie and me put together.

Millie came in right behind me and saw the monstrosity, "Where did that thing come from?"

We looked at each other and said… "Mom."

Millie added, "Who else."

There was no way I was going to take care of this dog. I wanted my Spotty back. The dog was so strong, he dragged Millie along the street and when he decided to run, Millie flew in the air behind him.

Mom believed that a shorthaired dog would shed much less than a longhaired dog, like Spotty. But we didn't have the giant dog long enough to find out. The poor thing had a bad case of colitis, and Mom had the problem of cleaning up enormous amounts of shit sprayed over the walls and floors. It took her two seconds, and the dog was gone.

That Great Dane was Mom's way of trying to make up with us. It did break the ice, and we laughed our way into talking to her again. Still, she had betrayed our trust, and we *never* forgave her for the deceitful way she got rid of Spotty.

We were about to choose up sides for a game of stickball when we discovered we were one man short.

"We need another body." Sergie noticed that Melvin wasn't there and looked at me, "Has any one seen Melvin?"

"What the hell are you looking at me for?" Melvin was the one person I couldn't stand, and they wanted me to find him?

"He lives in your building, so I thought..."

"So he lives in my building, so what? Who died and left you a cripple? Go get him yourself."

"I can't. I'm buying the Spaldeen and getting the broom stick."

"Then get somebody else."

"What the fuck. Are we gonna play or fart around arguing?"

"Yeah, okay, I'll get him."

Yetta answered her door, "Solly, do you know where my little Arab is?"

"You mean he's not home?"

"No. Maybe you can find him for me, and tell him to stay close to the house."

Yetta left her door open, and I could hear her and Aaron giggling. I stuck my head into the apartment to see what they were giggling at. There was a stranger in the hall by the kitchen, a bald-headed man in a dark blue suit. From inside the kitchen, a woman's voice was resisting the bald-headed man. He was clawing at her and pulled her out into the hall.

It was Mrs. O'Conner, Tommy's mother. There was no need to say she was drunk, she was always drunk... just different degrees of drunk. Today she was half-drunk, fighting off the man's attacks. He lifted up her dress and put his hand between her legs, and started to undress her.

Mrs. O'Conner screamed, "No! Stop! Stop that! Enough!"

Aaron egged her on, "Go on, let him do it. If you do I'll give you an extra five bucks."

I couldn't think of anything more disgusting than watching someone fucking Mrs. O'Conner. Just the thought of it turned my stomach. I had to get the hell out of there.

Shit! Melvin was outside with the rest of the guys, and they were already choosing up sides without me.

"Why the fuck didn't you get someone to tell me Melvin was out here? And why did you start without me? You know you're all a bunch of fuckin' hard-ons."

Junior looked at me, "Solly."

"Yeah."

"Go fuck yourself."

There were two captains, supposedly the two best players, who were the ones to choose up the sides. Sergie and Junior always accepted that roll and no one questioned them. A broomstick flew through the air, and Sergie caught onto the middle of it. Then Junior and Sergie went up the stick, hand-over-hand, until no space was left. The one on top was the winner and got first choice of players.

The sewer by my building was home base. The fender on a parked car was first base, the other sewer by Hoe Avenue was second, and the fender of another car was third. Today I was playing the outfield by Hoe Avenue. I always made spectacular dives off the roofs of cars and into walls, but I could never hold onto the fucking ball. I couldn't figure out what I was doing wrong. My friends dubbed me banana fingers.

Back, back, back... the ball was almost in my hands. I jumped into the air, and it bounced out of my hand, and I bounced off the hood of a moving car. The driver chased me for a while, but got frustrated and gave up.

Melvin was up at bat when Paulie Weinmann, in his cool paratrooper uniform, watched us play. Melvin missed the ball, but hit Paulie right on the head, which slowed down the game. The very next batter was Junior. He swung and the stick flew from his hands, and we screamed to the people on the sidewalk, "Heads up!" The broomstick crashed through Mr. Jacobs' window. We saw a cop car turning around Faille Street onto our block, "Chickie, the cops." I grabbed the broomstick and tossed it under a parked car. We separated and blended into the background.

HIT ME, MOTHERFUCKER

ONE OF THE most respected kids in the neighborhood was Johnny Anderson, from around the corner on Faille Street. He was a tall, quiet guy who kept to himself. Jackson, on the other hand, was the leader of a gang, the Simpson Street Midgets, one of the biggest gangs around at that time, and picked a fight with everybody. He was constantly bragging about being Sugar Ray Robinson's cousin and was always looking for a fight.

Jackson challenged Johnny to a boxing match in front of Jack's candy store. A crowed gathered and encircled them, creating a human boxing ring. Sergie, Junior, and I had the best seats, on top of a parked car.

Jackson was shorter than Johnny, but walked up to him threateningly. He knew what he was doing. Fear was his first punch. He twisted his face in forced anger, trying to scare his opponent into submission. He stuck his chin out, pointing it at Johnny, and with his arms pulled back at his sides, he left himself wide open and defenseless, taunting, "Come on, motherfucker, hit me! Hit me!" So Johnny obliged him... and proceeded to kick the shit out of Jackson.

After the so-called fight, Jackson peeled himself up off the sidewalk and put his hand on Johnny's shoulder, announcing to the crowd through his bloody face, "If anyone ever touches Johnny, they'll have to answer to me and my gang." He put his arm around Johnny's shoulder and shook his hand, "You're my man." Johnny walked away with Jackson limping beside him.

After the fight, Sergie and I followed Jackson to P.S. 75's school-yard and through the perennial hole in the cyclone fence. A bunch of guys were playing softball, and Jackson started arguing with Ramirez. They were working their way into a fistfight.

You'd think Jackson would have learned his lesson from his fight with Johnny and would be using a different technique. Nope. He led with the same open stance, hands at his sides pushing his chin out, pleading to Ramirez, "Okay, motherfucker, go on, hit me. Go ahead, hit me, motherfucker!"

This time it worked. He scared Ramirez just long enough to knock him to the ground. With a dull thud, Jackson slammed his combat boot into Ramirez' head, leaving his footprint on his face. But it end-ed like all Jackson's fights did... he and Ramirez became great friends.

Walking along Longfellow Avenue, one of our short cuts to the Bronx Zoo, the brick buildings and concrete streets reflected the heat of the sun into my face.

Junior, Sergie, Melvin, and I found our secret entrance to the Zoo. A breeze blew through the trees, dropping the temperature to a bear-able level. At that time, peacocks roamed the zoo freely along the crisscrossing asphalt paths. We bumped into one and it fanned its tail of colorful eyes at us and screamed a piercing scream, like we were in a dense jungle. I expected Tarzan would be swinging through the trees around the next turn.

We passed by a few machines, where for a nickel, you could buy a handful of pellets and feed the animals. The elephants would take them right out of my hand with their trunks, feeling like Manny's stub-bly five-o'clock shadow. The llamas tickled the palm of my hand as they nibbled it with their soft muzzles.

On our way to the waterfalls, we came across the alligator pit near the reptile house. The pit was enclosed by a small wall and sur-rounded by an outside fence. It had trenches leading into each other that were sometimes filled with water and alligators. This morning they were empty, and Sergie and I went under the fence, climbed the wall, and jumped into the trenches.

There were doors along the trench walls, hatches that the zoo-keepers would open to release the alligators. My heart raced, know-ing that at any moment they could open the doors, and the alligators would rush into the trenches – and the guards wouldn't know we were in the pit.

Sergie and I were joking around out of nervousness, and then we heard a clicking sound and water trickling into the pit. That was too much for me. All you could see was a blur as Sergie and I narrowly escaped, in Chapter Two of *The Bronx Zoo Pit of Doom*.

On our way out of the Zoo, we crossed Westchester Avenue to the entrance of the Bronx Park, where you could rent rowboats for a dol-lar. A dollar was way out of our league, but we brought our bank with us – Melvin. He always had money, lots of money, and always swore he didn't have a dime. This time we shook him down and promised to pay him back – which we had no intention of doing.

Rowing up the Bronx River, we played pirates and had sword fights with sticks we found. We jumped ashore and pulled the boat behind us onto dry land in search of a place to hide our stolen treasure.

Junior whispered, "Hey guys! Come here. You've got to see this. Shhhh... keep it down."

Through the tangle of bushes, there was a clear spot in the shade of a tree. Sitting on a blanket, an older kid and his girlfriend were in a clinch. Every time he moved his hand up her skirt between her legs, she sighed. He unbuttoned her blouse and unfastened her bra. Her red nipples stood at attention and he put them into his mouth making sucking sounds. Then he got up onto his knees and started taking his pants off.

One of us stepped on a dry twig, and at the same time, a shaft of sunlight penetrated through the bushes lighting us up like a flood-light. The kid turned and saw us. By the time he got his pants back on, we were down the river. He ran along the shore screaming, "You little pricks!" and chased us down the riverbank until he couldn't go any further.

All day, our block had baked under a hot sun, melting the tar on the street. The guys and I cooled off on Junior's stoop, in the darkness of a moonless night, under a halo of light from the lamppost, rehashing what we saw in the park.

Sunday morning after an early mass, Johnny, Bobby, Sergie, and I were walking home from church, and we got so caught up in talking and kidding around that we found ourselves on Aldus Street. With nothing to do, we continued walking down to the Swing Park next to P.S. 75, then crossed Bruckner Boulevard over the railroad bridge to the creek.

The tall weeds were reaching up to touch the sun. They were crowded together in bunches and absorbed the street sounds. It was so quiet there I felt I was far away from The Bronx. In an open field at the edge of a ditch, we discovered some rusty sheets of corrugated metal and junk wood left over from the Quonset huts. Whatever we found we used to build walls for an improvised clubhouse. Without nails or hammer, we secured them with piles of rocks and, with nothing up our sleeves, Poof! We had a clubhouse.

We squatted on the ground inside and started our game of telling stories. We heard a creaking sound... and knew what that meant. We jumped clear of the clubhouse as it folded in on itself and came crashing down. A sharp, rusted metal corner swiped across Johnny's knee and cut it open. A fleshy, tube-like thing stuck out of his knee and, without thinking, I pushed it back into his knee with my finger.

Bobby had a handkerchief and used it as a bandage, wrapping it around Johnny's knee. Johnny was in shock. He didn't know what to do. Blood was gushing out. Sergie quickly took off his belt and put it around Johnny's thigh, just above the knee. I found a stick and made a tourniquet by twisting the belt to stop the bleeding.

"How are we going to get him home?" asked Bobby.

Sergie and I devised a human chair by crossing our arms and holding each other's wrists. The two of us shared his weight, and without too much trouble, carried Johnny all the way home.

We delivered him to his mother. She almost had a heart attack and blamed us for what happened to her Johnny. And, after we had worked together to save his life, she chased us away.

A group of Yentas circled their wagons with their chairs, and as we walked past, we overheard their gossip.

"Did you hear about Mrs. O'Connor?"

The rest of the Yentas were vultures salivating for some juicy news. "What about her?"

"Well... You know she's pregnant."

"Yes, yes, we know."

"She's going around trying to trade her unborn baby for a television set."

"Nooo! You're kidding me. She wouldn't do that."

"So help me God, it's the truth."

"Who told you that?"

"Everybody knows..."

No one ever knew if it was true, or if it was just coming from their ugly thoughts. My mom said that, most of the time, their stories were untrue, and they hurt a lot of people with their gossip. Mrs. O'Connor had two boys, Tommy and Dennis. Tommy was closer to our age and wanted to hang out with us. He was a good kid, and we accepted him as one of us, and never talked about his mother in front of him.

One day Melvin disappeared from the block, and my life seemed so much better without him. We learned he had a mild case of Polio on his mouth... so much for wearing camphor balls. The day he came home, his mother Yetta, invited us to their apartment for cake and milk, trying to get Melvin back in the swing of things and help him bond with his friends again. My mom wasn't too happy with Yetta for that, thinking that Polio was something you could catch... like the measles.

Wow! Melvin's toys knocked us for a loop. I mean he had an actual BB gun! But not just a BB gun, it was a Red Ryder Rifle. It was beyond what I could ever dream of. Sergie asked if he could borrow it. Melvin knew that if he let Sergie have it, he'd never see it again. He always looked up to Sergie and wanted to be accepted by him in the worst way. He would have done anything to please him, and his BB gun was the price.

Sergie, with the brand new, shining blue-metal Red Ryder Rifle in hand, raced up the hall stairs with the rest of us to the roof of my building. Mom happened to be walking into our apartment when she spotted me in the hall, "Sollinue, come, I wanna talk to you."

"Aww, Ma, my friends and I are..."

"Shush, it will only take a minute."

Mom sat down in the kitchen and poured herself some coffee and cream, while I was jumping out of my skin and shifting from one leg to the other.

"Vhat is it? Do you have to pee or something?"

"No Ma. Go on, go on."

She took a sugar cube and held it in her mouth and let the coffee sieve through the cube, "Sollinue, darlink..."

She definitely wanted something from me. I didn't care what the hell it was; I just wanted to get up to the roof with my friends.

"Please do me a favor. I can't find Millie, and I've got to pick up some work. I'll be gone for a few hours. Please take care of Ronnie for me."

"Yeah. Okay, okay... where is he?"

"He's in the living room. Now keep a good eye on him." And with that she was gone.

One of Mom's rules: Never go on the roof, especially with Ronnie.

The guys were already there, shooting at the top of chimneys. While I was taking my turn, Ronnie, who was two and a half years old, was wobbling toward the edge of the roof.

Melvin screamed out, "Solly, your brother!"

"Holy shit! Ronnie! Stop! Stop! Don't move! Please stop!"

Ronnie turned and looked at me, smiled and continued walking toward the edge. One step more, and my baby brother would fall like a rock into empty space – and there was no way I could stop him. This can't be happening. Mom's gonna kill me! In a couple of seconds, a thousand things went through my mind. If Ronnie fell off the roof, I might as well have joined him.

But Ronnie hesitated, and that was all I needed. I grabbed his arm and pulled him back from disaster. I picked him up and crushed him in my arms and took him downstairs. Millie was in the apartment, and I left Ronnie with her and ran back up to the roof.

Sergie was pointing the gun at people in the street. He spotted his brother Tony on skates. The first shot missed him and almost hit Crazy Leo, who looked up and raised his fist, "I saw you, Solly! I'll get you for this!"

A quick, second shot from Sergie hit Tony on the neck. I was surprised he screamed from pain. I thought BB guns were harmless, especially from this distance. Tony got out of his skates and rushed into his building. Sergie handed me the gun and ran down the steps. I got rid of it as fast as I could and gave it back to Melvin. Now, if we were caught, the blame was on him.

"*Abbot and Costello Meets Frankenstein* is playing at the Ward, you wanna to go?"

"I don't know..."

Sergie needed an answer, "Come on, Solly, you goin' or what?"

We took the usual short cut across the creek. Halfway there, two kids jumped out from behind a boulder blocking our way, one colored, the other Spanish. The Spanish kid looked at Sergie.

"Hey kid, what's your name?"

"Garsha."

Sergie was ashamed of being Puerto Rican and changed the way he pronounced his last name from Garcia to Garsha, thinking it was more American sounding.

The two kids pulled out switchblades, "Okay, Garsha, now empty your pockets or we'll cut yah."

If we could only get past these guys, we knew we could outrun them. Sergie and I put our hands in our pockets, as if we were giving in, offering the switchblade kids a false sense of power. We gave each other a knowing look and took off like a rocket all the way up Bruckner Boulevard, leaving the two kids behind us. We turned onto Boynton, around the corner to Westchester Avenue, and onto the waiting line at the Ward.

We couldn't get in fast enough and bumped the kids in front of us, constantly looking over our shoulders. We worried that the switchblade kids would catch up with us, and didn't feel safe until we got into the theater.

The matinee started with a *Superman* cartoon: *"Superman, who leads a never ending battle for truth, justice, and the American way."*

The *Superman* cartoon drew me into its atmosphere of darkness. What made them different was that Superman was a little more human than in the joke books. Even though he had super powers, his body could be punished by pure evil and he had to strain all of his powers to fight back whatever dangers challenged him.

Finally we got to see *Abbott and Costello Meet Frankenstein*, featuring Dracula and the Wolf Man – the reason we came here in the first place. They made a joke out of the monsters that had always scared the shit out of me. It was the best Abbott and Costello movie ever.

After we saw the whole matinee, we took the long way home up Westchester Avenue, not taking any chances of bumping into those guys. When we turned onto East 165th Street, a blast of wind whistled across my ears and a sheet of newspaper attached itself to my legs and wouldn't let go. I tore the paper off, and the two pieces chased each other down The Three Hills. No one was on the street or in the stores.

A voice cut through the ominous stillness. It was Frankie, Sergie's oldest brother, yelling from his window.

"Hey, Sergie, do me a favor. They're having a sale at B & J's. Here's a buck..."

Two fifty-cent pieces wrapped in brown paper clanked on the sidewalk.

"Stop fucking around and listen to me. I want you to buy me the record, *Nature Boy*, by Nat King Cole. Remember, it has to be Nat King Cole, or forget it. And also, get me, *Golden Earrings*, by Peggy Lee. You got it?"

"Yeah, I got it!"

Even the Boulevard was empty of people. Now I was really getting worried. I had to be alert, or I was next to disappear. Thank God, B & J was filled with people, it made me feel secure.

B & J had booths where you could listen to records and choose the ones you wanted. Sergie and I used their policy to our advantage and had fun listening to music for free. We listened to Spike Jones making fun of *The William Tell Overture* and squeezed in one more song, Vaughn Monroe singing, *Dance Ballerina Dance*, before the owner came to throw us out.

"Okay, kids, I know what you're doing. If you're not buying, I want you outta here."

"But Mister," said Sergie, "I've got the money to buy a couple of records. See?" We bought Frankie's records and left.

As we were crossing Hoe Avenue on our way back, we cursed at an ambulance that almost sideswiped us. It stopped in front of Sergie's building, and we pressed though the crowd, enjoying the excitement. A gurney came out of the front door with Sergie's mother right behind. It was Mr. Garcia, Sergie's father.

"Cookie! Come here, sweetheart." She put her arms around Sergie, "Your father is very sick. I'm going to the hospital with him, and I want you to stay here with your brothers."

Sergie didn't say a word. He stood there numb, like he wasn't there. His eyes were staring at nothing, and he never cried. His brothers, Frankie and Tony, took him upstairs. Mr. Garcia died at the hospital that night. Sergie was outside the very next day, playing on the street with the rest of us.

Metal skates on the sidewalk vibrated through me from my head to my toes, until my teeth rattled like a pair of dice. When I finally stopped skating, my hearing was numb to the street noises and everything felt like it was filtered through wads of cotton stuffed in my ears.

Crazy Leo snuck up behind me and twisted me around, "Gotcha, you little prick!"

I tried to fight him off, but my squirming only made him angrier, and he hit me in the balls. I couldn't catch my breath. Leo freaked out and took hold of my dick and pulled until it felt like he was tearing my penis from my body. He showed me some mercy and let me go. I hopped up the stairs on one skate with a burning pain from my prick.

Mom heard me skating and limping into my room, "Vhat's dis? Look at you. Vhat happened to you?"

Most of the times when something happened to me, I never said a word. But this time Mom caught me in a vulnerable moment.

"Crazy Leo hurt me, down there."

"Let me see."

My pants were already halfway down and my white underwear was full of blood. Leo had torn through my skin.

"Oy, yoi yoi!" Mom rushed me into the bathroom and I shuffled behind her with my pants still down around my knees. I was twelve years old and was more embarrassed than hurt. After she cleaned it up, it didn't look as bad as it felt. I was relieved that my prick was still there.

"Harold! Come here. I vant you to see dis."

"Ma! No! No! You can't do dat."

I started to suffocate at the thought of Harold seeing me like this. I guess Mom heard the desperation in my voice.

She understood, "Okay, mein boychick, get some clean underwear and put your pants back on."

Mom was near my room talking to Harold, "Look, look at his bloody underwear. Leo Meisel made his little thing bleed. His hands should only fall off."

"That little prick. I'll teach him a lesson he wont forget."

What?!! Harold was sticking up for me? The world must be coming to an end! Then I remembered how much he hated Leo. He was looking for an excuse to kill that arrogant Jew.

Leo was out on the street and saw Harold coming for him.

"Big man! Come on and get me big man!"

Harold said nothing. He charged at Leo with those mean, hateful eyes I knew so well. They ended up on Faille Street and Westchester Avenue. Out of breath, Harold stopped and raised his fist in the air, "I'll get you, you little prick."

Leo was taunting him, "Yeah? You and what army?"

Harold tried but couldn't take another step, "When I get you – not today, but maybe tomorrow – I'll break your fucking neck."

"Ahhh! Go tell it to the Marines."

Why was Harold doing this? It was as if he owned me and no one else was going to touch his property. I was his to do with whatever he wanted. Harold left Leo, came upstairs and shoved me against the hall wall. Ahh, back to the Harold I knew and loved.

"You stupid little prick. You turn my stomach. Why didn't you fight back? You're just another Jew coward like the rest of them in the concentration camps."

"I didn't see him coming. And he's older and bigger than me."

What the hell did I just do? I actually answered Harold. This was a no-no... Never say anything, maybe just shake my head. Even that was too much.

"You retarded little shit." Harold grabbed my mouth with his vice like hand. The combination of whiskey and beer cooking inside of him sweated out of his skin and filled my nostrils with his stink.

"You say another word, and you'll think what Leo did to you was nothing. Did I say think? You can't think, you're a mentally defective imbecile."

Harold was in good form tonight. The physical punishments that he inflicted on me were pretty bad, but Harold's verbal beatings were worse, and I believed them. His words never left me. They were always with me, beating me down every moment of every day and night.

THE END OF THE WORLD

IT WAS SATURDAY, nearing the end of summer vacation. The five of us thought we'd treat ourselves to a double feature, *One Touch of Venus* and *The Three Godfathers*. We had a plan to get all of us in for the price of one. The idea was for one of us to pay, and once inside, wait by an emergency exit until the lights went down and the movie started. Then he could open the exit door for the rest of us to sneak in. Junior lost the toss, and it was his job to open the exit door.

In order for us to get to the exit doors, we went to Hoe Avenue and walked through an alleyway between the apartment buildings, into a huge, empty back lot hidden behind the stores that fronted on the Boulevard. It was filled with rubble, what must have been the remains of old apartment buildings. To pass the time, we found a couple of broomsticks and picked up marble-sized pieces of stone to practice our hitting skills. We hit them at the blank wall of the Boulevard Theater where the exit doors were.

Sometimes, when no one was around, I'd come here by myself and practice my swing. After a while when we played hardball, the ball looked to me like the size of a watermelon, and the bat felt like the size of a tennis racket. I never missed or struck out. The pitchers could throw any kind of crap at us, and I could hit the ball wherever I wanted to. Too bad I was never discovered. At that time there was no such thing as Little League... well, not where *we* lived.

While still playing in the rubble, we could see the back of the Chinese restaurant where they were preparing food for the day.

Finally, we could find out the answer to the neighborhood myth that the Chinese actually cooked pigeons, telling us it was chicken, and that the soy sauce was pigeon blood. There were pigeons all around them, probably getting free handouts. They never did kill or cook a single pigeon. But it was more fun to believe in the myth and not what we saw.

When the exit doors opened four small, shadowy phantoms scurried through, breaking the rays of sunlight that flashed into the darkened theatre... the matron in hot pursuit. By the time she got to the door, we were already innocently sitting in our seats.

A raging fire swelled into a tidal wave. The furious inferno cascaded off the jagged stonewalls and surged down the railroad tracks through a narrow tunnel. Spy Smasher desperately pumped a handcar, trying to outrun the angry river of fire that chased him through the tunnel. His long cape billowed behind him, outlined in a blinding halo of rushing flames that reached out, licking at his heels. The blazing fire exploded and swallowed him up, engulfing the movie screen with white, hot flames.

NEXT WEEK: CHAPTER TWO
HUMAN TARGET

Beethoven's Fifth played, *"Da-Da-Da-Dum..."* over the end titles. Then the screen went totally blank. Kids began screaming and stomping their feet. I stuffed the end of an empty Good and Plenty box into my mouth and blew. It vibrated with a raspy whistle, tickling my nose. When the picture finally appeared, the whole theater fell silent, like someone had switched off a radio.

The main feature began and I could hear the crinkling of brown paper bags throughout the children's section. The theater filled with mouthwatering aromas – the foods of the different cultures of my neighborhood. During the second feature, Sergie and I snuck up to the balcony so we could watch the movies over again. We usually got away with it, but not this time. The matron chased us out of the theater into an unexpected rainstorm.

As kids, we didn't listen to weather forecasts. If it rained or snowed, that's what it was. The rain was coming down so hard we had to duck into the doorway of the Army & Navy Store, right next to the movies. Sergie and I looked at all the neat stuff in the window and spotted a long rectangular plastic cover. We looked at each other and knew we had to have it.

"Yeah, Solly, let's get it. It'll be cool. We'd be able to walk anywhere in da rain and we won't get wet."

"What are you crazy? It costs a whole dollar. How da hell are we gonna get a dollar?"

Sergie didn't have to say a word. I knew the answer to my own question. All the way home we ran close to the apartment buildings, under awnings, in and out of doorways, dodging the people and the rain.

I never got an allowance, never even heard the word. When I desperately needed money, I had to find it for myself in any way and anywhere I could. First I looked for a lump under the linoleum. Another favorite place was behind the cushions of the couch, where loose change would spill out of drunken Harold's pockets and roll down into the cracks. If it wasn't raining, I'd offer my services to Abe, delivering groceries for tips. In a pinch, my friends and I would coax a drunk from Harry's Bar into giving us some change. If he passed out, we hit the jackpot and picked his pockets. The very last thing I'd do, if there was no other way, would be to steal change from Mom's pocketbook.

When I got to my building, I found Mom talking to Harold at the stairwell by the mailboxes. Two weeks ago, Harold was in top form and hit my mom hard enough to send her to the hospital. During his violent rage, Mom made sure Millie, Ronnie and I were safely together in my room. With the door closed, it was like listening to a radio show... but this show was for real. We were afraid even to breathe out loud, afraid we'd be his next victim.

When the police showed up and took Harold away, Millie, Ronnie, and I emerged from my room to an empty apartment. We didn't know what to do or who to turn to. Later, when Mom came home from the hospital, she found us in Millie's room by the window.

"Everything's okay. Come, children, come, we'll eat something at the Chinks."

During the two days Harold spent in the Tombs, Mom learned that she had the legal right to kick him out of our lives. And when he was released from jail, Harold found his things packed and outside in the hall.

We had two glorious weeks without Harold, and now, he was trying to come back. I'd never seen him cry before, but there he was, spiffed up in a suit (something that wasn't in plaid) crying and sobbing like a baby. Even I felt sorry for him... but not sorry enough to want him back.

"I'll be good, Molly. I'm sorry. I promise, I'll be good. Please Molly, you've got to take me back. I'll never touch you again. Look, look Molly." He took out a wad of money. "I saved every penny of my pay for two weeks. And I didn't touch a drop."

Looking at all that money helped my mom decide. "Well, okay... but if you raise your hand to me or the kids, just one single finger, out you go for good."

Of course he lied. In one week, Harold was back to his violent self. And of course, my mom still let him stay. We had our chance, and Mom blew it.

While she was selling us out, it gave me the opportunity to go upstairs and rummage through her pocketbook. Her loose change sometimes escaped the coin purse and found its way to the bottom of her bag. It was my lucky day, and I helped myself to two nickels and three dimes. I passed Harold and Mom as they were coming in, and escaped with my ill-gotten loot. I was ten cents short of my half. Where the hell am I going to get the rest of the money in this weather?

I ran through the rain down to the garbage cans in the alley searching for deposit bottles. In those days, you could return the broken top of a dated milk bottle, and if it was unopened, the grocer would exchange it for a new bottle of milk for free. The broken bottle tops I found were already opened, so I couldn't get anything for them. Still short ten cents, I met Sergie at the Army & Navy Store, and he had his share, plus the extra ten cents we needed.

We stepped out of the Army & Navy Store and slipped the opaque, khaki tent over our heads. It dropped down to our ankles, completely immersing us in plastic. The only proof of our existence was our protruding shoes. There was a clear horizontal eye slit enabling us to see where we were going as we stepped out into the rain.

It was a relentless and heavy rain, like sleet beating rapidly off the plastic, reverberating around inside and distorting the sounds outside. But the rain was wasting its time – we were safe and dry in our protective plastic womb.

At first we walked hesitantly off-sync; Sergie was going one way and I was going another. After a few tries, we found a rhythmic flow and marched on. We looked like a new form of biological life, with four feet waddling toward Aldus Street.

We were surrounded by our own tiny universe, taking it with us, as we traveled in someone else's world. When we strayed from our block we didn't belong. We walked among the people and knew their faces, but still they were strangers to us, and we were strangers to them.

At the corner of Faille and Aldus across from P.S. 75, not more than twenty feet from us, a man stood on the edge of a roof top holding a glass in his hand. He lifted his arm over his head, pointing the glass to the sky and drank. As if it was the most natural thing to do, he leaned forward like the world belonged to him, jumped, and plunged through the air, headfirst. He didn't make a sound as the rushing air cushioned his flight. He floated down with dignity and grace until his head broke his fall, hitting the concrete alley and landing with a dull crunch. His head splattered all over the place. We stood there with bits and pieces all around us.

From nowhere, a police car and an ambulance appeared. They took the body away. What was left was a sugary, red mound that I thought were his brains. I could feel my legs push back at the hardness of the concrete sidewalk. Hot sour phlegm lingered in my mouth as I swallowed at a lump in my throat.

The mound of granular red blood melted away in the pounding rain. The red stream swirled around a drain and we watched as it was sucked down through the grating and disappeared. The alley was clean again, like it never happened. No blood, just rain beating down over our heads. Sergie and I never said a word to each other. Alone with our own feelings, we turned and waddled away. Hearing the ghostly clanging of a trolley told me I was almost home.

The front door slammed shut, "Is dat you, Millinue?"

"No, it's me, Mom."

"What's happening here? You come up yourself without me calling you?"

"I'm hungry."

"Where's Millinue?"

Millie shouted, "I'm in my room!"

"Good. You also go to your room and I'll feed you supper."

Eating alone in my room, was my clue that Harold was back.

During my dinner of spaghetti and meatballs, I heard Millie screaming at Mom and ran to see what was happening.

"After what he did to you, you're taking him back?!"

"Shush, he'll hear you. Don't start trouble."

"Who the hell does he think he is? He's not even my father! What gives him the right to treat us that way?"

"Vils vista from meir?"

"Why did you take him back?"

"Shut up, he can hear you. You'll get him mad."

"I don't care. I don't want him back. How dare you take him back!"

Mom bit on her index finger. When she bit on her finger, you knew she meant business. "Are you going to shut up?"

Millie wouldn't stop. Mom grabbed Millie's plate of spaghetti and sauce and dumped it over her head. Well, that shut her up. Millie gulped as the sauce dripped in globs through and around her hair, over her face, off the tip of her nose and chin. Noodles draped themselves over her ears. Mom looked at me, and at Millie, nudged us several times, until we gave in. Millie did a spit-take through the sauce, and we cracked up laughing.

In my room finishing my dinner, it became awfully quiet outside. The driving rain had abruptly stopped, like a faucet that had been turned off but was still dripping. Heavy drops trickled off the clotheslines and out of drain spouts, splashing down onto the alley pavement and off of tin garbage cans, inventing their own kind of music.

On my way out to play, I heard mom talking in the kitchen, and I hesitated in the hall, listening to her telling Millie what happened on her way home from work.

"I was on da platform with such a big crowd. You never seen such a crowd. Two trains come, but before I could get into my train, the crowd of people coming out pulled and pushed me around, taking me to the wrong train. Oy, I fought so hard. And then dey pulled at me so hard dey pulled my sweater off and carried it away to the wrong train." She chuckled, "I watched my sweater leave me in da other train. So, I waved goodbye to it, 'cause I'll never see it again." They laughed and I left.

Down on the street it was hot and muggy. The clouds were gone, and the setting sun glistened off wet dripping buildings. The rain left a miniature river racing along the gutter, looking like rapids as it rushed over and around the daily trash that filtered out onto the streets.

The guys were in front of my building, hunched over and busy catching live ants. I joined in the hunt. We put the ants on used ice cream pop sticks and laid them carefully onto the fast flowing river. The ants, trying to escape, scurried around looking like a crew of pirates working their ships.

By accident, I stepped back on Bobby's stick, putting it out of commission. To get even, he deliberately smashed my stick into the stream.

"Hey! What the fuck's the matter wit ya? What the hell did ya do that for?"

He turned away from me and walked toward our building.

"Where da fuck are you going? Come back here and I'll break your fuckin' ass!"

Bobby turned, "Tough shit."

"I'm not kiddin' ya."

"Yeah, you really scare me," Bobby retorted. "I'm shittin' in my pants."

At that moment, all of the unfair things in my life that left me powerless were bottled up inside me, ready to explode. Bobby lit my fuse. I lost control and ran after him. Gone were my senses of taste, smell, and reason. A cold heat flushed through my shaking body. The stranger who was wearing my clothes and whose blood was swimming with hate, made a mad dash at him.

My anger spilled all over an astonished Bobby. I was so pissed, I didn't know whether to punch or push him, so I sort of punched and pushed him at the same time. And to my surprise, he crashed through the front door window of our building.

Bobby didn't get hurt, but the noise of breaking glass brought the old Yentas to their windows. Anthony ran to his apartment on Faille Street, and the rest of us were off like a shot around the corner to Westchester Avenue and down through the metal doors of Junior's basement.

Junior's basement had little crooked rooms made of damp second-hand wood. It smelled of rusty pipes and mildew. To us it was a place of refuge from the prying eyes of adults. We stayed in our snug sanctuary until we thought the coast was clear, keeping ourselves busy playing G-Men vs. Enemy Spies. Even though we were old enough for playing experimental sex games with the girls, we were still young enough to enjoy G-Men and Spies.

Melvin, as usual, fell victim to our game and ended up tied to a chair as a spy who wouldn't talk. But we went a step too far and left the basement, locking the metal doors behind us, leaving Melvin in the kind of darkness your eyes never get used to.

The sun was beginning to set as we turned the corner on our block and found a bunch of empty tin cans. We stomped our shoes into the center of the cans, and as they flattened, the ends of the cans wrapped tightly around our shoes. Sounding like an army of tap dancers, we clanked the rest of the way home to our block.

We took the air caps off the tires of parked cars and put them between our knuckles and blew. As the air skimmed across the open end, it produced a piercing whistle. When I spotted Kathleen Doogan walking toward us, I threw my air cap into the gutter. By the time my friends turned in the direction of my eager gaze, I was already sitting on the fender of the nearest parked car, with my knees sticking out as far as I could without sliding off.

While Kathleen was talking to my friends, she maneuvered herself to my knees, her two soft thighs pressed lightly against my left knee. I could feel her thighs gradually part, as she slowly slid along my knee, stopping at her pussy. At first she delicately leaned against me and then, pressing harder and harder, she gently rubbed her pussy up and down against my knee. The longer she rubbed, the hotter her soft pussy got and every inch of me tingled with a fever radiating from my cock.

Meanwhile, she was chatting away, pretending like nothing was going on. And when she had had enough, Kathleen detached herself from me, leaving me sitting there trembling with a thrilling buzz, on the verge of exploding out of my body.

"Melvin! Melvin!" shouted Yetta. Holy shit! We realized we forgot all about Melvin! We left him tied up and locked in the basement for over an hour.

"Solly, have you seen my little Arab?"

"Yeah, I know where he is."

"Would you get him for me and tell him to stay close to the house where I can see him?"

"Okay Mrs. Melnick, Junior and I will get him for ya."

"You're such a good boy, Solly."

Junior and I ran to the basement, unlocked the door and untied Melvin.

"What the hell's wrong with you guys? I'm going to tell my Mother!"

Junior said, "If you do, I'll beat the shit out of you."

Melvin swallowed his anger and joined the rest of the guys as if nothing had happened.

Our friends were standing by Harry's Bar, talking to Mrs. O'Conner. She was a tall, gaunt woman with thin features and the kind of limp stringy hair that drunks always have. She was drunk. What am I saying? I never saw Mrs. O'Conner any other way but drunk... for all I knew she was born drunk. Funny though, she always reeked of whiskey, and yet, I never saw her take a drink.

Melvin, Junior, and I got there in the middle of a conversation. Mrs. O'Conner was sitting on a stoop saying, "And I've got something to show you, something I know you'll like to see."

She spread her legs as wide as she could and pulled up her dress. She wasn't wearing any underwear. Mrs. O'Conner was very proud of herself as she showed us her wide-open pussy. What I saw was her dirty, wet pubic hairs, stuck together in wiry clumps, and I imagined the foul stench emanating from that sweaty black hole.

I was as horny as the next kid, even to the point of pumping on pillows, but when Mrs. O'Conner showed us her cunt, it gave me a sick feeling in the pit of my stomach. The embarrassment of knowing she was the mother of our friend Tommy got to me and the rest of my friends. We all turned away in disgust.

"Where are you boys going? Don't you want to pet it? I know you do. If you each give me a nickel I'll let you pet it. Where the hell are you going? Didn't you hear what I said? I'll let you pet it for only a nickel."

Her voice faded as we crossed the street and strolled over to Shirley's building. We sat on the stoop and leaned against parked cars by her window. It was a warm night, the weekend before the new school year. There was something in the air brushing across my face, a cool undercurrent, telling me the weather was about to change.

We hung out by Shirley's window, taunting kids who had to go through our block to get to Longfellow and Bryant Avenues. Kevin was our first unfortunate victim. He had enormous ears that stuck out from his head, and we shouted at him, "Hey Dumbo ears, where you goin'?"

"Careful with those ears, you might fly away."

Seeing he was about to cry egged us on, "Hey Dumbo ears! Where ya goin' Dumbo ears?"

We switched targets when we saw Hollender coming up the block. He always looked like he just woke up. His feet pointed outward in opposite directions, and when he walked it looked like he didn't know which way he was going. He was haphazardly carrying books and loose papers pressed tightly against his chest like any second they were going to spill over, but they never did. He wore thick eyeglasses that hung at a tilt. Bravely, he ran through our gauntlet of merciless insults.

Hollender looked at me with pleading eyes, as if he saw something in me that made him think I understood him. He cried out in frustrated anger. I thought to myself, Why? Why, do I do these things to people? I don't want to... but I do it anyway.

After Hollender escaped down the hills, Sergie said, "You know Hollender was in a German concentration camp."

He said it like it was important, but I didn't know what that meant. I *did* know that what we were doing to these poor kids, could easily have been done to me by my own friends.

Our supply of unfortunate victims eventually dried up, until our old graybeard Hasidic Jew came along. Over the last couple of years, we had developed a routine with him. Every time he walked by, we jumped in front of him scratching our imaginary beards on our faces. In return, the Hasidic Jew scratched his ass and said, "You scratch your face, I also scratch your face."

Shirley leaned out on her ground floor windowsill, a short girl with dark hair and a round face, a little on the pudgy side. Outside her apartment, Shirley was just another kid like the rest of us, but leaning from her windowsill, she was transformed into royalty holding court.

We gathered under her window, and while the guys were talking, I was fooling around with an empty spool I had in my pocket from my mom's sewing thread. I wrapped a rubber band around it to make a catapult, inserted a wooden match in the hole, and pulled back the rubber band like a bow and arrow. It shot through the air, hit the brick wall of Shirley's building, and burst into flames.

While I loaded up another match, Shirley looked at my friends and declared, "If he doesn't stop that, I'm going back in." My answer was to shoot a couple more flaming matches.

Sergie said, "Solly, why don't you cut that shit out."

Shirley got up and turned to leave.

"Okay, okay, I'll stop."

Sheldon and his sister Selma walked out of our building. Well, Sheldon never actually walked, he bounded forward on his toes, more like a half-skip, in his own irregular rhythm. Strangely, the whole sky lit up, from black night to a bright yellow orange. One of the gods had turned the night into a neon sky. My first thought was that this unearthly glow happened because of the man who jumped off the roof. Sheldon, splattered with freckles, and his sister Selma, whose nose wasn't her best feature, looked up at the sky with fear and disbelief in their eyes.

The whole block reflected the eerie orange sky, which loomed like a threat to our lives. If there was anything I could feel guilty about, I felt it at that moment. Some all-seeing power knew all the things I'd ever done wrong and was about to confront me with them. We all kind of bundled together, watching the menacing night around us with a feeling of impending doom.

Shirley said nervously, "What's happening?"

I answered her in an evil, threatening voice, "It's Doom's Day, the end of da world."

Anthony joined in, "Yeah, it's the beginning of da end."

Sheldon resisted, "Bullshit."

"The orange sky is a message from God," Sergie taunted.

"Are you kiddin' me?"

"God is coming down to punish you."

Sheldon asked, "Why?"

"After all, you killed his son, Jesus," Sergie declared. Then he looked at me, "You too... everybody knows you Jews killed Christ!"

I gave him the finger. "Fuck you! I never touched the guy!"

Sheldon replied nervously, "Ahh, I don't believe it."

The guys concentrated on their more vulnerable victims, Sheldon and Selma. "Yeah, the Jews murdered Christ and someday they'll be punished... and tonight looks like the night."

We'd done such a good job making up the story about the orange sky that Sheldon was starting to believe it. And we were starting to believe it ourselves. Sheldon and Selma were at the point of tears and the more they pleaded for us to stop, the more we kept it up, until finally, Sheldon pumped his left fist into the crook of his right arm.

"Kiss my ass!" Sheldon cried out, as he and his sister ran back into the building.

After about an hour, the orange sky melted away. The night was very still now, and we were in our own thoughts. I stood there with a cigarette cupped in my hand, took a last drag, and flicked the butt into the street, acting real tough and cool. We knew the night was over, and one by one, each of us went our own way.

Melvin and I raced up the stairs in the dark, playing our usual game of spitting at each other to see who would have the last spit before Melvin disappeared into his apartment. I lived one floor above and continued up the steps, until I bumped into what felt like a dead animal blocking my way on the landing. As my eyes got used to the dark, the lump shifted its shape and turned into drunken Harold, who had passed out before making it into our apartment. I gingerly stepped over him as if he was just another part of the hall and walked in the door.

"I want you to stay in your room, Harold will be home any minute."

"No Ma... he never made it. He's lying in the hall by the stairs."

Mom rushed to the front door, "Oy! People are gonna see him." She got him to his feet and helped him to their bedroom. What did they do together in their room besides sex? Did they ever talk about anything? I saw the hate, but never the love. Were there any tender moments between them?

Riding my pillow like a horse, I threw myself at the bad guy's pillow and both of us tumbled to the ground. I put up a good fight, but the bad guy got the better of me and hung me off the edge of a cliff (my bed). He subdued me, and tied me up, and dragged me to the entrance of a cave (my closet). Then, gloating, he carried a sweating bundle of dynamite (spool of thread) and wedged it over my head into the crack of a boulder (top shelf of my closet). He struck a match and lit the fuse. The thread dangled down from the shelf, steadily burning up toward the spool. I desperately tried to untie myself. Will I get loose in time to stamp out the fuse?

NEXT WEEK: CHAPTER FIVE
NO ESCAPE

HOT LIPS

AT NIGHT I could hear the mice clicking their nails on the hall linoleum, sliding into walls. I was too terrified to go to the bathroom at night, afraid I'd be eaten up by the mice. When I couldn't hold it in any longer, I'd pee out my window into the alley before I'd walk through the infested hall to the bathroom. There was nothing pretty about roaches – shimmering, oily skeletons, long feely antennas, fast-crawling legs hugging the floor, scurrying every which way. No matter how hot it was, I covered myself with my blanket to keep the roaches from climbing up my nose and into my ears to eat out my brains.

"Sollinue, it's hot. Come, I put a mattress on the fire escape for you and Millie."

Lying on the fire escape three floors above the street, I stared up at the sky and stars. I floated and swayed in the vast openness above me, feeling like a kite pulling at the string, wanting to be free. Sergie was out on his fire escape too, in the building next door to us about ten feet away. He was on the same floor as ours and we talked and told stories to each other until we fell asleep.

Scattered, unclear sounds surrounded me, and gathered together, focusing into my mom's deep voice.

"Sollinue! Get up! Breakfast is ready."

It was the usual day, until that night after supper. Harold was in the living room and started to spew out his drunken hate for me. His anger was building until he couldn't hold himself back. He was heading in the direction of my room. Before he even turned into the hall, I was out the front door, escaping into the street.

One of the older guys, Oscar, joined us on Junior's stoop. He brought a handful of dirty comic books, with famous comic strip characters, like Popeye, who gets a super hard-on from eating his spinach and is able to break down doors with it. He was selling the hot books for fifteen cents apiece. I had fifteen cents for the movies that weekend. I gave it up to buy myself a hot book instead. But fifteen cents was a lot of money, and I couldn't make up my mind which one I wanted.

"Come on, come on. Pick one out already!"

I finally picked out what I thought was the best, "I'll take this one." It was *Secret Agent X9*, investigating a sexy Chinese woman, slinking around her apartment in an open silk robe, showing off her tits and pussy. Agent X9's hand is rubbing her pussy on the couch, while at the same time he's sucking her nipples. Throughout the book she keeps calling him Hot Lips. I kept the book well hidden under my mattress, and only took it out to jerk off.

One day I reached under my mattress and the hot book was gone. I looked for it again and again, but it just wasn't there. No matter how hard I tried I couldn't remember where I put it.

Because of Harold, we never had company. But one afternoon we had a very special visit from Harry and Walter and their wives. The whole time they were here, Harold was a perfect gentleman. After everyone settled in, my brothers started calling me Hot Lips. Oh my God! Mom must have found *Secret Agent X9*! Every time they saw me, they called me Hot Lips and laughed, even in front of Sylvia and Sonny. Worst of all, my own mom called me Hot Lips.

I escaped into the bathroom and locked the door. I stayed inside for a long time, hoping the whole thing would blow over. Mom tried to coax me out, but only made it worse. "Vhat are you doing in dere, jerking off?"

When I was no longer a part of the conversation, I snuck out of the house and stayed outside until everybody left. More than the embarrassment, the worst part was that I never got my *Secret Agent X9* back.

The street was filled with a sweet, nutty odor of roasted grain. It was Monday morning, and I was reluctantly walking to school, wondering what to expect from Junior High School.

Besides not being in grammar school, there were many reasons why this school year was different than any other year. First I was unprepared for the abrupt change of not having girls in my classes anymore. In a way, it felt good not being shamed in front of the girls.

Then there was Sergie. All through grade school, Sergie and I were in the same class, inseparable. Now for the first time since the first grade, we were separated. They had severed our umbilical cord. But I made a lot of new friends, like Julio Reyes and Victor Jorrin. I missed Sergie at school, but we still had our block.

In grammar school, we had the same teacher everyday, all day. Now, we had a different teacher for each subject and had to go from room to room. My homeroom teacher was Mr. Kamil, whose right knee was frozen, causing him to walk with a stiff limp. The story was that his knee was a war injury, and he still had pieces of shrapnel in his leg. He wore the same suit everyday, with permanent food stains on his jacket. His face matched the color of his gray suit, and his black hair seemed confused and didn't know which way it wanted to go. He always needed a shave. Everyday his beard was the same length... how did he do that?

Mr. Kamil dragged his leg in front of the blackboard and chalked a circle representing the earth. He told us, "We can't win a war with Russia. It is too big, and they outnumber us with people and soldiers. We would have to use atomic bombs. But if we use too many, more than say five atomic bombs, the earth's thin crust will crack open." With his chalk he broke the thin, circular line, "And the Earth will explode into pieces and float into space."

We heard there was a new teacher in school, named Mr. Zuckerman. He was a tall, thin man who swam in his oversized suit. He looked very fragile, like all you had to do was touch him and he'd collapse. One of his students was Jackson of the Simpson Street Midgets, and for the whole class period, he tormented and teased Mr. Zuckerman, showing him no respect.

"Mr. Jackson, I see you're the only one who didn't turn in your test paper."

"Hey, Teach, you don't know what your talkin' about. I gave you my test. You must have lost it."

"Mr. Jackson, if you don't have your test on my desk by tomorrow, I'll have to fail you. And if I fail you, you won't graduate."

"You better think twice about that. If you fail me, you better keep outta my way."

"Are you threatening me?"

"No, just tellin' ya."

After the end of the class, Jackson's argument with Mr. Zuckerman spilled out into the hall and Zuckerman tried to ignore him. I was in Workshop, building a wood tie rack, when I heard the commotion outside in the hall.

Mr. Zuckerman was losing his patience, "Mr. Jackson, you had better think about your actions. I won't be responsible if you persist."

Jackson laughed at him and elbowed Zuckerman in his chest, "Get the fuck out of my way."

What happened next was a scene right out of a movie: Zuckerman used tricky moves I'd never seen before and effortlessly handled Jackson like he was a ragdoll. Jackson didn't have a chance. He flew and twisted in the air, looking like he was on an amusement park ride, and landed on the ground with Zuckerman's foot on his throat. Later on, we learned that Mr. Zuckerman was in Special Forces during the war and had seen a lot of action. He had killed a lot of Japs in hand-to-hand combat.

From that day on, Jackson showed a lot of respect for Mr.

Zuckerman, and so did the rest of the class. Every time they entered and left his classroom they would affectionately chant, "Zuckie's Chain Gang..." grunting, "Uuh-huh, Uuh-huh... Zuckie's Chain Gang, Uuh-huh..."

The first week of school was over and a terrible head cold kept me in bed with fever, chills, stomachache – the whole works – and a nose that wouldn't stop running. Where was all this mucus coming from? This one could keep me home for at least a week. Most of those days I spent in bed, listening to my radio, suffering with the boring daytime radio shows. It was all worth it to not be in school.

My first day out of the house was Sunday, when Mom decided to take Millie, Ronnie, and me to the movies to air me out. She took us to the Star where we saw two detective mysteries, a *Charlie Chan*, and *The Falcon*, and a western. The Star had no balconies, only orchestra seats, and even with your eyes closed, you knew what theater you were in, because your shoes would stick to the floor with each step.

Before our movies ended, we could hear the wind whistling from outside of the theater. The management interrupted the film and announced that a hurricane might be hitting our neighborhood. We didn't wait for the end of *Gene Autry* and rushed through the lobby out into a stormy scene, with rattling street signs, fighting back the wind.

At first, we leaned against the howling wind, but that didn't get us anywhere. We had to lower our heads and plow through it. Every once in a while, a strong gust would almost carry us away. Poor little Ronnie was off the ground, flying in the air behind Mom, whose tight grip was his only anchor.

Another gust and metal garbage cans flew past us. Signs on rooftops tore away from their moorings and toppled down, bouncing off the sidewalks and sliding past us. We were the only people on the street, dodging everything that came our way. A sudden heavy downpour of rain, hit my face so hard, I could barely open my eyes. I couldn't make out any of the stores through the wall of rain. Millie and I just followed Mom as we fought our way home.

The storm was taunting us, but through all of the danger, some- how Mom saw the fun in it. Her laughing made me feel like nothing could happen to us. She got us home safely into the vestibule of our building. We had cheated the storm out of swallowing us up, and the wind screamed its anger at our escape.

The rain knocked at my window as the wind whistled around in the alley. Our building was my fortress, and the wind could do its worst. I was protected in my room in warm dry clothes, eating a warm supper. The rain against my window washed away all thoughts of Harold.

The next day, school was closed because of the storm, and my holiday continued. The hurricane had torn at a row of huge trees around the corner on Faille Street, ripping their roots out of the ground. The power of their crushing weight crashed down into the street and crisscrossed each other. Their twisted trunks and branches tangled them together, desperately holding on to each other, leaving tunnels and hidden caves.

Faille Street didn't look like The Bronx anymore. It had become an impenetrable jungle, a gigantic toy for me and my friends. There was no end to the games we played, like a safari marching through Tarzan's jungle, or Marines fighting the Japs on an island in the Pacific. But our three days of fun came to an end when a cleanup crew started taking our super toys away... and we were back to reality and back to school.

It was a cool evening in September, and after meeting Mom at the Simpson Street Station on our way home, we stopped at Mr. Siegel's Hardware next door to Chester Drugs. The store was crowded and while we waited our turn, we watched *Arthur Godfrey's Talent Scouts Show* on a round television screen the size of a soft ball.

Most of the television sets were owned by the businesses in the neighborhood. Whenever I had a chance to watch one, it felt unreal standing inside a store staring at a radio with pictures.

Godfrey's slow nasal tones and pointed remarks came out of the circular screen. Mom could care less about the waiting crowd, because she had *Arthur Godfrey* to watch. She was mad about him and always listened to his radio show. Now she had a chance to see what he looked like.

Mr. Siegel interrupted Mom's love affair, "Molly! Molly, can I talk to you for a second?"

"Vhat is it?"

"A friend of mine belongs to a Jewish organization that helps people. He knows this Spanish couple with a new baby.

They got here today, from... Jesus, I can't remember where they're from. Well anyway, they're from another country and need help. They don't have a place to live."

"So?"

"Well it's an emergency... with the baby and all. They'd like to rent a room until they can find a place of their own."

"Vhere did you meet these people?"

"Don't worry Molly, they're good people. I'd like you to meet the wife and baby. She's over there by the dishes waiting for her husband. Mrs. Alvarez, over here!"

"Si?"

"Mrs. Alvarez, this woman is a good friend. Her name is Molly, Molly Havener, and she has a room to rent."

"Wait a minute, I didn't say dat."

Mr. Alvarez walked into the store and joined his wife. Just by looking at the couple and their baby, Mom took a liking to them.

"I have a bedroom right next to the front door, near the bathroom and kitchen. You'll have lots of privacy. I can give it to you for five dollars a week."

Oh shit, just like that she was giving my room away.

"Vhat do you think, is five dollars too much?"

Mrs. Alvarez could hardly speak English, but her husband spoke it fluently, with a slight accent, "No, that's fine. It will be only for a short time... until we can find a place of our own."

"Dat's okay, darlink." Mom looked at the baby, "Oh, vhat a beautiful baby."

"Mrs. Havener."

"No, please call me Molly."

"Okay, Molly, would it be asking too much, or be too inconvenient for you if we move into the room tonight? We don't have anywhere else to go."

"Sure, why not. Where's your things?"

"They're at the Penn Station check out counter. I can pick them up tomorrow."

Mom looked at Mrs. Alvarez and her baby, "Dahlink, don't you worry. Everything's going to be alright."

And now I had to sleep in the living room again, right next to Harold. But there was no need for me to worry. As long as strangers were in the house, he'd be on his best behavior. And sure enough, while Mr. and Mrs. Alvarez were living with us, Harold spent most of the time in his room and left me alone.

Mom helped Mrs. Alvarez with her baby and took them for a tour around the neighborhood. She showed Mrs. Alvarez the Triangle where she could shop for food and get what she needed for the baby.

New smells filled our apartment with the fragrance of Spanish cooking. As always with the people she liked, Mom made friends easily and treated Mrs. Alvarez like a daughter.

I really liked them, not because they kept Harold in check, but because they treated me like they really cared for me. Still, I wanted to be back in my dungeon, where I could be alone, away from everyone else's lunacy. I wanted to be alone and free, even if it was with my own deranged mind.

After only two and a half weeks of living in my room, Mr. and Mrs. Alvarez moved out, we never knew where. I missed them, but I was happy to get my room back. I also got Harold back.

My room was one of the places I could be invisible to everyone, except for the people who hated me. They seem to have this radar that penetrated my defenses. Harold was either super quiet or a raving maniac, nothing in between. And now with all that pent up hate he had stuffed inside, he couldn't hold it back any longer.

Harold trapped me in the hall, "You! Yes, you… get over here!"

He sat me down in the kitchen, "I want to talk to you."

Here it comes… I closed my eyes and prayed for him to do his worse and get it over with so I could get back to my room, but he kept punching my shoulder to punctuate every point he made. Each punch weakened my control, and I couldn't block him out anymore. I had to sit there listening to his non-stop crap.

"Look at me, damn it! Look at me when I'm talking to you!"

To Harold I was an annoying paper cut, a sore that never heals, always reminding him I was still there. He grabbed me by the chest, pulled at my shirt and skin, picking me up from the chair and throwing me back down, almost toppling the chair. He pulled me from the chair again, but this time threw me to the floor.

Lying on my back, I started to walk the ceiling with my eyes trying to keep from looking at him. I wasn't reacting to his violence and it frustrated him. He didn't know what to do with me, "Get the fuck out of my sight, you fucking idiot retard!" Before Harold could take another breath, I was gone and out the front door.

IMITATION OF A FART

THE LEATHER SOLE had worn down and pulled away from one of my shoes, and before Mom left for work, she gave me money to have it fixed on my way home after school. So I spent my day in school, flopping through my classes. After lunch, all the kids in Junior High were lined up on the caged stairway to receive free injections. We didn't know what they were for, but if the school said it was okay, then it was okay with us.

While waiting in line for my turn, Seymour Schwartz was standing at my side. I watched the pale, syrupy snot hanging from his nose. It dripped down toward his chin, but at the last second, he sniffed it back up into his nose. When he breathed out, it dripped down out again, up and down in a never-ending ride – earning him the nickname of Yo-Yo.

Yo-Yo was a hell of a baseball player, the best in the whole neighborhood. He was equally great at any position, including pitching, but was constantly harassed by the guys. I tried to be kind to him, but I avoided him whenever I could.

Not having girls in our classes opened up new possibilities for me, like becoming the class comic. It all started while we were waiting on line for our vaccinations. I was surrounded by my new friends: Reyes, Jorrin, Wozar, and Paratory. Their favorite nickname for me was Rothballs.

I was inspired to cup my mouth around my forearm and blast away, making an excellent farting sound. To my surprise they laughed.

This urged me on and I went a little further, adding to my act the flopping of my shoe sole to accompany the sounds of my imitation farts. They broke up, infecting the whole stairway filled with kids, from top to bottom. Those fart sounds brought me fame and started my career as a comic.

It was 3 pm, the end of a very satisfying school day for me. I had learned I was actually able to make a whole group of kids react to something I did.

My shoe flopped up Faille Street alongside Anthony Santangelo's house, where there were still a few open morning glories peeking through the crew cut hedges. I flopped on to Westchester Avenue to get my shoe fixed, but hesitated... this would mean I'd be losing part of my comic routine.

It was early on a chilly morning and my friends and I were out on the street. My kid brother Ronnie was about four years old and in my care for the day. We all made a beeline to Jack's candy store, the first to open on the block.

Before spending our hard-gotten money on a Spaldeen, we first had to test them for the highest bouncer. Poor Jack was awfully patient with us, and we paid him back by robbing his candy. Ronnie was so little and on the chubby side, and we figured that no one would notice him if we stuffed him with candy while Junior kept chickie on Jack.

We did better than we expected. Ronnie was so top heavy with candy, he could hardly walk straight, and we practically had to roll him out of the store. After divvying up the candy, we saved it for the movies.

To pass the time while waiting for the Boulevard Theater to open, we played a game of flies up. We wouldn't tolerate cheating in any game. If there was any disagreement about whether a ball was caught on a fly or not, we'd argue until there was a standoff. Then we'd call for a do-over.

I was up at bat, and before I even got my first swing, Junior called out, "Truck! Truck comin'!"

The Spaldeen got loose and the truck smashed it, popping it open. But that didn't stop us. We just cut the ball in half and started a new game. When the half ball was pitched to the guy up at bat, it danced all over the place. We couldn't control it or predict where the ball would go, and it became a joke. If you could learn to hit that insane ball, you could hit anything.

It was almost time for the movie to open and Barbara Erb and Annie Denner joined us – an unexpected pleasure. Sergie and I had a super crush on Barbara. I could tell she liked us both. We sat on either side of her in the orchestra.

While we were watching the movie, *City Across The River*, all of my attention, no, my whole being, was concentrated on Barbara. I-wrapped my arm around the back of her chair, and inch-by-inch, I raised it. It took me almost the entire movie just to reach the top of her chair. I was feverishly throbbing, sweating, and shaking, but Barbara never felt a damn thing... it was all me. At the end of the movie, I could hardly stand up and stumbled out of the theater. Do-over!

The background noises were empty sounds going nowhere and a swollen buzz filled my consciousness. Nothing else existed. I was breathing into myself, thinking if my life ended right now I wouldn't care. All my pain was gone. Harold wasn't important, school wasn't important, but I *was* important. When the gas wore off, I felt cleansed of all my fears. The dentist had cured me. At least for a little while, I felt satisfied being myself.

It was Thanksgiving Day and my dentist visit had been an emergency, an unforgiving, throbbing toothache. Even my pain was screaming from the pain. It sucked out all my strength. Mom had to help me to the dentist, but left me there to rush out and buy the turkey.

On the way home from the dentist, the air was cold and snow-flakes were drifting down, tickling the un-numbed parts of my face. Past the church on Hoe Avenue, I watched a bunch of kids looking up into the sky, coaxing the snowflakes down onto their faces. Crossing Westchester Avenue, I expected to see the trolleys, but remembered they were gone. They had disappeared overnight. All that was left of them were the tracks pointing the way for the cars to follow. Part of the background music of my neighborhood had been the ringing of the trolley bells. Like an amputation, I could still hear the phantom trolley bells ringing on Westchester Avenue.

When I got to my building, the snow had changed to a cold rain. Our apartment was saturated with the smell of Mom's turkey. She was cooking it with strips of bacon on its breast and the whole turkey was covered with a brown shopping bag to keep it moist in the oven.

To me Thanksgiving never meant family. It meant only a holiday from school and hot, delicious turkey dinner served in my warm room. I ate with my radio, listening to shows that had Thanksgiving as part of their plots. Harold took this holiday off and left us alone, a Thanksgiving we had something to be thankful for.

Mom brought me a plate with a turkey wing, the neck and some slices of white meat. What I really wanted was a drumstick, but of course, they belonged to Harold. Around the side of the plate were sweet potato, cranberry sauce, and the best stuffing, together with my mom's super gravy made from the drippings of the turkey.

By the time I ate, the numbness was beginning to wear off and it was hell trying to chew on one side of my mouth. But it felt good to be alive, and I stared at the window, watching the downpour hitting the glass pane. My ear was glued to the radio speaker. The announcer's voice echoed above a drumroll: *"Mister District Attorney! Champion of the people! Defender of truth! Guardian of our fundamental rights to life, liberty, and the pursuit of happiness."*

THE MUMMY'S CURSE

ALONE IN AN empty apartment, Mom and Harold's bedroom doors were wide open, begging me to investigate. I found a sealed-off, undiscovered chamber where Harold jealously hid his secrets. His closet door separated his world from mine. I broke through the tomb's entrance and a foreboding voice spoke to me, *"You enter my secret chamber at your own peril. You have been warned."*

I knew that if I entered the mummy's tomb, there would be a mummy's curse on me. After thousands of years of being closed off from the world, the light entered the dark vault with me. The chamber was filled with a treasure of artifacts, all intact, unseen by other eyes except Harold's. Each object warned me to be very careful, or I'd trigger the curse of the tomb. The voice promised it would tell Harold I was there, touching his secret things.

Hidden behind three big, petrified tree stumps was a rifle, a real rifle with a hexagon barrel. I had never seen a hexagon barrel before. It must be an ancient gun. Beside it was a box of strange tools; and amongst the tools was a box falling apart from age, filled with bullets.

Very gently, so as not to disturb anything else, I slid the gun out of its hiding place and out of the tomb. As I was about to close the vault door, the chamber came alive, shouting out an alarm in Harold's loathsome voice, *"I put a curse on you. You cannot hide from me. I will have my revenge…"*

I slammed the door shut, cutting the voice off in mid-curse, and ran to my room to examine the rifle. The gun had a pump action, but it seemed to be stuck. I had to use both hands and some body English to pump the rifle. I couldn't wait to show my friends and hid the rifle down the leg of my pants and up under my shirt, so I could carry it out onto the street. I called Bobby, Sergie, and Junior over to the entrance of the alley and uncovered the rifle.

Junior's eyes popped open, "Wow!"

Sergie couldn't believe it, "Holy shit! Is it real?"

"Yeah, damn right it's real. And I also got bullets!"

Off to the creek we went and found a secluded spot by a huge boulder. It took a couple of us to pump the gun, but we finally got off a shot.

A hand punched through the air from behind me and grabbed the rifle from my hand. Some kid, maybe three years older than us, appeared from nowhere. "Here let me show you how it's done." And with one quick pump, he loaded the chamber with several bullets.

I said, "Wow! That's cool. Let me try it?"

"No. Nobody's going to touch this gun but me."

Hearing that, I knew we were in for a lot of trouble. The guy pointed the rifle in our direction and pulled the trigger. Either he was a lousy shot or missed on purpose. Before he could get off another shot, we jumped behind the granite boulder.

His shots rang out in quick succession, off the boulder. I was too afraid to feel afraid. He started to walk toward us, shooting all the way. The bullets got awfully close, some just barely missing us. He was acting like he was in some cowboy movie. We looked at each other and couldn't believe this was happening. Were we really going to die? If I wasn't always constipated, I would have shit in my pants.

His rifle ran out of bullets, and while he was reloading, we didn't need an invitation. In a "...*cloud of dust and a hearty Hi–Yo, Silver,*" we disappeared leaving him behind us, a little dot surrounded by puffs of smoke, firing at our trail of dust.

Out of breath after our narrow escape, we rested at the old broken down swimming pool on Whitlock Avenue. Two tough guys, about seventeen years old, walked up to us.

"What's da matter, someone chasin' ya?"

Another guy looked at me, "Nice sneakers, kid."

The tone of their voices meant trouble. They definitely wanted to start something. We had left one problem and stepped into another... It was the mummy's curse.

"Hey stupid. You're blocking my way. Get the fuck outta my way."

No one was in his way, but he pushed Sergie hard into Bobby.

"Hey you, you little punk. Let me see those sneakers."

These guys were bad news, and our only escape was to jump over the fence that enclosed the pool. I was halfway over when one of the guys got a hold of my foot and tried to pull me back. He ended up with one of my sneakers. I didn't stop running, and caught up with my friends as they ran past Bryant Avenue.

At that moment, my tic decided to act up. All I needed was for my friends to see me looking like a freak. Now, I was deep into the mummy's curse. I ran ahead of my friends and ducked into my building, hiding under the stairwell until I was able to transform myself back to a normal human being.

I held my breath as I limped into our apartment with one sneaker on. No one even noticed me. It would be a long time before I'd see another pair of sneakers again. How was I going to explain losing my left sneaker, when I wasn't supposed to be by the creek in the first place... one of my mother's cardinal rules. But I didn't have to worry after all, because the very next day, I took a chance and went alone down to the pool. There was my sneaker waiting for me, sitting on top of the fence.

Harold never did find out about his missing rifle. It was a mystery to me that he never noticed it was gone, but if just one single piece of his fucking candy was gone, all hell would break loose.

Millie was crying uncontrollably in the kitchen. It was almost impossible to hear what she was saying. I got closer and heard her pleading to Mom, "But Ma, it's my sixteenth birthday, my special birthday."

Mom had been planning to give Millie a surprise party for her birthday, but Millie's best friend, Veronica, accidently, or knowingly, told Millie about it. When Mom found out that Millie knew, she called off the party.

"I'm sorry, Mom said gruffly, the idea was to be a surprise."

"So it's not a surprise. It's still my sixteenth birthday."

"It's not the same ting."

"Damn it, it's still my sixteenth birthday. I never had a fuckin' birthday party because of Harold, and I never complained. Why? Why can't you... just this one time?"

"Don't you curse. You watch your mouth."

"Jesus Christ, Ma, just this once? So it's not a surprise... it's still a special birthday."

"But dat's not the same ting. I wanted to make it special by surprising you."

"Don't hand me that shit! How can you do this to me?"

Mom walked out of the room, "I vill not talk to you if you keep on cursing at me."

"Where are you going? I hate you! You hear me? I hate you! I'll never forgive you for this!" Millie went to her room and cried herself to sleep, and she never had her special day.

Maybe we couldn't afford such a big party. I think Mom felt relieved there wouldn't be one. She thought very little of herself, and maybe she thought she might botch it up or was afraid Harold might act up during the party. Whatever it was, Millie still got a royal screwing.

Leaning forward in a squat, with a snap of the wrist and a little body English, my baseball card cut through the air, flying toward its destination up against my building. My friends and I took turns tossing our cards. The one that came closest to the edge of the building won the other kid's cards.

Sheldon walked out of our building all dressed up in a dark suit. He was wearing a yarmulke, which looked like a black bald spot on the back of his sandy red hair. Most of us went to P.S. 75 or St. John's Catholic School, and Sheldon was the only one who went to Hebrew School. In his own peculiar gait, he bounced across our baseball cards.

Bobby yelled, "Hey! Get the fuck offa da cards!"

"Hey, where are ya going all dressed up like dat?"

Sheldon looked at me with his freckled face, "It's my Bar Mitzvah. I'm going to my party."

Sergie asked, "Where's da party?"

"It's on Longfellow."

"Can we go?"

"Maybe I could get a couple of ya in."

No one was interested except for Sergie and me.

I asked, "Don't ya have to be dressed up?"

"Nah, it's okay. I can sneak you in."

The party was held in a large apartment. There was a big crowd surrounding a long table piled high with deli and neat rows of glasses filled with red wine – and it was all for free. Sergie and I found a corner of the room where we could drink all the wine we wanted without anyone noticing us. After two glasses each, we got real dizzy, my first time getting high. Everything softened and slowed down. I didn't care if people noticed me, and I didn't have to be constantly on guard. Whatever I did or said flowed out of me without any fears. I just didn't give a shit.

Before the grownups noticed how high we were, Sergie and I slipped out of the party, laughing all the way home. Climbing the stairs, I was stopped in the hall by Mrs. Meisel, who was Crazy Leo and Sydney's mother.

"Solly, could you please help me move my couch. I think I dropped an earring behind it, and there's no one home to help me."

She must have been kidding. I was so small for my age, how the hell was I going to help her move that heavy couch? Together we inched it slightly away from the wall, and Mrs. Meisel reached over the back of the couch, searching for her earring. Her ass was in my face and gave off a sexual signal I couldn't refuse to answer.

The wine gave me a false sense of courage, and I leaned against her ass. My cock fit into the crack between her warm cheeks. Her ass squeezed into my groin burying my cock as I pressed hard against her. She must have felt me, but she didn't move or say a word. I couldn't help myself. No matter what the consequences, I couldn't stop. Just before I exploded, she stood up, thanked me for my help, and showed me out the door. My legs had turned to rubber, and by the time I got to my room, I was still so horny I grabbed one of my pillows and pumped away.

THE DOUBLE-HEADER

SYDNEY MEISEL WAS older than me and had the reputation of screwing around. The Meisel's lived right across the hall, and I saw them leaving their apartment without her. Before she had a chance to close her door, I said, "Hi Syd."

"Hello, yourself."

"I've got some great hot books, would you like to see them?"

"Sure, why not."

With the money I made delivering groceries for Joe and Abe, I bought some hot books and always carried a few with me just in case. You never know.

Just the idea that Syd was sitting there in her kitchen reading the hot books in front of me turned me on. My dick pressed against my pants, trying to break free. I took a chance and pressed it against her shoulder. She didn't seem to mind it. I could feel her body shaking with excitement, but it wasn't for me, because she got up from her chair and said, "Solly, I think you better leave. Now."

She shoved me out of her apartment and ran downstairs. Out on the street, she met an older boy she knew and brought him back upstairs. They left the door slightly open and I could hear them fucking. Here I get her all excited, and she screws somebody else.

Mrs. Meisel came home unexpectedly early and caught Syd in the middle of doing it. Mrs. Meisel screamed like she was being murdered. The boy rushed out of the apartment with his pants down to his knees and hobbled down the stairs, tripping as he tried to pull his pants up. Ah, justice!

Sitting by a table at the back of Jack's candy store, Anthony and Sergie ordered chocolate egg creams. Jack made his egg creams with a little milk, seltzer, and U-Bet chocolate syrup. It had to be U-Bet. If it wasn't, it didn't taste like a real egg cream. I never knew why they called it an egg cream in the first place, when there was no egg in it... just another mystery of life in The Bronx.

I thumbed through Jack's new joke books while drinking a chocolate malted with a salted pretzel stick. The pretzels were made for eating with a malted, and I couldn't think of having one without the other.

It was a week before the Fourth of July and Junior raced into Jack's. "Hey guys! I've gotta show you somethin'."

In Junior's hall was a large cardboard box filled with all kinds of firecrackers. He was actually trying to sell them to us. We begged him for a few free ones, but no dice. We kept on nagging him until he finally gave each of us a two-incher. Sergie and I decided to hold onto our two-inchers until it got dark. When night finally came, and we felt safe from patrolling cops, we set them off. Wouldn't you know it, after a whole fucking day of playing it safe, we got caught.

The cops chased us, pounding down on us like bulls, and caught us both. Sergie broke loose and ran up the long flight of steps to Junior's house with one of the cops right behind him.

"Where do you think you're going, you little Spic?"

The cop grabbed Sergie and threw him down the long flight of steps. When he got up, the cop pushed him to the floor again and kicked him. He dragged both of us to the wall by Harry's Bar. The two cops made us spread eagle and searched us. We were two skinny little kids, and they treated us like we were the most wanted criminals of The Bronx.

My mom ran across the street screaming, "That's my Solly! Vhat are you doing to him? He's a good boy."

One of the cops opened the police callbox and called for a patrol car. Mom kept screaming, "He's a good boy!"

They took us to the 41st Precinct, but that was all for show. What they really wanted to do was scare us. And they did. But I got an education that night. The cops treated me differently than Sergie. They were much rougher on him and kept referring to him as, "the little Spic."

It was a Sunday morning and nothing was happening. Sergie and I were the only ones on the block, and there was nothing we really wanted to see at the movies. Sergie's brother Frankie told us that the Yankees were at home for a Double-Header, so we opted for the Yankee game. We carried our brown paper bags filled with sandwiches and took the 167th Street bus near St. John's.

We paid 60 cents for a bleacher seat, and walked down a ramp into the belly of the stadium. Out from the brick buildings, gray concrete and tar streets, we saw an island of vivid green grass... like seeing color for the first time. From our seats in the bleachers, we heard the delayed, hollow sounds and disconnected muffled voices from the distant practice, carrying back to us on the damp, soft morning air.

Joe Page was a relief pitcher when the specialty of relief pitching was new. A handful of us bleacher kids leaned over the wall of the Yankee bullpen nearby. He smiled and talked to us, asking us about school and what positions in baseball we played at home. Sergie and I shouted back that we didn't play hardball – we played stickball.

"That's great. Stickball is great for eye and body coordination. So keep practicing your stickball, and when you're ready for hardball, you'll have a head start."

Here was a Yankee player really talking to us kids and interested in us. He was enjoying himself. Then there was Joe DiMaggio, who stood in center field by the monuments. When we shouted out his name, all he did was grunt back at us.

Today Sergie and I were going to put a plan into action that we had talked about many times at home. Half the people in the Stadium never stayed for the second game. So after the first game ended, Sergie and I took a gamble and left the Stadium, even though we knew we couldn't get back into the bleachers once we left. The grandstand gates were rolled open and the crowd piled out onto the street. Sergie and I mingled with them walking backwards, creating the illusion we were walking out with the crowd when we were really walking back into the Stadium. The guards couldn't tell the difference.

Once inside, we raced to the empty box seats and sat right behind the Yankee dugout. No one paid any attention to us. There we were, looking at our heroes close up, no longer the tiny walking shadows we had seen from the bleachers. Walking just a few feet from us were Jerry Colman and Yogi Berra. I could reach out and almost touch them. Not only could I see the game up close, but I could also feel the action.

One of the great moments of going to a game at Yankee Stadium was, after the game was over, the guards let everybody exit out onto the playing field. We found ourselves standing on the same grass where the legends of baseball had stood. That day Sergie and I had a special treat. Exiting from the box seats close to the diamond, we beat the guards to the bases. I slid, smashing my foot up against Second Base. I was Joe DiMaggio, stretching a single into a double. All the way home, DiMaggio, Berra, and the Scooter were with me on the bus.

TREASON AT POE PARK

FOR LUNCH I had a salami sandwich with a healthy spread of hot mustard on white bread, with a bottle of cream soda. I ran out past Crazy Leo and Yeager, leaning against our building. They were always leaning against something... doorways, parked cars. Yeager was somewhere between heavy and fat, and even though he didn't wear a yarmulke or payot dangling down in front of both ears, he carried himself as if he did. He was very tight with Crazy Leo and anytime I looked up from playing, they were standing together, leaning, watching the rest of us.

When my friends and I were on the roof, it was like living in a secret clubhouse separate from the rest of The Bronx, where no one could see us, not even Leo and Yeager. Everyone on the block was walking below us, never thinking of looking up. Here, we had the power of seeing and not being seen.

Anthony, Sergie, Junior, and I chipped in and bought homing pigeons. We kept them in several orange crates on the little roof above the doorway. We trained them, and once they got used to their coop as home, we chucked them. This involved taking them a distance away from the coop and letting them go. They would fly right back to their rooftop home.

One day Mrs. Levine discovered our pigeons, and we had to get rid of them. It was impossible for her to have found out – someone must have squealed on us. I suspected it was Melvin. Anthony got permission to set up a coop down in his basement, near a few windows that opened onto their backyard. Now our pigeons had a home where Anthony could raise their little chicks. He even trained one to sit on his shoulder as he rode his bike through the streets.

Crazy Leo caught Anthony on his bike and grabbed the pigeon off his shoulder. He put its head between his fingers and swung it around until its neck cracked. The pigeon ran around with its head flopping to one side until it quivered and died. From that day on I lost any affection I had for pigeons. I never had anything to do with them again. I couldn't even bear to look at them.

About a week later, we were on the roof, flying kites. Every time the kite tugged at my hand, I felt like I was a part of it, flying and free. But some days, we played a dangerous game patterned after the WW II dog fights. We attached razor blades onto the tails of our kites and maneuvered them into the strings of each other's kites, cutting them free. The cut kites would take a nosedive and fly off into the distance, never to be seen again.

While flying our kites, we could see into the windows of a hotel across Westchester Avenue where two naked people were fucking. We all got excited and our pants bulged with hard-ons. When the couple got up from the bed we got the shock of our lives, they were both men! We were devastated and ashamed for getting hard-ons while watching two guys, and now our manhood was in question. So we made a blood pact by pricking our fingers, mingling our blood, and promising never to mention this to anyone for the rest of our lives.

Late that afternoon, Millie was in my room trying to talk me into going to a public dance at Poe Park as her dancing partner.

"You don't have to worry, I promise I'll be with you all the time. You won't have to dance with anyone but me. There's nothing to be afraid of. And anyway, there'll be so many people, they won't even notice you."

Millie had taught me how to dance, and we knew each other's

every move. And now she was going to make it pay off. I think she was using me to break the ice with the boys. They would see how good she was and want to dance with her.

We took the bus to Poe Park. It was twilight, when the green leaves appear black against the turning sky, just before both are obliterated by the night. I thought I knew all the different parts of The Bronx, but I'd never been in this section before. It felt like another country.

Floodlights lit up the surrounding little piece of the park into daylight. A gazebo was in the center of a clearing with a real band, surrounded by kids laughing and talking. One of Millie's friends, a girl I'd never seen before, flirted with me.

"So this is your little brother who's a wonderful dancer? He's awfully cute. Solly, is that your name?"

I nodded my head, "Yes."

"Well, Solly, save a dance for me."

Then, before Millie and I even had our first dance, she walked away from me, leaving me alone in the crowd of strangers. The traitor! There I was standing all by myself, trying to hide from the strangers darting in and out around me. A pain started in my stomach, and built into terrible cramps. I knew that pain like it was an old buddy – diarrhea bubbling in my stomach.

Millie came back and I told her, "I've got to go home."

"Oh, no you don't. We just got here. Just one dance and you can go. You'll see, it isn't that bad."

"You don't understand. I'm hurting. I've got to go to the bathroom."

"Why don't you go to a bathroom in one of the restaurants outside the Park?"

"I can't."

She didn't believe me. She thought I was faking pain as an excuse to go home. "Ehh, do what you want." She gave me carfare and left me standing there alone. The cramps grew and the pain was getting out of control.

Like Millie said, there were restaurants on my way to the bus, but I was too afraid to ask to use their toilets. I'd rather die of the pain than have all those people, eating at their tables, hear me ask to use a toilet and look at me with disgust. They probably would have kicked me out anyway, because I was just a kid. And maybe all I would have done would be to miss the bus... I had to get home!

It was a long time before a bus came, and by then, I had doubled up in pain. It felt like I'd been given an enema and couldn't hold it in any longer. I was ready to explode.

The bus finally came. Thank God, it was empty so I could hide in the back. The bus didn't move. It just stood there for what seemed like forever. What the fuck is he waiting for? You damn bastard, move the fuckin' bus! Sweat ran down my forehead, and puddled in the notch of my throat. The bus driver finally had some pity on me and started on his route.

Meanwhile, I was folded in half banging my head in desperation against the top of the chair in front of me, which temporarily took my mind off of the cramps in my stomach. I almost bit through my fingers trying to hold the shit in. I didn't know if I was going to live long enough to get home. My clothes were drenched in sweat.

The bus stopped at Southern Boulevard and Westchester Avenue, and I made a mad dash for home, ran upstairs, sat on the toilet and relieved my pain. I stayed there for about an hour, afraid to leave in case I might get another attack.

Outside the door of the bathroom, I heard Harold take in a deep breath and clear his throat with a growl. "What the hell are you doing in there? Get outta there, or I'll get you out!" Harold screamed, "My God, it stinks in here. Just like a Jew to smell like shit."

Harold pushed me into the kitchen, and sat me down on a chair. He stared at me, very close to my face. Was this going to be one of his talking-at-me times?

My urge to shit began to grow, and Harold became the bus that wouldn't move. The pain took over every function of my body and mind. I couldn't even think. The only thing that was going through my mind was getting into the bathroom, just a few feet away. The walls became a blur and were closing in on me.

The painful cramps became stronger than my fear of Harold and I didn't care if he was there or not... I ran into the bathroom almost shitting in my pants. The stink was so bad that Harold decided to leave me alone.

ON THE JOB

WHEN THE GUYS and I stepped out of the Boulevard movie, I was groggy from being cooped up for hours in the dark, watching cartoons, a serial, some shorts, and two movies, *Twelve O'clock High*, with Gregory Peck, and *The Hasty Heart*, with Ronald Reagan. I had been living in WW II again. Now the streets seemed unreal, and I had to readjust to being in 1949 again.

The guys were in a playing mood. They took my Navy cap off my head and teased me by keeping it out of my reach, passing it from one guy to the other. A shit game, especially when you were "It." I got really pissed off and chased them across Westchester Avenue, where the El made the sharp turn onto Southern Boulevard.

I was running by the bicycle store and something caught my eye in the window. It was a brand new, green Shelby bike. The Shelby Company tried to imitate the design of the Schwinn bike, the "Cadillac of bikes." The Shelby wasn't in the same class, but it looked awfully good dressed up with its shining new fenders, chain guard and a streamlined green barrel attached to the center bar. Leaning up against the bike store window, I forgot all about my cap.

There was a sign attached to the bike that said, "Super Sale." On my way home, I couldn't think of anything else but that bike. My friends had bikes. I was the only one who didn't. There were days when they would disappear from the block, traveling on their bikes to foreign neighborhoods and new adventures, leaving me home alone with my radio.

"Solly, it's so nice outside. Vhy don't you go out and play wit your friends?"

"Ma, they all have bikes, and I don't."

"How much is a bike?"

"There's one I saw for only eighteen dollars."

"Vhat are you crazy? I don't have dat kind of money."

"No Ma, you've got it wrong. I'm not asking you for the money, I'm going to pay for it myself."

"Darlink, I love you, but how are you going to get dat kind of money... rob a bank, maybe?"

"The man told me all I need is a dollar for a down payment to hold the bike for me. Could you give it to me? I swear I'll pay you back. I can get it on the lay-away plan, and I've got two months to pay it out."

"Still, how are you going to get such money?"

"I'll find a job."

"I'll tell you what. If you can find a job, I'll give you the dollar and you don't have to pay me back."

I was way ahead of myself. Where the hell am I going to find a job? Delivering groceries for tips wasn't enough.

Mom never said anything to me about what she was thinking. She took me with her to Chester Drugs to buy aspirins, so she said. While there, she struck up a conversation with one of the brothers and asked him if he needed any kind of help. Since Mom was a steady customer, he gave it some serous consideration. Before we left the store, he said, "We could use someone to stock supplies and do deliveries." He looked at me, "Can you handle it?"

"I can do that."

"Alright then, we'll start you off with a dollar a week plus tips."

On my first day, a truck emptied boxes full of supplies onto a slide that went down into the basement. How many times my friends and I had looked at the boxes being pushed down the slide into the bowels of the Chester Drug cellar and wondered where those boxes went? I was standing in the mysterious pit, looking up into the street, and I was the only one of my friends who knew what it was really like down in the drug store cellar.

My job was to sort and stack the boxes into the right places. It took all of my strength to push the boxes and lift them to where they belonged. I thought I was alone in the basement, but I had company... creeping, fat, juicy water bugs, almost as big as my hand. Every once in while one would jump out of a dark corner and flutter into me. Euggh! I did the whole job with goose bumps. Thank God, I only had to do the stocking once a week.

I worked at Chester Drugs three days a week after school, and all day Saturday. During the summer, I worked full time with two days off, Saturdays and Sundays. I figured if I also delivered groceries for Joe and Abe, plus tips from the drug store deliveries, plus the dollar a week salary, I'd be able to pay for the bike before the two months was over.

A bunch of older guys from Hoe Avenue learned I was working at Chester Drugs. One day they cornered me outside the drug store and threatened me into robbing some scumbags for them. And if I didn't, they'd take care of me. My friends and I would always call each other scumbags, but I never saw one. When I searched through all the drawers at the store, I found a box full of loose, thin rubber things I thought were scumbags, and I gave them to the guys. What they actually were, were finger protectors. If it had been possible for any of the guys from Hoe Avenue to get one of those suckers on, which I doubted, it would strangle his cock, cut off its blood supply, and his dick would develop gangrene and have to be amputated.

The next day the guys from Hoe Avenue caught me after work and shoved me into an empty alley. "What are you a fuckin' wise guy? You trying to make fun of us?" They thought I was making a statement about the size of their dicks.

"What's the matter? I got the rubbers like you asked for and a whole bunch of them, too."

"Are you kidding me? You thought that shit was rubbers?"

All four of them began to laugh. "You're a lucky kid, we believe you. We'll give you another chance. Rubbers look like what you gave us, but much bigger and each one is wrapped separately. They usually come in a box with the name Trojan condoms on it. You got it?"

"I swear to ya, I didn't know."

"Take it easy kid, we believe ya. We'll see you tomorrow. And make sure you bring the real stuff." They walked away, "What an asshole..." and laughed themselves out of the alley.

The next time I got it right. Most important of all, I learned what a scumbag looked like... and my boss never found out.

"Berra got a hold of one and hits it high, back, back, back, and into the bleachers. How *about* that?" My boss' radio was on, with Mel Allen keeping him company as he filled out a prescription for me to deliver.

He worked on a marble counter in back of the store by an open window. The counter had smooth indentations scooped out of its surface for measuring and counting pills. He poured white powder from a jar onto the counter and, using a miniature, flat metal ruler, he slid it effortlessly into several even piles. On the other end of the thin metal ruler was a tiny spoon that he used to shovel each pile of powder, guiding it into separate small, white envelopes and taping them closed.

For years I believed Chester was my boss' name. I didn't know it meant Chester as in Westchester Avenue. My bosses appreciated how hard I worked and decided to give me a raise. They said they were promoting me to work the cash register. That sent a cold chill through me. There was no way I could do it.

The register looked at me, threatening me with its complex machinery. I knew I'd louse it up. Chester Drugs would see me counting on my fingers and find out how stupid I really was. How was I going to make change for the customers when my math sucked? The only way I could survive the shame was to quit. The Chester brothers tried to talk me out of it, but it was no use. I'd commit suicide first before I'd tackle that machine.

It was the end of July anyway, and I had enough money to buy my bike and pay Mom back. And I had a whole month of vacation with my new bike before school started.

My friends and I spent almost every day of August traveling to every corner of The Bronx, from Orchard Beach to the Grand Concourse. Never the same place twice. My bike was a green tank... the damn thing was bigger than me. Whenever I wanted to use it, I had to drag it down three double flights of stairs. But dragging it back up the stairs was hell. I had to maneuver each step like I was scaling a mountain and brace myself against the sheer weight of the bike taking me down into a great fall. My love affair with the green tank didn't last very long.

The summer ended with a gruesome scene I'll never forget, and will never understand. My friends and I heard a girl screaming as if she was being tortured. I recognized the voice. It belonged to Larraine, from the corner of Faille and East 165th street. She was a shy and pretty girl, with a terrible scar on one side of her face that she kept covered with her long black hair. The rumor was that when she was about six years old, a pot of boiling water accidently spilled onto her face, leaving a permanent scar from her forehead to the bottom of her cheekbone.

A group of guys I'd never seen before had spread her arms and legs apart and tied her to a tall, black metal gate. They were laughing as they tried to shove a broomstick up between her legs. Larraine franticly tried to twist herself free, but the rope wouldn't give.

She screamed out to the people on the street, "Stop! Stop! Please! Somebody help me!" But everyone ignored her screams, as if nothing was happening.

One guy was feeling her breasts while another was forcing the broomstick up her skirt. She saw us watching, and with tears filling her eyes, she begged us to help her.

"Help me! Please help me!"

Sergie was first to respond, "What the fuck are you guys trying to do?"

"Get away kid, if you know what's good for ya, or you'll join her."

I answered his threat, "Ahh, you're talkin' out of your asshole."

"Hey, I'm warning ya. Get the fuck outta here, or I'll beat your ass in."

"Yeah... you and what army?"

Why were they doing this? What were they getting out of it? My friends and I couldn't watch. We had to do something. We ran and told her parents what was happening. They called the cops and saved Larraine. The cops caught one of the scumbags. The others got away. Larraine disappeared for a while, but returned to the block a few months later.

Eyes bulging, spit dripping from his lips, a patchwork of scars held his face together. He plunges the large kitchen knife in his hand into a bodiless square head and carries the head on his knife, as blood gushes out from the open wound.

"Let's see what you've got there, Mr. Rothman?"

Embarrassed at being caught, I tried to hide my drawing from my Eighth Grade homeroom teacher, Mrs. Kalinson.

"Nooo, don't hide it. Let me see it. Mmmm... this is very good. I didn't know I had an artist in the class. Mr. Rothman, did you ever think of going to an art high school?"

"No."

"Well, you should definitely think about it. I can help you find the right school."

"Okay." I didn't know what she was talking about.

"Good. I do know several art schools that might be perfect, The High School of Industrial Arts, and the other one is The School of Music and Art. I'll get their addresses and information for you. I've heard a lot about the School of Industrial Arts. I think that's the one for you."

That was too much at one time. Me going to a special school scared the shit out of me. I wasn't sure I wanted to do this.

During the lunch break, a few guys were in the schoolyard playing a dangerous game that was becoming very popular. They offered me a chance to try it and the smart part of me refused. They teased me for a while, then, to prove it was harmless, they demonstrated it on Wozar.

"Hey Wozar, let's show Rothball how it's done. You take ten deep breaths and on the last exhale, I grab you from behind like this, and squeeze hard on your chest until you pass out."

Wozar passed out and a few seconds later he started convulsively jerking, and then came to.

"That's all there is to it, see? It's real easy."

It didn't look like fun to me. Why, oh why, did I sometimes do things I didn't want to do? And this was one of them. It was a bad experience, like being dead for a few seconds. Afterwards I felt terribly weak... Who needs that? I didn't give a shit how much they teased me, I never did that crap again.

After lunch Mrs. Kalinson told me she called the High School of Industrial Arts, and they told her what was required to get into the school. I'd have to show them a few pieces of my artwork. Mrs. Kalinson suggested I should have at least twelve drawings. The thing that really scared me was that I also had to take an exam. Tests were my waking nightmares. Every time I took one, my mind would freeze and go blank. I always failed, and I'll fail again. Why should I embarrass myself? Test? No way... forget about it!

"Mrs. Kalinson, I've changed my mind. I don't think an art school is for me."

Mrs. Kalinson felt my fear, "It's not that difficult. All you have to do is some sketches, which you do all the time. And you're very good at it. It should be easy for you. Look at it this way, no one will ever know if you fail the exam. If that happens, you can go to a regular high school, so you have nothing to lose. But I believe you'll make it."

JEWS ARE NOT ALLOWED

IT WAS A little early to meet my mom at the train station, so I took a walk around the Boulevard and stopped at Vim's appliance store. The window was full of brand new TV sets, round glass eyes that stared back at me. I pictured having one in our living room, and I could just turn a knob and have all the movies I wanted on any day of the week. Vim's was having a special sale on the lay-away plan, with no down payment. Still, it would be a long time before I'd see one in our house.

Mom did her usual shopping, and we ended up on Simpson Street where they had recently opened the very first supermarket in our neighborhood, the A&P. The store was always empty. People were smart enough to know the difference between quality food and processed food. The only reason Mom would ever go to the A&P was for their Eight O'Clock coffee beans, freshly ground right in front of her at the checkout counter.

It was 1949, a month before Christmas, when mom and I got home and heard a busy commotion in the living room. Not the usual loud cursing... It was different. There was an excitement in the air. Taking a chance I wouldn't be seen by Harold, I snuck a peek at what was going on.

Harold was home early that day, bent over in one corner of the living room. He was blocking whatever he was working on. When he stepped back, there in front of him was a new piece of furniture in our almost empty living room – a brand new, 12-inch Admiral TV. Harold was connecting wires when he noticed me watching.

He ordered Millie and me against the living room wall and set down the law, "I bought this television for my son. And from now on, no one – I mean you two – will be allowed in the living room at anytime, for any reason. And if either of you are found watching, or even being near the TV, you will suffer the consequences."

Harold spent about half an hour farting around with the rabbit ears, trying to get some sort of reception. The best he got was a double image of ghosts and shadows. Even if I couldn't watch his damn TV, I did get something out of it – it kept him busy and away from me.

Finally, Harold decided he would have to invest in an outdoor antenna, and he put one on the roof of our building. Whenever he adjusted the antenna on the roof, he would shout orders down to Mom from the alley. In a few short months, the roof had become a jungle of metal trees.

Every evening when Harold came home from work, he'd use his superior intellect and apply his brilliant idea of touching the TV to see if it was warm. If it was, he knew we had been watching his precious television. Didn't he realize that, given a certain amount of time, things do cool off, especially in the winter? What an asshole.

Once a year, on Christmas Day when Little Harold visited us, we were allowed to watch his fucking TV. I could feel Harold seething inside because his law was being broken, and he couldn't enforce it. He didn't want Little Harold to see him for what he really was, a fascist bully. There was an hour-long special on Christmas, *Walt Disney's Disneyland*, which showed clips from Disney's cartoon films and advertised Walt's dream of eventually building Disneyland. Even if all we got were glimpses of Disney's cartoon characters, it was a hell of a lot better than the garbage cartoons they usually showed on TV – flat, old animated line drawings with nightmare squeaky voices that were out of sync.

We still mostly saw TV outside the radio repair shop windows by Harry's Bar, or if I was really lucky, at a friend's house. But when Harold wasn't home during the afternoons, Millie and I sat in front of the TV, staring at the test pattern as if it was a show in itself. It looked like an official government stamp over a circular pattern of lines. At the top was the head of an Indian with a full, feathered headdress. Words would appear across the pattern, "PLEASE STAND BY." To us those words meant that at any moment something was going to appear... but nothing did. Just the idea of having TV in our home was enough for Millie and me to feel like part of the future that had been promised to us in the World's Fair and in the movies and joke books during the war.

Eventually, when the programming would finally start, there was nothing to see but kiddie shows. One of the programs was *The Howdy Doody Show*, which wasn't too bad because they interrupted it to play cliffhanger serials. I also didn't mind watching Princess Summer-Fall-Winter-Spring, and if no one was at home, I'd jerk-off watching her. On some of the kiddie shows, they played old cowboy movies – very, *very* old cowboy movies – with washed-out faces and metallic voices. Anything was welcome as long as it moved and talked.

We commandeered a table at the back of Jack's candy store. Bobby Frick was already there and told us the bad news that his family was moving to Brooklyn. I couldn't believe it. "You've got to be kidding me. Why Brooklyn?"

Sergie added, "Jesus, couldn't you have moved anywhere else but to Brooklyn? I don't believe it."

"It's true... you can axe my Mother. We'll be out of here by this weekend."

Sergie asked, "Why are you leaving?"

Junior smirked and interrupted, "Y is a crooked letter." That was Junior's specialty, his pat answer whenever anyone asked Why?

Sergie answered back, "Why don't you shut your face. It's not funny."

"Go fuck yourself. And Y is still a crooked letter."

I looked at Junior, "What a fuckin' shmuck."

Once we believed Bobby was really moving, Anthony said,

"Hey, we're going to miss you."

"Yeah, I think this is it."

Melvin asked, "Why can't you come here on the weekends?"

"Y's a crooked letter."

"Holy shit," Sergie yelled, "Why don't you stop with the Y shit."

Music was playing in the background from Jack's radio, Vaughn Monroe singing, *Someday You'll Want Me To Want You*. Bobby pulled up a chair, his last time to hang out with the guys, and we rehashed and embellished our stories of our sexual experiments with the girls over some chocolate egg creams.

A simple twist of my foot and the muscles in my thigh pulled at each other, tightening into a hard rock. There was no way of stopping the pain. Jack rushed over and punched my thigh several times. That relaxed my muscles, but when I tried to walk, my thigh started to seize up again. My leg became a metal rod of pain. Jack punched it harder and the pain subsided, but I was afraid to walk on it. Bobby and Sergie carried me up the three flights of steps and deposited me at the front door of my apartment.

I never invited any of my friends home. Who knew when Harold would act up? I was too ashamed of how we lived, with a violent, fowl-mouthed drunk, and didn't want anyone to know.

When Bobby Frick moved away, the block wasn't the same for about a week. But life went on and someone else filled the empty space.

Millie and Mom were talking in the kitchen.

"Dhat's a shame. You two were more like sisters than friends. Vhat happened?"

"Veronica wanted to go to dance parties with me and..."

"Vhat's wrong with dhat?"

"Ma, let me finish. All the dance parties were at the Catholic

School. I went to some of them, and the kids talked about church things and it made me feel out of place. And when they learned I was Jewish, they stayed away from me and no one wanted to dance with me."

"Those son-of-a-bitches! To hell wit them. Can't you take Veronica to regular parties?"

"I tried, but she just wants to go to the church dances."

That year, Millie and Veronica began to drift apart and eventually never saw each other again.

I AM ONLY PART
OF WHAT IS

IT WAS A dreary, boring winter with lots of freezing rain keeping me indoors, and I spent most of my time either in my room or at the movies.

Stashed away in my closet, I had two cardboard boxes filled with hardcover books that I had salvaged from the garbage cans in the alley. They were too difficult for me to read, but I saved them anyway. I loved to look at them and when I touched them, I felt I was absorbing what they were saying between their covers. Most of them were technical, science, or philosophy books, and some storybooks without pictures.

I devised a game: With each page I turned, I closed my eyes and let my pencil drop randomly on an open page of the book. Whatever word the pencil point landed on, I would write it down on a blank piece of paper. If the word was too difficult, I left it out. The simpler words that I understood, I wrote down on my piece of paper in columns, until I accumulated pages full of words. Sometimes they would read like sentences... and they were trying to tell me something.

Never before did I have this kind of patience. I went through volumes of books as they opened up to me. I wish I could remember now what they said, but I can't. There was one short line that stuck in my mind, "I am only part of what is." I didn't exactly know what it meant, but I always remember it.

During those winter months I thought of lots of things to do. One of them was something like I'd done before using an empty shoebox, but from here on in, it was very different. This time I divided the box into little compartments. I cut up magazines and joke books, and using both the background art and the figures, I glued them one behind the other in perspective. Instead of having only one scene, now I could have many scenes in one box. And now I could tell a continuous story of my own! I had invented my own three-dimensional comic book!

That winter I discovered I had a special magic – I could change nothing into something.

PART TWO
BRONX: SURVIVAL OF SPECIES

THE END OR THE BEGINNING

IT WAS ONLY a week and a half before the SIA entrance exam, and I had nothing to show. I told Mrs. Kalinson that I couldn't do it.

"Mr. Rothman, you'll be sorry for the rest of your life if you don't try. You still have enough time to do the twelve drawings they asked for. Don't disappoint me. I already gave your name to the school. You're on their list for the entrance exam, and if you don't show up, you'll make me look bad. I know you're scared, but I'll be with you every step of the way. You still have time for the drawings."

"But I don't know what they want."

"Just use your imagination. Do what you love doing. Draw what is the most fun for you. When you finish each drawing, show it to me."

I brought my first drawings to Mrs. Kalinson: a car careening off a mountain road, and a giant octopus strangling a diver with its tentacles.

"This is wonderful. And you were afraid... Keep it up."

Two days before my trip to SIA, I had finished all twelve pieces. I also threw in a couple of advertisement drawings, and now I was ready. Julio Reyes, who was in my homeroom class, was taking the test with me. Julio had never been in the same class with me until Junior High. We got to know each other better when, in the first week, he saved my life. It happened when Mrs. Kalinson left the room for a few minutes. One of the guys in class snuck up behind me, and for no fucking reason, got hold of both ends of my necktie, and started choking me with my own tie. I couldn't break loose, and passed out. From what I was told from the other guys, he continued choking me, and if it wasn't for Julio stopping him, I might have died.

Julio and I took a liking to each other, and over the years, developed a close friendship. He remembered my mom, and she treated him like he was one of the family. He told me, "We have to stick together," and set himself up as my protector.

On the morning of our trip to SIA, I wanted to dress right. "Ma, do you know where my good pants are?" Actually, they were the only pants I had.

Mom watched me rushing around, and asked, "You're not going to school?"

"They gave me and my friends the afternoon off to take a test."

"This is true? Sollinue, you know you're not getting into that school, so vhy are you wasting your time with this art crap? Don't do it, you'll only get hurt."

"My teacher, Mrs. Kalinson, said I can pass the test, and I can get into the school."

"She said that? Alright, alright... But you can't go like that. Here let me iron that shirt."

Julio and I got off the train, and walked to 79th Street, to the High School of Industrial Arts. Inside was a spacious room with a low ceiling, dotted with pillars that held up the floor above. Kids carrying portfolios were wandering around the room, looking for the auditorium. The SIA seniors who helped run the event, made me feel like I was invading their territory. The auditorium was filled with eager faces, all kids my age with the same goal: Art. For the first time, I was in a place where art was important. This is where I wanted to be.

The kids settled down as soon as the teachers sat behind their desks along one side of the auditorium. They began to call out our names alphabetically, and out came the artwork to be reviewed, huge oil paintings and beautiful watercolors. This was all new to me. These kids were my age, with artwork that looked like they didn't need an art school. I sat there numb. All of a sudden, I didn't belong anymore.

Here I was, with my 11" x 12" penny paper pad, browning at the edges from being on Jack's shelves for twenty years. My fears were suffocating me. I had to get out of there. I was sitting close to the aisle and could overhear the teachers commenting on the students' work.

"Magnificent!"

Another teacher said, "These are wonderful!" And they were.

"Excellent!"

"Outstanding!"

Each compliment was like a sledgehammer, beating me down deeper and deeper into my chair. What the hell am I doing here? I had to get the fuck out. Folding my drawings in half, I stuffed them in my back pocket. I was so short, I felt no one would notice me sliding off my chair, and slipping out the exit. A little bit more, and I'd be out of there. Then they couldn't find out I was a fraud, and didn't belong.

Just as I maneuvered myself to the back door, I heard my name being called above the chattering voices... not once, but three times, each one louder than the other. I ran to the teacher's desk, just to shut her up. Everyone in the auditorium looked in my direction. I felt like I'd been caught committing a crime.

"Mr. Rothman?"

"Yes!"

"What do you have to show me?"

There was nothing I could do. I took my drawings out from my back pocket, and unfolded them. She watched me rub out the creases on the edge of the table. I closed my eyes, and handed them to her. My mind flooded with fear as she scrutinized each piece, acting as if they held her interest.

"Did you copy these?"

"No. I thought copying would be cheating."

"I see. Hummm… Very nice. Very imaginative. Why do you want

to be an artist?"

It was the first time anyone ever asked me that question, and without thinking I blurted out, "Because that's all I know how to do."

"Thank you, Mr. Rothman. Well...? You can take your seat now."

After the teachers had finished and left the auditorium, a senior student took over. "In front of you, you will find two blank sheets of paper and a pencil. On one sheet of paper, you are going to draw a composition using these four elements: a boy, a dog, a man, and a pile of newspapers. Just use your imagination in anyway you like. You've got fifteen minutes."

I drew a boy standing by a johnny pump, holding his dog by a leash, watching a man setting up his newspapers in a wooden newsstand, while the dog raises its hind leg, and pees on the johnny pump, leaving a puddle.

"Sorry, but your time is up. Now, on the second sheet of paper, you will sketch from a model. We're going to have one of the seniors model for you. Her name is Alice. This time, you'll have half an hour to complete the sketch."

This was my last chance to prove myself, but I tried too hard, and smothered whatever talent I thought I might have. My drawing was awful. I gave up, and erased what I had done. I knew now I would never be able to get into this school.

I started to daydream, and doodled away the rest of the time. I ended up with a collage of detailed sketches of different parts of the model's anatomy, disconnected and floating all over the page. When the fuck was this going to end?

"That's it! Thank you for coming. We'll let you know by mail if you were accepted or not. Before you leave, make sure your name is on your test papers. Thanks again, and have a safe trip home."

I knew what the inevitable outcome would be. I got on the Lexington Avenue subway, and headed home, defeated. Mom was right, why do I need this art crap?

A few weeks later I received a letter from SIA:

"Mr. Rothman,

I am happy to inform you that you have passed
our entrance exam. We will be proud to have you as a
student at SIA. However, (and here comes the kiss-off)
we are very sorry we cannot admit you at this time,
because we have an unexpectedly high volume of
new student applications. Please be assured there will
be room for you at Mid-term.
Respectfully,
John B. Kenny, Principal"

The day of our graduation from Junior High, all of us kids ran
around getting our classmates to sign our autograph books. Mom insisted that I should have Harold sign my book. I got so angry at her
that we got into a screaming match. This was the first time I had ever
argued with my mom. She was surprised I fought back. But as always,
I finally gave in to her.

The bastard had the balls to sign it, "Your Father."

On the first page of the book, I drew a heart as large as the page,
and asked Mom to sign inside it. I knew she couldn't write, but she
could sign her name. I begged her – but she never did. I still have that
page with the empty heart.

The saying Sergie chose for my book meant the most to me: "It
is chance that makes brothers, but hearts that make friends. Your pal
and best friend, Sergie."

No one in my family showed up at my graduation. When I got
home after the ceremony, I pinched a few of Mom's ladyfingers. Millie
and I were not allowed to touch them because they were Mom's favorites, and very expensive.

When Mom got home from work, I noticed she had bought herself a new watch. She gave me her old one, and congratulated me for
graduating. It was the first watch I ever had, and the only real present
that Mom ever gave me. It even had dials that glowed in the dark.
It didn't make any difference to me that it was her old watch, and I
didn't care that it only lasted for a few weeks before it broke down.

Everyday of those few weeks, I was high with the knowledge that I wasn't wearing a toy, but a real grown-up watch.

My friends and I kicked off our summer vacation before high school, with the discovery of a pair of wood construction horses. They were there on the corner of Hoe Avenue, just waiting for us. We carried one of them back to our block, set it up in the gutter between Sergie's and my buildings, and used it as an "Olympic" high jump.

We were going through a fad of jumping everything in sight – johnny pumps, parking meters, car hoods. Before, it would have been impossible for me, but now my body was doing whatever I asked it to do. Our contest started with the five of us, and our jumping point was the edge of the curb. Up and over the horse we went. After each jump, we pulled the horse farther out from the curb. Sergie and I were the last two standing. There was no stopping us. When we got to a point where I felt the jump was too far for me, I threw in the towel.

Sergie teased me, and called me "Chicken." When that didn't work, he tried to cajole me into doing it. "Jesus, Solly, you can at least try."

He could have called me "Chicken" for the rest of my life, and I still wouldn't do it. I had this bad feeling that I couldn't make it. No matter how many times the guys tried to talk me into it, I refused to play their game... and it pissed them off. So Sergie took the last jump without me.

Like a ballet dancer, he flew gracefully through the air and landed down hard on his balls. His legs got twisted around the horse, and he and the horse flew in the air. They came crashing down, and splatted into the street. Sergie doubled up in pain. For some weird reason, he blamed me for his stupid decision to jump. He wanted to fight me, but was out of commission, and got Anthony to take me on.

Neither of us wanted to fight, but Sergie kept egging Anthony on. It was like he had some kind of spell over Anthony. For a long time, we just stared at each other. I thought I had an advantage because he was gay, and punched him solidly on his nose. His snot poured all over my hand.

With that, Anthony blew up like a mad man, and threw me to the ground. He came down on me with both knees, and beat me to a bloody pulp. Then he turned and walked away. I could hardly move. With my clothes bloody and torn, I pulled myself up on one arm and shouted, "I'll kill you! Come back here, I'll kill you!"

"Oy vayz mir, my Sollinue! Vhat happened?" Mom looked at me as if I was going to die.

"Vhat's da matter wit you? Have you gone crazy? Look at you! Ever since you were run over, every time I hear an ambulance, it eats out my kishkas."

The very next day Sergie, Anthony, and I were close buddies again. It was always that way with us.

A bunch of the guys were standing at the brick wall across the street, choosing up sides for a game of Johnny-on-the-Pony. A kid from Hoe Avenue got into an argument with Eddie Ramirez, and really pissed him off. Eddie was just shy of fighting the kid, but instead, blew off steam on an innocent, metal garbage pail, and kicked the shit out of it just as a patrol car was driving by.

The car stopped and out came a grizzly bear with fiery hair – it was Big Red. Once he got his hairy claws on you, there was no escaping him. He enjoyed beating us up, especially if his victim was black or Puerto Rican.

He politely invited Ramirez into the police car. Big Red and Ramirez sat in the back seat, while Reds' partner drove the squad car away, disappearing down Hoe Avenue. We stood there not talking, but we were all wondering the same thing – what was Big Red going to do to Ramirez? Half an hour went by before the cop car pulled up to the curb. Big Red dragged Ramirez out, and threw him onto the sidewalk. Eddie's face was red and swollen with welts, just for knocking over a garbage can.

We spent the rest of the day playing Johnny-on-the-Pony, and beating each other up, without any help from Big Red.

PILOT TO BOMBARDIER

ON A SUNNY early morning, Melvin and I were rained out of a game of box baseball. Without warning, a driving rain hit the ground with a wall of sound, bouncing off buildings, garbage cans, and windows, creating a wavering mist as far as I could see. In two seconds, Melvin and I were drenched.

I ran upstairs into my room, and changed into some dry clothes. I slammed my window shut, keeping the storm outside, and stared at the steady downpour attacking my window. The storm gave me plenty of time to finish my model plane. Patiently I glued it, rib by rib, exactly how a real plane is built. The quick drying cement was so potent, that by the time I was done, I was high.

The very next day, I took my model biplane to the roof, and wound up the rubber band connected to its propeller. I poured lighter fluid on its tail, struck a match, lit the tail, and threw it off the roof. As I watched it fly, blazing through the air, I was in the cockpit of that burning plane, going into a tailspin and crash-diving into the street. In a few seconds my plane was gone.

We didn't have to play games with Terry. With her, everything was out there. We were hanging out by Junior's stoop, trading hot books. Terry was the only girl there, and she got interested in reading Mandrake the Magician. She pointed her finger on a page, "How would you like to try that? I never did that before." Mandrake was doing 69 with an exotic Asian woman. Terry flipped the page, "Ah, I'd really like to try this one. How about it? How about one of you guys go to the roof with me and give it a try?" Her eyes were wide open, and her face was a blotchy red. The hot book shook in her hand. We all wanted to go, but she would have none of that. She told us to choose, and I won.

She and I climbed the five flights in Sergie's building, and stopped on the landing by the exit door to the roof. We started kissing and feeling each other up. I could feel every contour of her body – her breasts, her thighs, her pussy – pressing hard against me. We rubbed against each other in matched rhythm, like fucking with our clothes on.

I felt like I was in a World War II movie. When the B-17s flew bombing raids over Germany and reached their target, the pilot would say to the bombardier: "You're now flying the ship… the plane is all yours."

I was the pilot, and my hard-on was the bombardier now flying the ship. I was on the beam, and just about to unload the bomb, when Terry warned me not to touch her pussy.

"Why not?"

"If you have to know, I have my period."

I choked up as soon as she said, "period," and my hard-on gave the ship back to the pilot.

"Don't stop now!" she insisted.

The idea of the blood scared me, and put the ship in danger. I had missed the target, and was getting lots of flack. I wanted out of there. When I found a chance, I peeled away from the formation.

"Where the fuck are you going?"

I ran down the stairs with Terry in hot pursuit. Lucky for me, Sergie and Junior were walking up the stairs.

"Hey guys, help me out! Terry's on the warpath right behind me! We escaped into Sergie's apartment and slammed the door.

Terry knocked at the door, "Solly! I know you're in there." She heard us giggling, and started banging at the door, "You lousy fuck, get out here!"

She waited for fifteen minutes, and finally walked away. I circled the field for another half hour before I landed the plane, and snuck over the rooftop to my building.

WHAT ARE YOU DOING
IN THIS SCHOOL?

WHEN WE GRADUATED P.S. 75, we were told which high school we each would be assigned to. I had to go to Morris High, at least until I could transfer to SIA. At the front entrance of Morris High School, a tall tower from the Dark Ages loomed over me. There wasn't one guy I knew crowding into the school. Outside the sky was overcast, and inside, the halls were dark and disapproving. A bell rang, and everyone disappeared into the classrooms. I didn't know where to go, what room I belonged to.

Everything was gray, with lonely creaking noises echoing through the halls. I didn't want to be there. If I didn't leave soon, I felt the building would swallow me up. Fear carried me out of Morris High. I didn't care what might happen to me, but I wasn't going back in there. It reminded me too much of Lincoln Hospital.

On my way home, black clouds gathered and darkened the sky. The streets were empty and still. A can scraped along the street, traveling in my direction. No matter how far away I got, the school chased after me with flashes of lightening and thunder. The clouds opened and the rain came down. As the wind picked up, it blew sheets of rain into my face, blinding me the rest of the way home. I had to stop every other block, and duck into a store vestibule to get my bearings. Finally, I made it home, and listened to the thunder rumbling outside my window.

"Vhat are you doing home?"

"I'm not going back to Morris High."

"So vhat are you going to do? Make sense. You've got to go back to school."

"Sergie said I could transfer to another school, if I do it right away… before it's too late."

"Vhat school?"

"Sergie, and a lot of the other guys I know, are going to Samuel Gompers. That's where I want to go."

"Vhat is dis transfer business your talkin' about?"

"To get into the school, I have to bring my school records to Gompers, and I need you to come with me to get me registered there."

"Oy, that means I have to take off from work."

The next morning, Mom and I walked to Kitsel Park, across the street from the Hunt's Point Palace, and down into the subway. Mom put a dime in the coin slot for each of us, and we walked through the wooden turnstiles. On the platform, I leaned against the pillars that kept the station from caving in, not knowing exactly where we were going, or what to expect. We took the Lexington Pelham Bay Local train, screeching through the winding tunnels, and got off at the Cypress Avenue Station.

The Gompers Annex was small, very much like P.S. 75, and wasn't as overwhelming as Morris High School. It would be a good place to bide my time until I could go to SIA.

"Excuse me sir, I have to register my son. Vhere is the office please?"

A man with one clouded eye showed us to the office. Mom was right; it didn't take very long. And I got a reprieve – I didn't have to start until tomorrow.

We got lost looking for the train station on our way back. Mom spotted a cop, "Hofficer, we're a little lost. Vhere is da train to Horseshit Bitch?"

I cringed when the cop did a double-take at Mom, "Excuse me, Lady, but what did you say?"

"I'm asking... vhere is da train to Horseshit Bitch!?"

Mom had an innocence about her that the cop picked up on. He could see she was sincere, but he still couldn't understand her.

"Vhat's da matter vit you?! Don't you understand English? Horseshit Bitch!"

I was afraid of cops, but mustered up some courage, "My mom means Orchard Beach."

That's vhat I said, Horseshit Bitch!"

The cop smiled and pointed us in the right direction.

I rolled out of bed, and for a brief moment I didn't know where I was. As I prepared for my first day at Gompers, I felt home sick even before I left the house. Looking at myself in the bathroom mirror, all I could see was spikes of hair springing up from the back of my head. For the longest time, no matter what I did, nothing would keep my cowlick down – until our neighborhood barber introduced me to this dark green glop. When it dried, it turned my hair into concrete strands.

With my plastered-down hair, I took the Lexington Local to Gompers, wondering what to expect in my new school. Standing by the door, staring out of the train window, I lost my sense of location and felt myself in an in-between world, watching the metal beams rapidly pulsing by.

The green glop did the trick, and held down my wild patch of hair. I fondled the glued clumps between my fingers as my train slowly passed a station. The opposite platform was filled with a congregation of short plaid skirts, with long white socks... a group of girls from a Catholic high school. All us guys knew Catholic girls were easy, you could talk them into anything. To get their attention, I stood on my toes to look taller, and imagined that a passing glance was directed at me.

At Gompers, there were students who looked more like adults, that didn't belong in the schoolyard. Some of the guys were leaning against the fence shooting up, others were sniffing horse or smoking shit. Who are these guys I'm going to have to deal with?

By the time I got into Gompers, it was three days after school had officially started, and everyone else was pretty well settled in. But everything was new to me. When I found my homeroom, four guys I knew from P.S. 75 were there, which made me feel at ease. Our homeroom teacher, Mr. Bookerman, had a young, open face, but a body like a bulldozer. His skin was Arab brown, almost as dark as Manny's. His black hair was cropped close on the sides of his head, with longer hair combed straight back on top.

My eyes were fixed on Bookerman's suit, which appeared to be several sizes too small. The stiches on his sleeves pulled at the seams of his shoulders, and looked like at any moment, they would burst through. When he stood in front of the class, in his own quiet way, Mr. Bookerman demanded attention, and got it.

While filling out my Delaney card, the bell rang to start the first class of the day. Ramos was one of my friends from P.S. 75, and saw the confusion on my face.

"Hey Rothballs! What's your first class?"

"Print Shop."

"Hey, that's my first class. Let me see your list. Hey! Don't worry, we've got all the same classes. Hey, just stay with me, and everything will be cool."

Inside the Print Shop, all the kids grouped together at one end of the room. I was the smallest and thinnest in the class. A few of the guys must have been trapped in their first year of high school... growing old. These men-children instantly found something about me they disliked. From that day on, they bullied me every morning, and forced me to sing songs I never heard of. If I didn't know the words or went off key, they didn't hold back, and punched me hard on my shoulders. By the end of the first week, I couldn't raise my arms, and the constant punches blended together into large tattoos of black and blue.

One morning, the Print Shop teacher, Mr. Miller, walked into the room in his blue smock, and caught the bastards in the act of terrifying me. The whole school knew the stories about Mr. Miller's service record. He was a submarine captain during the war, a war hero with a chest full of metals for his bravery. He had been wounded several times, and no one fucked with him.

He grabbed one of the guys by the collar. The look of cold anger coming from his eyes sent chills through all of us. What I saw in his eyes must have been the hell he went through in the war. He threatened my persecutors, and they stood down – and never bothered me again.

The Print Shop wasn't like a regular classroom, with desks facing a black board. Instead, a huge printing press commanded the center of the room, looking naked with all of its wheels and gears exposed. The press radiated such power that I was afraid, once I started it, I wouldn't be able to control it.

In front of the press was a long table with metal keys, and wood blocks that the keys fit into. Hugging the walls of the room, were tables with side-by-side wood boxes. Inside each box, little compartments held small slivers of metal, with letters of the alphabet, from A to Z, on the end of each of the metal slugs. I enjoyed working in the Print Shop, typesetting paragraphs, and placing one letter after the other in a hand-held, metal slide that looked like a foot-measuring device in a shoe store.

Funny how little things can quickly leave a lasting impression. My teachers always said, "Watch your Ps and Qs." And here they were, the Ps and Qs, right next to each other. It was hard to tell them apart, and very easy to confuse one for the other. What seemed just abstract words to me became something real I held in my hands.

Our first assignment was to set the type for several paragraphs of copy in the shape of a Christmas tree. I placed the type in the shape of a tree in the middle of one of the square frames, filled the empty space around it with wood blocks, and locked it in place. Setting the type was easy; my challenge was using the press.

We had to hand-feed each sheet of paper into the monster press. Before my turn came, some wiseass kid was showing off behind

Miller's back, playing chickie with the press by sticking one of his fingers on the edge of the press plate. At the last second, just as the press came down, he'd pull his finger away. But one time he played his game too close, and the press came crushing down on his finger.

It was weird to see it; his finger was actually flat, like Looney Tunes. Miller took him down to the nurse, and he ended up in Lincoln Hospital – Good luck with that!

When Mr. Miller came back, he warned us. "I told you guys, pay attention, and don't screw around. If anything goes wrong, don't worry, there's a brake on the side of the printer that will stop the press. So if you're not sure of what you are doing, there is no reason to panic, use the brake. I cannot emphasize it enough. Use it, use it – *use it!*

"Okay, Mr. Rothman, you're next."

As I fed the paper, I could feel the weight of the press with each heavy, pounding beat, "Voom-voom-voom, voom-voom-voom..." At first, it felt like a giant out of control, but after awhile I began to get the hang of it. When I looked at each page I had printed, I imagined I was working on the *Daily News*, turning out copy for the front page.

At Gompers, I never knew what was going to happen. Between classes, a teacher I'd never seen before stopped a group of us kids in the hall. He was tall and thin, and his suit dangled off his angular body. The teacher picked me out from the rest of the guys, and instructed me, "Watch my right hand." His hand shook, "Are you watching?"

"Yes."

"Well, keep watching... keep watching."

Out of nowhere, his left hand slammed hard on the back of my head. The other guys thought it was real funny.

"Always keep your eyes open for the unexpected."

Whatever that meant. I never saw that teacher again. He just appeared and disappeared... like he was never there.

My next class was English, with Mr. Bookerman. "I see we have a couple of new students, so I'll repeat what I told you a few days ago. During this term, you are required to read *Captain's Courageous*. As soon as we get that out of the way, we'll have some fun.

"I'm not going to give you a written exam on this book, but we will talk about it in class, so be prepared. The school will lend you the books, but there's not enough to go around, so the rest of you will have to find a copy at your local library. I suggest you get yourself a library card, if you don't have one already. Don't worry, you'll have plenty of time, so no one should feel any pressure."

My afternoon class was Sheet Metal. The room was one big open space, with a high ceiling, and long worktables lined up along the windows. The center of the room was dotted with oddly shaped machines, like parts from an alien space ship. They turned out to be simple metal-folding machines. A section at the far end of the room was partitioned off with metal mesh from floor to ceiling. Locked behind the fence stood cabinets, and the walls were filled with tools hanging in neat rows, each in its own dedicated space.

Mr. McGraw walked into the room. The only thing about him with any color was the explosion of red and blue curlicues on his suspenders. His white shirt ballooned out from his pants, and his bristle-brush hair was peppered with gray. He was completely blind in one eye, and his blind eye would stare at us through a cloud of scars. His voice sounded like a car driving on a road of gravel, and his face was the kind that had lived a hard life.

In one corner of the classroom were a couple of those men-children sleeping under a stiff, white blanket. McGraw tiptoed quietly toward them, and whispered instructions to two of us. He lifted a fire extinguisher from the wall, aimed it at the unsuspecting guys, and as he motioned to us to lift the blanket, sprayed them with the extinguisher.

"If you want to sleep, go home and do it. You're not doing it on my time, in my classroom. So what are you two waiting for? Get the fuck out of my classroom." The guys sauntered out the door.

"Good riddance. Before we start the class, I have to demonstrate some safety rules. The blanket those punks were sleeping under is an asbestos blanket, which is fire proof." He said it like he just wanted to get it over with. "If there's a fire anywhere in the shop, you take this blanket, and throw it on the fire. It will smother the fire.

"Here, let me show you. Anyone got a match? Ah, a cigarette lighter, much better… here, give it to me." McGraw put the flame on one corner of the blanket, "See, it won't burn."

The blanket blew up in flames. He grabbed the fire extinguisher – but now it was empty.

"The sink, assholes! The sink!" We found pails under the sink, filled them with water, and put the fire out.

"If there are any questions, keep them to yourself. Okay, so much for safety demonstrations… let's get to work. Okay, get around me, and I'll show you how to use these ovens. They're for heating up your soldering irons."

We stood in a semi-circle around him. When the iron got white hot, McGraw pulled it out of the oven. Then the idiot swung the glowing hot iron around the semi-circle of guys. If we hadn't jumped out of the way, we'd have been branded. Is this guy for real?

At the end of his class, one-eye McGraw made us line up by the door, and with a hard rubber hammer in his hand, he swung randomly down on our heads. We escaped into the hall, but a few of us got slammed on the head. At the end of my first day, I didn't know who was crazier, the students or the teachers.

The book, *Captain's Courageous* – I didn't even try to read it. I was not sure if my understanding of what I read was what the writer intended to say. I had to find ways to straighten out the outside world, by creating my own rules to understand theirs.

The title of the book suggested pirates to me, so I took a chance, and illustrated my own interpretation. I drew swords crossing beneath the head of a pirate wearing a patch over one eye, with a pirate ship behind him.

Mr. Bookerman loved it so much he hung it up in the classroom. Of course my illustration had nothing to do with the book, and Bookman knew I hadn't even read the book jacket. But he was very kind, and said nothing. During the class discussion of the book, I knew how to play the game by melting into the background, and avoiding being part of the discussion.

Before the class ended, Mr. Bookerman said, "That should take care of the required curriculum for this semester. From now on in this class, the most important word for you is: Question! I believe questioning is the true meaning of learning. I don't care if an expert in his field of study tells you that what he believes is true. Your job is to question him. Through questioning, you might even find out you know more than he did. But to do that, you've got to keep an open mind.

"This is not going to be just another English class. We are not going to follow the rules that you've had your whole life, for the sake of having tests. No! My class will be all about books of ideas – many different kinds of books, magazine articles, short stories – all with new views in science, history, and philosophy. I'll be giving you copies of articles that will make you think in different ways, and question the norm with new ideas of your own. No matter how stupid you may think they sound, don't be afraid to say what you're thinking. Anything goes. But what I don't want, are parrots repeating what you have read. Are there any questions?"

The room was silent, but soon it dawned on us what he wanted.

"We're going to start with a short article, a theory about how the

Egyptians built the pyramids. The article is only one page long. I want you to take it home, and see if you can add to the theory with something of your own that the experts didn't see. Feel free to develop a whole new theory. Remember don't hold back, no matter how stupid it might sound to you. Many of the stupid ideas of the past, turned out to be the brilliant discoveries of today.

"There are no tricks here. There's no right or wrong... just have fun with it. You've got a whole week, and weekend, to work it out."

That weekend I went to the movies alone to see *Destination Moon*. In the lobby, I was greeted by a man in a space suit handing out snap shots of the moon. Before the movie started they showed a travelogue about the Panama Canal, and how ships crossed the Isthmus of Panama, through a series of locks, to the Pacific Ocean. A flash of recognition jumped off the screen. I kept seeing in my mind the pyramids of Egypt.

It was so simple and clear to me how the Egyptians had built the pyramids, but before I could put my thoughts together, I needed a little more information about the Panama Canal. I couldn't wait. I left the theater after the first feature, something I would never do, and walked over to the Public Library on Southern Boulevard, a few blocks south of the Hunt's Point Palace.

I filed through the card catalog drawers, and found a couple of books on the Panama Canal. The books had lots of pictures and simple captions, which made it easier for me to understand. There it was, the answer, right in front of me. As I was walking to the front desk to check out the books, I heard, "Mr. Rothman!" I didn't know where the voice was coming from, "Over here!"

I turned, and there was Mr. Bookerman, working at the front desk.

"Mr. Rothman." There was surprise in his voice. "What are you doing here?"

"You know that problem you gave us about the pyramids? Well, I had an idea that I think works, but it's so simple I think someone else must have thought of it."

"It's a quiet night tonight, and I have plenty of time. So how about if you tell me your theory, and then I'll let you know if its been thought of before."

"I'll try."

Mr. Bookerman and I sat down at an empty table. Normally, I'd be terrified to say a word to any adult, especially to a teacher, but once I started, I got caught up in the excitement of my discovery and forgot about my fears.

"Isn't it possible that the Egyptians built deep canals leading from the Nile to where they were building the pyramids? Isn't it possible they created water locks, like the Panama Canal? Then, maybe they floated the giant stones on a raft from the Nile, along the canals, and into the building site. By controlling the locks, they could raise the water level inside the pyramid, and the raft would float up, carrying the stone on it. And then, they would slide the stone into place, creating the walls of the pyramid. I'm thinking, the Egyptians repeated using the locks for each level, raising the water higher and higher for each layer of stones, until they reached the top of the pyramid."

Mr. Bookerman sat there, dumfounded. The first thing out of his mouth was, "What the hell are you doing here in this school?"

"I'm not going to be here much longer. The School of Industrial Arts accepted me, but I have to wait because it's over-crowded."

"Call them. You don't want them to forget about you, so keep reminding them. I want to tell you something, Rothman. Egyptology is my passion, especially theorizing how the pyramids were built. I have my own theories, but I've never heard anything like yours before. I believe you've hit on something completely original. There are some kinks to be worked out, but as a whole, it's brilliant."

Why was he saying that? How could Mr. Bookerman believe I was brilliant? That was a new one on me. Maybe it was because most of the students at Gompers were so dumb they made me look smart. Bookerman's belief in me gave me something I had very little of, confidence in myself. His encouragement made it possible for me to call SIA and remind them that I was still out there, waiting. It was my first step in realizing I wasn't retarded after all. But it would take many hard years to fight that image of myself, within myself.

When I made my first call to SIA, I couldn't speak the words that were in my head. My sentences made twists and turns, and got stuck in my mouth. Everything was backwards. Nothing came out right, except for a few crippled words. I tried to straighten them out, but they didn't make sense, and I had to hang up.

But I didn't let this stop me. Everyday I reminded myself I didn't belong in Gompers. I was afraid I'd get used to being there. Each day took me further away from SIA, and I was afraid they would forget their promise to me. After a while, Gompers would feel like they owned me, and wouldn't let me go. But I refused to be nothing. I refused to accept what I could and could not do. This was my time, and I was going to take it. I was going to fight hard to get into SIA.

I called SIA almost everyday. They got so annoyed with my constant calls, they told me to speak to Mr. Kenny, the principal, and gave me his office phone number. I'm sure they were sorry about that, because I also called him every day, asking when I would be transferred to SIA. I pleaded and begged him until he couldn't take me anymore. He said if I'd stop calling him, he would find a place for me, even before this semester was over.

In One-Eye McGraw's class, I was selected as the tool monitor. My job was to keep tabs on who borrowed a tool, and when he returned it. Unfortunately, McGraw discovered one of the tools was missing.

"Okay, you fuckin' assholes, one of you stole a soldering iron from the cage. Mr. Rothman, you're the cage monitor, and I'm holding you responsible for that missing tool."

As punishment he grabbed a metal chain, wrapped it around my neck, and locked it high up on the cage, so that I was just barely standing on my toes. He left me hanging there, stunned. I watched as One-Eye gave another one of his famous demonstrations, showing how easily pig iron could be melted. Whether accidentally or not, he dropped the melted metal, almost splashing it on the students. From that day on, we all feared the words, "We're going to have a demonstration." We learned to stay far, far away from One-Eye.

While hanging off the cage, I got the class' attention by imitating McGraw, shutting one eye, and pulling my lips to one side. Holy shit, that's it... One-Eye McGraw looked like Popeye! I had the guys in stitches. McGraw knew I was doing something behind his back, and turned quickly to try to catch me in the act, but just as quickly, I changed my face back to my normal self.

Every time I lost my balance, the chain would tighten around my neck. The danger became very real, and I broke out in a cold sweat. At first my toes tingled with a slight pain, but the longer I stood on them, the more the pain increased. I didn't know how much longer I could hold on. I was hoping that any second One-Eye would release me, but he just left me there, dangling. I was losing the strength in my legs. They began to shake, and were about to cave in. I wondered, was he crazy enough to let me choke?

I screamed, "Get me offa here! "

One-Eye McGraw laughed, and unchained me. I could have choked to death, and he was laughing – a real funny guy. I've got to get out of this fuckin' madhouse.

One-Eye took me off being the cage monitor, and gave me the job of keeping grades on the student's Delaney cards. My math wasn't very good, and I didn't know how to figure out percentages. I thought, what the hell, and gave everyone passing grades. Even the guys who made me sing became very friendly to me. I think it was the very first time they'd ever passed anything. I was taking a chance doing it, but McGraw didn't notice anyway... or just didn't care.

FIRST DAY AT SIA

THE DAY FINALLY came for my transfer to School of Industrial Arts. It was a sunny Monday morning; the weather was warm for early spring, and I was ready to get the hell out of Gompers.

Mom was about to leave for work, "Solly, why are you up so early?"

"I'm changing schools today."

"Again wit the changing?"

"Don't worry, this time I can do it myself."

"And vhat school you changing?"

"To the art school."

"What kind of money can you make with art? This art school garbage, it's a vaste of time.

I fortified myself with my usual hearty breakfast of hot coffee, and a hard roll with butter, topping it off with a cigarette.

I was going from an all-boys school, to a new school filled with girls. I was ashamed of being so short for my age. I thought I could correct nature's mistake, and before I left for school, I cut newspapers to the shape of my heels, and stuffed them into my shoes. This made me about an inch taller, but I felt like I was walking on high heels. My ankles would twist and slide to one side, but with a little practice, I was able to control it. That one-inch made a great difference to me, as I walked tall to Simpson Street Station.

When I saw the SIA Annex on 51st Street for the first time, it looked like a little old shack compared to the surrounding buildings.

Eventually, I learned that the Annex and the Main Building had been used as hospitals for wounded soldiers during the Civil War. My destination was to find the main office, and check in. I wandered around, and crossed a rickety bridge between buildings several times. It was a creaky, makeshift walkway suspended over an open yard, and in the winter, you'd freeze your balls off getting from one building to another.

Instead of the office, I found the library, but no one was there to point me in the right direction. There was a boy sitting on the edge of a table who looked much older than me, but then everyone looked older than me. A girl was snuggling into him between his legs. She was real sexy in her tight skirt, with her breasts tight against her blouse. Every once in a while, she'd sneak a peak at me, looking as if she was about to say something like, *"You want me don't you? Wouldn't you like some of me?"*

Damn right I would. I had the passions of a 15-year-old, but unfortunately, not the body to match. She was teasing me, and the guy didn't notice. For the life of me, I couldn't understand why she kept looking at me. Compared to her boyfriend, I was only a little shrimp.

Then, both of them looked at me, and started laughing. Other kids in the hall were giggling at me, too. I walked away, and with each step I got shorter and shorter. I turned around, and saw a trail of newspaper pieces working their way out of my shoes. I never looked back again. I just kept on walking out of the building... all the way to Broadway.

My eyes followed the Paramount movie marquee wrapping around the corner of the building. The price of admission was not much more than the Boulevard or the Spooner. I still had my lunch money, and bought my ticket with it. Maybe the movie would help me wash away the shame of being laughed at in my new school.

I sat in the front row of the orchestra, and watched *Saturday Island*, with Linda Darnell and Tab Hunter. When the picture ended, I waited for the second feature, but it never came. Instead, the lights came on, and a live band appeared onstage. I was stunned to find out they were going to have a live stage show, and I'd only paid the price of a movie. Maybe they made a mistake, and here under the bright lights, they'd find me out. I used my powers of invisibility, blended into the background, and sank down into my chair.

It was midday, but this was the kind of stage show that people got dressed up for at night. Three women in sparkling costumes lit up the stage, and the audience applauded like they knew who they were. These beautiful women were introduced as, the McGuire Sisters. I was so close I could practically touch them. The audience enjoyed their songs with polite applause.

The Sisters looked over the audience and spotted me. They focused all their attention on me, and I lost my invisibility. They looked at me as if I was somebody special, and sang their next song directly to me, *Teach Me Tonight*. At first I couldn't believe it was me they were singing to. I looked around, thinking it must be someone else, but the Sisters were all pointing at me, gesturing "Yes, you!" Then they sang, *Sincerely* – to me, a little boy who was a nobody.

My face was burning, and the more they sang to me, the deeper I sank into my chair. The Sisters smiled, and kept directing all their attention to me. The audience got caught up in the fun, and the show came alive. The more I squirmed, the more the Sisters smiled, and the audience laughed.

The McGuire Sisters ended by throwing kisses to me. One of them asked me to come up on the stage so she could hug me, but I couldn't do it, and they knew it. They were kind and didn't insist. The audience loved the show, and the McGuire Sisters had a hard time getting off the stage. Afterwards, I walked away feeling as tall as everyone else on the street.

Mom's workplace was on West 29th Street, between Seventh and Eighth Avenues, not too far from the Paramount. The elevator was having a hard time. It clanked at each floor, and had to give itself a little shove to make it to the next. At the eighth floor, the elevator door hesitated, and opened with a sudden jerk. *Scherzer and Hect Furriers* was painted on the frosted glass office door in front of me. While I was standing there, Millie walked out of another elevator.

"What are you doing here?"

"What are *you* doing here?" We both laughed.

I rang the doorbell, and a buzzer answered back. Millie and I sat in the waiting room, while one of the salesmen got Mom. She was so happy we showed up unexpectedly at her job, she didn't even ask us why we weren't in school. Just seeing us there thrilled her; it was like seeing a part of herself.

"Did you eat?"

"No, Mom."

"Neither did I," answered Millie.

"Come, I'll take you to the deli."

On the way, we passed the superintendent of the building, "Your kids, Molly?" A salesman came into the lobby, "Hi, Molly. Your kids?" Everyone knew my Mom. She took us to the corner deli for a late lunch, and she had great joy in showing us off.

Nick, the deli man, asked, "Your kids, huh, Molly? They *must* be... they look like you." We sat at the counter, "What'll you have, Molly?"

"I'll take my usual, and the kids'll have pastrami sandwiches on club, and a cream soda." Mom turned to us, "What are you doing here?"

"I went to the Paramount movies, Millie answered, and it was close to your job, so I came here to see you."

"So did I... I went to the Paramount, too!"

"So Solly, did you change schools? And vhere did you get the money for da movies?"

"I used my lunch money."

Millie asked me, "Where did you sit?"

"In the orchestra... in the front row."

"I was in the balcony. Did you see how the McGuire Sisters were singing to someone? I couldn't see who it was, but everyone loved it. Could you see who it was?"

"It was me! They were singing to me."

"Yeah, sure they were."

"I swear it. They were singing to me!" No matter how hard I tried to convince her, she never believed me.

A movie poster spelling out, *THE THING,* in bleeding red letters, greeted me every morning on the Simpson Street train platform. It sent me off to school, and welcomed me back home again. SIA was in the middle of Manhattan, where everything was happening. Thousands of new faces, all kinds of people constantly on the move, carried me along with their energy.

My first day at SIA was actually my second day, but the first day didn't count – and this time I found the office.

"Mr. Rothman," said the registrar, "you were supposed to be here yesterday."

"I'm sorry, I got the dates mixed up. I'm really sorry."

"Well, congratulations! I'm glad to see you've made it to SIA. Here's your homeroom number and class schedule. I'm sure you'll love it here. Good luck."

The students were already in their homerooms. They'd been together for a couple of months, and when I walked into the classroom they made me feel like I was invading their territory.

Julio, my classmate from P.S. 75, greeted me like a long lost brother. Seeing him there took the edge off and I felt less like a stranger. Julio had started at SIA only a week earlier. He had spent part of his semester at Harrod, the aviation high school.

"What is it like here?"

"It's great. Come on, I'll show you around."

He took me to the makeshift gym/lunchroom where they were setting up for dancing during lunch period. Imagine that, dancing in school...

But instead of staying for the dances, Julio took me out of SIA. We walked past Saint Bartholomew Church on our way to watch the ice skaters at Rockefeller Center. I especially liked the women in short skirts. I'd follow their long legs up to what looked like their underwear, hugging their asses so tightly. I could see every muscle on their streamlined bodies as they spun in circles.

Before we took the subway home at 3pm, Julio had something else to show me. Close by the school on Park Avenue, was the famous Waldorf Astoria. We watched the rich in their expensive, tailored clothes, stepping out of their limousines and having their asses kissed by the help. No one noticed us in our T-shirts, sneakers, dungarees, and jackets. Inside, the hotel looked like the Taj Mahal, with marble floors and golden elevators – a temple to the rich. The dark, shiny banisters were too tempting for Julio and I. We slid down a whole flight of stairs, upsetting the guests, and ran out of the hotel feeling the heat of the busboys at our heels.

Saturday, after the excitement of my first week at SIA, I treated myself to a movie. *The Day The Earth Stood Still* was playing at the Loewe's Spooner. For me, the most unforgettable thing about that movie was the magic phrase that stopped the giant robot from destroying the girl, and the whole world: *"Klaatu Barada Nikto."*

On my way home, the song *The Little White Cloud That Cried* was flowing out of B & J's music store. Johnnie Ray's voice had a new sound that haunted me. I leaned against a parked car by the store, absorbing every note and every word. Even if I didn't have a phonograph, there was no way I could go home without that record. I spent every penny I had scrounged, but when I got home with my prize, all I could do was stare at it.

Sunday, I was in luck. Harold disappeared for the whole day, probably on a drunken binge. For breakfast, I fortified myself with a bowel of Hot Ralston, the cereal of Tom Mix. With no one in the apartment to stop me, I tiptoed into Harold's room and borrowed his portable phonograph, took it to my room, and played my record. I sang my heart out with Johnny Ray.

I didn't hear Mom and Millie coming in the front door until they appeared in my open doorway, laughing at me singing from my heart. I felt like an open wound – too ashamed to open up and sing my guts out, ever again.

Before I had a chance to return the phonograph, Harold came home drunk. I was hoping he was too drunk to notice it missing, but my luck had run out. He screamed from his room, "Where's my phonograph? I'll kill him! I'll kill him! If that little Jew prick took it, I'll kill him."

Harold got to my room before I could escape. He stood over me and saw the phonograph. "I knew it. I knew it!" His eyes were dripping with anger and looking for blood. "You fucking mental retard! Touch my things will ya!"

Under my breath I kept repeating, "*Klaatu Barada Nikto... Klaatu Barada Nikto!*" I must have been doing it wrong, because it didn't work...

Harold heard me whispering the strange words. "What the fuck is that? What are you, some kind of imbecile?"

The towering monster came at me, "You little Jew scum! When I'm through with you, you'll never touch anything of mine again." He hauled off and whacked me across my face. I picked up his phonograph to protect myself, but still, he came at me. Without thinking, I shoved the phonograph into Harold's chest. He wrapped his arms around it to keep it from falling, and I ran out of the house, leaving him dazed and not quite understanding what had just happened.

I heard Harold yelling from behind me, "Don't bother to come back. If you do, I'll kill you!"

I stayed out and didn't come back for a long while, waiting for him to pass out into one of his deep, drunken sleeps. The next day, he either forgot the night before, or got too exhausted from all that hate and left me alone.

ROTHBALL MEETS THE PARK BOY TIMS

ON A WARM June night, just before the end of the school year, I met this guy, Keller, from Hoe Avenue. He was about my age but tried to appear older than he was. He always had a pipe in his mouth and wore a sports jacket with leather elbow patches, attempting to look sophisticated. Keller started a conversation with me about a girl named Jolene, who wanted to meet me. "She told me that you know her... I think she has a crush on you. You interested?"

"Really?"

"You want to meet her, or not?"

Jolene was sitting on a stoop and looked up at me, surprised and excited. She had high cheekbones and her brown, silky hair brushed across her face. She had an unusual and beautiful face. She wasn't just pretty, everything about her had the feeling of soft edges. I knew her from somewhere, but couldn't place where.

"You don't remember me do you?"

"I know you from somewhere."

"Remember Mrs. Davidson's class?"

"Yeah..."

"Remember when she had to leave the classroom for a long time, and you and I made a deal with each other in front of the black board?"

"Yes, yes, I remember now! You said if I drew on the blackboard what my dick looked like, you would draw your pussy."

Jolene's blush was more exaggerated on her pale skin. I didn't understand what I was feeling. It was beyond a crush. She was perfect, and I was afraid of her because she was too real. I didn't know how to handle these new feelings.

Jolene was serious and knew what she wanted – me. But I knew she'd eventually find out who I really was, and my heart would break. So I stayed away from her. Every once in a while, she would find a way to accidently bump into me, but finally we went our separate ways.

On the first day of my summer vacation, it was early in the morning, and I was outside with my kid brother, Ronnie. He stood by the blank wall next to Siegel's Hardware, holding a shortened broomstick, while I was at the curb lobbing a Spaldeen to him. A few pitches later, Ronnie got ahold of one, and amazingly for a five-year-old, hit the ball across the street, high in the air – up, up and over the roof of a two-story building. It's a good thing I had Melvin and Sergie to back me up, because no one would have believed me. Even though all three of us saw it, we couldn't believe it ourselves. Ronnie felt our excitement, and knew he had done something special.

It was getting to be 9 am, time to deliver Ronnie to Frieda. Ever since she started taking care of him, she'd been feeding him the food she ate, and he was changing from a cute, pudgy little boy, to a cute fat kid. After I dropped Ronnie off, I bumped into Susan at the concrete park, and talked her into walking with me to the creek.

The preparations for the new parkway had begun to change the face of the creek, making it almost unrecognizable to me. Gone were the tall weeds that would hide us from the busy streets. So Susan and I had a difficult time finding a private place where we could fool around... until I saw the large boulder where I hid with my friends when we were being shot at with Harold's rifle.

Susan and I got into some heavy petting. I unhooked her bra, uncovering her white breasts with red nipples, asking to be kissed.

Susan suddenly got nervous, "Don't do that."

"Why not?"

"The nuns say that having sex is a sin."

"What are you talkin' about? We're not fucking, so how can it be sex? This is just feeling each other up. It's not fucking."

Susan pressed my head into her breasts. I guess she agreed with me. I was working my way down to her pussy, when we heard a group of guys walking toward us.

"Hey! You! Whataya doing there?"

"Nothing. Why?"

I told Susan to take off. My first thought was that they might rape her. Before they had a chance to answer back, Susan was gone and out of sight. And I thought *I* was fast! I was glad she was safe, because I might not have been able to help her.

"Oh it's you, Rothball." It was Frank Wozar with a bunch of guys I knew from P.S. 75 and Gompers. "We know what you were doing. Couldn't you share her with us?"

"No, I couldn't. When it comes to sex I'm very selfish, and I don't share."

Paratory added, "Alright, alright... forget it. I'm glad we bumped into you, Rothball. You heard of da Lightnings?"

"No, I don't think so."

"You musta heard of 'em – the Manhattan Lightnings. You know, like they're one of the biggest gangs in the City, and they're forming gangs all over. So, you know, like we formed a new gang, and we're callin' ourselves the Park Boy Tims. We're part of the Lightnings. It's like them having a franchise in The Bronx."

Joey asked, "We'd like you to be part of our gang. How about it?"

"Maybe."

Joey said, "Since we know you, you'll only have to go through just one of the initiations."

"What initiations?"

Wozar added, "You have to run through two rows of guys swinging their fists and punching you. That's it. Nothing to it."

"Nahhh, I don't think so."

"Come on, Rothball," said Joey. "We'll always be there to protect each other. We're family. Come on, be part of the family."

"Look, I like you guys, but I don't want to be in a gang. Okay?"

"Alright, Rothball. We tried. See ya."

Who the hell wants to be punched out? Why do I need that shit? If I wanted to get punched around, all I had to do was go home, and Harold would be very pleased to take care of that for me.

For my whole life I had known myself with a part in my hair. This was the summer I combed it back into a DA. Once I got rid of my part, I felt a new sense of freedom. Finally, I didn't have to use that green gook anymore. And when the Chinese Laundry moved from Junior's building, to where the cigar store used to be in my building, Lee would let me constantly train my DA in the mirror just inside his doorway. Now, all I needed was a leather jacket, combat boots, dungarees, and a garrison belt, and I would be really cool.

WORKING MY WAY DOWN

I RECEIVED A phone call from my brother Walter, offering me a job in Brooklyn.

"Hi, Murphy. How'd you like to make some good money? This restaurant I work for needs some extra help... how about it?"

All the blood drained from my body, as if he was pushing me out of a plane without a parachute. The idea of being in another country – Brooklyn – with unfriendly natives, gave me stomach pains, and I had to take two charcoal pills. When I was thirteen, the doctor told Mom I was developing an ulcer, and prescribed the charcoal pills. Mom couldn't understand why her boy would be getting an ulcer when he ate well, and got lots of exercise in the street.

Walter heard the fear and hesitation in my voice. "Hey Murphy, you don't have to worry about a thing. I'll be there with you. Just keep your eyes on me, and you can't go wrong. You can make nice money. Come on, Murphy, it'll be fun."

He talked me into it, but I was terrified. After I hung up, I got the runs. Everywhere I went I carried a bottle of Pepto-Bismol as my close companion. I felt safe knowing it was with me in case of an emergency like this. I drank so much of the stuff that the blood in my veins turned pink.

Carstairs was a soda fountain and restaurant on Flatbush Avenue, not too far from Church Avenue, and next door to a movie theater. They were noted for their good food, but mostly famous for their ice cream – freshly made downstairs in their basement.

Part of my job every morning was to prepare the tuna fish salad. Walter demonstrated how it was done, how to finely chop the celery and onions. I wanted to be really good at it, and chopped them even smaller than Walter did, until they blended together into one smoothly indistinguishable, savory schmeer.

Everyone wore a white shirt, a black clip-on bow tie, and black pants. I didn't have any of those things, and Carstairs had to lend me whatever they had in their back closet. All the workers looked like they were wearing a uniform. On me, it looked more like I was wearing a tent. I didn't know a damn thing about being a waiter, or how to serve a customer. The other waiters were annoyed with me because I was so slow, and made mistakes. They didn't think it was fair that I should split the tips with them.

The parts of the job that terrified me most were making change, and spelling out the orders. In two more seconds, I was going to run out of there screaming, "I quit, I quit!"

Just before I exploded, Walter took me aside, "I'm sorry, Murph, but the boss feels that waiting tables isn't your thing. But he got lots of compliments from the customers on your tuna salad, and he wants you to keep doing it. He's gonna switch jobs on ya, and from now on, you're gonna be at the soda fountain."

One morning, while I was preparing the tuna salad, Walter called me from the other side of the open grill. I couldn't see him, and without thinking, I leaned forward with my hands on the hot grill. They sizzled as they cooked, just long enough to iron out all the wrinkles.

Walter ran over, "Are you alright?"

"I'm alright... I'm alright."

Walter laughed, "What the hell were you thinking?"

"I didn't know the grill was on."

"Here let me make the tuna salad."

"No, no really, I'm okay."

My new job also included preparing the morning coffee in a Silex coffee pot. I only knew how to make percolated coffee in my mom's metal pot. The Silex was a puzzle to me. I watched the other guys use it, and tried to imitate what they did. I didn't know what the hell I was doing, and I think I missed a step – the Silex exploded, splattering coffee all over the walls. Broken glass was everywhere. Lucky the restaurant wasn't open yet, and no one was hurt. Walter sighed, and helped me clean up before the boss got in. Everyone kept my secret.

One morning, the boss came over to me, "Everyone is too busy, and I'd like you to go downstairs to the basement, and bring up the container of freshly made chocolate ice cream. Do you think you can handle that?"

"Yes, I can do it!" I mean, how difficult could that be?

The ice cream cylinder was almost as tall as me. What did I get myself into? It was too heavy to carry, so I had to drag it over to the wooden stairs. I found the special handle for the cylinder, hooked it on, and pulled it up the long flight of stairs, one step at a time. But I made one miscalculation – the handle never clicked into place.

When I got the ice cream almost to the top, the handle worked itself loose, and the cylinder crashed down the steps like a torpedo. I stood there with the handle still in my hand, but no cylinder at the other end. I hoped that no one heard it. I closed my eyes and made that noise in my head.

The boss pushed his way through the rest of the guys at the basement doorway. Instead of being angry, everyone was laughing. That was strike three for me, and I should have been called out. But Walter worked his magic charm, and I was given another chance. I wished he would stop doing that. I'd rather be fired, and go home, and end this torture.

Closing time at Carstairs was 11pm, and Walter thought it would be safer for me to stay at his apartment in Brooklyn than to travel all the way to The Bronx late at night. But I refused. So every night for the next couple of months, I chose to face the dangers of the subway at night, to be home in my room in The Bronx, rather than stay in Brooklyn.

Before closing at night, everyone took turns cleaning the restaurant. One of the waiters, Jerry, was very quiet. He only spoke a few words at a time, just enough to get by. As we were cleaning up, he took me into his confidence. He was an ex-Marine who had fought in the Pacific. He never talked about the war, but he opened up to me. He showed me the metal plate that replaced part of his skull, and told me how he got it.

"When I was on Guadalcanal, me and my buddy scrambled for a bombed-out crater, with bullets whizzing by our ears. A wave of fanatic Japs, thousands of them, charged at us in an open field, like they wanted to die.

"My buddy got hit by a mortar shell, and I was trying to keep his brains from spilling out of his head." Jerry held back his tears. "I could hear the Japs all around me, but couldn't see a thing through the clouds of smoke. I could only see a few inches in front of me. Suddenly, a screaming Jap broke through the smoke, almost on top of me. He jumped into the crater, and we fought each other for our lives. Then I heard an explosion, and the next thing I knew, I was in a hospital with my head bandaged. Part of my skull was missing. They replaced it with a piece of metal."

I wondered why he trusted me with something so devastating to him.

I had no problems working the fountain, until this prick of a guy gave me a hard time. He didn't like the way I made his ice cream soda, and bitched every step of the way as I was putting it together. Either it wasn't enough ice cream, or it was the wrong flavor. I knew I'd heard him right the first time. I don't know what his problem was, but he refused to pay for the ice cream soda.

The boss heard the whole thing, and took the customer's side, soothing the prick, and agreeing with his complaints. He told me the guy was a long-time customer, and he didn't want to lose him. So he took me off the fountain, and I ended up washing dishes. Here, I think I found my niche. I was an excellent dishwasher, but I wanted to be better. I thought if I did it faster, I'd impress the boss. Instead, I started breaking dishes, and a piece of broken glass sliced my thumb open.

The boss had had it. He tried to let me down easy by telling me that this was a slow time for the restaurant, so he wouldn't need me anymore. I hadn't worked my way up at Carstairs, I'd worked my way down.

As I walked out of the front door, Tony Bennett was singing, *Because of You*, from a table top jukebox. The restaurant and the music cooked together into a stew, until I couldn't separate one from the other. Whenever I heard that song again, I felt the restaurant door slamming behind me.

I may have lost the job, but I did save enough money to buy myself my first leather flight jacket. I got it from the Army & Navy Store next door to the Boulevard Theater, and if it was from the Army & Navy Store, you knew it was authentic. Now I could play the part of a tough guy – short, but tough.

Millie quit school at the end of her Junior year, just after she turned seventeen. She said she wanted to start living her real life, but soon found out it wasn't any better than school. She got a job at Ohrbach's, on Union Square at 14th Street, in Manhattan. She worked at checkout, and later in the office for several years. There, she developed a friendship with a fellow worker, a young woman named Colette. When she talked, Colette put on airs, gesturing pretentiously with her hands, so Millie and the other girls nick-named her Miss Park Avenue.

After a late double date with some guys from their job, Millie brought Colette home to stay overnight. I didn't expect a dark brunette to walk gracefully through our front door. She had a dimple on her chin, and dark red lips that were puckered on the verge of a kiss. Colette peered at me with her penetrating, cat-like eyes.

"Millie, you didn't tell me your kid brother was so cute."

While Millie prepared her room for her guest, Colette stayed in my room, asking me the usual, simple kid questions like, "How do you like school?"

I cut her off, "Excuse me, I have to go to the bathroom."

"Can I watch?"

Those three words made my balls tingle, and in my sophisticated way, I answered, "Okay."

"Maybe you'll let me hold it for you?"

Before anything could happen, Millie walked in, "Everything's ready."

Colette looked as disappointed as I was. "Solly, maybe another time."

At least I had the satisfaction of knowing this wouldn't be the last time I'd be seeing Colette.

PUMPING IRON

DURING THAT SUMMER I grew faster than the speed of light, but without gaining weight. My wrists continued on up to my armpits. Oh hell, my whole fucking body was the size of my wrists. You couldn't tell by looking at my face that the rest of me was a walking skeleton. I needed to find a way to build myself up, and went to see Lefty.

Junior's name was now, Lefty. I don't know why, but he wanted to be called Lefty. I guess he thought it was cooler. Junior... I mean Lefty, had become a bodybuilder, and had created his own little gym down in his basement. He had developed connections in the land of muscles, and the neighborhood knew him as, "Mr. Muscles."

He said he knew this drug addict who desperately needed a fix, and if I had the cash on me, the guy would sell me a brand new set of weights for four dollars. That's 250 pounds of gold-colored, metal weights for only four dollars. As soon as I got the weights home, I started pumping iron, and very quickly started to look human again.

Even though I had grown older, my tormentors still owned the dark night in my room. They had never changed with me, and still haunted me. The same old witch hovered over me, holding her sharp knife, waiting for me to move so she could plunge the knife into my chest. And the room was still closing in on me, about to devour me.

Now that I had turned sixteen, this had to stop. I just couldn't live this way any longer. In one quick, angry challenge, I threw my quilt off my body, forced myself to open my eyes, and screamed into the blackness.

"Go ahead! Do whatever you want to do to me!" Nothing happened. I screamed again, "You hear me? I'm taking my room back!" Again, nothing happened. Then, through the sides of my eyes, I saw something flutter past me. I didn't wait to see what it was, and threw the quilt over my head.

Every night I challenged them, and every night I became less afraid of the dark. Once in a while I lost the fight, but eventually they evaporated from the dark corners of my room.

Harold's slippers stood in the same exact spot by his bed for so long, they created a groove in the linoleum. Every morning when he got up, he slipped effortlessly into his slippers without looking. And just as easily, he'd slip in and out of his angry rages.

This winter, he smoothly and quietly slipped out of our lives. There weren't any fights. I just woke up one morning, and he and his stuff were gone. It was difficult to be enthusiastic; how many times had he left us before, only to return? Each day, Millie and I waited, expecting him to show up. Harold never came back, but he had already left his mark. I still carry him with me.

Now that he was gone, Millie and I could watch the TV any time we wanted to. We watched everything that moved on the screen, from kiddie shows like *Kukla, Fran, and Ollie*, to old serials like *Nyoka*, and *Flash Gordon*.

My great discovery was *Your Show of Shows*, with Sid Caesar, Imogene Coca, Carl Reiner, and Howard Morris. They kept me on the floor, laughing till I cried.

Julio and I were in the lunchroom, watching the girls dance. He pointed to one of the girls I'd seen around school, but never met. All the guys at SIA had the hots for her. Julio started telling me his plans for a way we could rape this girl, and get away with it. I went along with him, thinking it was only part of a story game, like the ones I played with Sergie, and the rest of the guys on my block. But Julio was serious, and was seriously including me in his plans.

"Hey Solly, this can be done, and no one will ever know."

"You've got to be fuckin' kidding me!"

"No. It's so easy it'll really work…"

"What're you out of your fuckin' mind, Julio? Go fuck yourself. I'm not raping anyone."

"Then how come you went along, and planned it with me?"

"I thought you were playing a game."

"What're you some kind of asshole?"

"Yeah, that's me, an asshole… and this asshole's not raping anyone!"

With me knowing his plans, he decided it would be smarter not to go through with it. The girl was never raped, and Julio and I didn't talk about it again.

On our way home, we stood on the subway platform, waiting for the Uptown Lexington Express. As the train came screeching out of the tunnel, someone grabbed me, and pushed me over the edge of the platform. Julio dangled me off-balance over the tracks, as my toes tried to hold onto the edge of the platform. He held me there, playing chickie with the oncoming train.

"What the fuck are you doing!?"

"Don't worry I've got ya."

I was desperate, "You son of a bitch! You fuckin' bastard! Get me outta here!"

A ton of metal was roaring closer and closer to my head. I was about to be crushed, and torn apart. At the very last second, Julio pulled me back onto the platform.

"Get the fuck away from me!"

"Come on, Solly, can't you take a joke?"

"Some fuckin' joke. Up your ass, Julio! Just stay away from me!"

I thought I could trust Julio. I never expected him to do something like that to me. What the fuck was he on? After that, we were still friends, but I was very wary of him and learned to watch my back.

When I got home Mom was pacing the floor. "Oy gutenue! It's my fault. It's my fault!"

"What happened?"

"Oy, mine boychick! My Sollinue, it was all my fault. I read it in the cards. I told Sally her fortune, and it came true. All of it came true. I'm never going to tell fortunes anymore."

"Ma, what are you talkin' about?"

"Oy vayz mir, mine Sollinue... Sally killed herself. She opened da oven, put her head in, and died. It was all in da cards. It was my fault."

"Ma, the cards are wrong most of the time. This is only a coincidence."

"Sollinue, you don't know vhat you're talking about. Coincidence, shmo-incidence... you don't know vhat you're talking about."

At sixteen, I started rebelling, and arguing more often with my mom. And some of our fights became screaming matches.

"Ma, you've got to stop believing this crap."

"Vhat do you mean, crap? You're too stupid to understand."

That hit home, and I blew up, smashing my hand into the wall until it bled.

"Vhat's wrong with you? I can't talk to you anymore."

What she meant was, I refused to do what she wanted me to do, and wouldn't believe what she wanted me to believe.

"You're acting like a crazy man. If you go on like dis, I'll put you in a crazy house."

EMPTY EYES

IT WAS A very cold day in February 1952. At each block, Millie had to ask a stranger for directions to Mount Sinai Hospital. Manny had gone to the hospital for an appendix operation, but when they operated on him, everything went wrong. They found he had cancer, and as soon as they cut him open, it spread like wild fire.

Each time they operated, they took out another piece of him. The man I saw in the hospital bed wasn't Manny. My mother called him Manny, but it couldn't have been him. Manny was always very heavy, but this man weighed under sixty pounds, with empty eyes looking back at me.

Every inch of his fleshless arms was covered with black and blue marks from the constant barrage of needles, and tubes were stuffed up his nose. Every time Manny took a deep breath, I could hear an almost inaudible gurgle coming from his throat. I couldn't look at him. I spent the whole visit ignoring him, and watched the busy street outside his windows.

Toward the end, Mom was there almost every day to feed him her homemade chicken soup. One of the last things he said was, "I loved you, Molly. I always loved you."

I was there at the end, standing by Manny's bed. He took a deep breath, and I heard that gurgling sound again… but this time he stopped breathing. Manny died, and I felt nothing. I just wanted to get out of the hospital, and home as soon as possible – back to my routine of having my supper alone in my room, and listening to my radio.

At the front desk of the hospital, we learned that Manny's brother, David, had taken away all of Manny's personal belongings. His things were gone, as if he never existed. All that was left was a ring, with a dark red gemstone that kept falling out of the setting. A doctor personally met us at the front desk and asked us for permission to have an autopsy done on Manny. Millie and I refused the autopsy. We knew what they wanted – to cut him up into pieces, and experiment on his body. Hadn't they cut him up enough?

Millie and I never knew that Manny had a large family, but we found out when most of them showed up at his funeral. All these strangers were related to us -- aunts, uncles, and cousins. Millie and I had never seen them before, and would never see them again. David came in with the woman my mom referred to as Manny's Whore. Millie and I never knew her name. To us she was, and always will be, The Whore. She wore her heavy make-up in such a sloppy way it made her look like a clown. She hadn't been invited, and they pushed their way into the funeral parlor. Manny's family disliked David, and ignored the both of them.

Mom coaxed Millie into asking The Whore why she was there? She started screaming, "Who the fuck are you?! You've got your nerve!" She looked at the crowd staring at her, "No one here has the right to Manny's money! It all belongs to me! Manny promised me!"

Manny's relatives pleaded with her to calm down, but the more they tried to quiet her, the louder and more violent she became. I don't know who they were, but three big guys looking like wrestlers wearing yarmulkas appeared, and practically carried her, kicking and screaming out of the building. They warned David and The Whore that if they didn't stop interfering with the funeral, they would call the police, and have them arrested.

Manny's taxi union paid for burial plots in Philadelphia for all of its members, and it was a long drive in my brother Harry's car.

He wasn't buried in a coffin like I'd seen in the movies – dark, well-polished hardwood, with curlicue edges. Manny's coffin was a plain, unfinished pine box with knotholes, like an orange crate I'd use for my scooter. It was as if he wasn't worth anything better.

When I heard the hollow sound of the shoveled dirt, drumming on the pine box, I realized Manny was inside there, and that I would never see him again. It began to rain, camouflaging the tears that quietly dripped down my cheeks. I was suffocating. The suffocation I felt was for the hopeless boy who choked on his fears, a worthless boy who hid his pain so well.

Two days later Mom, Millie, and I visited Manny's apartment on Simpson Street, David and The Whore had been there first and cleaned out the apartment. They took every stick of furniture. They even emptied the kitchen drawer where Manny always kept a jackknife hidden for me to find.

When I returned to SIA, I used Manny's death to get sympathy from the kids, especially the girls. They felt so sorry for me, and hugged me so close I could feel their bellies breathing against mine. Manny was gone, and here I was using his death for my own advantage, getting whatever I could get out of it.

MOLLY'S STORY: THE OLD COUNTRY

IT WAS MARCH 1952. My father Emanuel Rothman, alias Emanuel Roth, had died at the age of 55, succumbing to complications due to cancer of the liver.

A week had passed since Manny died, and I found Mom in the kitchen telling her own fortune with playing cards. She laid out the cards on the white porcelain kitchen table, surrounded by four Shabbos candles, their flickering yellow flames reflecting off of her face. Mom's fingertips hovered above the cards, as if they had eyes and were reading the meaning of each card. Every so often, her fingertips lightly touched the cards, going back and forth, and adding up their meaning.

"Ma, I thought you quit telling fortunes."

"Oy, Sollinue, I had such a dream." Mom spit three times, and knocked on the wood cabinet. "It was so real. Manny, my dead baby Harvey, my mother, and father – all of dem came to me trying to tell me something, and they won't stop bothering me until I find out what it is. And they want me, every Friday, to light candles for dem."

"So, why are you reading the cards?"

Mom stopped laying out the cards, and looked up at me. "Sollinue, my totala, my dream told me to."

"Mom, how did you learn to read fortunes? Did your mother teach you?"

"You really vant to know?"

"Yeah, I really do."

What I know about my mom's past is from the accumulated bits and pieces she would tell me over the years to come. Whenever she told her story, she would add new pieces to her life's puzzle that we didn't hear before. But she always started the same way, every time.

"It all started vhen I was a little girl. My name then was Esther Malke Sauce, and I lived in a small country called Bessarabia, on a farm near a small town called Brachun. My mother's name was Surah, and my Father's was Avroom."

"But Ma, what about reading the cards?"

"Vait, vait... let me finish. I'll get to it. Anyway, don't you vant to know about your grandma and grandfather, and how we lived in the old country?"

"I'd love to know, but I thought..."

"Hold your horses, I'll come to it."

For the first time in my life, Mom was actually talking to me, and telling me her story. I was thirsty to know anything about my grandparents, and my mother as a young girl. Once she got started on her story, there was no stopping her – her past took over.

"Okay, now vhere was I? Oh yes, our house. Ah, our house... you should have seen it. It had fruit trees all around it. The house was very large, with a straw roof. It was a yellowish house, and vhen da sun... oy, vhen the sun shined on it, the house became a golden fire. The windows had wood shutters, hand-carved designs, and painted red. On the edges of the house, also had beautiful designs.

"And my father... oy, my father was so handsome, with a red beard and mustache, with blue eyes. He was very religious, and always wore a yarmulka. He was tall, like your brother Harry. And, oy such a voice! All over he sang... a beautiful voice. My father was a cantor, not for money... didn't need it, he was rich.

"For a Jew to own their own land in Eastern Europe was impossible. My mother, Surah Goldsmith, inherited the land from her grandfather, who went to America. One of the reasons my father married

391

my mom, besides her being beautiful, was for her land. My mother and father had so much land. They owned half of the town land. Wherever you go, it was their land. They had acres, and acres, and acres – one farm for sheep, one farm for cows. My father made all kinds of cheeses. And goats, we had goats. And we had lots of horses."

Mom's voice rose and filled with joy. Like an excited young girl, her words couldn't come fast enough, "Fruits! Ah, we had fruits everywhere. Orchards full of fruits! My father also grew tobacco. He had so many houses to dry the tobacco, and many horses and buggies, because you couldn't walk so much land. In the summer time, they use ta rent the land out. Besides all that, he was a furrier. He got the skin from the animals; they trapped them. He had men working for him, lots of people working for them."

Mom's voice got more excited and short of breath, "They cleaned the furs, and made coats. You have never seen such coats, Russian ones, with the fur inside. And the top was all white, not dyed like here. And on the top, it use ta be sewed on with red, and all different designs on it. And a fur on the bottom, you know, like the real Cossacks, and the kind of hats they wore.

"My mother, my mother... Ah, my mother, she was absolutely gorgeous! She had long black hair. You should have seen her... she had dark brown eyes, and red cheeks, and white skin, like milk. She was beautiful. I resemble her very little, no not too much, my mother. Her lips were like rubies. And her cheeks, I'm tellin' ya, like flowers – like roses. When my mother use ta walk in the town, everybody use ta admire her. That's how good-looking she was.

"My mother had two sisters, very good looking, too. One was here in America, and the other in Bessarabia. And she had two brothers, both in America. Most of the family was in America. Did you know I had an older sister? She died before I was born. My mother gave me her name.

"Ahh, my mother was some famous painter, believe me. All my tings, whatever I wore, she made it. And, and you know, she sewed pictures on long pieces of material that covered the walls. You know, uh …uh, what's it called, tapestries. Yeah, that's it, tapestries. If she saw something, a bird flying with beautiful colored wings, she use ta do them. Whatever she saw…

"You know, I had a painted horse. You couldn't separate us. A pinto, you know, with different colors. Oh, it was a beautiful horse. Mom painted a picture of him. I had it in my room. She painted everything, my cat… and I had a curly chicken she painted. She also sculpted people, and animals, too.

"You should have seen… there was one room, from ceiling down to the floor, the whole room was full of things she did. All the rooms had painted beautiful pictures hanging on the walls. She painted people, and flowers. My mother use to make people… nicht, not the way you make people, it's not people the way you know.

"She weaved beautiful blankets, all different colors, even made her own linens. She never sold her work. She use ta do all those things because she enjoyed it. And she was so rich she didn't need the money. Whatever she did, she kept it. All of it was stored away. It was for me, when I get married. My mother made it all by herself, with one hand. Vhy one hand?

"You see, when she was young she got polio, and paralyzed in one hand. Her left hand closed, like this, and one foot was back in a little bit. She walked okay. She cleaned and made meals and stuff. My mother didn't have any servants to help her. She didn't want it. She was a very plain woman. She did everything herself. My mother was really something.

"My mother was a very young person. She was a very young person when she died." For a moment Mom wasn't talking to me, she was talking to herself. "Ah, yeah… when she died, I died with her."

I interrupted my Mom, "My grandmother was an artist? Ma-aa! Why didn't you ever tell me that? You never cared about my artwork. Why?! You call it "that art crap," and tell me it's a waste of time. I never knew there was an artist in the family. Why didn't you tell me?!!"

Mom looked at me with her hand over her mouth, taking in what I said, and without answering me… "Vhere was I? Oh, yes. When the women came, the Christian women every Sunday, my father use ta have wine for them, and my mother use ta bake cakes. There was like, a little gathering. My father was very friendly with all the people there. They use ta call him, Ponya. I think it was Ponya. Uhhh... it's like a king, like somebody big, you know, like a general or something. And the women use ta come, and they use ta go all over in the house, and were never tired looking at the art.

"The people use ta talk of my mother's art, and how wonderful it was. Neighbors from all over use ta visit our home, and loved her art. She did art for the Christian people for nothing. The word traveled throughout Russia, and finally reached the Tsarina, that my mother designed and painted the most beautiful Russian eggs. She was famous for them.

"I'll never forget it, Sollinue, you should have seen the carriage, the way it was. Ah! It all was designed with beautiful velvet things, and gold trimmings that curled around the carriage. The horses were dressed up in all different colors, silver straps against the dark horses, with sparkling jewels in them. And standing up on top of their heads, were colorful feathers fanning out.

"Tsarina Alexandra came with a lot of guards. There must have been a couple of dozen guards there. And the Tsarina came to my mother, and looked in da whole house, and saw everything. She loved it all, and wanted dis one, and dis one, and dat one.

"Tsarina also saw what she came for, the Russian eggs my mother painted and designed. They excited the Tsarina, and she had to have them, and took them with her, and a bunch of paintings.

"When the Tsarina came into the house, she really touched me. The Tsarina touched me, and talked to me. From then on, every year, she sent some solders to pick up some art from my mother.

"We lived in a big house – it was one floor – a wonderful, beautiful house. The walls were made of clay," Mom giggled, "and horse's shit mixed in, and no bricks. The walls were smooth, and painted. I don't remember what color. The roof was made of straw; it never leaked. Attached to part of the house, was the stable. The horses, and other animals, their bodies helped keep the house warm.

"When I woke up in da morning, the branches of a pear tree went into my window. All I had to do was reach out, and pull off a pear. Forget it, they were so sweet, and juicy, and tasty – and that was my breakfast. Holding a pear in my mouth, I climbed out of my window, and called my horse. And from around the back of da house, my Pinto came running to me.

"Oy, my horse... Ah, what a horse!" Mom interrupted herself, and her eyes were tearing, about to cry, "Ahh, such different colors! It had white, and reddish on its face and back. Oh, it was a beautiful horse. We went everywhere together. That horse knew what I was thinking. He knew me better than anyone.

"I ride... vhat's da word? You know, no saddle? Ahhh, that's it... I jump on my horse, and ride bareback. I was very vild. I was very mischief. My mother use ta pray to God, I should come home in one piece. Got an extra pear for my horse, and we rode off into the fields, and into da woods. As I left, I heard my father scream, "Where is that girl? She's so dam spoiled!"

"Shush, you'll wake her."

"She should be awake. Malke is old enough to be working around here. You spoil her."

"I rode across da field, and was on my way to the Gypsy camp. I also brought sugar cubes with me for the little ones.

"They were camping on the edge of our farm. They had my mother's permission for when they traveled through, they could stay on our land. Every time, they gave me lessons for telling fortunes on regular playing cards. I loved their stories about werewolves, and vampires. We lived near Romania, where they lived. The Gypsies loved my vildness, and they also taught me to dance Gypsy. Their camp almost was my second home. They taught me the ways of the Gypsy.

"One time, one of the Gypsy wagons left the others, with me still inside. They had the idea of kidnapping me, thinking they'd get lots in ransom because my parents are rich. And if that didn't work out, they'd make a slave out of me, and sell me.

"The Gypsies loved and respected my mother and father, who were always good to them when no one else would. And they volunteered to help find me. They joined the Sheriff of the town, and its people, to find me. The town also loved my mother and father because of their generosity. Every week, my mother fed the townspeople who had nothing, and gave others work on our farm. My parents never had any problems with pogroms.

"The other Gypsies knew the way of their own, and were the ones who found the kidnappers. When the Gypsies found the wagon, I couldn't scream. They had my mouth tied, and I couldn't scream. But the other Gypsies searched the wagon, and found me, and turned them over to the Sheriff, which was unheard of – Gypsies and Sheriffs don't mix.

"I went to Hebrew School, but not long. They had no school in Russia; maybe in large cities they have them. The people were workers, so there's no schooling. But the Jews had schools, Hebrew Schools. Yeah, there was a Rabbi there, he teached the children, but I didn't go all the time. I knew how to read Hebrew, but I was so goddam fed up with school.

"Oh, was I a devil! The Rabbi use ta get fresh with all the little girls. He use ta play with them all over, and I use ta see it. What he did to those kids, you don't want to know what. So before I went into Hebrew School, I went to, uhhhh... to a ditch, and I took mud, and put it all over my face, and into my hair, and all over, so he shouldn't touch me. He never even looked on me." Mom looked at me, and laughed deeply, "I use ta do that."

"My mother saw me, and said, "What the hell is that?" I was full of mud in my hair, my whole body, and all."

She said, "What are you doing that for?"

"I use ta tell her... other children use ta be afraid to tell, but the hell with that. They then kicked the Rabbi out of there. That was really something.

"The Holy Days were coming, and just before Easter, the town had no wine. My girlfriend's father was too busy, and sent us for wine. He sent me, my girlfriend and his three sons. Kids, imagine, just kids should go to another country, and get wine. We had to have horses and wagon, naturally, and we had to cross the water, over to Romania, for the wine. We put the horse and wagon on a boat. We were in Russia, and had to cross to the other side of the Prut River to Romania.

"We were told, Make sure to get nice, sweet wine. So wherever we went, we first tasted it, and we got drunk." Mom punched me, and laughed. "So we had headaches... we was sick, so we asked for a hospital. And in Romanian, a hospital is a crazy house.

"I'll never forget, we were trying to pull one door open of the hospital, but it was locked. And the other door was banging, from the crazy people who tried to break down the door to... to get a hold of us. And we tried to open it up. We didn't know what the hell was happening. We thought the door was jammed. We found a window, and looked into the window. We saw them... they were jumping into the window. They went towards us, and we started running.

"We ran into the garden. They had gates, you know, with points on them, and everything. And there were the ones who were a little bit crazy, outside with the guards who had guns and all. And one of the crazy guys saw us, and went crazy. He jumped over the big gate, and his whole bathrobe got caught. He ran, and was naked, and he was running after us. Solly, he was this far away from us." Mom showed me with outstretched arms. "And his mouth was full of foam, you know? If he got a hold of us, maybe bites us, or something – we would have been done.

"So the guard had to shoot him. He ran after him, and shot him. We saw that! We were so scared stiff. We ran until we couldn't run anymore. The crazy man was so close he got ahold of my long hair – that's how close he was. So the guard had to shoot him. I was so sick.

"So on the way back, we was so scared, and then we had to pass the cemetery, down a hill. We was so frightened from what had happened to us, we forgot to put the brake on the wheel. The horses... you know, when you don't put the brakes on, the carriage goes on the horses' legs, and they get wild, and that's it. That's what they did. The horses threw us right in a ditch." Mom laughed over her words. "We got up from dere, we had all different animals on us – frogs, and long black things, you know, those blood-sucking worms... what is it?"

"Leeches."

"Leeches, that's vhat they were, leeches. Ahhch, disgusting! I got chills thinking about dem. Ah, that crazy house – that was a terrible thing. I never forget it as long as I live. It gave me nightmares.

"When we got home, my mother looked at me and said, "Oy! What am I going to do with her?"

"My mother spoke Jewish, but I didn't know how to speak Jewish. I learned mostly Romanian and Russian, not Russian exactly, it was Bessarabian. The real Jewish language is really Hebrew. I learned how to speak Jewish over here in America, with my grandmother and my aunt.

"Sometimes I slept at my neighbor's house, where my girlfriend lived. My mother was a great cook, but I hated lots of things she cooked. But at my friend's, I ate everything, even potatoes which I hated. It was delicious. Isn't that something?

"Well, anyway, I stop by my neighbor's house, where my girl-friend lives. They are having a party. They do that a lot. You get a lot of people, and they come to your house, and have a party, and paint. And that's the way they use ta having it.

"Sometimes for a week, we'd spin wool. You know, we make all kinds of different linens. The cotton over there, we make it very thin, and it comes out like pure silk it's so thin.

"I stayed over my girlfriend's house, and I woke up hungry for food, when I heard breaking dishes in the kitchen. My friend's mother thought it was her children. She started calling their names, and an animal answered, making a noise... whatever it was... Grrr, you know? So we all sat down together, and the mother held us so we shouldn't be afraid. Who the hell knows what it was? It found food, and ate it, and went out. It must have been a werewolf because there were large footprints, bigger than a regular wolf, everywhere. And the thing was able to open the door and closed it behind itself.

"In the early part of the evening, lots of us go out to a Bazaar. They usually go on until late. It was twelve o'clock, and the horses started to go around and around and around... they never went nowhere. Until after midnight, they were normal again. A evil spell was put on them. It was frightening. From then on, everybody use ta go out only during the day, and before midnight they made sure they were home.

"A war was on, I think the revolution, where Russians were fighting Russians. I didn't see exactly the fighting, but when we went outside in the evening, we can see the fireworks. I saw big wagons with soldiers piled up on each other like fire wood, with blood all over the road trailing behind them. Some was still alive, groaning and screaming and crying. And there were Cossacks on their horses, sounding like thunder as they rode by, with hard faces looking to do something. I saw that.

"They were raping and killing our friends and neighbors. My mother hid me down in our cellar, so when the soldiers came they wouldn't rape me. A lot of our friends were killed. So the others moved, and they left everything, and left their homes so they couldn't be killed.

"In that winter, there was so much snow our house was filled up. And we was prepared, we had barrels of water in the house, and everything. We couldn't dig ourselves out. Spring soon came, the snow melted, and it was quiet again.

"Late one night, I had a nightmare. I woke my mother. She got up, and went into my room to make me feel good. She took my mind off my nightmare by telling me of her dream she just had, about a rose.

"In the dream, a beautiful princess told her that, during the night she will wake up and find a rose by her pillow, and for her to drink the morning sweat on it. And when she woke up, before she came to my room, she found the reddest rose she ever saw next to her pillow. And she had it in her hand, and she drank the teardrops on the rose. Then she went back to sleep, and when she woke up in da morning, she wasn't paralyzed no more.

"I know you won't believe it, Solly, but I swear to you it is true. But dat didn't last long, she only enjoyed her freedom for only a week, and very soon afterward she came down with da flu, the kind that killed millions and millions of people, all over."

Mom started to cry, "Yes, yes, I died with her. When she died, the whole town died. It was such a day. You know in Europe when somebody dies, in the streets they put carpeting – nice, beautiful, red carpeting in the yard. It was a long, and big night. My father had fires burning in bunches everywhere. The people stood in line to see my mother. And after, you eat a lot, and drink, and dance. All the people celebrated. That was the way of the Russian people.

"My father got married right away to a woman with three girls. He tried to make me do things I couldn't do, like he wanted me to learn how to sew with a machine, but I was so short, I couldn't reach the pedal. He didn't care. No matter how hard he wanted me to do it, I couldn't. He'd pinch me hard until I was black and blue, I still couldn't reach it.

"He wanted me to work for his new wife, do whatever she wanted, and to be a servant to her three kids. I refused, and he came after me with an axe handle, wanting to kill me. I ran away, and never came back. My father didn't care. He didn't want me anyway. I tried to stay with friends, but they were afraid of my father. I didn't know what to do, and cried hysterically.

"Then I found my aunt, and she took me in. I worked, and she took my money. Then my aunt sent a letter away to my rich uncle, who lived in New York City. She told him I was the only one of the family left in Russia, besides her, and told him to help out. My uncle sent money, and she took the money away from me.

"The only fun I had was every Saturday night... no, Friday nights. They had a beautiful park there. It's gorgeous. The trees, the flowers, and everything, was so pretty. And I met my boyfriend, Yankel, there. I came to an empty part of the park. In the bushes came wild dogs, and they chased me. I remembered someone telling me not to move. Saliva dripped from their mouths. I slowly lied down. They were all over me. I was too frightened to breathe, and I didn't move a muscle.

"Yankel appeared from nowhere, and chased the dogs away. You know, Solly, I forgot that he was tall, and so handsome. It just happened that he was living next to my aunt, not far from the park, and he took me home. And in just that one night, Yankel fell in love with me.

"When I got home, it was late, so my aunt went and beat me up. My aunt took my clothes, and threw them out, and says, "Get out!" My boyfriend was around, and saw everything in the window. So, Yankel came, and picked me up on his lap with my clothes, and he brought me into his home with his family.

"Oy, my aunt found out where I was, and came to his home, and wanting my uncle's money, she said she feels sorry, and apologizes,

"I didn't mean to do all that to you."

"I went back to my aunt, and from then on, Yankel and I started going together. I was very sick, and when I got well, my Yankel made a party for me. I had a good voice when I was young. I use ta sing and everyone danced. And... and we drank, and I got high. And my boyfriend had a gun with him. I didn't know it. I kissed another boy, or he kissed me, and Yankel got mad. I told him I didn't mean it. I mean, what did I know... I was young.

"He says, "Sure, I was right there, and you kissed the other boy."

"Yankel's love scared me, I was too young to understand. He told me again how much he loved me, and he wanted to run away with me.

"My uncle found out that my aunt was taking his money. His letters told me to hide the money, and that he had paid for a carriage to take me to a train that will take me to Paris. There was an aunt who will meet me in Paris, and take me to America.

"Yankel found out I was going to America, "When you go to America, you won't even think about me."

"He wanted to shoot me. And all of a sudden, I don't know why, somehow there was a big storm. Oh my goodness! The entrance to the park had a giant iron gate, a real high one, you know, with doors and all that stuff. We walked in the side street, and those doors fell from the wind, and one of them fell on Yankel. I had to pull him out. He didn't want to kill me anymore. But he knew it was over, and he went and got drunk, very drunk. He got very sick, and was found lying down in a horse stable.

"They went to call his mother, and he didn't want it. He chased everybody away. He says he wants me. I had to go, and I brought him home to his house. He didn't let anybody touch him but me. I put cold compresses on, and took care of him, and all that.

"The day came when I left for good. It was in da wintertime. The snow over there is impossible... it blinds you. You gotta wear dark glasses, otherwise you can't walk out in it. There was a beautiful sled with four horses to take me to a train. I don't know where the train was going, but I knew I was going to America.

"All of a sudden, Yankel ran in front of the horses on the trail. He started waving his arms. He didn't want to let me go. Then he threw himself under the horse's feet. They had to drag him away, and as they took him away, he shouted a curse on me. Maybe that's why I had so much bad luck all my life. Since then, the rest of my life turned into garbage.

"Yankel calmed down, and handed me a piece of paper with his address and picture. There for a while, I was very much in love with him. As we rode away, I heard Yankel scream, "Somehow I'll find you!""

"Oh yes, I almost forgot something very important. My best friend's father worked for my uncle in America, and he helped my uncle to get me to America, and got a visa for me. By the time he sent a visa to his daughter, he was too late. The white Russian soldiers had already raped her, and killed her. I got to America, and she didn't... my only best friend.

"I took a train to France, met my guardian there, and we missed the ship. We had to wait in France for the next ship. I was so excited to come to America, just to get away from the life I had with my father and aunt.

"There are lots of things to see. Today I recognized places from pictures I saw. My guardian, an old man, had us stay at a big place for all Americans from America. We stayed at the place for nothing. They use ta give us the meals everyday. Ehh, the old man never had enough, no matter what they gave him.

"I wore Russian clothes... you should've seen me with those clothes." Her hands sculpted the air around her. "I wore a white skirt gathered all around me, you know, with red trimmings, and red boots. Then I had a red apron with designs all around it. And I also had a little red babushka, and my hair was down to here..." she pointed to the bottom of her ass. "Yeah, my hair was very long. Den I had those white, uhh... linen blouses my mom made, all gathered around, dis way and dat way, and puffed sleeves, and red long earrings that my mother also made for me, with real gold. The boots I wore... my boyfriend, Yankel, was a shoemaker, and he made these boots with buttons – he made for me.

"There was this French woman who loved my clothes. She lied to me, and said I couldn't go to America unless I wore American clothes. And she bought me old, brown clothes to go to America. I left all those pretty things in France. The old man said the French woman didn't really give a damn about me going to America, she just wanted my pretty clothes. I was too young to realize dat.

"And den... Wait, I forgot to tell you. In Paris, there was a lot of guys over there, with Russian banjos and things. There was big, long table, and they made me dance on it. You should of seen me den, like those gypsy dancers. I was like a little doll, you know, with long hair, and all that. I was dancing Russian dances in my Russian clothes, while they played the banjos. Because I did dat every night, they gave me extra food, the old man, too.

"There was the top deck, and da bottom. My uncle in America gave me money for first class, but with the money – the old man took it, and paid for tickets for his sister, daughter in-law, and his niece, and nephew. So instead of first class, we were way down in the basement, sleeping with a whole bunch of people. There was so many people, I could hardly move. After my mother died, my whole life went down into the basement.

"On the boat coming here, there was a big storm. We almost got drownded. I was so sick. We all had these, uhh… life things on, you know, in case we sink."

"When I came here, my uncle got me off before Ellis Island. Uncle paid extra to do it. We ate at the Chinks. We had roast duck and milk. I was very religious then, because of my father and mother, and I told my uncle, "You're not supposed to have milk with meat."

"Don't ask any questions. You're now in America, and everything here is different."

"They lived in the Grand Concourse. Everyone who lived there was rich. When we got home, they gave me Epsom salt to clean me out. I was such a greenhorn, and when I went to the bathroom, the bathroom was so beautiful – it was gorgeous, like a dining room. In Bessarabia, we used the outhouse. I was sitting there, sweating. I didn't want to make in there because I didn't want to dirty the place up, and make it smell. After a half hour, and I'm still in the bathroom, my aunt opens up the door, and sees me sweating. I had to go, I had terrible cramps, and felt sick.

"My aunt said, "What the hell are you doing? You sit down over there, and don't mind the smell, and you do it. Then press this handle, and it all goes away."

"My uncle's wife really wanted me to be a maid. They took me to be a maid in her house. She wanted me to wash dishes, clean the house, and all dat stuff. I didn't like it because I was very vild at home, running around all over with my horse, and all dat.

"If she thought she was going to make a maid out of me, she had to have her head examined. So she saw I didn't like it. She gave me old clothes of hers, and I didn't like that. Then she gave me dishes to wash, and I didn't do them. So she went and told my uncle.

"So my uncle said, "I'll talk to her." My uncle sits me down on his lap, and he says to me, "In America you work, and make money that you give to parents. And what would you like to do? Would you like to work here in the house, or would you like to go out and work?"

"I want to go out and work. I want to meet people. I want to see people. I want to go places. My uncle was so happy. He was so happy tears came out of his eyes. I had to wipe his tears. "I'm smart. I don't want to be a maid."

"So, alright, I'll send you to school because you're still young."

"I was very young when I got here, about twelve years old. That's why I had to have a guardian. Otherwise, they wouldn't let me come to America.

"My mother's sister, Tovah, and my grandmother made dinner for my uncle and his wife, and told him that she has a daughter my age. It will be easier, and better for me, to live with her a couple of weeks. And I went to her for a couple of weeks.

"While I was there, she was very good to me. Tovah would sew clothes, and made me a couple of sets of clothes, of skirts and dresses. And then she started talking me into staying with her.

"Why are you going over there? Your uncle works a whole day, then comes home late at night. I'm your mother's sister, and your grandmother is here. Stay here. Tell your uncle you can stay here. You want to stay here. You don't want to go there."

"It was hard for me to tell my uncle that I wanted to stay with my Aunt Tovah, because he was so good to me. My uncle agreed to let me stay with my aunt. Then my problems started. If I refused to do what my aunt said, she'd start pinching me, and smacking me across the face. I wanted to go back to my uncle. Tovah wanted me to be her slave. Oy, she use ta kill me!

"They kept me down in the basement, with the dogs and cats. I couldn't eat, couldn't sleep... I kept thinking about Yankel. I wrote lots of letters to him, but my aunt found out, and she took his address, and my letters, and ripped it up, and burned them. He wrote me back many times, but she never gave them to me. How could she be my mother's sister?

"Aunt Tovah had a big house in the Rockaways, where she rented rooms out for the summer. I had to wash all those rooms clean. During the summer one of the rooms caught fire. In Romania, the word for fire is "foc," which sounded like fuck. So I ran, knocking on all the doors, screaming, "Fuck! Fuck! Fuck!" The people thought I was crazy. My aunt had to explain to the borders that I was a greenhorn, and couldn't speak English, and was confused.

"My uncle got me a job in Manhattan working on furs, which I had experience on my father's farm. My aunt wouldn't let me wear lipstick and makeup. One day, I found on the subway a roll of red crepe paper. I took it to the washroom, and wet it, and put the dye on my lips and cheeks. Hours later, my face began to bleed, and I had to go to a hospital.

"Wherever I went, it was no good for me. So that's why I married Nathan Schnell. I'd marry anybody, as long as I can get away from my aunt. You know, you can't blame me, right? I was so goddamn poor. I was sixteen when I had my first baby. His name was Harvey. Then starts all my troubles... I never had a good day. I really mean it... in my entire life.

"When I got home from work, Nathan would always take my money, and gamble it away. One time, I had no money to feed the baby, and Nathan wasn't home. I refused to wait for him in our apartment because his father lived with us, and I was afraid of him. His father would get fresh with me. I didn't want to be alone with him. I waited outside in da snow, with my baby in the carriage, until Nathan would come home. He didn't come home until two o'clock in the morning.

"The baby got sick. I couldn't afford a doctor. A neighbor called the doctor, and she paid for it. By the time the doctor came, the baby died. He was only fourteen months old. Why did he die – because of that son of a bitch Nathan.

"I had two more children with him, Walter and Harry, which was short for Harvey. Nathan was supposed to mind them while I was at work. Instead, he left them outside while he fooled around.

"What happened was, you know fur work is seasonal work, so it wasn't busy, and I only worked a half a day, and got home early. I opened up the door, and there they were in the bedroom, my best friend and Nathan, doing it on my bed. She was supposed to be my best friend. She lived right next door. She ran out like a whore. So I went and hit Nathan over the head with a chair, and the blood started gushing.

"I got scared, so I ran out and called the cops. The cops came in, and they called the ambulance. I told da cops what happened. They asked me if I want him home? I said, "No!" And that was the end of that. I never saw him and his father again. I divorced him.

"Some marriages, they have some good in it, but all my husbands were no good. Really… no really, I had a very tough life."

Tears welled up in her eyes. "I had it very good when my mother lived. She was so good to me. She was an angel, my mother.

"When I worked, I left Harry and Walter in a day nursery. The nursery was in a basement. Walter fell down all the steps, and was badly bruised in the ribs, and all over he was bruised. Harry was able to talk, and told me that they didn't feed him, and he's very hungry all the time. I stopped in a candy store… you should have seen the way he ate, whatever I gave him, it disappeared. I paid the nursery to feed my boys, and they kept the money, and never fed them. So I got a woman to stay in the house, and I wouldn't trust day nurseries no more. Then I had to marry Manny or live in the streets.

"All my life I worked as a furrier, and for what? Thank God, I had kids. God bless them all. They're the only reason my life was worthwhile. But my mother, she was so good to me."

Mom stopped, breathed deeply, and went back to her cards.

"Then what happened?" I asked.

"Please Darlink, I'm tired. Another time. Dat's enough… I don't want to talk anymore." She started crying, and left the kitchen.

TOO LITTLE, TOO LATE

ON AN EARLY Saturday evening, the street sounds slowed down to a trickle in the soft, warm air. I walked our new puppy... that's right,

Mom got another dog. It felt good to be alive without Harold being in my life. I could walk through any part of our house without that bastard being there, without having to smell his sour beer breath, or the shit squashed in his pants, spreading its smell throughout the apartment.

But I wasn't completely through with Harold. I couldn't break the habit of eating alone in my room, or listening to my radio whisper into my ear. And a sudden noise from any of the rooms still made me jump with fear.

The puppy and I sat outside on Lefty's stoop, enjoying the quiet, when I heard a playful voice behind me, "Hellooo, Solly."

"Hi."

It was Nina and Susan, "Whatcha doing?"

"Sitting."

"Poor Solly is all alone."

"Yeah, I'm all alone. My mother took Ronnie and went visiting somewhere."

"You mean, no one's home?"

"You've got it."

We talked for a while, and then I got up and walked toward my building. "Well... I'll see ya."

Nina and Susan followed right behind me into my building.

"Hey, Solly, do you mind if we keep you company?"

Acting like I didn't care one way or the other, I said, "Sure, why not."

We were watching Harold's TV, when Nina moved very close to me. I leaned over and kissed her... or did she kiss me. I could feel her up for as long as I wanted to, without any interruptions from some stupid kissing game. We found ourselves sinking deep into the soft, dark maroon couch, where Harold had passed out so many times.

While we were arranging ourselves for the best strategic position, Susan sat on the floor ignoring us, and continued to watch the TV. Surprisingly, it all worked out smoothly. But every few minutes, I'd look over my shoulder expecting to see Harold standing over me, threatening. But not even Harold's phantom could stop me. Both of us were pumping away, when I heard someone at the front door. Ronnie ran into the living room, and right behind him was my mom.

"Solly, vhat is dis? What are you doing there?"

I couldn't face my mom. I never wanted to know her private life, and I certainly didn't want her to know mine. I wanted to bury myself into the couch. But instead, being the true coward I was, I pulled up my pants, and ran out of the house, leaving Nina to face my mom alone.

Nina told me that my mom was very nice to her, and treated her with respect. She promised Nina that it would be their secret – but Mom didn't speak to me for a couple of days. A week later, she called me into the kitchen.

"Sit down, boychickal. I think it's time we had a special talk."

Oh, no, here it comes... she's going to give it to me about Nina.

"I understand that, being a man, you have certain needs, and I know you can't help yourself. Now listen good. When you find a girl, make sure she's a stranger, and never take her home. Give her a wrong name, and go to a hotel, bring a fake ring and a cheap suitcase. That's it! Den, you can screw her belly off.

"One more thing, a very important thing: Wear protection. Do you understand, bubbala? You don't vant to make the poor girl pregnant...

And then go have fun."

Mom left me in the kitchen, stunned. I had just had my sex education talk – Molly's version. It wasn't exactly *Love Finds Andy Hardy*.

In Jack's candy store, I was looking over the joke books, and saw a new one on the rack, called *Mad Comics*. It was from EC Comics, so I naturally thought it was going to be horror stories. When I thumbed through it, I didn't know what to make of it. I'd never seen anything like this before!

Mad was really insane, with each panel filled with visual slapstick going on in the background that had nothing to do with the main story line. I finally got it. They were making fun of everything that was sacred to kids... they took *Superman,* and changed him to *Superduperman*, and turned *Tarzan* into *Melvin of the Apes*. I was hooked.

GOING IN DIFFERENT DIRECTIONS

THE DAYS WERE dwindling down to the end of summer vacation, and all my friends started to drift away from our block. Eventually, Sergie hung out with a group of Jewish guys on Faille Street, and felt like a stranger to me. From time to time, I'd run into him on the Boulevard, but he wasn't that constant friend, discovering and experiencing new adventures with me. I pretty much became a loner.

But on the weekends, I still had Lefty's parties. Dancing to the hot Latin music left me throbbing in a sensual high. Besides Lefty, the only friend I had was my childhood enemy, Melvin, who didn't really count, because being with him, I still felt alone. But as the months went by, Melvin and I became inseparable, we even began to like each other.

It wasn't only that my friends left the block; I was also going in a different direction, not because I was an artist, but because of the different way I was thinking. I felt very strongly that there was something I had to do. I didn't know what it was, but it was there inside me, waiting, and wanting to get out.

That September, without warning, Mom moved us to Brownsville, Brooklyn. She did it so quickly I didn't have time to get angry. It was a temporary move, but her reason for it was to live closer to Walter – which would make it easier for her to go house hunting without traveling all the way from The Bronx. Mom and Walter had this plan of buying a home together on Long Island. The houses there were sprouting up like mushrooms, and Walter wanted to be part of it.

We were on the fifth floor of the apartment house on Pacific Street, looking down into the courtyard of a Catholic School for wayward girls, which looked more like a prison than a school. Its building was in the middle of the courtyard, surrounded by a high brick wall with broken glass embedded on top.

I got ahold of Walter's field glasses, and searched for the wayward girls... but never found any. I did see the nuns sunning themselves in wicker chairs. They would pull their robes above their thighs, and... they had legs! Human legs, pretty legs, soft white legs. They sat there, thinking they had complete privacy, so they felt free to open their legs, and let the cool breezes circulate between them. I felt guilty for getting excited, but the guilt wore off very quickly.

It was a Saturday morning, when we got together at Walter's apartment near Avenue H, to go out looking for a house. Millie, and her friend Colette, met us there. Hunting for a house bored the shit out of me, so I looked for an excuse not to go. I volunteered to stay home and take care of the kids, Walter's son, Brucie, and Harry's daughter, Caryn. They loved the idea.

Before they left, Colette suddenly came down with a terrible headache, and stayed behind with me, and the kids. Just the idea of being alone with her made my body feel the thrill of that sudden dip on a racing roller coaster. As soon as everyone left, I suddenly didn't know what to do. It was as if I was alone with this delicious pastry, locked in a glass case right at my fingertips – I could see it, but I couldn't have it.

Almost as if she was reading my mind, Colette said, "Solly, this headache has made me very tired. I'm going to lie down in the bedroom. Don't be afraid to make any noise. When I'm like this, nothing can wake me up, even if the house is collapsing." That was my key to the pastry case.

I gave Colette about fifteen minutes to pretend to fall asleep. It was just another game to be played. While the kids were in the living room watching TV, I tested the rules of the game, and loudly called her name. Then I went in and shook her real hard. When she didn't move, we both knew she was pretending. Well, if that's the way she wanted it, it was okay with me.

I told Caryn I was very tired, and was going to take a nap with Colette... could she please do me a favor, and watch TV with Brucie, and not bother us? Under the covers, I slowly took off my pants, and peeled off her panties, keeping the illusion of trying not to wake her from her pretended sleep. Her legs sleepwalked their way around me.

Caryn came in with Brucie, "Uncle Solly, we're hungry. Could you peel this apple for us?"

"Yeah, okay, but after I peel it, I want you to stay in the living room."

With her legs still wrapped around me, I twisted myself to the side, and hanging partially off the bed, I peeled the apple with the speed of light. The kids left, and I was back in the saddle again. As soon as I left the bedroom, Colette woke up and joined us.

"I had a wonderful sleep, and my headache feels better now."

Later on Mom, Millie, Walter, and Sonny came back to the apartment with tired, unhappy looks on their faces. Searching for a house together had turned out to be a struggle. Mom and Sonny just didn't get along. Sonny tried to control all of the house decisions, leaving Mom out of the picture. It was clear this wasn't going to work out, and the whole idea fell apart. Our one-week move to Brooklyn was happily over. We moved back to The Bronx – but I had lost my block forever.

We rented the first floor of a two-family house in Pelham Parkway. I loved being back in The Bronx, but it was no fun living on Matthews Avenue. Bad things kept happening to us, like the time a group of kids took a disliking to Ronnie, and tried to set him on fire. Mom and I searched the area, but were never able to find the bastards. Then the landlord's little brat kept invading our apartment with his mother's keys, and taking whatever he wanted. Things just kept getting worse. We lived there for only a month, and Mom went bankrupt. She couldn't pay the rent, and gone were the days of the free-month's-rent. Now we had nowhere to go.

To keep us from living in the street, Mom had to break up the family temporarily, until she was able to save enough to pay her debts, and keep us together. Lucky Millie got to stay on our old block with a close friend, cockeyed Cindy. I went to live with Walter. Yes, damn it – back to Brooklyn. But that didn't stop me from traveling to The Bronx every weekend to hang out on East 165th Street. Mom and Ronnie stayed at Harry and Sylvia's house, in Paramus, New Jersey, in the attic that I had helped Harry build. When we all lived together – Millie, Mom, and Ronnie – we hardly saw each other, but now I felt lost without them.

During the summer, Millie was still working at Orbach's, and I worked with Walter for an awning company, Atlantic Awnings on Atlantic Avenue. Every week, Millie and I gave Mom our paychecks. We realized that the sooner we paid our family debts, the sooner we could move back together again. But Mom knew we needed some money for our expenses, and whatever she didn't need she gave back to us.

There were no home-cooked meals at Walter's. Sonny only cooked out of cans, or we ate out. I stand corrected... one day, Brucie freed their pet canary from its cage, and it accidently flew into a pot of boiling water. Sonny screamed, then just stood there, watching it being boiled. That was the first time their apartment ever smelled like real food.

Our day started at 5 am. While the whole apartment building was still sleeping, Walter would wake me up, and we would leave the quiet morning behind us as we went out the door. We always stopped for coffee on our way to the awning shop, and brought an extra cup with us.

The early hours of our morning were spent preparing our truck with supplies and awning fixtures. Walter taught me how to use a stock and die for threading pipes, which came in handy on the job. Anything I did, no matter how small the task, I gave it my all. I didn't do it to be rewarded; I did it because it made me feel good, especially if I did the work well.

There were two other trucks packing up, besides ours. One morning, Walter was bending a pipe, using a special tripod that was bolted to the basement floor. The ground under it was thick with grease, and when Walter jerked at the pipe, his feet slipped from under him, sending him sliding across the floor, and into a wall. He looked at me in an odd way, just like Mom, and we both started to laugh. Mom and Walter were made of the same stuff.

The other guys in the shop took it seriously. They couldn't understand why we were laughing. Walter looked at me, made a silly face and rolled his eyes. Without a word, he was telling me: These guys are idiots. He made me feel like we knew, and they didn't have a clue.

After packing up, we were on the road by 8:30 am. Each truck was given a clipboard with lists of possible jobs for that day. The boss, Mr. Greenberg, never expected anyone to complete the list, but with me as his helper, Walter and I completed the list on the clipboard everyday. We made a great team.

Mr. Greenberg was amazed. Since he started his business, this was the first time anyone had been able to do that. He gave us praise, but no bonus. That didn't stop us though. We felt pride in our work, and I enjoyed crossing off each job on the list.

Before our first job, we stopped at a diner for breakfast. The jukebox was playing Frankie Lane's, *Jezebel*. Someone had a sticky finger, and kept on playing it over and over again. Walter introduced me to a sandwich of two sunnyside up eggs, over lightly, in a hardroll dripping with melted butter and egg yolk – and with a cold, chocolate milk – I was in heaven. After that, like a trained dog, every time I heard the song, *Jezebel*, my mouth watered for my absolutely favorite breakfast.

All the hot housewives smiled at me, but fucked around with Walter. When we were leaving a job, they would shout out, "Remember, call me!" The midday sun's heat was intensified under the canvas. Walter told me that sometimes the canvas could heat up to 120 degrees, or more. When I had to work up close to the awning, the heat got so dense, I couldn't breathe.

We were about to leave a job on Long Island, when the owner called us back, "What kind of job is this? The awning is hanging crooked."

"Don't worry, lady," Walter said, "I'll take care of it. This is a normal occurrence, and we have something specifically made for this problem. It will only take us a few minutes."

Walter told me to get a few odd pieces of canvas from the garbage bag in the truck. He unrolled the awning to its end, and while it sagged, he stuffed a rolled-up piece of canvas into the loose end, so that when he rolled it back up, the awning was perfectly aligned. He called to the owner, and showed her.

"That was fast. What did you do?"

"We have this special packet, a Dutchman."

This sounded much more professional than a couple of rags. The woman ate it up. Boy, Walter was a great bullshit artist. I loved him, but after a while, I found it hard to believe him.

Mostly, my job was to get Walter whatever he needed from the truck. This included threading, and cutting the pipes to size. Then, at the end of the job, I had to put everything back, ladders and pipes, and tie them down to the truck. The first time I attempted it, I did a sloppy job, which almost killed us. Walter had to make a short stop at an intersection, and one of the loose pipes flew to the front of the cab – a couple of inches either way, and the pipe would have gone through one of our heads.

Walter got out of the truck to check on the pipes. As soon as he touched them, they all broke loose, and came crashing down on him. Lucky he didn't get hurt. Instead of being angry with me, he showed me how to tie everything down by using a slipknot, and some great Navy knots. Since that time, I over-tie everything.

We traveled all over Brooklyn, Queens, and Long Island, working in the houses of the rich and famous, people like actors and songwriters. This was all new to me. I couldn't wait to go to The Bronx to tell my friends about it, but by the time I got there on the weekend, the thrill was gone.

On one of our Brooklyn jobs, we stopped to install some window awnings on the tenth floor of an apartment building. Walter told me it was a cathouse, and as I walked down the hall past each door, I pictured some woman inside, fucking. I could swear I heard their moans and groans. Every girl who passed us in the hall, I imagined was a prostitute, inviting me into one of the rooms.

When we were about to install the awning, Walter told me to hold him by the waistband of his pants, so he could hang out the window to put up the awning. The only thing stopping him from falling ten flights – was me. What was he, nuts? How could he trust me after the loose pipes incident. I must have lost ten pounds in sweat on that job.

Our very next job was in Little Italy. We had to replace an old roller, with a new canvas awning. Before we left the shop that morning, the boss had told us to use an old, rusted roller, and make it look like new by painting it with a metallic, silver paint. He said no one would know the difference, and he was right. It was hard to tell the roller wasn't new. Even with all the crap I pulled in The Bronx, I felt this was a dirty trick – to make this poor guy believe he was paying for a new roller.

The old roller we were taking down was very long, and made of wood, which made it extra heavy. It was hanging outdoors, directly over the storekeeper's vegetable stands. Walter was at one end, and I was at the other and, as we lifted it at the same time, Walter shouted, "You got it?" I said, "Yes," thinking he was checking to see if I had a solid hold on my end. I didn't know he was going to let go of his end. The sudden weight of the roller pulled me off balance, and if I hadn't let go, it would have taken me down with it. The roller went crashing down onto the fruits and vegetables, crushing everything in its path, and careened into the street, rolling to a stop by two parked cars.

The storekeeper screamed at me in Italian, and ran after me for blocks, biting on his bent finger. I stayed away from the store, while Walter resolved the situation. Whatever he did, it worked. Walter picked me up a couple of blocks away, laughing. To make me feel better, he treated me to a creamy, chocolate Italian ice. It was completely and deliciously different from the ices we had in The Bronx, and I couldn't get enough of it.

Working with Walter that summer, my diarrhea attacks reappeared, especially on the hottest days. The pain was too much for me. It slowed us down, and we couldn't complete our job lists. Cold chocolate drinks seemed to be my enemy, so I had to give up my favorite breakfast of eggs and chocolate milk. Once I did that, we got back to getting our job lists done. While driving from one job to the next, Walter started teaching me how to drive the truck.

On the weekends, Walter was using Mr. Greenberg's shop without his knowledge, to produce his own awnings, and install them. He talked me into canvasing door-to-door with him. I was scared shitless to open a conversation with a stranger, especially selling something I didn't know anything about. It was like asking me to throw myself on a live grenade.

"Murphy, it's really very easy. Don't worry, if you need me, I'll be right across the street. Here's what you're going to say: "Excuse me Ma'am, would you be interested in a canvas or aluminum awning for your home?" That's it. That's all you have to do."

As I walked to my first door, I practiced the words over and over again. When the door opened, my mind ran away from my body, and a strange voice said, "Excuse me Ma'am, would you be interested in a canvas or aluminum awning for your home?"

The woman smiled, and very politely said, "No, thank you."

Wow, that was easy. The more the homeowners refused me, the more confident I got. We were about to call it a day, and I was at my last house. I got a little creative, "Excuse me, Ma'am, would you be interested in a canvas or aluminum awning for your windows, backyard, or doors?" I was very proud of myself for adding those few words.

The woman smiled like the others, and said, "Yes. I'm very interested." I just stared at her… I didn't know what to say.

She repeated herself, "I said, yes, I'm interested."

I went blank. I saw Walter across the street, and screamed, "Walter! Walter!"

I scared the shit out of the woman. She was about to slam the door in my face, but Walter got there in time to calm her down, and made the sale. After that, no matter how much Walter tried to convince me to help him sell awnings, I would never do that again. From then on, I spent my weekends back in The Bronx.

The summer vacation was coming to an end, and we were installing an awning over the windows of a new bank in Queens. The bank was all-windows, so we only had a thin strip of wood at the corners to work with. While I was screwing in some fixtures, I heard Eddie Fisher's voice coming from nowhere, belting out the song, *Tell Me Why*.

I was working very carefully, but no matter how careful I was, I tapped ever so slightly into the window, and the glass cracked. It was such a tiny crack… maybe no one would notice it. But slowly, the crack began to grow. I pressed my hand against it, trying to hold it back, but it wouldn't stop. The crack raced throughout the plate glass window, like jagged branches of a tree. Helplessly, I watched it race across the whole storefront, and then around the corner to the other side.

Walter couldn't help me out of this one. So that was my last job, and the last time I would ever live with my brother, Walter. Mom had paid off all her debts, and saved enough money to get us together again. We all moved back to The Bronx, onto Boynton Avenue, between Westchester and Bruckner Boulevard – by bus, only minutes away from my old neighborhood.

FROM THE ANNEX
TO THE MAIN

AT SIA, THE Annex was a temporary holding pen, where we waited for the real thing – our move to the Main Building, on East 79th Street, in our Junior year. Over the summer, I had worked out everyday, and now that I was taller, everyone at school was treating me like I was a new kid on the block. Even the girls were paying more attention to me. With this new self-image, I felt like I belonged at SIA.

A girl flashed by the doorway of the classroom, laughing and screaming, her long hair flying in the air. Right behind her, in hot pursuit, was our Sculpture teacher, Mr. Cavallito, grinning and running on his toes, squirting a water pistol at her. She turned out to be his star pupil, who was sculpting a huge, detailed figure of a Roman soldier in full armor. She was working on that sculpture every day for months. It looked finished to me, but she was never satisfied.

The Sculpture classroom had one long worktable in the center, where we created our sculptures. There were a couple of little tables at the end, with taut wires strung across them, used for cutting through blocks of wet clay to find impurities. If a sculpture was fired with pieces of foreign substance in it, it would explode and destroy the other students' works, at the same time. One whole wall was lined with shelves filled with our sculptures, in different stages of being worked on.

My strongest memory of that classroom was the pit. It was a

wooden barrel filled with unused pieces of dried clay. Some of us called it "the black hole." For punishment, Mr. Cavallito would make a student soften that rock hard clay with water. It was a hard and dirty job. The clay would squish through and between your fingers, and dry on your arms like *The Mummy's* decaying skin.

Mr. Cavallito had one lesson we all had to do: create a bust of ourselves. We were on our own with no instructions. After that, he allowed us the freedom to sculpt anything we wanted. I was working on a sculpture of a naked, native woman. While detailing her nipples, the girls in the class giggled, and acted embarrassed. They complained to Mr. Cavallito, who ignored them, and cheered me on.

After two years at SIA, it finally dawned on me what the purpose of the school was. It wasn't like most high schools, stifling the creative urge, but fueled it, and gave it all the freedom it needed to grow. SIA's different way of seeing education started a change in my life.

At lunchtime, I explored the new neighborhood for places where I could afford to eat. As the weeks went by, I learned about a deli around the corner that had the best, and cheapest hero sandwiches. There was a corner restaurant that wasn't too bad either, but a group of Italian girls hung out there, and they were constantly playing the jukebox – Italian singers like Tony Bennett, Connie Francis, and Vic Damone – they played them non-stop until I couldn't take it anymore.

I was wearing my usual leather flight jacket, combat boots, and garrison belt, leaning against the school building with a cigarette dangling from the corner of my mouth. My hair was combed back into a DA, with a long, wavy curl pulled down on my forehead. But inside, I was still that little kid, acting out the movies. The other guys all looked the same, and I thought they were really tough. I wondered if they felt the same way I did.

I took a last drag on my cigarette, flicked it off my thumb, and it shot across the sidewalk into the gutter. An old guy wearing a sandwich board spotted my butt, picked it up, and smoked it like it was his dessert. His gray beard looked like a wet bunch of Brillo rusting under the basement sink, his overcoat was crusted with dirt and dried food, and his feet pressed out of the sides of his torn shoes. The sign he wore advertised the art store around the corner, and he was always in front of SIA.

For his lunch, he would scrounge around in garbage pails for leftover sandwiches, and put some in his pockets for his dinner. He made room for the empty soda bottles he collected for the nickel deposit. Talk was, he was filthy rich, and had savings accounts collecting interest at different banks. It bothered me that some of the kids treated him like shit, and I spoke up for him.

"Why don't you leave the old guy alone? He's not doing anything to you." I walked over to the old man to show him that I cared.

He looked at me and said, "Hey! Why don't you mind your own fucking business and leave me alone, you fucking asshole!"

He saw right through me, and put me in my place. From that day on, I treated him like I would anybody else.

Julio and I were in the train on our way home, when I spotted a cute Spanish girl. I asked Julio how to say, "pretty," in Spanish.

He said, "chinga."

I walked over to her, and as smoothly as I could, said, "chinga."

She hauled off, and slapped me so hard, it knocked me off balance.

"Hey Julio, didn't I say it right?"

He laughed, "Yeah, you said it right... but chinga means fuck!"

"Very funny."

When we got on the train, I started joking around with Julio, and this guy I'd seen around the school got into my face. "Why don't you shut the fuck up, or I'll shut it for you."

He was taller than me, and twice my weight, with hairy Popeye forearms that ballooned out from his rolled-up sleeves. I never did anything to this guy, he just didn't like my face.

"Are you kidding me?"

"No, you little shitface."

He shoved me into Julio, who had a short fuse, and unlike me, loved to fight. He had to have a fight every so often... it seemed he couldn't live without one. He was pissed off, and shoved me aside, "Okay asshole, you want to fight?"

"Hey look, I have nothing against you. My fight is with this little shit."

"And my fight is with you – you big shit!"

The train stopped at the Jackson Avenue Station. Julio and I, the Popeye forearm guy, and six colored kids who were rooting for Julio, all got off the train, and onto the El platform. Without hesitation, Julio threw the first punch. I don't think poor Popeye ever got in a punch. The colored guys got caught up in the excitement, and two of them grabbed Popeye, and hung him upside down over the railing. They held him there by his ankles, out over the street below.

Holy shit, what the hell was I doing here? It was too late to run, I was trapped with these insane guys.

Julio was wearing a club jacket that had the word, "Tiger," embroidered on it. "Hey Tiger, you want us to drop him?"

They were really going to drop him! My stomach felt like it was about to give up whatever I had in there.

"Hold it guys," said Julio, "I think he's had enough."

Popeye pleaded, "Yes, yes, please... I've had enough! Don't drop me. Please don't drop me!" I felt sorry for Popeye, and didn't want any part of this.

They hauled him back up onto the platform. The poor guy was shaking, and so was I. We all got on the next train, and Julio and I got off at Simpson Street Station – and home. These guys were even crazier than Julio!

The smell of snow was in the air, but this year it wasn't the same. My childhood friends were gone, along with the muffled sounds of the trolley bells. Walking to the train station, I felt the few joys of snow I still had left: the thick snowflakes melting off my face, the crunching of fresh snow under my feet, watching the snow trim the trees, and cover the hard concrete in waves of white fluff. From nowhere, a song came rolling up and down, through the valleys of the snowdrifts – *You Belong To My Heart*. I was stuck in time; I couldn't go back, and I couldn't go forward.

When I got to school, my first class was Photography, which I liked – especially being in a darkroom with the girls, and imagining what things could develop in the dark. Maybe a girl would accidentally brush against me, or lean her breasts on my shoulder. With these random touches, I could build a whole story of sensual possibilities.

During lunchtime, we had choices... we could dance, or go to the auditorium to watch old, classic movies with our lunch, or hang out on the street. Over the summer, I fell in love with this new music I'd been hearing at B & J. It wasn't really new, but I had just discovered it, and I was excited to bring a couple of records to school, and introduce something new to the dance floor. One record I brought was called, *Night Train* – really hot stuff – along with a couple of songs by Johnny Ace.

There was one thing I knew I was very good at, and that was dancing, but I'd never danced in the 3 years I'd been at SIA, because I was just plain scared. I would stand around the periphery of the gym at lunchtime, watching the others dance, until I became just another one of the supporting pillars of the gym.

The kids who danced every lunch hour, acted like they owned the dance floor, and condescended to let me play my records. They heard only twenty seconds of *Night Train,* and hated it. How the hell could anyone not like it?

I snuck in my Johnny Ace record, and they let it play... it tugged at my heart until I felt it would burst if I didn't dance. Standing on the other side of the room, was a Spanish girl with black eyes, sneaking flirting glances at me. I was electrified by her charms, and something inside me pushed me across the room. Her long, wavy hair framed her dark, creamy skin. I had never seen anyone with such black eyes.

Johnny Ace was singing, *My Song*, a slow Fish. I took her hand. She softened, and became more nervous than I was. We didn't say a word to each other, and I breathed her into my arms. The curves of her body melted, molding into mine. I felt the heat and softness of her naked arms. My thighs rubbed against hers to the rhythm of the music. We were so close I could feel where her thighs met. My heart was pounding so strong I began to lose the beat of the music.

I looked away from her and saw the other kids in one blurry swoop. There was shock and surprise in their faces – shocked to see me out on the dance floor, and surprised that I danced so hot, and so well. Abruptly, they turned off Johnny Ace, and went back to dancing to their white bread, pop music.

I peeled myself away from Black Eyes, grabbed my records, and strolled through the halls. I heard singing coming from one of the passageways. Four colored kids, singing accappella, had found a spot where the acoustics increased the richness of their voices. Holy shit, these guys were great! My record of Johnny Ace was called Rock and Roll. The acappella guys said they were singing R & B – Rhythm and Blues. They were as good, and maybe better, than anything I heard on the radio. I was their best audience, and spent most of my lunch hours listening to them sing.

"Twenty-five cents for a gallon of gas. One gallon oughta do it. Solly, ya gotta dime? That'll make it an even gallon."

It was springtime, and Julio was taking us to SIA in what looked like a bunch of dented metal from a junkyard, pieced together to re-semble a car. I knew it was a convertible, but I didn't know if it was a car. Everything in the damn thing rattled and complained to let it die in peace. Julio was acting funny, and I got to thinking the car might be stolen. What gave me a clue was, when I met him at Simpson Street, he was hurriedly changing the license plates.

On our way to SIA, Julio was teasing me, chanting a saying that was going around, "Arms for the Arabs, Sneakers for the Jews."

By that time, I knew about what had happened in the concentration camps. Everyone I knew believed that Jews were cowards for taking all that crap from the Nazis. I didn't know yet, that Jews had fought back.

We got to school early, and Julio invited a group of guys and girls for a short ride in his convertible. We piled in, and after a few blocks, we found ourselves on Madison Avenue, going the wrong way. It was too late to turn around. We had already gone halfway up the block, when the light turned green, and the oncoming cars and trucks charged at us like a stampeding herd. All we could hear were our own screams.

I must admit, Julio kept his cool, and at the last second, he turned off the Avenue, onto a side street. It was so close I could feel the breeze of the roaring traffic, passing behind us.

I announced to Julio, "I'm not going home with you in that death trap. I mean do you even have a driver's license?"

"How could I, asshole, I'm not old enough. But I do have a learner's permit. Come on, Solly. Come home with me. It'll be fun."

"I'd rather walk all the way to The Bronx, than ride in that rattling pile of junk."

At lunchtime, I bought myself a Dagwood sandwich at the deli – a delicious pile of salami, cheese, and stuff. I could hardly get my mouth around it, and by the time I finished it, my jaw ached. I took a walk, and before I knew it, I was standing by the Roxy Theater, just off Times Square. I had walked too far, and now it was too late to get back to SIA on time. The Roxy was one of those grand movie cathedrals, and tempted me with its marquee. Its large billboard was selling a new kind of movie, called Cinemascope. The screen was so huge it was supposed to make you feel like you were actually in the movie. I was sold.

The movie was called, *The Robe*, a spectacular ancient Roman costume movie, staring this new guy, Richard Burton. All the movies set in ancient history, used British actors. This made me believe that everyone in ancient times spoke English with a British accent.

There was one scene, where the Roman soldiers were on a boat with this Centurion guy, Richard Burton. Having Jesus's blood on his hands sends him a little bit off his rocker, and in his best Shakespearean accent, he shouts, over and over again, "Were you out there? Were you out there?" After the movie, I left the Roxy with his words reverberating in my head, wondering in perfect diction, "Was I out there? Was I out there?"

One of my friends at SIA, Bermuda, filled me in on what I missed the afternoon I cut school. "You know that regular high school, down the street? Well, when we were walking by, a group of guys there were picking on the gay kids. They called everyone who went to SIA a bunch of fags, "Look at all the little girlies going to school… where are your dresses, sweetheart?""

"That was it! All of us guys had had enough. We came back with Julio, and a few other guys, and found those bastards still hanging out in front of their school. Julio went up to the tallest, toughest looking kid in the bunch. He must have been over 6 foot, and Julio's half his size, but they got in each other's faces.

"The kid said, '"What are you going to do, you little Spic? Why don't you scram and take your cute boyfriends with you?"

"Julio jumped up, and knocked the tall kid out. He fell like a tree. Someone even shouted, "Timber!" That was the last we heard from those bastards."

Julio came to school that June, loaded with firecrackers. We took off into the rich neighborhood with a handful of ladyfingers. They were as thin as toothpicks. Even if they exploded in your hands, they wouldn't hurt you. Uptown was where the rich people lived, and downtown was where they did their business. The Marx Brothers' humor wasn't lost on me; I found my own ways of putting down the rich.

I walked with Julio through the Upper East Side streets, until we found an easy mark: a woman strolling in her expensive clothes, with a miniature poodle at her side. When we passed by, we lit the ladyfingers, and threw them at their feet. They exploded with sharp, snapping sounds. Her dog yelped, and ran wildly around its mistress, tangling the leash around her legs.

"You fucking little bastards!"

Those words coming out of such a sophisticated mouth surprised me. We could hear her screaming for help all the way back to school. At SIA, Julio had another dumb idea. He wrapped a cherry bomb in a piece of newspaper, lit it, and stepped away to watch the kids react to the explosion as they walked by.

A tall, stringy, colored kid, with a cigarette dangling from his mouth, was looking for a light. He saw the burning newspaper, and with his cool, rhythmic stroll, sauntered over, and stuck his face right into the burning newspaper. He got his smoke lit, but lingered there for a moment.

What the hell was he waiting for? Why doesn't he get the fuck out of there? I was about to warn him, but he walked away just as the cherry bomb went off. The kid seemed vaguely surprised at the explosion, but shrugged it off, as if nothing had happened.

After that, I told Julio he was on his own. He was certainly on his own when he lit the next cherry bomb, and dropped it in a metal garbage can at the bottom landing of the school's main stairwell. One of the girls was passing by, and when it exploded, she screamed hysterically. She couldn't hear anything at all, and they took her to a hospital, where she quickly recovered. There was an all out search for the guilty person, but no one ever found out who it was... and I didn't say anything. I couldn't understand why I was this guy's friend?

With Julio, it just never ended. On our way to the subway, he was carrying a leather briefcase, acting like a little kid bursting to show me what he had in the case. It was a short-nose 38 – the fucking idiot had a real gun. When he took it out to show me, it was pointing at my stomach.

"What are you, fucking crazy?"

I pushed the gun away from me, "Don't you ever point a gun at me! This isn't the way to treat a friend. What the fuck's the matter with you?"

"Don't worry, I know what I'm doing."

He put the gun back in the briefcase, and it went off.

"Don't worry, you say? If you're going to carry a gun, that's it – you'll never see *me* again." I guess I meant a lot to him, because he never carried a gun again. At least, not when he was with me.

Some of these guys I knew scared the shit out of me, but I never let them see it. I had to keep up a tough front, when all I really wanted was to be back with my old childhood friends, and back in my old room. If these guys ever got an inkling of who I really was, it would have been all over for me. My real self was inside myself, well hidden from the outside.

TOUGH GUYS OF
THE BRONX

WHEN I STEPPED outside onto the street, after sitting in the Boulevard movies for a few hours, I had to adjust to the real world that had been going on without me. Meeting Sergie in front of the theater helped steady my movie legs. Growing up together, it was easy to read when Sergie was upset.

"Hi Sergie, what's up?"

"Oh hi, Solly. I'll tell you what's up. You know Kornblew, and the other guys from Faille Street? We formed a club called the Centaurs."

"Yeah...?"

"Have you ever heard of the Park Boy Tims?"

"Well, sort of."

"These shmucks think the Centaurs is a gang, and accused us of invading their territory. No matter how many times we told them we're just a social club, they won't believe us. They challenged us to a gang war for tomorrow afternoon."

"Don't show up."

"Come on, Solly. You know we can't do that, and still live here. I don't know why the Tims are so angry."

"Maybe part of the job of being a gang, is to be angry."

Julio was the leader of a Puerto Rican gang, called the Tomahawks. When I told him Sergie's problem, he was willing to help. It wasn't that he wanted to help Sergie; he just wanted some action. I met Julio and his gang, and showed them where the fight was going to be, and when. My job was done, and I turned to leave.

"Where the fuck do you think *you're* going? Hey, you're part of this shit. You're not goin' anywhere."

How do I get into these things? All I wanted to do was help Sergie out, and now I'm in the middle of a gang war. Walking to the Centaur's basement clubhouse, I was desperately thinking of how I could get out of this mess.

When the Tims finally arrived, they were surprised to see the Tomahawks, a real gang, waiting for them. I stuck close to the walls, as far from both gangs as I could get. The room was as crowded as a subway during rush hour. It didn't look like we'd have enough room to fight.

The Park Boy Tims quickly checked out the situation, looking for a way out of a fight. Paratory, the leader of the Tims, said to Julio, "There's no fight here, now that we see the Centaurs are only a social club, and not a gang." He turned to Sergie, "You guys should stop wearing club jackets with Centaurs printed on them. People will think you're part of a gang."

One of the Tomahawks wasn't satisfied with Paratory's bullshit. His name was Loco, and he looked like he just stepped out of a wrestling ring. He carried a baseball bat, and was all worked up for a fight. "None of this talk-talk-talk shit, let's fight!"

He started wildly swinging his bat. He didn't care who was in his way, even if it was his own gang. Loco just wanted to fight. Julio was the only person in the room who had some control over him, and talked Loco down in Spanish.

To my relief, the fight was called off. The crazy thing about it was, the Tims and Centaurs all grew up together in grade school. Now, for no reason at all, they were enemies. After that day, all these guys were showing me respect, for being so cool at the potential fight... if they only knew.

Melvin, my new close buddy, and I, had just left the Boulevard Theater after seeing two great movies, *Stalag 17* and *War of The*

Worlds. Still dazed, we walked along the Boulevard, and took a short cut along Bruckner Boulevard, to Boynton Avenue, to my new apartment. Melvin stayed for supper, and we spent the evening hanging out.

It was late, and the streets were empty – a dark night with no moon, and the trees blended in with the black sky. I didn't know where one started, and the other ended. I was a stranger to this street, and it was a stranger to me. There were no lights coming from the rows of two-story buildings, just scattered streetlights, leaving a circle of concentrated light outlining the edges of a few lonely trees.

As Melvin and I headed to the bus stop with our usual tough Bronx swagger, I stopped to light a cigarette. Out of the shadows of a dark doorway, a hot, red glow flashed in answer to mine, like fireflies signaling to each other. I heard girls giggling. Reflected lights from a passing car, flickered off the faces of a group of people, sitting on a stoop.

A voice broke out from the dark shadows, "Hey, looka here. There go the tough guys of The Bronx."

And like a shmuck, I answered, "Yeah, that's right."

That got the voice pissed off, "You fuckin' punk. Come over here, and we'll see how tough you really are."

What was I doing... why didn't I keep my mouth shut? "You really scare me. I'm shitting in my pants."

"If you want to live, you better not come back this way," the voice was followed by girls giggling.

We stood under the El on Westchester Avenue, waiting for Melvin's bus home. "So, Solly, what are you going to do?"

"You mean you're not going back with me?"

At that moment, Melvin's bus came, and true to his nature, he said, "No way!" The fucking bastard got on the bus, and waved, "See ya!"

I stood alone on the corner of Boynton and Westchester Avenue, deciding what to do. I could circle around Ward Avenue to Watson, and back to Boynton, and avoid having my ass kicked. But those wise guys knew what I looked like, and sooner or later, I'd bump into them. I had to face them. I walked back on the same side of the street, hoping they weren't there anymore.

The streets were empty, with only the sound of one person's foot steps... mine. I was almost past the row of two-story buildings, when this guy pulled away from the shadows, and jumped in front of me, blocking my way. Another guy joined him. I was scared shitless.

"Well, looka here, the little prick came back."

The girls were always giggling, but never said anything. My problems with tough guys always seem to happen when there were girls around.

At first, I couldn't see his face, then he stepped under the streetlight, and I was able to see my protagonist clearly. He was older, and a head taller than me. He had a wide scar along his cheek that split off in two different directions. His close crew cut accentuated the beefy rolls of skin on his neck.

"Who the fuck do you think you are?"

My legs shook uncontrollably. It took all my strength just to stand there. I was dead... I knew I was dead. This guy was going to kill me, and there was nothing I could do about it.

"I warned you to stay away, motherfucker. So, shitface wouldn't take my warning... I'm gonna break you into pieces, you fuckin' asshole."

I just wanted to get it over with, "Do you want to fight, or are ya gonna talk me to death?"

Just before punches were thrown, another guy stepped in between us, "Hold it! Hold it. Hey Lynch, can I talk to you for a second?"

"Make it fast, I want this asshole."

"I know this kid. He's all right. He doesn't mean any harm. Like you say, he's just an asshole." He moved toward me, "I'm tellin' ya, I know this guy. Believe me, he's all right." He put his hand on my shoulder, "He's all right."

Scarface finally turned away, "Okay, kid. If my friend says you're okay, then you're okay. But next time, be careful wit your mouth.

Now, just get the fuck out of my face."

The guy that intervened, decided I better get lost while I could, and walked me home. "My name is Tony. I know your mother, Molly. She's a friend of my mom, Mary Zappala. Your mom is a good woman. I've seen you with her, and guessed you was her son. Man, you don't know who you were dealing with. You're lucky you're still alive. I've seen Lynch take on 3 or 4 guys at one time, and send them to the hospital."

"You really saved my ass. Thanks a lot, Tony. I don't know what to say, but thanks a lot."

"It's okay, kid. He won't bother you anymore. But you've gotta learn when to keep your mouth shut. If not, it's gonna get you in a lotta trouble."

I was cold, and shaking with built up adrenalin that had nowhere to go. My kneecaps vibrated from being so cold. That night, I lay in bed, thinking how odd it was that there were times when I'd act like a coward, and other times I'd face danger, even if it meant being hurt. Tonight, I'd either been a fool, or I'd been brave. Either way, it was a lucky night.

DICK IN HAND

BEFORE MELVIN AND I went to the movies, we ate at the deli on Westchester Avenue. A little bell tinkled over the door of the deli, and we walked across the sawdust floor to a small table in the back. Moishe, the waiter, took our order. He was bald, thin, and bent over, and so brittle it looked like he didn't have much longer to live. His every step was pre-planned; instead of walking, he fell forward into his steps. It surprised me that he could even make it across the room.

We each ordered a Pepsi, and a couple of the best franks in New York. I found a cockroach doing a backstroke in my Pepsi. When I complained to Moishe, he said, "Stop complaining. Look, I won't charge you extra for the roach."

It was Saturday, and we ended up at the Boulevard movies, where they were playing *Quo Vadis*. We made sure we sat next to a couple of girls. They looked so much alike they must have been twins. One of them gave me a good looking-over. I joked around with her, and she loved it. After awhile, my twin said to me, "Please be quiet, I'd like to watch the movie."

I held her hand, and she held mine back. I put her hand on my thigh; it burned through my pants. I moved her hand toward my cock, and very carefully, I unzipped my fly. She took my cock out of my pants, and closed her hand around it. She knew exactly what to do. I covered the whole action with my jacket. She sat there, frozen in her seat, staring at the movie screen, pumping my cock.

My hand found its way under her skirt, and between her legs, working its way up to her pussy. She didn't make a sound. My hand slid up her thigh in slow, calculated moves, stopping each time for a reaction. She didn't move a muscle. My hand started to shake involuntarily, the closer I got to her pussy. I was just about to collect my prize, when she jumped away from me, as if she was being electrocuted.

"What the hell are you doing? I'm not that kind of girl!"

She said this while her hand was still holding my cock. I pulled my hand away, and everything was quiet again. She continued her business of jerking me off. My twin spoke to me, while I was coming in her hand. She said she liked me, and wanted to see me again, and suggested we could meet on the walkway over Bruckner Boulevard, by Boynton.

I had cum all over my club jacket, and ran to the restroom. I was cleaning it in the sink, when Moose, Monk, and Ramos walked in to take a leak. Their eagle eyes spotted the wad of scum on my jacket.

Monk said, "What the fuck were you doing? Jerking off?"

I was ashamed that they thought I was so low I'd jerk myself off in a public place, like the movie theatre. To save face, I told them the truth. "Okay, asshole, if you have to know, I didn't jerk off. There's these girls, twins - one of them jerked me off."

Moose gave me five, thinking what I did was really cool. And before I could get another word out, they were gone.

When I got back to my seat, there were at least twenty guys collected around the twins, acting like starving scavengers picking at the leftovers. Melvin stopped me in the aisle, and told me that some of the guys took the twins' pocketbooks, and stole their money. I left the theater with Melvin, not feeling too good about myself... and I wondered what the girls might be going through. I couldn't face them, and never met them on the overpass. Without my realizing it, the guys in the neighborhood were slowly building a reputation for me of being cool.

Melvin and I took a walk around the Boulevard, and back to 165th Street, by way of Westchester Avenue. It must have been about eleven o'clock at night, and the busy traffic had slowed down. We noticed several dark shadows stretching out to the gutter. It was a couple guys, sitting on a stoop.

One of the shadows spoke to me, "Hey! Solly."

It was Sergie, with two of his friends from the schoolyard, and a couple of girls. The girls were bragging about how they could predict the exact size of your dick, before and after it grew into a hard-on, just by looking at the crotch of your pants.

No matter how much Sergie and his friends tried to coax the girls into touching their dicks, the little cock-teasers refused. Finally the guys begged them, but teasing was as far as the girls would go.

These guys weren't getting anywhere, so what the hell, I thought I'd give it a shot. I had this hunch to ignore the girls, and spoke to Sergie, instead.

"I don't believe them. They're just yanking your chain."

The girls were annoyed. The short, plump one said, "No! I really can do it!"

"I think you're full of shit."

"I'm not full of shit... I really can do it."

"Yeah, right. It's impossible. She's pulling your leg, Sergie. It can't be done."

"I know what I'm talking about."

"Okay, prove it. Actually, the only way you can prove it is, if I take my dick out."

I took my dick out, and she studied it like she was reading my palm. "Your thing will definitely grow to a hard-on of six inches." And then she held my dick in her hand, as if she was weighing it, and started petting it. Which, of course, gave me a hard-on.

"You see? Six inches!"

"How do you know its six inches?"

Still holding my cock in her hand, like a hot dog in a bun, "Because I know!"

I didn't count on her letting it go just yet, because I was just about to come in her hand, so I thought fast and said, "I don't know, it looks larger to me. Let's ask your girlfriend here what she thinks?" Now, both of them were holding onto my hard-on.

"I think it's longer than six inches," said her friend. That did it – I came in their hands. Sergie and his buddies were amazed at how easily I got the girls to touch my dick. I even amazed myself.

The guys I knew from public school, were seeing me in a new light. Word got around about the gang fight that never was, and my part in it became exaggerated. I wasn't trying to make a reputation for myself. I was only doing what all the other guys just bragged about. I never heard any of the stories that were circulating about me, but I did see a difference in the way the guys were treating me.

FROM THE FRYING PAN INTO THE FIRE

MOM PARKED THE car across from her royal highness, the Plaza Hotel, which looked down on her subjects, bumping into each other in the streets.

We were there to surprise Millie, at her new job as a switchboard operator at the Plaza Hotel. Ronnie had to go to the bathroom, so Mom took him by the hand, and off they went, right into the main entrance of the hotel, looking for the restroom. Strangely, not one of the wealthy guests, or any of the workers in the hotel, noticed my mother in her housedress, with chubby Ronnie in his striped T-shirt and baggy corduroy pants.

Mom asked the desk clerk, "Sveetheart, I'm waiting for my daughter, who works here. Maybe you know her? Her name is Millie, a short, blond girl."

"I'm sorry, I don't know her. How can I help you?"

"My son, here, is busting, and has to go to the bathroom. Do you have one?"

"Turn right up ahead, and you'll see it."

"Thank you, darlink. That's to the da right?"

"Yes."

In front of them, was a floor-to-ceiling mirror reflecting the room behind them. Thinking it was another room, Mom crashed into the mirror. She laughed, and the passing guests tried to ignore her.

"Vat kind of place is dis? They make it so hard to find a place to pee." She was still laughing, when she got back to the car with Ronnie. Just then, Millie came out of a side entrance. "Look! Look, there's Millie. Millinue! Over here!"

Millie saw us waiting in the car. "Mom! Solly! What are you doing here?"

"I've got some news. Come, get in... we'll talk on the way home."

"What is it?"

"Do you remember Bob Rosenfeld?"

"Of course, I do. I used to have a crush on him."

"Vell, listen to dis, I found out he wants to meet you... I guess to go out with you. I said, "Okay." Is that alright?"

"Jesus, Mom, why doesn't he axe me himself?"

"Do you want to, or don't ya?"

"Yeah, I guess so."

"How's tomorrow night? He axed me if he could come pick you up for a date."

"Yes, I'd like that, but why can't he axe me himself?"

"He's very nervous."

Bob lived with his mother, next door to Mrs. Levine. My mom and his mother never got along. We very rarely saw Bob, because he always hung out by the schoolyard, playing baseball.

I was on my way out to visit my old neighborhood, and when I went to open the front door of my building, the wind opened it for me, taking me with it. Bob was pressed between the building and the doorway, trying to protect himself from the wind.

"Solly, you remember me... Bob Rosenfeld?" Bob had brought the storm with him, foretelling things to come.

"Sure, hi."

Bob had changed. He had lost a lot of hair, but he was still good looking – dark, tall and thin. He was shaking, but not from the weather.

"I haven't seen Millie in a long time. How does she look?" His cigarette flared up from a gust of wind.

"The same."

"I'm kind of nervous to meet her."

"There's nothing to be afraid of, she's just Millie. In fact, she's just as scared as you are."

That gave him confidence in himself. He threw his butt away, and walked into the building.

This was the first hurricane they gave a name to; it was called Barbara. I leaned into Barbara, and walked toward my old block, East 165th Street. The storm got worse, and almost lifted me off the ground. I decided I'd better turn back, and plowed through the wind. The hurricane was testing me. I felt like Jon Hall in the movie, *Hurricane*, trudging through a torrent of rain. But unlike Jon Hall, I survived the storm without lashing myself to a palm tree.

About a year and a half before her date with Bob, Millie was riding the subway on her way home from work, when a soldier, a total stranger, approached her and introduced himself.

"Hi. My name is Chet, and I'd like to apologize for staring at you. I know this is going to sound crazy to you, but I swear I'm telling you the truth. At first, I thought you were someone I knew because you look so familiar to me. You won't believe this, but where I saw you, was in one of my dreams. What is your name?"

"My name is Millie, and yes, I don't believe you."

"Look, I don't go around picking up women on trains."

"And I don't let strange men pick me up on trains."

"I can't let this go. I've got to see you again."

"I don't know anything about you."

"Yes, you're right. Let me visit you at your home, with your parents, until we get to know each other."

Millie agreed, and that weekend Chet showed up at our apartment. He was a perfect gentleman to Mom. He reminded me of Noah Beery Jr., when he played the airplane mechanic in the old movie serial, *Ace Drummond*. Each weekend after that, they took a walk in the neighborhood, and Millie learned he was a Sergeant in the Air Force, and was actually a mechanic for airplane engines.

One time, Chet took me to the airfield where he worked, and let me sit in the cockpit of a real fighter plane. The instrument panel was practically in my lap. I was living my fantasy, sitting in that cockpit. None of my friends were going to believe me – I hardly believed it myself.

During that Christmas, Chet brought everyone presents. Millie told him that I was thinking of being an architect, and he gave me an expensive drafting set. I finally got a real present! But Mom made me give it back to him because it was too expensive to spend on me.

Millie was too ashamed to tell Chet about Harold, who was still with us then. Chet, wanting to please her, tried to get close to him. For a while, they went out drinking together. This gave Millie second thoughts, and she decided to tell Chet the whole truth about Harold. So Chet stopped being Harold's drinking buddy. But when Millie went out with him on dates, he still drank a lot... this worried her.

It bothered Mom that Chet was Christian; it didn't seem to bother her about Harold. She didn't trust Chet, and she was such a good judge of people – like Harold, for instance. Millie was caught in the middle, between Mom and Chet. Mom won out, and Millie didn't see Chet again.

Now, Mom was playing matchmaker, and brought Bob back into Millie's life. Boy, did she make a big mistake! I don't remember anyone not liking my mom, except for Bob – he despised her. Bob wanted to have complete control over Millie, and he wouldn't be able to do that unless he tore Mom down in Millie's eyes. How many times did I hear him talking against Mom to Millie, until she couldn't think anymore, telling her how Mom was holding her down by lying to her all the time, saying that Mom was just using her, and wanting to control her – all for her own selfish reasons.

Hearing his lies pissed me off, but I couldn't say a word because I promised Mom not to make trouble. One Saturday night, an all-out fight developed between Bob and Mom, in the hall of our apartment. With Millie at his side, he screamed at Mom, telling her she was a liar, and didn't want Millie to be happy. Millie agreed with everything he said. Mom was frustrated, and hurt, because it wasn't all true. Then, Bob twisted the knife. He announced that he and Millie were getting married, and Mom wouldn't be invited to her only daughter's wedding. They turned their backs on Mom – and Millie walked out of her life.

That evening, Mom was so upset she didn't know what she was doing. She turned on the oven, then forgot about it, and left the kitchen. When she came back later to light the oven with a match, it exploded in her face. The doctor said she was lucky to be only slightly burned, on her face and arms, and she should heal quickly.

Mom and I stayed up for most of the night, playing Knock Rummy. I kept winning, and she kept doubling the bet, until she owed me some ridiculous amount, something like ten thousand dollars.

"You son of a bitch, aren't you ever gonna stop winning?"

"Ma, if I'm a son of a bitch, and I'm your son, then you must be the bitch."

Mom knew she'd been had, and gave me a good shove. Smiling, she pushed me again a little harder, "You son of a bitch!"

I burst out laughing, and pinched her shoulder.

"Don't pinch, you'll give me cancer."

Mom kept on playing, and with each deal, said, "One more game, double or nothing," knowing she would eventually win. And when she did, she laughed as if she'd put one over on me. I didn't say a word, and laughed with her... and our lives went on.

Millie and I fought a lot, but we deeply loved each other, and we had shared a lot of fears and pain together. Now, the support we had for each other was broken, and torn apart. That night when she left, Millie broke my heart.

Bob and Millie got married, and very rarely came back to see Mom. When they did, it was because they were having a hard time. Whenever Bob needed to use Mom, he permitted her to cook them free meals. Throughout these dinners, he would whisper into Millie's ear, laughing at Mom.

SENIOR YEAR

THE MORNING STARTED in my Cartooning class, with Mr. Bad Breath Zoretsky. I was penciling in some background art, and Zoretsky was looking over my shoulder, "That's good, very good – but what's this?"

"Yeah, I see. It doesn't work."

"So, change it."

No one ever told me I could do that. Up to that time, I assumed you had to do it right the first time, and if you erased your mistake, that would be cheating.

Zoretsky grabbed an eraser, "You've got an eraser, use it. That's what it's made for." He erased my mistake, as if he was angry at my artwork. "There. Now, correct it!"

I was in shock when he attacked my artwork with the eraser, but it taught me that you don't have to be perfect the first time. You could correct your work, and it would still be a work of art.

Zoretsky's class was interrupted by an unexpected Senior Assembly, with special guest speakers, the artists from *Mad Comics*: Bill Elder, Jack Davis, Wally Wood and William Williams. They were my comic book heroes. To me they were great artists, with an insane humor to match. The auditorium was filled to capacity, with students gathered outside the open doors, into the hallway. The *Mad* artists didn't have to say, or do anything – just being there was enough.

They spent most of their time on the stage sounding each other out. Bill Elder said that William Williams was a terrific artist, but too slow for comic books.

"By the time it took him to finish one panel, I could have gone to lunch, seen two movies, and come back... and he'd still be working on that same panel."

They were joking around with each other for an hour, and we loved it. In a million years, I would never have believed that, someday, these same guys would be doing freelance work for me, at Will Eisner's Studio.

Several guys in school organized a group they called, the Bottle Club. You had to be cool to belong. The president of the club was Unger, the hairy ape. He was the kind of guy who would spit a lump of phlegm high up into the air, then maneuver himself under the thick green slime, and catch it back into his mouth. Sometimes he'd miss, and it would splat on his forehead, and ooze down his face.

Each lunchtime, Unger and friends would set up a bar in the men's restroom. They got ahold of a long, wide plank of wood, and rested one end on a toilet seat, and the other end on a wooden box. Once they had transformed the plank into a bar, they would sell drinks. I didn't ask to join that dumb club, but somehow, I was automatically a member.

After lunch, and a couple of beers, I reported to my Illustration class with Mr. Vanier. I was working on an illustration, my version of the *Silver Chalice,* from the book of the same name. It was the first time I was using tempera paint, and I surprised myself. I was doing a pretty good job. Vanier must have picked up on something, and called me to his desk. He asked to smell my breath, then handed me a note, and told me to bring it down to the Dean of Boys, Mr. Haggerty. In the note, Vanier suggested I should be kicked out of school for drinking.

A cold numbness froze my mind. I couldn't think. By the time I got to Haggerty's office, I was shaking, as if from a fever. Inside his office, I knew I couldn't show that I was afraid. If I did, I was lost. Mr. Haggerty asked to smell my breath, and being an expert on drinking, wrote a note to Vanier, telling him that he was mistaken. "Mr. Rothman does not smell of any kind of alcohol. The boy's breath is clean."

Before Haggerty sent me back to Vanier, he said, "Mr. Rothman, I don't want to ever hear that you've been drinking. Not even a sip of beer. Do you understand me?"

That day, I quit the Bottle Club.

Graduation wasn't far off. The closer it got, the more anxious I became. I was worried that I was too stupid to graduate, proving Harold and Mom right. I couldn't live with that possibility. If I quit before graduation, they'd never know, one way or the other. And why should I prolong the pain of finding out I wasn't an artist, unlike the rest of the kids at SIA? I'd never find a job in the art field anyway, so what good is a diploma?

I went to Mr. Haggerty's office to quit. "For the life of me, I don't understand it, Mr. Rothman. Why do you want to quit now, when you are so close to graduation?"

I didn't know what to say, and I gave him a poor excuse, "My family really needs the money."

Haggerty saw through it, and told me bluntly, "You know, you're not going to find a decent job without a diploma. Can't you hold off for a couple of months? Believe me, those months will pass very quickly."

"No, I have to quit now."

"I'll tell you what, I'll make a deal with you. I'm going to hold off putting the paperwork through, just in case you change your mind. I guarantee you, without your diploma, it will be almost impossible to find a job."

I answered all the want ads for start-up jobs, but everywhere I went, like Haggerty said, I was turned down without a high school diploma. I ran, not walked, back to SIA, and straight for Mr. Haggerty's office. Even though I was only away for a few days, when I walked back into the building, I felt like a stranger, and didn't know if they would accept me back.

"I'm so glad you're back, Mr. Rothman. You're making the right decision. You know, it didn't make sense quitting after four years, with only a couple of months left to graduate. It really bothered me that one of our better students would quit."

Who was he talking about? My grades weren't anything special. For all those years, I never thought he knew I was alive.

Toward the end of every year, the artwork that would represent the school's best was exhibited at SIA. To my surprise, one of my pieces was displayed on the celebrated walls. At first, I thought they made a mistake. It was only a simple pen and ink, a stylized line drawing of London's Piccadilly Circus, but there it was with the others. For four years, none of my teachers had said anything to me about my art. It made me proud to be recognized as an artist.

Voices were dulled in the folds of the water, swishing against the boat's hull. Familiar faces boarded the boat. Wherever SIA students went, we didn't need a building – we were the school, tied together by being artists. Every year, the school had a field trip. This year, they rented a boat for a Bear Mountain excursion, and for that one day, the boat became the School of Industrial Arts.

The boat slowly pushed away from the pier, and we were on our way. Traveling under the George Washington Bridge, I looked up at the naked girders, and felt the raw power of its weight suspended over my head. The Palisades rose up out of the Hudson, and surrounded us on both sides, an endless forest of trees and open sky. Going from my concrete world into a living, breathing world was too much, too fast, and it took me a while to readjust to a new way of seeing and feeling.

Around a bend of the river, waves materialized into hundreds of WW II ships. They were pickled, and parked uniformly at attention next to each other, waiting. They looked like phantom ships, manned by invisible ghosts of the fighting men who put their lives out there for us. Untold stories must be trapped inside each ship, stories of great battles of life and death. Now the glory was gone, and they sat there, homeless, and ignored. Watching them rise and fall on the waves, I wondered if maybe Walter's ship was among them.

After passing the ships, the trip to the park was uneventful. The boat docked, and we were released into real nature. I expected wild animals to jump out of every bush. Julio and I separated from the others, and went on an adventure of our own. It wasn't called Bear Mountain for nothing. It must be loaded with bears, and we decided to go bear hunting. We climbed up a steep slope, past a ski jump that looked down on the manmade park. We yelled down to the park, and its echo yelled back at us.

Higher up on the mountain, we threw some heavy stones down the hill. They ricocheted off some larger stones, and loosened them, creating a growing avalanche of small boulders, crashing down, and making hollow crunching sounds as they hit the trees. I don't know about Julio, but I got worried they might hurt someone. But they stopped harmlessly with a thud on the soft, muddy ground below.

Bear Mountain, what bullshit. There wasn't a single bear on the mountain... but there *were* a helluva lot of bugs. The hotter and muggier it got, the crazier the bugs got. They came at us by the thousands, buzzing in our ears, and biting through our clothes with stingers made of steel. We were feasts of fresh blood, and they hunted us as we raced down the mountain. As soon as we thought we were rid of them, new bug recruits would come out of the woods and take their place. We had almost reached the bottom of the mountain, when Julio and I tripped, and fell into a road filled with mud, and instantly, we became invisible to the bugs.

At the bottom of the hill, we discovered a swimming pool filled with SIA students, cleaned the mud off our clothes in the shower, stripped down to our bathing suits, and dove out of the heat into the cool water of the swimming pool. I swam nonstop until I couldn't swim anymore, and took a rest on the edge of the pool. Sitting next to me was Katherine, one of our fellow subway travelers.

Katherine was a good looking girl, but her plain, unappealing clothes made her look frumpy. She had just come out of the water, and when she sat beside me, her thin bathing suit sucked tightly to her pink skin, and caressed her belly button. In her bathing suit, she had a body that wouldn't quit, perfect from head to toe, begging for attention.

We sat side by side, her shoulders leaned up against mine, and the bare skin of our arms touched. We didn't talk much, but we did lie down on our backs, and watch the puffy clouds transform into floating pictures. Time didn't exist, only the pleasure of being with her. Walking back to the boat, our hands found each other, and we held on tightly so as not to lose the moment.

Katherine and I climbed to the top deck of the ship. I sat on the edge of some sort of shelf, with Katherine between my legs, bringing back memories from my first day at SIA, and that boy and girl in the library locked in the same position. We both still had our bathing suits on under our shirts. A gust of wind would blow open her unbuttoned skirt, revealing her legs, and our naked thighs would touch.

Then she was in my arms, pressing her thighs tightly against me. You'd need a crowbar to separate us. Her lips were relaxed, and softly gave themselves to me. Katherine's shirt scarcely hid my hands searching the curves of her body. I kissed the part of her breasts that swelled out from the top of her bathing suit.

If we rubbed against each other any longer, we would burst into flames. When I came, my body jumped into a spasm, as if I had stuck my finger into an outlet. At this point, I usually lost interest, and wanted to get as far away from the girl as possible. But this time, I couldn't get enough of Katherine. Even after I came, I still wanted to be near her, touching her.

When we docked at the City Pier, I became conscious of who and where I was. As Katherine and I stepped off the boat, we got knowing smiles from the other kids. After that boat ride, you couldn't keep Katherine and me apart. We secretly met in SIA's unused staircases, and made out as often as we could.

Soon after the Bear Mountain cruise, the principal called an emergency assembly in the auditorium. It must have been serious, because the speaker was Mr. Kenny, himself. He stood at the podium.

"Ladies and gentlemen... I hope I'm not using those words too loosely... I'm here to speak to you about an incident that took place on the way back from Bear Mountain. I have been informed that a couple of our students got carried away aboard the boat." All the kids in the auditorium cracked up laughing.

"Ahem, ahem... I know we stand for creative freedom, but what happened aboard the boat wasn't freedom. It was license to do whatever you please." He looked pointedly in my direction. "Freedom comes with responsibility. What happened between two of our students was not acceptable behavior. Normally, the two of you would have been punished, but because it's so close to graduation, I'm going to be lenient. I'll end this short assembly with a warning: Anyone... *anyone* caught sexually experimenting in our school, will be suspended from SIA permanently.

"I have nothing against what you did, but there is a proper time and place to do it, and that's not in *my* school." Kenny smiled, "I know you're a good bunch of young people, and this isn't personal. I have nothing further to say. Thank you for listening, and I wish you good luck on your up-coming graduation."

We were given a choice of graduating in cap and gown, or in our own individual suit or dress. Since we were far from being alike, we took a vote, and decided unanimously to wear suits and dresses to express our individuality.

Mom had to chip in to help me buy a suit, my first suit since I was six years old. There was a clothing store for men I'd never noticed before, on the corner of Aldus Street, and Southern Boulevard. It was musty smelling, with a distinct odor of wet cardboard boxes. When we walked into the shop, the owner materialized from nowhere. I could see in his thirsty eyes, he thought he had an easy sale.

"How can I help you?" The old man's breath complemented the smell of the store.

"My son, here, needs a suit for his graduation."

"I've got something special for you."

The old man was wearing an open vest and baggy pants. His back was unnaturally bent over, and his head thrust way out in front of his body, pointing the way to the back of the store. He disappeared through an open doorway, and reappeared with a light beige, almost-white suit, that must have been hanging there since WW II.

"Here, try this on."

The suit hung loosely off my shoulders. The old man grabbed the back of the suit, bunching it up in his hand. "See, it was made for the boy. It fits him like a glove."

"Don't hand me that garbage," Mom said. "Who do you think your talkin' to, a greenhorn? Look, mister, I work in the garment business, and I know your tricks. Do me a favor, and let go of the back of the jacket."

With a straight face, he said, "Everyone's wearing this style."

Mom loved the cheap price, "We'll take it. But for the same price, you've got to take it in to fit the boy." The old man groaned, but was happy to get rid of a suit he couldn't even give away. The finished suit jacket had oversized shoulders, and tapered tightly down at the hips. The button was so low, if I lifted my leg high enough, I could very easily step right out of the suit.

Mom and Millie showed up at my graduation. It was easy to spot them, they sat real close to the stage. There I was, walking across the stage to receive my diploma in my new, light beige Zoot suit. I waved my diploma at Mom, "I did it! I've got my diploma!"

The audience joined in, cheering, and laughing. And here I was, stupid Solly, the first in my family to get a high school diploma. The diploma said I was an adult now, and the world belonged to me. Outside on the street, I was bursting with pride on becoming an artist. Look at me! Look at me!

A few of us guys wanted to do something in a big way, to celebrate our graduation. We decided we'd all get laid, or get a blowjob, but we didn't know where to go to get one. Bermuda, and I, and a couple of other guys, hopped on a train, and took it downtown to Times Square.

We walked along Broadway, past Dempsey's Restaurant, and the Newsreel Theater, heading for the Automat next door. We sat drinking coffee, trying to come up with a plan, but no one knew what to do. We ended up seeing this new movie *Them* about some giant, radio-active, mutant ants trying to take over the world.

PART THREE

THE LITTLE HOUSE
ON 32ND STREET

ARTIST, NO EXPERIENCE NECESSARY

THE WEEKEND AFTER my graduation from SIA, my elation wore off, and I had little expectations for a job in the art field. But this particular ad pulled me in: "Artist, no experience necessary." What the hell… I might as well give it a try.

Standing on the platform of the Simpson Street El, with my wavy, light brown hair piled high on my head, a curl pulled forward on my forehead, and the sides combed back into a DA, I waited for the Lexington Uptown Express. In my beige, single-breasted graduation suit, I walked from Grand Central Station, to the corner of 5th Avenue and 42nd Street.

The closer I got to the employment agency, the more I began to lose my nerve. Finding the address was easy, and yet I hesitated. I stood there, frozen to the sidewalk, as a continuous flow of people rushed about me. I thought of turning around and going home. After all, I did get this far. But the rushing crowd, with their determined eyes, bumped against me as if I wasn't there, pushing me one way and then another. I escaped the unrelenting waves of people by ducking into the agency building.

ABC Agency was printed on the frosted glass door. I hesitated… thinking I could come back another day. My portfolio felt awkward; every time I tried to open the agency door, it got in the way. When I finally got synchronized, I entered a long, narrow office with a row of empty desks lined up on each side, one in back of the other.

Sitting alone behind a low, gated barrier, a thin woman with blond hair looked up, "Yes, can I help you?"

"I called you about this ad in the times: "Artist, no experience necessary."

"And what is your name?"

"Solomon Rothman."

She took the ad from my hand, "Let me see that... Ah, yes. Why don't you take a seat, and fill out this application?"

She noticed that I was struggling with the application, "You know, you're a little early, and I have some free time, so let me give you a hand with that."

When she opened the little gate and invited me to her desk, it put me at ease and soothed my tension.

"My name is Linda. Come... sit down, and we'll talk. What school did you graduate from?"

"The High School of Industrial Art."

"Ah, I've helped place lots of kids from SIA. I see you have a port-folio, let's take a look. Mmm... very nice. Mmm... I think I know the perfect place for you."

Linda thumbed through a stack of index cards, and pulled one out, "Here... here it is. These are great guys. I have placed several people with them, and you'll be a perfect fit. Now, this job is for a shipping clerk, but the good news is, it's a place where you can im-prove your position. The other applicants I've sent also started out as shipping clerks, and now they are working on the board."

Linda felt my indecision. She read me wrong. She thought I didn't want the shipping job, but actually, I was scared. I didn't know what working on the board meant. "Look... I don't want to send you up there if you're not sure. So, let me know right now."

"No, no... I really want this job."

"Good. Now, if you get the job, you'll have to pay us one week's salary. Okay?"

"Yes."

"You won't have to pay it all at once. We can break it up for you into four weekly payments. How does that sound to you?"

"Sounds good." Things were going so fast, I'd say "Yes" to anything.

Linda started to dial the phone, "I'm going to try and get you an appointment... "Hello? I'd like to speak to Pete Eisner. This is Linda Klein, from ABC Agency. Thank you.""

Covering the phone with her hand, "I think you're going to like this place... "Hi, Pete? This is Linda Klein, from the ABC Agency. I'm fine. Look, is that position still open? Terrific! I have this young man here who will be a perfect fit for you." She paused... "Did I ever steer you wrong?" Linda looked at me questioningly, "11:30 okay?" I nodded. "Okay Pete, he'll be there at 11:30 this morning.""

Linda hung up, and wrote down the address: 161 East 32nd Street, between 3rd and Lex.

"The place you're going to is called, Will Eisner Productions. Your appointment is with Pete Eisner. Make sure you remind him that I sent you. You couldn't work for two nicer guys. Good luck!"

Having plenty of time, I decided to walk to Will Eisner Productions, this way I'd save on carfare. It was a warm day, and the air was filled with unrecognizable, sour smells that changed from block to block. Without knowing how I got there, I was carried along the streets to a little house on 32nd Street.

The two-story, buff brick building was jammed between two giant buildings, making it appear even smaller. Seeing it sitting on the concrete sidewalk in front of me, made the job very real. I was sweating through my suit jacket, and my wet shirt was pasted to my skin. I leaned away from the front door, afraid to take the next step, ready to walk away. Why am I worrying? I'm not going to get the job anyway.

Inside, there was a stairway to my left, and behind it what looked like a warehouse, smelling of machines and grease. Maybe I had the wrong address, and was in the wrong place. But there, on the wall at the bottom of the stairs, was a sign: *WILL EISNER PRODUCTIONS,* with an arrow pointing up the flight of stairs.

At the top was an open office, with a desk facing me. Janet the receptionist, stood beside her desk. She was top-heavy, and very thin below the waist, making her look off-balance – like any moment she might fall over. Her short, platinum blond hair was tightly waved, without a strand out of place.

"Can I help you, honey?"

"The ABC Agency sent me. I'm supposed to see Mr. Eisner."

Before she could answer me, a voice shouted out from the front office, "Give me a couple minutes, and then send him in."

Janet said, "How the hell did he hear us? I swear that man has ears behind his balls. What's your name, honey?"

"Solomon Rothman."

"Okay, Mr. Rothman, just knock on that door."

She pointed in the general direction of two doors. I was a little confused.

"That's it, sweetheart, right through there."

"Mr. Eisner? My name is Solomon Rothman. Miss Linda Klein, at the ABC Agency, sent me."

Pete stood up from behind a half-circle desk that almost trapped him from the front door. He was a balding, pear-shaped man. His shirtsleeves were rolled up to his elbows and his slacks were held up by a pair of bright red suspenders. Pete put his hands inside his waistband, acting very important and businesslike.

"Have a seat."

Without thinking, I opened my portfolio, and put it on his desk. He closed the portfolio without looking at it.

"Did the Agency tell you what this job is?

I couldn't remember anymore. "No."

When I was a kid, I never had any hope or expectations of being anything at all; I always believed I'd end up sweeping floors.

"Well… you'll be sweeping floors and other odd jobs."

Pete studied my reaction to what he said.

"Do you know what I'm saying?"

"No…"

Okay, I'll lay it all out for you."

Pete walked back and forth behind his desk. "We're not looking for an artist. What we need is a shipping clerk. Your job will consist of mailing, cleaning up the office, and other odd jobs. This is not a dead end. Eventually, you'll have the chance to work your way onto the board. It's all up to you.

"If you accept, you'll start at twenty dollars a week. Remember, you'll have a great chance to improve your position, and accordingly, your salary will increase. Personally, I think you're a perfect fit. Well... do you want the job?"

I was so happy to get a job in an art studio, and so relieved that I didn't have to look any further. "Yes! Yes! I'll take the job."

Pete was taken back for a moment by my sudden enthusiasm, "Okay. You'll start at 9 am, on Monday. Be a little early, say about 8:00, and we'll get you started."

Pete sat down in his swivel chair, put his legs up on his desk, and as I started to walk out, I heard a great crashing sound. I turned around, and Pete had disappeared. A group of people ran into the office, and a head popped up from behind the top of his desk.

Pete's face was all red, "It's okay, I'm alright. Something's wrong with this damn chair, I've got to get it fixed. Okay, everybody, I'm alright."

The train rushed out of the subway tunnel, onto the El station at Jackson Street. I stood inside the car, leaning against the door, and looking through its window. As the wheels screeched to a stop, the doors hissed open, and then hissed closed. Reluctantly, the wooden platform released the train, and with a sudden powerful jerk of the engine, the heavy cars, one-by-one, pulled away from the platform. I was hoping to see some kind of drama being acted out in the apartment windows, as the train sped from station to station, to Simpson Street.

Mom was in the kitchen when I burst in with pride to tell her,

"I got a job as an artist!" I lied, making the job more important than it was. "And it was the very first place I looked for a job."

She could have cared less. "So, how much are you making?"

"Not much, but..."

"I thought so." I could never please her. "You know, my Sollinue, you should stop mit this stupid thing about art."

"But they promised me I'd get raises."

"Yeah, yeah."

That was the end of our conversation. I knew what "Yeah, yeah" meant. It meant, Why are you making a fool of yourself.

Mom walked out of the kitchen, and I caught her looking at herself in the mirror, remembering the girl she was in Bessarabia, on her father's farm... a girl in a body that grew old. Still looking closely at her face in the mirror, she said to herself, "I've earned every wrinkle I have."

Monday morning, I got to Will Eisner's extra early, which was very dangerous, because it gave me too much time to think. Today, I'll be starting a job that I found by myself, without the help of family, or friends. I'm going to be a shipping clerk, whatever that means. What if they ask me to do some artwork? What would I do? What I'll do is lose my job, when they discover I'm not really an artist. Ehh... what am I worried about? For chrissakes, my job is only sweeping floors. That's fine with me.

In The Bronx, I was Solly, a streetwise kid with odd jobs in my neighborhood. I knew the streets, and the people in them. But in Manhattan, I was completely naïve, and lost. This was a real job, and I was entering a new world of sophisticated adults.

I didn't have too long to wait at the entrance of the building. A tall, thin man, with short gray hair wrapped around his baldness, fumbled in his pocket for his keys.

"Hi. Waiting long?"

"No."

"Are you the new shipping clerk?"

"Yes."

"My name is Chris Christensen... And you are?"

"Sol Rothman."

"You don't talk much, do you?"

The keys jingled in his hand, "I'll have the door unlocked in a second." Not only was he opening this new world to me, I entered it with a new name – from Solly, to Sol.

Chris took me through an open room filled with art tables and taborets, and led me to a narrow room in back.

"You can wait here. Pete should be in soon."

Alone, not knowing what to expect, I watched the artists filtering in, and saying their good mornings. They looked at me with as much interest as a chair out of place.

Pete greeted me in the back room, "I'm glad you got here early. Now we can get you started."

When Pete spoke, he had the habit of putting his hands inside the waistband of his pants, looking like he was trying to keep his belly from overflowing. When he was thinking, he'd put the side of a forefinger between his lips – every once in a while, releasing a sucking sound.

Pete called out, "Coop! The new guy is here." Coop had a weight-lifter's body, and walked with a slow, heavy, awkward shuffle as he lumbered toward us. He had staring green eyes, and light brown hair that was so thick it refused to stay in one place.

"Sol, this is Ernie Cooper, the person you're going to replace. Coop, this is Sol Rothman. Coop is going to be with you for a while, to help show you the ropes. If you have any questions, just ask him. Okay? You'll be fine."

After Pete left, Coop asked, "Where you from?"

"The Bronx."

"Yeah? So am I. Like, where in The Bronx?"

"By the Simpson Street Station."

"What high school did you go to?"

"SIA."

"So did I. Like, I must've seen you there. So, you're from Hunt's

Point... do you know a guy named Lefty?"

"Yeah, he's a friend of mine. He lives on my block." I should've known that Coop, being a body-builder, would know Lefty.

"That's it... I knew I knew you. Like, I've heard about you."

Coop did a turn around, and treated me differently. He told me how he had started out as a shipping clerk, and worked his way onto the board. For now, his job was to train me. And once I got it, he'd be on the board fulltime.

Coop spent the rest of the morning telling me my duties: delivering packages when needed, allocating flyers to be mailed to disc jockeys for the RCA account, and keeping the place clean by emptying waste baskets, and sweeping floors at the end of each day. I also got to do other odds and ends, like trim the *PS* dummies with an awesome cutting machine. After a week, once I got the knack of it, Coop spent less time with me, and I was mostly on my own.

Will Eisner Productions would only print the exact amount of flyers to be mailed. On this day, I ended up with hundreds of extra pieces. I felt the heat build on my face as I counted, and recounted them, and I still ended up with extra flyers. By now, I had geographical landmasses of sweat, marking my shirt. Somewhere, somehow, I had made a mistake, and I couldn't figure it out.

I decided to hide my mistake with the regular mail. While delivering to the Post Office, I threw my mistakes into a corner sewer when no one was looking. I was so relieved when none of the disc jockeys complained about the missing flyers.

One morning, as I was loading my wagon with packages to be mailed, one of the guys in the bullpen was listening to music on the radio, and the *William Tell Overture* traveled across the room. Without thinking, I shouted out, "That's *The Lone Ranger!*" The whole Art Department laughed. I didn't know that the theme for *The Lone Ranger Show* was taken from classical music, and I ran my mail wagon out to the street in shame.

My whole childhood was spent trying not to be noticed. It was tattooed on my soul. I kept my mouth shut, and my opinions to myself. Because my thoughts were formulated through my dyslexic way of seeing the world, I didn't want anyone to know I didn't know, and be marked stupid. My life was in my heart. That's who I was, and that is where I lived.

When I was crossing 34th Street, my packages came untied, and spilled all over the street. As I desperately tried to collect the packages, the light turned green, and the tunnel traffic, like a herd of buffalo, came charging at me. The cars whizzed by awfully close to me, others screeched to a stop, and blew their horns. I rushed, and fumbled the packages, dropping them all over again. Out of fear and frustration, I angrily kicked them to the curb, sat down, and stared at the street, trying to make up my mind if I should go back to the office, or go home, and never return.

I decided to go back, and face my ridiculers. When I did, it turned out that *The Lone Ranger* incident had broken the ice. The artists thought I had done it on purpose, as a joke, and everyone started to introduce themselves.

Pete and Will's secretary, Wilma, sat in the same office as Janet, and took care of all financial matters, including the payroll. She was tall and thin, not an once of fat on her, but her weight was distributed in sensual curves, in all the right places. Something was always going on in her head. When she looked at me, I could practically hear her thinking.

Across the way, was the office of Joe Sapinsky, Art Director for the RCA Account. Joe, a William Holden type – tall, handsome, and soft-spoken – was in the Navel Air Force Reserve, and piloted a jet fighter on the weekends. He looked like what you would imagine a pilot should look like. His job was to protect the home front. Joe was full of clever little tricks, and at all times, had to prove that he was cool. He acted like he had just climbed out of his jet to share some of his wonderful self with us.

There were two Joe's, both Art Directors. Little Joe directed *PS Magazine*. He was wiry, thin, and much smaller than Sapinsky. The rumor was, that Will used him as the character for *Joe's Dope*, in the four-color section of *PS Magazine*. His desk was in the middle of the bullpen, back-to-back with Dave Madeline, his Assistant Art Director. Dave was tall, with straight blond hair, and doughy white skin – a very funny guy.

The bullpen was an open room, with windows only on one side, and the artists sat along the window wall. The first thing I noticed about George Conradson, the artist who did the technical art, was his dark brown hair, which he combed in a tuft like a cardinal bird. In back of him, sat Daniel Zonarovitch, a heavy Russian, who looked like the Slavic meatballs he ate for breakfast, his biggest meal. He loved laughing at other people. Before he worked for Will, he used to ghost for the comic book character, *Captain Marvel Junior*.

Against the opposite, windowless wall, sat all the Production people – Bob Gee, Ernie Cooper, and Sondra Lanzman. Bob had a perfectly round head, with hair neatly parted on the left side, and he was always very well dressed. Watching Bob Gee, was like watching a silent movie. He did everything in sharp, quick motions. He was always on the move, even if he was standing still, as if his body wanted to be somewhere else than where he was.

Next, came Ernie Cooper, and behind his desk, sat little Sondra, who had a crush on Joe Sapinsky. She was short, with dark hair, and sad eyes, that opened up when she laughed. Behind her, was an empty art table... waiting for me. As for Will Eisner, I hadn't met him yet; he was on business in Washington DC.

WILL EISNER RETURNS

WE HAD A heavy delivery to take up to Grand Central Station, and Coop wanted a favor from me. "This is my night to weightlift, and I don't want to pump up my arms, so would you be a great guy, and carry both packages?"

He had his balls... He's standing there, actually facing me, with his muscles pulling at his shirt, and he wants me to carry the heavy packages?

"Are you putting me on?"

"No, I'm serious."

"Sorry, but I can't carry both of them all the way to 42nd Street."

"Okay, maybe we can take turns."

Coop was so thick that, with each step, his thighs pushed away from each other in opposite directions. As we were walking, he turned to me, "Hey, I bet you never thought you'd be working for Will Eisner."

"Why? What makes him so special?"

"You've gotta be kidding me. Lots of guys would give an arm and a leg to work for Will."

When we got back to Will's, Coop found some color tearsheets of *The Spirit,* and showed them to me. It did look familiar – the masked hero, the police chief, and the little colored kid – I remember thumbing through *The Spirit* joke books at Jack's. But Will was still just a boss to me, like any other boss. Anyway, Pete was the man I had to deal with.

Whenever I had some free time, I'd talk to Chris Christenson, an expert comic book balloon letterer. He used this special plastic tool that had little holes in it. With a blue pencil point in one of the holes, he slid it across his T-square, drawing in blue guidelines where he planned to place his lettering. Chris let me watch him, and without realizing it, he was actually teaching me how to create balloon lettering. Sometimes, he would edit as he lettered, adding or subtracting words that didn't fit the picture, proving to me that hand lettering was an art in itself.

Chris told me that if I wanted to get on the board, I'd better start learning right now. If not, it probably wouldn't happen. "First, you have to know what you're going to be working on. It's called *PS Magazine*. It's a monthly magazine that takes the Army's technical manuals, and simplifies their instructions into comic book drawings, making it easier, and more entertaining for the GI to understand. There are four main characters: Connie Rodd, Sergeant Half-Mast, and Sergeant Bull Dozer, in the two-color pages, and *Joe's Dope*, in the four-color section, referred to as "the continuity."

"For now, you should be concentrating on doing the mechanicals. Listen and watch the others, and imitate what they do. And if you have any questions, just ask me. By the way, how would you like to make some extra money?" Chris didn't wait for an answer.

"Every so often, I work on Saturdays, and I need some help straightening the *PS Magazine* back issue files, and organizing Will's original artwork of *The Spirit*."

I was always enthusiastic about any job thrown my way. Almost jumping out of my skin, I answered, "Yes! What time should I be here?"

"Calm down... save some of that energy for Saturday."

Riding the train home, somewhere in the middle of the trip, I'd change from an innocent kid in Manhattan, to the streetwise Bronx kid. Will Eisner's and The Bronx were my two worlds, and would eventually converge – the subway was the wormhole that connected them.

Saturday morning, Chris was already working when I got there, pulling files out of floor-to-ceiling bookcases. My job was to climb a ladder, get the files at the top, and then help him carry them to a table, where he would switch them from one place to another, for no apparent reason. I couldn't understand what we were doing.

"I can see you're wondering why I'm switching files around..."

Before Chris explained, he made me promise never to tell anyone. I said, "Yes," and even though he hardly knew me, he trusted me.

"After I tell you, you and I will be the only ones who know my secret. Ahh, there *is* a reason why I do this. You see I switch the files, so no one can ever know where anything is, except me. That makes me indispensible."

Chris was a heavy drinker, and every so often, asked me go to the liquor store across the street from the Underwood Building, on Park Avenue South, to buy a couple of bottles of whiskey. No matter how much he drank, he never got drunk. The only change in him was in his eyes... they got watery.

"Sol, we're going to cut off early today, but I want you to report a full day's work. And before we leave, let's clear off that extra art table and taboret, in the corner there. Monday, I'll find a very simple mechanical for you... don't worry, I'll show you exactly what to do."

On Monday afternoon, Chris set me up with a T-square, a triangle, rubber cement, a rubber cement pick-up, and a few single-edged razor blades.

"All you have to do is paste up this one word, on this acetate overlay. It fits in position with the line of copy on the original page, you see? This is a color overlay; anything on this overlay will be printed in color. Now, go ahead, and have fun."

I did what he told me to. I rubber cemented the type and the overlay, and tee-d up the type, moving it into place with a razor blade. When the cement dried, I cleaned the excess with the pick-up. The type stuck to the pick-up, and pulled away from the overlay. I went through the whole process again, but this time, I cleaned it very gently. Just when I thought I had it, the pick-up pulled the type away from the overlay again.

This little, fucking piece of type, that should have taken me a minute or two, has taken half an hour, and it's still not pasted down. Chris was probably wondering what happened to me. Sweat dripped down my nose, and I hoped no one was watching me.

Why can't I do this? What was I doing wrong? After being at it for all that time, I was too ashamed to ask Chris for his help. I gave up, and left the type loosely flopping, with excess rubber cement on its edges. When no one was looking, I put my page in the middle of a pile of finished pages, and hoped no one would notice my botched-up attempt. At this rate, I'd never be able to get on the board.

When that *PS* issue came out, I found the word I had partially pasted up. It looked clean, and straight on the page, making me feel that I was a part of producing the book.

Will returned from Washington, and I got my first glimpse of him, standing by Joe Sapinsky's office. Joe was sitting at his art table, with Will leaning into his doorway. Slowly walking by the two, I overheard Joe saying, "Why name it?"

"Because sequential art is as important as any other art. It has great possibilities that no one is realizing. I'm naming it because it has never been seen as a worthwhile art, and it deserves respectability, and recognition as an art form. My idea is in the early stages... it's been rolling around in my mind for years, but now it's starting to come together."

That wasn't the last time I heard Will use the words, sequential art. It was always on his mind, and whenever he had the chance, he'd use it, each time changing it, and adding new ideas.

Will seemed to be a gentle man. He was good-looking, bald with a fringe of brown hair, and had a serious face that was easy to smile. Will smoked a pipe; it seemed to be glued to his face. I don't think he could function without it. I came to the conclusion that his pipe had a spell on it, and fed him all of his creative ideas.

Every so often, Will found himself off balance, and he'd trip over objects around him, objects that would get in the way of his concentrated thoughts. He would stumble while in a conversation, and catch himself before falling, looking like a dancer discovering a new step - and then he would continue to talk as if nothing happened. He seemed to accept it as part of who he was. Will never said a word to me. I don't think he even noticed me, so I was able to watch him whenever I had the chance. Sometimes he'd stand, unobserved, by the entrance of the bullpen, digesting everything and everybody in the Art Department.

Little Joe and Dave Madeline saw Will standing there at the doorway, and called him over to their drawing tables. I quietly worked my way near their art tables, until I could hear what they were saying. The great thing about being a shipping clerk was that no one paid attention to me. It was like I was secretly tapping their phones, and listening to their private conversations.

Little Joe said, "Will... we're in a jam. These guys from the Arsenal are killing us. The Army wants this issue to be all about the maintenance for their new tank. I requested the photos, but they refused, and said it was top secret. Dave and I even tried the Pentagon... still no dice. What the hell are we supposed to do? Have pages without art? Doesn't that defeat our purpose?"

Will took his pipe from his mouth, and used it as a pointer, extending his index finger to emphasize what he was saying. "I know exactly what you're going through. A while back, I needed a picture of an experimental sub. I went to Washington DC, and before they would let me near their Top Secret files, I had a thorough security clearance by the FBI and CIA.

"A Major took me to the Pentagon, and we went from room-to-room, until we finally stopped at a huge metal vault. Inside, was a room full of files, marked in bold red letters: TOP SECRET. I was warned not to take anything from this room. The Major opened the file for the sub, and (Will started laughing as he talked) took out a tearsheet with a detailed photo of the sub – on the front page of *Life Magazine*."

That was the first time I heard Will laugh. I can't describe the sound of it, but it was an open laugh, like we were all in this together. Will had one of those voices that was completely his own. There was an eager, innocence to it and I could recognize it anywhere. Little Joe and Dave laughed with Will at the insanely stupid way the military works.

Getting back to business, Little Joe said, "All joking aside, Will, what are we going to do? We still need that picture of the tank for the next issue."

"Wait a minute, Joe, there was something I was going to tell you the other day, but I forgot. Now, what was it? It had something to do with the magazine tearsheet in Washington... Nooo, that's not it. Ahhh, yes… I remember."

Holding back from laughing, Will continued in short, breathy giggles, "Boys, our troubles are over. I remember passing a hobby shop on 5th Avenue a couple of days ago, and in the window – sitting right there in the front window, open to the world – was an exact model replica of the new Top Secret tank we need."

"Get outta here!"

"Nope. That's the military for you."

Will caught sight of me standing in the aisle, listening to them – his first inkling of my existence – and broke through the silence between us. "What's your name?"

"Sol."

He spoke to me like I was one of the guys, "Okay, Sol, I want you to go to Polk's Hobby Shop... Do you know where it is?"

"Yes."

"Good. Get five dollars out of petty cash, and buy a tank model kit for me." He wrote down the name of the tank kit. "You got it?"

"Yes!"

I was alert, ready to go, and eager to please. I almost sprang out of my shoes, willing to do anything. Will smiled at all that energy, "Good man." I didn't have any trouble picking up the tank kit, but I did keep the change.

Working in the backroom I felt like a stranger, separate from the guys in the bullpen. Someone had their radio playing music from the early 40s: *Juke Box Saturday Night* and *Amapola*. When I heard them, I was a little boy again and I could feel Walter and Harry standing right at my side.

During the morning coffee break, Coop called out to Little Joe, "Joe! I bet that music brings back memories of the war... like, you must have lots of stories."

"Yeah, I do."

"Were you at Normandy? Did you see, like, lots of action? Did anything, like, happen to you?"

"I don't want to talk about it."

"Ah, come on, just one little story, and like, I promise I'll never ask you again."

Dave was a good friend of Little Joe's, and asked him, "Let me tell him just one of your stories, and maybe that will shut him up. Come on, Joe, let me tell him the story about you being surrounded by German soldiers."

"If you want to, go ahead. I really don't care."

"Joe was a regular dogface, and was on a scouting mission with a group of other guys from his outfit. Joe and one of his buddies got separated, and trapped behind the German lines. They found themselves surrounded by Germans, who were setting up camp. The only thing they could do, was hide in a thick clump of bushes at the edge of the camp.

"When Joe and his buddy saw that the Germans were Nazi Elite SS troops... Holy shit! They just stopped breathing. Joe had heard about what the SS did to prisoners, and knew that, at any second, they might be discovered. They had to hide there for two days and nights, forcing themselves to stay awake."

"But, like, what did they do when they had to go?"

"They had to shit and pee in their pants. And when they ran out of food and water, they lost all hope. But at the last desperate moment, the SS broke camp. Just before they left, a Nazi soldier walked in their direction, stood at the edge of the bushes where they were hiding, and looked right at them. He opened his fly, and pissed all over them, and Joe and his buddy had to sit there, and take it.

"Two hours later, the camp was gone, and so were the SS. Joe and his buddy were able to get back through the German lines to their regiment, and spent the next few days in a nearby river, washing their skin raw."

Coop smiled, and said, "Come on, you're pulling my leg, aren't you?"

Dave answered, "No, it's all true, every word of it." It was hard for Coop to believe the danger this quiet little guy had gone through in the war.

Around four o'clock that afternoon, I was returning from a delivery. Will stood in the shadows of the hall, smoke twisting out from his pipe. He was listening intently to a discussion in the Art Department, but his status as the boss kept him from joining in the fun.

George Conradson was speaking to Bob Gee, "Do you sometimes believe you're not real?"

"No, I can't say I ever did."

"Is the reality of our individual selves, the way everyone else perceives us?"

Bob Gee asked, "What does that mean... that I'm not real to myself? That's a crock of shit."

Dave Madeline joined in, "Give the guy a chance to explain."

"You see, if how I see myself is colored by my subjectivity, then how I see myself can't be true, because it's colored by my hang-ups."

Dan added, "Is there any truth?"

"I don't know, said George, but I do know, it's just me and my feelings..."

Bob Gee interrupted, "You're all screwed up. That's your problem... you're all screwed up."

I couldn't understand what the hell they were talking about. I
never heard that kind of thinking before. They had these discussions
almost every afternoon. I guess they broke up the tensions and monotony of the day. Anyone could join in, and it was always, anything
goes.

Will never interfered, as long as the *PS* issue was finished on time.
His attitude toward these free-for-alls, helped encourage them in the
first place. The idea of having discussions at work was new to me.
Actually, it was similar to the storytelling my friends and I used to
do... except this storytelling was about abstract thoughts.

The guys in the Art Department saw me as a fresh, blank canvas
that they could dab at with their paintbrushes. George Conradson
noticed the blank look in my eyes, and called me over to his art table.

"Sol, that's your name right?"

"Yes."

"Well, Sol, you look a little lost. I think I can help you understand
what we're doing here, so you could join in sometime, if you'd like.
We're playing a game of ideas, talking about, and then questioning
those ideas. To begin with, I'd like to suggest a book to read that
might help you see things in a different way. It's called, *Generation of
Vipers*, by Philip Wylie."

With my first paycheck, I found a really good baseball glove for
Ronnie, at a pawnshop next to Chili Charlie's, on 34th Street. After
making a payment to the ABC agency, I still had enough money to
buy the book, *Generation of Vipers*. I had never tried to read a whole
book before. I was too afraid I wouldn't understand it.

Somewhere in me, the feelings and thoughts were already there,
but I couldn't put them into words. Philip Wylie's book gave me a
voice to question, even question the book itself. I might have read
it wrong, but no matter how wrong I got it, it still made me think in
whatever direction my mind wanted go. Working at Will's, created in
me a burning curiosity about the world. The artists there opened my

eyes, and I spent most of the winter, and the rest of my life, reading. Their discussions began to make sense to me.

It was 1954, the day before Christmas. That morning, the dummies for the next *PS* issue were finished, and needed to be trimmed. The cutting machine waited in the corner of the back room; an iron arm, four feet in length, was locked in standing position, like a guillotine ready to plunge its sharp blade down on its next victim – me.

I was very proud in finishing my jobs in the fastest way possible. It was the same pride I felt working with my brother Walter, putting up awnings faster than anyone else.

I put a stack of *PS* dummies on the cutting table, and released the sharp blade. I got the idea to save some time, by not putting the blade back into the lock position between cuts. Instead, I threw the heavy metal arm up into the lock position, and quickly readjusted the dummies on the cutting line, for a second cut. It was working out better than I expected, until one time, I threw the handle up, but not quite high enough. It missed the lock, and the razor sharp blade came rushing back down toward my hands.

I've always been told to use my head in dangerous situations. Well, I did… and lucky for me that I did. The iron handle hit the top of my head, stopping the blade from cutting through my fingers. I carefully locked the arm in place, and then allowed myself to sit at my art table, and feel the shock of almost losing all my fingers.

I watched Wilma and Janet, decorating the place for the afternoon Christmas party. This would be my first office party. After what just happened to me, the party couldn't come fast enough. I couldn't wait to have a drink. I didn't know what I was drinking, and I didn't care. My Christmas present was not cutting my fingers off.

Little Sondra had eyes only for Joe Sapinsky, who paid no attention to her. He had his eyes on Wilma, who ignored him. When the music started to play, Wilma pulled me into a corner of the room, and we danced to the creamy smooth voice of Nat King Cole, singing *Pretend*.

This wasn't like the usual dances I'd been to. Wilma was a woman, not a girl. She was in control, and knew what she was doing. She danced so close to me, it felt we were glued together. Her cheek was burning, as if she had a fever, and she pressed hard against me, until it hurt. I was too high to feel the music, and stumbled my way through the dance. I didn't want to leave the party, but my head was beginning to hurt, and I couldn't wait to get home.

I got off at my old neighborhood. Even though I didn't live at East 165th Street anymore, it was my comfort zone. The alcohol numbed the pain in my head, and I walked on my old block, enjoying the streets and people I was part of. No matter where I lived, this was still my home.

GREETINGS

WHEN I GOT back to Boynton Avenue, there was a letter waiting for me from Washington DC. It read:

> *The President of the United States*
> *Greetings:*
> *You are hereby ordered for induction into the*
> *Armed Forces of the U.S.A.*

It told me the date, and where I was to report for my physical examination. Just when I had found a job that was building my confidence, now the Army was taking it away from me.

The Induction Center was at the southern tip of Manhattan, facing the Hudson River. I showed up with a letter from Dr. Parato, stating that, because of my accident, I had severe arthritis in my left foot, which lacked normal flexibility. The Army didn't give a damn. The Korean War was dragging on, and if I was walking, that was good enough for them. No way was I going home today.

There was nothing soft about that building. It was cold, and hard, and told me, "We mean business." Inside, there was just a big empty space, five stories high. Looking up, I could see the roof of the building above me. Fractured rays of light from the skylight, bumped into each other on their way down to the lobby. I felt like I was in an abstract painting... painted with light.

I followed the crowd of inductees, walking to the worn marble stairs on the left. The soldiers wore white lab coats over their uniforms. Two of them ordered us to strip down to our underwear, and pee into the paper cups that they provided. We were an assembly line of young men, holding our little cups in front of us. I was surprised to see that every cup had a different shade of pee. One was yellow, another yellow-green, others were light and clear as water, and some were shades of dark gold with heavy foam on top. What the hell were these guys drinking?

A couple of soldiers called our names in alphabetical order. I watched each guy getting stabbed in the arm, and saw their blood filling the syringes. That didn't look too bad... what was I worried about? My veins naturally popped out of my skin, like worm tunnels, but these two assholes couldn't find my veins. They kept probing me with the fuckin' needle, digging and twisting it into my arm, searching for a vein that any almost-blind person could see. By the time they were satisfied, I was on the verge of passing out.

We were marched into a large, empty room, told to form two single lines, and take off our underwear. I stood there, naked, and freezing my balls off, with a bunch of guys who had every weird, possible combination of shapes.

A doctor came into the room, and said, "Good morning, gentlemen. I want you to bend over, and spread your cheeks." We all did what we were told, but there was one guy who didn't understand, and was holding his thighs, instead of his ass. The doctor got impatient with him, and took him off the line. "Come here, son, I want you to look at the others." The kid walked down the line, looking into every one's asshole. The doctor looked at him, "What the fuck are you doing?" Disgusted, he threw the kid back in line.

Then, the doctor stood us at attention, and officially viewed our assholes, walking down both lines, tucking two fingers under each set of balls with a flourish, and saying effeminately, "Cough... cough... cough. Okay! Now, I want you to hop on your right foot... and now, on your left foot."

I refused to hop on my crushed foot. I stood still, while the others

479

kept jumping up and down. "What the fuck do you think you're do-ing? I said, "Hop on your foot!""

"Sorry, Sir, I can't. My foot hurts."

"Look, you little shit, hop on it anyway." I did, but with great difficultly.

"Look, you little prick, don't fuck with me."

Someone came in, whispered in the doctor's ear, and I was taken off the line. "Get your clothes on, and follow me." I was put into a small room, where two doctors were waiting for me. One of them tried to bend my left foot back, but it refused to move.

"You little cocksucker! You're faking it, aren't ya!"

I really couldn't bend my foot; but I lied about the pain. While they were developing the x-ray of my foot, I was left in the room for hours, without any lunch. It was getting to be the end of the day. They started closing up their offices, and leaving the building. I didn't know what to do. I thought they forgot about me.

Finally, two soldiers entered, and told me I was 4-F. "Okay, Buddy, you got what you wanted. Now, get the fuck out of here."

I never thought I'd be going home. Outside the building, I felt woozy from lack of food, and everything seemed unreal. I was re-lieved to be through with the Army, but that wasn't going to be the end of it. Every so often, for the next two years, the Army called me back in to see if my foot had healed. And each time, instead of only checking my foot, they made me go through the whole damn physi-cal, including the blood test. What a bunch of shmucks – after all those years, they expected my foot would magically heal?

A wall of piercing screams filled the Super Sale in Macy's Basement. Unafraid, Bob Gee dove into the crowd of women, and was swallowed up in the chaos. Coop and I stood against a wall for protection. Every once in a while, I'd recognize Bob Gee's voice above the deafening noise, and caught a glimpse of him fighting a woman over a paisley scarf. Each of them was holding onto one end, pulling, and screaming.

"Bob yelled, "I saw it first!""

The woman on the other end of the scarf, screamed, "No, you don't, I saw it first!"

Bob Gee yanked it from her hands, and won the battle. Coop and I couldn't take this madhouse anymore, and shouted out to Bob that lunch hour was over. While he was buying his scarf, Bob Gee said, "Too bad we have to leave… it's a great sale."

Coop answered, "What, are you crazy? You could get killed in there."

"You kidding? I love it… give me a chance to haggle, and I'm in heaven."

"Haggle?" I added, "That wasn't haggling, that was the Third World War."

When we stepped outside onto the street, my hearing was dulled to the sounds of the traffic in Herald Square. On our way back to Will's, I stopped to look at a novelty shop window, and a fake ink spill made of black tin, caught my eye. I had to have it. But when I got out of the store, Bob Gee and Coop were gone.

Back at Will's, I stopped by Janet's desk. Will walked by us into the Art Department, carefully holding the art he had just finished for the cover of *PS Magazine*.

Janet asked me, "Sol, have you seen Pete? I need to find him."

"No, but Where there's a Will, there's a Pete." Pete and Will were very close; if you saw one of them, the other wasn't too far away.

"Sol, you don't say much, but when you do, you're very funny and clever."

I touched Janet's hand by accident, and apologized.

"You know, Sol, once I had a climax just by touching a man's hand in the subway. You know, just the touch of a hand could be very romantic… as good, or sometimes better than fucking."

Her story excited me. It sounded like an invitation, and I leaned against her. She felt my erection, and pulled away.

"I know what you want. It isn't that I wouldn't like to, but I can't. I'm too mature for you. I've learned a lot about sex, and I'm very good at it. In fact, I'm too good. You're so young, and naïve, I know you'll drive me crazy wanting more. No, I'm sorry, but you're very sweet for trying."

At my art table, I thought I'd have some fun, and play a joke on Little Joe, who was still out to lunch. No one noticed me putting the phony ink spill on the art that Will had placed on Little Joe's table. The black metal ink spill glistened in the light.

Unexpectedly, Will walked into the room, looking for Little Joe. "Oh my God! Jesus Christ! My art... It's ruined!" Will kept cursing under his breath, as he carefully picked up the page, and attempted to balance the ink spill – trying not to cause any further damage.

The situation was getting out of hand. I had to get Will out of his agony, or I'd be fucking fired! I walked over to him, and acted like I was seeing the ink spill for the first time.

"Oh, my God! ...Wait a minute." And as if I'd just discovered what it really was, I went to touch the ink.

Will shouted, "What the hell are you doing?"

"But Will, it's not real," I said, and calmly lifted it off the page.

Will held back his anger behind a crooked smile, "Very funny, very funny. Who did this?" There was complete silence. Will believed my surprise at the fake ink spill, and never even considered that I might have been the culprit. And so ended the ink-spill caper.

With my fifteen cent token, I got onto the subway that evening, traveling into my tunnel through time – entering as Sol, and exiting in The Bronx as Solly – transported back to who I was, from where I'm going. I didn't know what I wanted to do with my life. Right now, I was just going along, letting each day dictate to me.

I spent most of my weekends at The Metropolitan Museum of Art, drawing bits and pieces of paintings. Many of my nights, I'd spend sketching ideas of my own... ideas that went nowhere. My art felt empty. I didn't have a style of my own, or any kind of voice in my art. There were days though, when I got a sense of who, and what I was, but just when I almost grasped it, it escaped me.

Maybe, in order to find myself, I needed to be alone in a place of my own. But I felt guilty, and responsible for my mother now that Millie and Harold were gone. I had to help her out. Still, I wanted my own place. I was giving my mom most of my pay, and from what I had left, I'd put aside a little for my own apartment. It was going to be hard to tell her that I was going to leave. But telling her wasn't my real problem. Every time I had enough money for an apartment, some emergency would crop up, and I'd have to start saving all over again.

During my second summer at Will Eisner's, there was a terrible heat wave. On the newsreels, they showed people frying eggs on the sidewalks. It was over a hundred degrees out there, and after five days of it, everything was beginning to melt. The newspapers told us that hundreds of people died during that heat wave in the summer of 1955.

Sitting at my art table, stuck in the windowless corner of the room, I could hardly breathe – what a time for our ancient fans to break down. Pete had promised to get new ones, but never did.

Will, Pete, Joe Sapinsky, and the rest of the art crew, were trying to work in the unbearable heat, when I let go with a bloodcurdling scream.

"It's too damn hot... I can't take it anymore!"

My clothes were drenched with sweat, and as I stripped them off to a burlesque beat, the guys were stunned. They didn't know I was wearing my bathing suit underneath, and I worked the rest of the morning almost naked. The whole bullpen went bananas! Except for Pete. Every time someone had to pass my table, they'd crackup laughing. Even Will laughed. That afternoon we got three, brand new floor fans.

The longer I was on the board, the more confident I became, and the more I was accepted in the bullpen. Sometimes, I'd interrupt the tedious repetition of the day by acting out little bits from *Caesar's Hour*. The more laughs I got, the more chances I took with my clowning around. I enjoyed showing them my funny self, but my real self belonged to me.

Nothing is colder than a subway platform on a damp winter morning; it penetrates your skin, and seeps into your bones. My kneecaps were shaking out of control. When I forced my knees to stop, it would travel somewhere else – my teeth would start to chatter, then my stomach would shake. I couldn't wait for the train to come, so I could stand against the warm bodies in a crowded car.

Working in a Manhattan office, surrounded by my own art table and taboret, meant I was officially a professional. I tried to play the part by wearing a corduroy sport jacket, with leather elbow patches, which I bought at Bonds. And I learned how to smoke a pipe. I even asked the tobacco store to make a special blend of tobaccos, just for me. My romance with the pipe didn't last that long. Soon, I was back smoking two packs of cigarettes a day, as usual.

Joe Sapinsky had been teaching me how to spec type, using a Haberule type gauge, which had the pica width and point sizes for all type fonts, and could count the characters of each line. The math was too difficult for me, so I invented my own technique for spec-ing type. It was a little slower, but it worked.

Little Joe gave me my first spec job, a page of the *PS Mag*. This morning, I was expecting the results. The type came back from the type house, printed on a sheet of onionskin – a crisp, lightweight, transparent paper, used to cut and paste the type to fit the exact layout for the *PS* dummy.

I forgot to bring my lunch from home, and Dave, Coop, and Little Joe took me with them to The Bank. At one time, it had been a real bank, but Paddy O'Reilly converted it to a restaurant. The entrance was on the corner of 3rd Avenue and 30th Street, and it looked like a turn-of-the-century bank. Inside, Paddy kept the flavor of a bank, complete with teller's windows.

The guys introduced me to Lowenbrau beer, and The Bank's juicy, homemade hamburger sandwich, dripping with melted cheese. From then on, it was the only lunch I'd eat at The Bank.

Paddy was not tall; he had a stocky compact build, like one solid muscle. His nose had been broken, and his ears were swollen and puffy – the trademarks of an ex-boxer – but you'd never believe he'd been a boxer if you measured him by his soft-spoken manner.

His mother, Mrs. O'Reilly, made delicious homemade meals. Her Irish accent was so heavy I couldn't understand a word she said. I needed Paddy to interpret. Dave talked me into trying her apple pie a la mode. I'd never heard of pie with ice cream on top of it before. When Paddy served it, the pie was steaming hot; its crispy crust was baked into a caramelized glaze, and the scoop of vanilla ice cream was melting into its hot juices. I was transported into pie heaven.

On our way back from lunch, we bumped into Will in the hall. Coop questioned him, "I don't understand, like... why aren't you doing *The Spirit?*"

Thoughtfully, Will took his pipe from his mouth, "I might do it again... but not right now. I have many other new things I want to do first."

I'd been here over a year now, and I still didn't know much about Will Eisner, or *The Spirit* – or understand why everyone looked up to Will the way they did.

Lately, I'd been staying home, spending my evenings reading books: Orwell's, *1984,* and Huxley's, *Brave New World* woke me up, and I saw that both their storylines, totalitarian state vs. manipulated control, were happening right now, all around me. The books only left me with more questions, and thoughts I'd never dreamt of thinking before. I was hungry for more.

There were unimportant things, familiar objects of mine, scattered on the floor. My feelings were also on the floor. I poured plaster in between my feelings and things. The plaster spread out along the floor, touching my feelings and things. I rearranged them to look less haphazard, and more pleasing to my eyes. When the plaster dried, I realized I had made a map of my life – and it showed me which direction I should go.

I woke up, and couldn't remember the answer *the* dream was telling me.

Today, some of us were preparing for our move to a new office, on Park Avenue South. Will was showing Joe Sapinsky, and Bida Bidelman, his announcement card for the move. The card had a picture of a hairy caveman, wearing a loincloth, and sitting outside of his cave, chiseling on a stone tablet: the date and new address for Will Eisner Productions.

Bida Bidelman had recently replaced Wilma. She was bow-legged, with wiry hair tied back in a puffy bun. She always had crusty cold sores at the corners of her mouth, and spoke her words dully, with lazy lips, like the cartoon character, Droopy the Hound. I liked Bida. She was nice to me. She taught me how to proofread, and I enjoyed our sessions together. When she couldn't take the boredom and tension of her job as copywriter, she would take a break, and stand at the threshold of her office, watching the artists like we were animals in a zoo.

PARK AVENUE SOUTH

DURING THE WEEKEND, Will Eisner Productions moved from the little house on 32nd Street, to a bigger space in a newer building on Park Avenue South, at 29th Street. It was my first day at the new place, and waiting with me by the elevator, was a young man with dark coffee-colored skin.

In the elevator, I pressed the button for the 7th floor, and asked him, "What floor?"

"Seven, thanks."

We were the only ones on the elevator, and we tried to ignore each other. All the way to the 7th floor, I wondered who he was, and why he was going to Will Eisner's. He was a good looking guy, with intense energy, looking like he was going to take off at any second. His black hair was cropped close to his head, and his muscles were tightly wound around his thin frame, looking like an anatomy drawing.

Both of us got off the elevator, and stood in a vacant lobby facing an empty glass showcase. Neither of us knew which way to go. We glanced at each other, saw that lost look in each other's eyes, and began laughing. Behind us, the other elevator door opened, and Joe Sapinsky walked into the lobby with Coop – saved from looking like a fool.

Joe asked my laughing friend, "Can I help you?"

"My name is Freddy Vales. I'm supposed to see Mr. Pete Eisner."

"Just turn to your right, and you'll find the girl at the desk. She'll direct you."

"Thanks."

I followed Joe and Coop to the Art Department. It was three times larger than the one back at the little house. Our old place felt like wearing comfortable clothes; the new place was more like getting dressed up. We had moved practically all of the old furniture with us, but we didn't move everything... some people were left behind: Little Joe, Bob Gee, Janet, and little Sondra. Besides Freddy, there were new additions: Chuck Kramer, Alex Polinsky, Darwin Robbins, John Pomeroy, and Tom Thunderbird. With Little Joe gone, his assistant, Dave Madeline, took over as *PS Magazine* Art Director.

Pete called me into Will's office, "This is Freddy Vales. He's taking over the shipping clerk position. I need you to show him the ropes." Freddy got the same deal I did. He would start in the mailroom, with the promise of getting on the board. It was more of a problem for Freddy, because there were no empty art tables available for him to learn on. Eventually, he got his table when Coop was drafted. In the meantime, I offered him the use of my art table, and taught him production during lunch and coffee breaks. By the time Coop left, Freddy was already trained, and it was an easy transition for him, from clerk to artist.

It took us several weeks to complete the move to Park Avenue South, and it gave us a late start on the next *PS* issue. Will thought he could save some time by taking a group of us to Raritan Arsenal, to get a head start. Will, and his merry men – mechanical artists and illustrators: Dave, Coop, Joe, Chuck, Daniel and me – packed into Chuck's car, and off we went.

The men we dealt with at the Arsenal, were big-bellied, pompous characters with heavy Southern accents. I needed an interpreter to understand their instructions.

On our way back, Coop plagued Will with questions whenever he had the chance. "Will, what does art mean to you?"

Will answered, "Art is what you need it to be." That shut Coop up, and everyone laughed.

Besides joking around, we found time to have one of our open-ended discussions, and this time, I was right in the middle of it. Dave started it by reading a passing sign, "Your savings are safe with us."

"Yeah," he said, "I'm sure they are. Like investing it in Wall Street."

Seeing the truth in what he said, I added, "So, that means they're gambling with our money."

Joe interrupted me, "That's not true. Banks do not invest our money."

Ignoring what Joe said, I continued, "And they even get away with not paying their equal share of taxes."

"You're being very naïve," said Joe. Those things are just not done in our democratic country."

Dave and Chuck backed me up. But Joe still believed in the crap they fed him in the Naval Air Force. This was the first discussion I was part of, and I surprised myself by standing up for what I believed to be true. Will Eisner Productions had become my higher education.

A growing resentment was simmering inside of me, coming to a boil each time I realized I was smarter than that bullshit everyone had always handed me – my family, friends, teachers, and especially Harold. They made me believe I was nothing. Now, I realized it wasn't true, and I felt cheated and angry!

The next day, I got to work extra early, and while waiting for the elevator, I watched the old man who ran the concession stand in the lobby, uncover his tobacco, candy, and magazines. I was so fascinated by him that I let the elevator come and go.

"Young man, vhy are you watching me?"

"I see you every morning and evening, but I haven't really been seeing you, until now."

"And today I have caught your attention, huh? My name is Sam Goldman. Vhat is yours, young man?"

"Sol."

"Sol, dat's a good name. Short for Solomon, I take it?"

I nodded my head. I wanted to talk to him, but I didn't know what to say. So I said the first thing that came to me. "Were you in the war? My brothers were. One was in the Navy, and the other was in the Army." I felt like an idiot. What does he care about my brothers?

He was kind enough to answer, "No. I vasn't in da war." He looked past me, gazing at the wall, and mumbled, "I was in a concentration camp." Neither of us said anything. I didn't know how to react.

"What... what happened to you?"

"Vhat happened to me? It was beyond living in a nightmare... because you never wake up from it. From the very first day, I knew I was going to die. When I arrived at the camp, the damn Nazis chose about thirty of us, and put us up against a blank wall." The tears in his eyes drew me into his pain.

"They made us face da wall, about three feet away from the wall... had us lean our foreheads against da wall. That's all. Just lean our heads against a wall, holding the weight of our bodies. Then, they made a game wit us. They took bets on who vould stop leaning first.

"This sounds like nothing, just leaning our heads against da wall... but do that for hours, and the pain becomes unbearable. They had rules: if you moved, you were shot. They forced us to lean like that for a day and a half. Only three of us, out of thirty, survived. They killed twenty-seven of us, as if they were shooting targets in a penny arcade. Eventually, they got tired of the game, but they devised other games to bet on."

Mr. Goldman felt embarrassed and out of place, realizing what he had just revealed. He had talked about the hell he always kept to himself, and tried to forget. He made me promise never to repeat what he had told me, to anyone in the building. It was a difficult promise to keep, as I watched people passing him by, like he was just one of the building fixtures.

When I got upstairs, Pete called me to his second office: the men's room. With his left hand under his belt, "I'm happy to say, you're doing a fine job, and we feel you deserve a raise. Business wasn't as good as we expected this year, so the raise won't be that much, but there is an opening position as Dave's Assistant Art Director, for *PS Magazine*. If you want it, it's yours. Doing freelance is another opportunity to make extra money. The work will be mechanicals and color separations for *PS Magazine*. You'll be paid per page, and you'll see how fast it will add up."

It sounded like a good deal to me. Except there was one problem, I didn't have an art table, or the other equipment I needed to do the job at home, and I couldn't afford to buy them. So I volunteered to work for a few Saturdays, helping Chris reorganize Will's art files. Every Saturday, I would take a piece from an old art table that was stored in the back room, and gradually, I reassembled it at home. I had to fight my way onto the subway carrying the art board, or the legs, bumping into people, and apologizing my way into the car.

There was one last thing I needed to complete my freelance gear, an extra long, metal T-square. I thought Chris and I were alone in the office, so I freely carried it to the elevator with me. Then I smelled Will's pipe tobacco, and heard him walking toward the elevator. I panicked, and slid the T-square down the leg of my pants. It was almost as long as my leg, and looked kind of like I had a giant hard-on.

Will and I stood there, waiting for the elevator together, not saying a word to each other. The elevator doors opened, and Will got in, but I didn't move. I was frozen to the spot. The doors began to close, and Will held them for me. "Well? Are you getting on?"

He watched me stiff-legging myself onto the elevator, dragging my leg along like *The Mummy*. He was smiling, on the verge of laughing out loud, and we both tried to ignore one another. The elevator stopped at the lobby. Will stepped out of the elevator, turned to me, and said, "I hope your leg feels better."

In the new place, my art table overlooked Tom Thunderbird's. I didn't know if that was his real name, or not, but he wanted to be called, Thunderbird, and that's what we called him. He had a crew cut with shaved sides, looking like an ex-Marine, and held himself at attention at all times.

Thunderbird would work on the board, mumbling comic book sound effects. Chuck, who ghosted for Will, happened to be standing by Thunderbird's art table. Thunderbird stopped working on his mechanicals, and looked up at Chuck, "Do you realize that from nothing, there is something?"

In between his pronouncements, he'd make vibrating space sounds to emphasize his point, "Vhwo-oo-oo."

"What the hell are you talking about?"

"From nothing... is everything."

Confused, Chuck said, "But before, you said, "From nothing there is something.""

"Well, I had a change of mind."

"You're nuts!" Chuck walked away, and Thunderbird went back to his sound effects.

I knew Thunderbird was putting us on. This was his way of telling us that, unlike him, we were shortsighted, everyday people who think alike, without any imagination. He started in on me, speaking pointedly in my direction, trying to get a rise out of me.

"Mysterious ceremonies... dark and dangerous cults are threatening. They tell you not to think, to become one of their mindless followers..."

Everyone was working away in his own concentrated world, ignoring him. The silence was deafening. Suddenly, a deep, rumbling lion's roar burst from my art table, electrifying the bullpen. Across the room, Freddy's screaming peacock answered my growl. From both ends of the room, a menagerie of wild jungle sounds invaded the silence, surprising even Thunderbird. I think we scared the shit out of him, and after that, he didn't want to mess with Freddy and me.

Freddy and I worked great together. Our work was more like a game. He helped me put my ideas into practice, to accelerate production on the *PS Magazine*. Like when I asked Pete to build us a long worktable, which turned out to be a big help in speeding up the process of putting the *PS* dummies together. With these new ideas, we cut off hours, sometimes days, in producing the *Magazine*.

One morning, Freddy came back from a delivery, and sort of danced through the Art Department to a rock and roll tune coming from Thunderbird's radio. I think it was Fats Domino, singing, *I'm Walkin'*. He called what he was doing the *Jailhouse Shuffle*, and taught me how to do it. But when the white kids on *American Bandstand* got a hold of it, they called it, *The Stroll*. That lunchtime, Freddy gave me some skin, and we both Shuffled out to the elevator. Coop tried to ignore us all the way to The Bank.

Coop thought being blunt made him superior and liked to goad people. Out of nowhere, he confronted Freddy, "Like, you must feel great now that you're not persecuted anymore."

Freddy was stunned, "They're still hanging us, and you say there's no persecution?"

"It's like, a fact that society's attitudes have changed."

"Facts! If you want facts, come and live in Harlem."

Coop wouldn't quit, "Come on, Freddy, you know things have changed for the better."

Freddy was frustrated, "The only thing that's changed is time, but the bigotry is still there. You're not colored, and you'll never know who we are, or how we feel. Look... until you're black, you have nothing to say to me."

Coop continued, "Look, being Jewish... like, I suffered, too."

I couldn't take it any more, "Hey, Coop, you say you suffered because you're Jewish? Then, give me one example of how you've suffered... you personally."

Coop tried to reach back into his memory but came up with nothing. He just stood there, stuttering. I ended the discussion by imitating the end of a *Looney Toons* cartoon, when Porky Pig stutters, *"Ah... a... tha... tha...That's All, Folks!"*

Freddy and I got back to Will's in time to set up for the fifth game of the World Series, the NY Yankees vs. the Brooklyn Dodgers. We hung up a huge piece of white wrapping paper for a scoreboard, and hung it on the back wall overlooking the whole room. While we worked on the *PS* dummies, Freddy took care of the scoring for his beloved Dodgers, and I scored for my Yankees. Freddy and I teased each other mercilessly throughout the game. The only run scored in the whole game was Mickey Mantle's home run – my Yankees won!

It was Thursday morning, the day after the World Series ended, when John Pomeroy joined the asylum. He was hired to be Art Director for Will's new publication called, *Hoods Up*. It was based on the same principal as the *PS Magazine*, but instead of being for the military, it would use Will's cartoons to make repair instructions easy for gas station mechanics.

Pomeroy was uncool, like puffy, white bread. He was a tall, big-boned person, whose clothes and hair were meticulously kept. He took his work seriously, but he was a very kind, giving person to me. John was openly gay, at a time when being gay was almost impossible. He was not what The Bronx had conditioned me to believe. Knowing him woke me up to the big lie. I started to trust my own eyes and feelings, and stopped listening to the bullshit.

SLOW DEATH IN NEW JERSEY

BACK IN THE Bronx, I bumped into Melvin buying cigarettes at Jack's candy store. He cornered me to ask a favor, "Hey Solly, I got this possible date…"

"What do you mean, a possible date? Either you have one, or you don't."

"Her name is Alice. She'll only go out with me if I can get a date for her friend. How about it? Be a pal… I'm beggin' ya."

"What does she look like?"

"Who?"

"The girl, man, the girl. My date."

"I don't know. I never met her."

"I'm not going out with any girl you haven't even seen. I won't go out on a blind date."

"Yeah, I understand… but, you've got to do this for me."

"Man, you're really horny for this girl… how come? Is she really that hot?"

"Look, it's only going to be for a few hours. We're taking them to the Paramount. You probably won't even have to talk to her. And I'm paying for everything." Melvin must have been desperate to offer to pay for all of us. I couldn't pass this one up. I had nothing to lose.

Melvin and I met at Alice's house. The girls weren't ready, and we had to wait in the living room, with Alice's mother and father. I sat on the edge of the couch my whole body looking like it had already left the apartment. Thank God, they were more interested in watching the *Huntley-Brinkley News* report about the McCarthy Hearings. The girls came floating into the living room, and the parents practically shoved us out the door, so they could get back to their news.

"Have a good time. Don't come home too late."

This was the first time I dated a Jewish girl. Her name was Elaine, not too bad looking. All the way to the Paramount, I asked her about herself, which she enjoyed. When she told me how much she loved dancing I asked, "Are you studying ballet, or the Broadway kind of dancing?"

"No. I'm going to be a Rockette, at Radio City Music Hall."

"That's great. I guess that's going to take you a long time to do."

"No, in fact, I expect to be part of the chorus line by next year."

"How can you be so sure?"

"My uncle is a very important person at the Music Hall, and he got me a tryout. I passed with flying colors. And he promised me, in about a year, I'll be kicking my legs with the rest of the girls."

After the movie ended, we were in for a special treat – the great Louis Armstrong, live! The girls were bored throughout his performance. I call them girls, because that's what they were.

On the way to their apartment, if our conversation veered away from her, Elaine had nothing to say. She made me feel she'd rather not be with me. So, I stopped trying to make it easy, and started having fun with my ideas.

"Did you ever wonder if your past, is actually your past? I mean, maybe, what you believe is you, is not really you. And maybe the only reality is how everyone else sees you. I guess the only way you see yourself, is all subjective and possibly untrue. So does that mean that we're all alone and unable to communicate our true feelings?"

Elaine looked at me as if I was from another planet, the same look that the guys at Will's gave to Thunderbird.

I was getting the effect I wanted. "Is there such a thing as truth between people? And can anyone ever know the truth of who you are? Are the feelings of other people colored by their own pains and hang-ups, filtering through and becoming their reality?"

I was scaring the shit out of her, and she stopped walking with me. With each step, she pulled further away from me until there was a cavern between us.

When I got home, Mom hit me with stomach-wrenching news. We were moving to Hackensack, New Jersey! Boring... boring... boring, New Jersey. For me to live there would be a slow death. If there was a purgatory, New Jersey was it – a place where you went and were never heard from again.

I was pissed off because she never told me what her plans were. "Why didn't you talk to me first?"

"Vhy?"

"Because I'm not a kid anymore. I also bring money into this house, and I should have something to say."

"You're still my little boy, and I know what's best."

"God damn it, Mom! What the fuck is wrong with you?"

"Don't you curse at me, I don't want to hear such language."

That was a joke – after living with Harold, and all that filth spewing from his mouth, for all those years. But there was no talking to her. When I tried, she would just frustrate me, making dismissive baby sounds at me: "Do-du-du-du-du... do-du-du..."

"I'm not helping you move. You can do it all yourself."

My anger toward Mom lasted a long time. But then, the day before we were going to move, she thought of a way to pacify me. When Manny died, his brother David and The Whore took everything Manny owned. But there was something of value that David didn't know about – a brand new, never-used car, hidden away in a garage. Only Mom's lawyer knew about it. The lawyer sold the car for payment, and whatever was leftover was given to me, Manny's only son, and placed in a savings account under my name. I didn't know it existed.

"Now that you're twenty-one," Mom said, "the money is yours." She suggested I use it for a down payment on a car so I wouldn't have to feel trapped in New Jersey. I got excited about having my own car, but now, the small amount of my pay I could set aside for my own apartment would be going toward payments for a car. And when that was finally done, I'd have to start all over again to live my dream of having my own place.

Before I started looking for a car, I gave Millie half of Manny's money. She was his daughter, and I thought it was the right thing to do. Mom drove me around New Jersey, searching for a car, but after a month I began to lose faith that I'd ever find one. On our last try, just before we got on the Parkway for home, we passed by a secondhand car lot. There was a green car, right in front, that stood out from the others. Mom wanted to stop, but I had already given up and wanted to go home.

She pleaded with me, "Just this last time. Come on, bubbala, give it a try." Reluctantly, I gave in.

It was a 1955 Ford Fairlane 4-door, with a v8 engine. Everything about it was clean, from its interior, to its humming motor. Mom flirted with the car salesman, told him that this was my first car, and talked him down in price. We found a nearby mechanic, who looked the car over thoroughly, and took it for a test drive. When he got back, he smiled, "Lady, this is a sweet car. It's in excellent condition, and for the price, it's a steal."

Mom gave the salesman twenty-five dollars to hold the car until Monday when I could give him the full down payment. On Monday morning, after all the papers were signed, I got into my car. Her powerful engine reacted to my slightest touch on the gas pedal, and with a sudden surge, the car blasted out onto the Parkway. With my new car, I was in The Bronx so often that New Jersey didn't exist.

COMICS ARE AN
ART FORM

COOP WAS UNEXPECTEDLY drafted into the Army. Now, at last, Freddy had a table of his own. It happened so quickly that Pete had to use a temp, until he could find a full-time shipping clerk to replace Freddy. This time, he found someone who wasn't looking to get on the board. His name was Henry Lee.

Henry was tall and thin, about my age, and wore glasses that enlarged his intense, owl-like eyes. His tight, curly hair was perfectly cut, close to his head, looking like Ming in the *Flash Gordon* comic strip. Though pale-skinned, Henry was proud of being black. Everyday, he would wear a long gray smock. Freddy and I had never thought of wearing one, but Henry made wearing a smock look like a professional uniform that all shipping clerks were supposed to wear.

Henry was going to night school to continue his higher education. He loved all the sciences, but was particularly fascinated with the idea of mind over matter. He would experiment at home to prove the power of the mind, trying to move a feather across the surface of still water in a basin, using his thoughts alone. His experiments always excited my curiosity, and I would try them myself at home.

We were coming to the end of another issue of *PS Magazine,* and the pressure was on. But then, the Good Ol' Boys from the Arsenal came up with last minute corrections, and additional instructions for the Connie Rodd character. When the job got to a feverish point, I dropped everything, and screamed. I jumped up out of my chair, and with a make-believe electric drill, I pantomimed drilling holes into my chest, accompanied by drill sounds. After each hole I drilled, I blew away the imaginary drill dust. The guys laughed – the tension was gone!

I had to get away from my art table for a change of pace, and I walked back to the mailroom. "Hey, Henry, got a minute?" He looked up from sorting.

"I had this dream, where I'm looking out through a window screen at a fence across the street. When I move my head slowly from side to side, like this, white blurry lines appear on the fence, turning into different designs that really aren't there. I had the idea that maybe that's the way we see things in space. We're seeing it all through the window screen of our own perception."

"Yes, I see. So, what you're trying to say is, we are not seeing the way space really is. It's only an illusion. I thought so, too, but today, science is dissolving that window screen, and now we can look into the past... and someday, maybe, see the beginning of the universe itself."

Talking to Henry would get my juices going, "Henry, if that's true, that we can look into the past, then isn't it possible that we can also see where space is expanding beyond us? Then, we would be able to see what the future of space holds for us. I mean, when we look out into space, aren't we actually seeing the past, the present, and the future? But we don't realize we're seeing it. Maybe, it all exists at the same time."

Henry answered, "I don't think we can, because human beings can't see beyond our senses. They're the only tools we've got."

"Well, we can create artificial tools that can see it for us..."

"Yes, I agree..."

"Or, are we just creating a world that's really not there, like looking through my screen?"

Thunderbird was standing close by, overhearing the conversation between Henry and me. It was too tempting for him, and he blurted out, "The stars in the sky... are they distant from me, or am I distant from them?" He walked away, leaving us with his little gem.

Later that week, when I got to work, Thunderbird was gone. No one said anything about his disappearance. It was almost as if he was an alien, whose physical body was designed to resemble a human being, sent to Earth to spy on us. He had never really been here; he was only a hologram, wavering in and out of focus. Now, he had vanished as quickly as he had appeared. I knew it... I knew he wasn't real.

Alex Polinsky replaced Thunderbird at the board, a thin, timid kind of guy, whose suit jacket looked like he was still wearing the clothes hanger. His straight, blond hair slid across his forehead, and his eyes peered at me through clear-rimed glasses. He always had a lit cigarette dangling from his lips, which somehow never moved when he talked.

Alex pretty much kept to himself, and didn't join in our discussions. At the rare times when he did say something, he was very polite, and hesitated before each word. Alex believed that producing mechanicals required artistry. He wasn't fast, but his work was clean and precise, meticulously moving each piece of copy and art with a pair of tweezers. He was never satisfied, and would move, and re-move, the copy until it was exactly in place, correcting it within the width of a strand of blond hair.

Alex was standing at his table, smack up against Joe Sapinsky's glass office, rubber-cementing a page for a large block of copy and art. As always, his cigarette was hanging from his mouth.

I asked him, "Isn't it dangerous to work over a cemented page with a lit cigarette?"

"Why don't you mind your own business. I know what I'm doing!"

I walked away, and a few seconds later, a live ash flicked off his butt, and the whole job went up in flames. Alex flew out of his seat, and franticly tried to put out the fire with his hands. The page fell to the floor, and he did the Flamenco on it until it went out. I wanted to laugh, but I decided not to rub his nose in it, and left him alone, giving him plenty of space to save face.

As Assistant Art Director, one of my duties for *PS* was to call freelance artists when needed. I called on the artists I loved, Wally Wood, Bill Elder, and Wills' former ward, Jules Feiffer, who still did freelance for him. They didn't need the work; they just wanted to be near Will, so maybe some of his genius would rub off on them. Maybe this guy Will was someone special. My respect for him was growing, but as a boss, he remained more of a regular person to me, than some sort of idol.

Dave had decided to leave Will Eisner Productions, and Pete and Will were seriously thinking of me to replace him as Art Director, for the *PS Magazine*. Will took me to Raritan with him, as a test, to see how I'd handle myself under the pressure of working with the Good Ol' Boys.

Pennsylvania Station was crowded, as we cut through the shafts of streaming sunlight from the high cathedral windows. We made our way through throngs of commuters in the cavernous interior, yet it sounded almost empty, with hollow footsteps and distant voices. Every few minutes, announcements bounced off the walls, "*West Gate: Newark, New Brunswick, Raritan... and Points South.*"

Will and I were alone with each other for the first time for more than five minutes. We felt awkward, and uncomfortable, and didn't know what to say to each other. We found our seats, and sat there, feeling the tension between us. This wasn't going well. I had to say something, or possibly say goodbye to my promotion.

"Will, the other day, I was looking at your tearsheets of *The Spirit*. Each frame was like a scene from a movie."

I must have hit the right note. Will turned, and gave me his full attention. "Ah... the comics were the forerunners of motion pictures. Before films, artists were inventing new ways of seeing things. And I believe that motion pictures were inspired by their vision."

"A new way of seeing?"

"Yes! Here, I want you to make believe your eyes are a camera you can place anywhere on your body, for instance, on your shoe, or your shoulder. Now, see what the camera sees. And the lens doesn't have to be on your body; you can even imagine it attached to a dog, and see everything from the dog's point of view. It will give you new perspectives."

"I never thought of that."

"Try it, and believe me, it will shake up your imagination, and you'll see things in a different light."

It was quiet again, which gave me time to inhale what he told me. While Will was still in a talking mood, I figured it would be a good time to ask him other questions that had been on my mind.

"Will, not too long ago, I overheard you talking to Joe Sapinsky, about sequential art. I couldn't understand what you meant. What is sequential art?"

What a change in Will, he lit up like a light bulb. "Comics are an art form of communication. It's an arrangement of pictures, or images with words, used to narrate a story, or dramatize an idea. I call it sequential art. Do you understand?"

"Yes, I think so."

"Good. I want to give comic book art its due. It is *more* than just art. What I'm actually doing here, is telling a continuous story with art and words. A book is all words, but I can make it come alive with my art, with strong emotions, and mood." Almost to himself, he said, "Yes... That's what I'm doing."

By bouncing his ideas off of me, Will, in a small way, was letting me into his creative process. During that trip, I got very close to Will.

At the Arsenal, Will and I separated. He kept some of the big shots busy, while I worked with the Good Ol' Boys, making notations of their corrections, and a few more complex changes. Will took my marked-up dummy, and left for Washington, while I took the train back to Manhattan.

As the train rattled through the dark tunnel under the Hudson River, I looked out the window, watching the passing lights of another train, going in the opposite direction. The girders that held up the tunnel passed in quick succession, its syncopated tune putting me in a dreamy trance. I began to think about how I'd reached a point in my life where I couldn't go back to what I was, and didn't know where I was going.

THIS GUY'S NUTS!

I GOT TO work real early, and as I stepped off the elevator, I noticed for the first time, the empty showcase window facing our elevators. The little access door in the back wall of the case was slightly ajar. It was so inviting... why not? It was begging me to use it for greeting my fellow workers as they arrived. I went into the conference room behind the case, opened the little door, and stuck my head into the showcase.

Just then, a stranger got off the elevator, and stood there, trying to figure out which way to go. I kept my eyes closed, and didn't move a muscle. The stranger walked over to the glass case. I opened one eye, and he stepped back. He took a closer look, and I opened my other eye. My head said, "Good morning." Stunned, he jumped back, and broke out laughing. I recognized him as one of my favorite comic book artists, Bill Elder, from *Mad Comics*.

Elder had an appointment with Joe to pick up some freelance work for RCA. While he was waiting, Joe called me to his office to do a mechanical job for him. The top half of Joe's office walls were all glass, which always reminded me of an aquarium. So, when I opened the door to his office, I pretended that an overflow of gushing water was trying to escape. I fought the wall of water, forcing my way in, and acting like I was a fish, I used my arms like fins, floating, and swimming around his office in slow motion, gulping air.

Even though the whole bullpen was laughing, Joe tried to ignore me, and handed me the job like I was his lackey. I went into reverse, and got flushed out of his office by a sudden flood of water, pouring me out the doorway. Bill Elder was still waiting, and saw the whole bit. When Joe called him into his office, and Elder took a seat, I found myself a chair with wheels and rolled around outside Joe's office. All they could see was my head, looking like a very short man gliding around outside.

Will saw what was going on, and I think he was enjoying my prank, because he had a wide smile on his face as he passed by.

As Joe was talking to Elder, I popped into his office, flipped a quarter on his desk, and said, "Here, Joe, get me a pack of cigarettes."

Joe was pissed, "Don't mind him, he's our town idiot."

I answered, "What makes you say that?"

"You know, Sol, you're always talking with your hands. I bet you couldn't talk without moving them, even if your life depended on it."

Joe thought he put me in my place.

"Of course I can." I sat down, folded my arms, and began to talk with my legs, moving them in all different directions... even Joe laughed.

Bill Elder turned to Joe, and said, "This guy's nuts!" Coming from a way out, *Mad* artist, this was great praise.

All of the guys in the bullpen were talking about the news: the Russians beat us into space with Sputnik. We were the Superpower, always the first, and the best. It was devastating that a second-rate power, our cold war enemy, beat us into space.

Chuck yelled, "How the fuck is that possible?!"

Dan answered, "I'll tell you how that's possible. We've got to wake up. There are Russian spies walking our streets right now. Look out the window, and I guarantee you, one out of ten will be a Russian spy. They're already in our government. I'll bet they sabotaged our Space Program."

I was so involved in my own changing life that, sometimes, I couldn't see what was happening around me... and I could care less.

George asked Dan, "What kind of people would hurt their own country?"

"I'll tell you: Communists! They're the ones that are hurting our country, and it's a fact that most of them are Jews. Look at the Rosenberg's... they betrayed us, and gave our atomic bomb plans to Russia. The Jews are a separate race from the rest of us... and didn't they betray Jesus?"

George was exasperated, "This conversation is beginning to be about your own bullshit bigotry. In the first place, Jesus was a Jew. According to your way of thinking, wouldn't that make him a separate race from the rest of us? It's so easy to blame it on the Jews when anything goes wrong. It's the easy way – if you're too lazy to think. Why don't you wake up, asshole." George walked away.

When I heard what Dan said about Jews, it reminded me of Harold, and my anger began to stir. "That's not true!"

Dan countered, "Sorry, Sol, but it *is true.*" The discussion ended with Dan talking only to Dan, "Lucky we had men like McCarthy, and the House Un-American Activities hearings."

The exchange between Dan and George woke me up, and made me care. I paid more attention to the news after that, and what was happening around me. I discovered I.F. Stone; his investigative reporting taught me to read between the lines, and separate facts from propaganda. During those years at Will's, I could feel the beginnings of change in the air. The biggest change of all was the non-violent, Civil Rights Movement, stirring the simmering pot of injustice in the country. The Communist threat, which had been fueled by Senator Joseph McCarthy's hearings, loomed over everything.

While waiting for a type delivery that afternoon, I wandered into the mailroom. I picked up a metal washer from the floor, and as soon as I touched it I was inspired. I felt like I was back in my room in The Bronx, devising a new toy. I attached two rubber bands, one on each side of the washer, cut a piece of wire clothes hanger, bent each end to hold the rubber bands, and wound them up tightly. I slid my invention under my thigh, and when I lifted my leg slightly, the washer repeatedly hit the seat of the chair, making a resounding fart sound. Holy shit, the damn thing worked!

Freddy looked around to see who laid one. George reacted, "Oh my God, get him out of here." And Alex said, "That's disgusting."

"Wait... wait a minute guys, I laughed, it's all right." I showed them my fart gadget, and they broke up laughing.

There was a pretty, young temp working in the office, who thought she was a gift to the world. I had tried to be nice to her, but she treated me like dirt. With perfect timing, she came into the Art Department with my type delivery, acting like she was my boss. As she was leaning over my desk, giving me orders, I secretly wound up the washer. I lifted my leg slightly, and released an enormous, and very realistic fart. The guys laughed, and she ran away into the front office, never to be seen in the bullpen again. This thing had great possibilities.

Freddy and I traveled home together on the same subway, and that day, the train was so jam-packed we could hardly lift our arms. I never wore a straight jacket, but this was what it must feel like. Nevertheless, I was able to maneuver my arms enough to wind up my washer. Then, I held it against a book I was carrying, and let it go. A juicy fart sound cut through the crowd, and in seconds, Freddy and I had part of the car all to ourselves. I did it again, and we even got seats.

Joe had this habit – when he talked to you, he would snap his fingers, and hit his fist into the palm of his other hand. He would do this repeatedly. It was damn annoying, and he knew it. But he kept on doing it to me.

Every so often, I'd bring in some hardboiled eggs to work. Joe loved to mooch an egg off me, and he'd always crack the eggshell on his head, thinking it was really cool. The next day, I brought in a few raw eggs instead. As usual, Joe took an egg from me, and cracked it on his head. The raw egg dripped down his face like snot, pulling away from his chin, and looking not so cool. From then on, my eggs were all mine.

Late that morning, while cementing together the *PS* dummy spreads, I accidently knocked over a large, metal pot of rubber cement, spilling it all over my pants. The cement soaked through, and the slimy gook clung to both my legs. I walked to the men's room with my legs wide apart, pulling at my pants to keep them from being permanently glued to my skin. They were completely ruined, and I had to surgically remove them. How was I going to get home?

John Pomeroy to the rescue! He came into the men's room with a pair of pants. "Sol, I found these extra pants in my taboret. They might be a little too big, but I think you can get away with it."

Now, Pomeroy was a big guy. On me, his pants looked like I was wearing a circus tent. You could put Freddy, Henry, and me into those pants, and still have some room to spare. I was walking around, holding Pomeroy's pants up with one hand, and trying to work with the other. I found some rope in the mailroom, and used it to keep my pants from falling down, but it made me look like a balloon figure in the Macy's Thanksgiving Day Parade.

Meanwhile, the rubber cement had dried on my legs. I tried taking it off with a rubber cement pick up, but all that did, was pull the hair on my legs... very painful. I had to resort to dissolving it using thinner, which irritated my skin until it was raw.

Everyone was out to lunch. I stayed in eating my homemade sandwiches, when Will came in and apologized for interrupting my lunch. He took one look at me, and started to laugh, "What the hell are you wearing?"

"I had an accident. I spilled a pot of rubber cement on myself, and I'm wearing Pomeroy's pants."

"And what is he wearing?"

"No, no, no... He had an extra pair in his taboret."

"Sol... you're really weird."

Will asked me to do him a favor, a small mechanical job. I worked on it, while he kept me entertained with a few of his stories.

"Years ago, these two young men came to me, to publish this way out character they called, *Superman*. I listened to their story about an alien baby from outer space, who had been saved from the destruction of his home planet. The baby landed on Earth with super powers. With that story, and the terrible art they showed me, I couldn't see them getting anywhere with it... and I told them so. I also told them to keep trying, and maybe, they'd hit on something worthwhile for publishing. And I wished them luck.

"Well, I sure screwed up on that one. But then again, maybe I'm better off for that mistake. I did become more open-minded because of it. After all, we are the sum of all the people we meet." Very often, Will ended one of his stories with such words of wisdom.

The rest of the day, I was working at a feverish pace, and to relieve the tension I did a little skit for the guys, still floating in Pomeroy's pants. "Here's what actually happened, when Frankenstein met the Wolf Man." I imitated the Wolf Man going down on Frankenstein, growling, and ferociously ripping at Frankenstein's cock. Instantly, I changed into Frankenstein, rolling my eyes, and groaning in ecstasy. The guys in the bullpen joined in the fun. They were all talented professionals in the arts – Broadway singers, dancers, a few actors, a classical violinist – and I loved that they enjoyed my antics.

There was a new girl in the office, Rita, who worked as an assistant to Will's secretary. She had wavy, short, blond hair, and when she talked, she ran her hands through it, lifting it from her forehead. When she looked at me, all I could see were her brown, almond-shaped eyes. Rita was a sexy girl, who walked like she didn't care where she was going, and took her time getting there.

On her first day at Will's, Rita watched Freddy and me build an intricate system of empty cardboard rolls, each four feet in length. We didn't know what the fuck we were doing, but we connected them into each other, cut open random holes, and joined them at odd angles. Our maze of tubes, held up with string, ran overhead around the entire bullpen, and back to us. We didn't know what the hell we were going to use it for, but it was pleasing to the eyes. It reminded me of one of Rube Goldberg's weird gadgets.

Then I had a brainstorm – Freddy and I would blow cigarette smoke through one end of the contraption, and see where it went. Nothing happened. I blew smoke until I almost passed out. The smoke was trapped somewhere inside, so we grabbed one of the floor fans, and faced it into the tube. After a couple of minutes, the smoke belched out in smoke rings across the room.

Freddy and I celebrated with the song *The Music Goes 'Round and 'Round*. But after that, we had no further use for it and took down all the tubes.

Rita came over to me after my questionable stroke of genius, and asked me where there was a good place to eat lunch. Freddy and I were going to The Bank, and I asked her if she'd like to join us. She lunched with us at The Bank for two weeks straight, and everyday, *The Lullaby of Birdland* happened to be playing. That song always reminds me of Rita. When we got back from one of our lunches, the office was empty, and Rita followed me into the backroom. I put my arms around her, and kissed her.

There were times when I was a little bit too much for Will. At the exact moment Rita and I kissed, he was walking by. Will didn't know if he wanted to smile, or be angry. He hit his forehead with the palm of his hand, "Jesus, Sol!"

Not too long after that encounter with Will, Pete called me into his second office, the men's room, where he dealt with important issues. When Pete put both hands behind his belt to support his belly, I knew it was serious.

"Sol… there is no kissing on the job; we can't have that. This is not your private playground. You don't shit where you eat. I know you know better. You're smart, you're a good young man, and I know I'll only have to warn you this once." Pete had me when he said I was smart. That one word from him made all the difference.

Pomeroy, and Randy Lithgoe, a sculptor who worked on the board at Will's, were part of the beginnings of SoHo. They found an empty factory building in the Cast Iron District, and took over a whole floor – a huge, unused space – for practically nothing. They broke it up into two lofts, and every day, I overheard them comparing notes on their progress, trading information on where to buy bits and pieces for their new homes. They even learned from each other, how to modernize the plumbing and electrical systems.

I wanted to be a part of it, but I didn't know how to begin. My ignorance of the complex decisions involved, and the possibility that I'd have to do it all myself, overwhelmed me. I couldn't ask for help, because I was afraid people would lose respect for me. I was lost.

Pomeroy invited Freddy and me to see his finished project. My mouth watered for what I saw. It reminded me of the Park Avenue penthouses where Walter and I had put up awnings. Pomeroy was a great guy. He introduced Freddy and me to Broadway musicals, and had a huge collection of record albums, from shows like *Music Man*, *West Side Story*, and *South Pacific*. The way he described the new exhibits at the Metropolitan Museum of Art, and the gallery openings he attended, made me see art in a whole new way.

Pomeroy always had lots of artwork around him, creating his own private gallery. His parties were like the ones I'd seen in the movies: sophisticated, with lots of talk, and cocktails. I felt out of place, but after a couple of drinks, I was open to listening to the odd opinions and attitudes of his guests. They liked me because I was a great audience. I didn't say anything, and listened attentively to everything they said. I was fascinated at first, but after awhile, it got boring, and everyone began to sound alike.

Freddy and I never cared that Pomeroy was gay. He treated us with respect, and after he left Will Eisner's, he became more of a friend to me, than a co-worker.

Pete was walking by my art table, "Pete! Can I talk to you? It's about a raise."

"Not here... follow me." He took me to the men's room, "Okay. What's the problem?"

"I think I deserve a raise."

Pete felt cornered, "And why do you think you deserve a raise?"

"I've reached the point where I'm doing every phase of producing the *PS Magazine,* and more. I layout the entire book, type-spec it, put together the dummies, do the paste-ups and mechanicals, plus the color separations. I also spec the four-color continuity, and run the stat machine... and do a little proofreading on the side. When the *PS* issue is completed, I work for Pomeroy on *Hoods Up,* and do odd jobs for Joe, for RCA."

"Hmmm, I see... Yes, you've come a long way. You certainly do deserve a raise. But it can't be much, you understand, this wasn't a very good year for us."

"But Pete, I've even started learning to run the offset machine."

"Yes, I see... hmmm... You do know that Dave Madeline will soon be leaving us, and we will need a new Art Director to replace him. I think you deserve that chance."

Instead of a full raise, they finally made the decision to promote me to Art Director for *PS Magazine.* From sweeping floors to Art Director, that was worth more to me than a raise. Me, an Art Director!

SHE'S NOT THE
GIRL FOR YOU

MY MOM'S DEEP voice reached into my sleep, and pulled me out of my dreams. She was talking into the phone, "I'm not a Mister... stop calling me Mister. Vhat's wrong vit you?" I walked quietly from my room so I wouldn't wake Miklos, who was sharing my room.

When I got to the kitchen, I teased Mom, "Good morning, Mister."

Mom punched me on the arm for making her laugh. "You're such a scundreck," she said affectionately.

Ronnie was already up, and at the kitchen table waiting for breakfast. Miklos walked into the kitchen. He was a young, good-looking version of Bela Lugosi, with a thick Hungarian accent, and about as tall as my brother Harry, six-foot, two. He walked with an innocent, straightforward movement to his body, like many Eastern European immigrants at that time. Mom rented out half of my room to him. I didn't know where she found these out-of-the-ordinary people, but somehow she did.

Miklos was a Hungarian freedom fighter who had run for his life from the Russians. He escaped at the Hungarian border by bribing the guard to look the other way, while he crossed over into Austria.

Now, Miklos was desperate, without much money in a far-away, strange country, trying to communicate in a language he couldn't understand. He and I hit it off right away – we spent many hours discussing in pantomime. Miklos was a quick learner. Each day, during our talks, he'd learn a new word.

I asked him, "What were the girls like in Hungary? Were they easy to have sex with?" He didn't understand me, so I punched my fist repeatedly into my open hand, saying, "Fuck, fuck."

Miklos got it right away, "Ah... ah yes, lots fuck."

Every weekend, Miklos and I would go into Manhattan. Just walking the streets, the girls would gravitate to him because of his good looks and foreign accent. One Saturday, he was excited to share his discovery with me, and took me to a Hungarian restaurant he found, on the Upper East Side. We sat in an open-air garden in the back, filled with tables. From the street, you'd never know a place like this existed in Manhattan. Miklos spoke Hungarian when he ordered for us. When the waiter found out he was a freedom fighter, we were treated like royalty, and given a bottle of wine out of respect for Miklos. The food tasted deliciously different.

One time, he brought home a friend from Hungary, a Gypsy. Mom enjoyed the visit, but after his friend left, she rushed around checking everything in the house. I got angry with her, but Miklos said, "Molly is right, Gypsies take things."

Satisfied that nothing was missing, she took off with Ronnie to visit Harry and Sylvia, while Miklos cooked one of his favorite Hungarian meals for me. Using a regular saucepan, he began by alternating layers of cooked potatoes with slices of hard-boiled eggs, seasoning it with salt and paprika, and lots of garlic. He was right, the blend of flavors was absolutely wonderful.

We sat at the kitchen table, and talked into the night. I asked him questions like, "Now that you've been here for awhile, how do you like living in America?"

Miklos used his hands to sculpt out the meaning of the new English words he had learned, "Not perfect, but good."

"Isn't it better than Communism?"

"Communism look good in book... not work in practice."

There was always a big turnover of workers in the front office at Will's, and this early summer was no different. A new temp appeared who had her hungry eyes on me. Little did I know that she had eyes on everyone who happened to be wearing pants. Her name was Myra Finkel. She was dark-eyed pretty, but nothing special. Her thick, black hair fell to her shoulders, which weren't too far off the floor... yes, she was very short.

Everywhere I went, Myra was there, and when we were alone, all she wanted to do was make out. She was a college student who came from an upper middle class family, and I felt flattered that she wanted me. Never did I have to coax her into having sex. All I had to do was look at her, and she'd drop her drawers. As a matter of fact, wherever there was a bed, she wouldn't miss the opportunity. She knew I was using her, the same way she was using me. Yet, she would try to manipulate me, crying to make me feel guilty for using her. But like a jerk, I felt sorry for her.

Myra met my family – Mom, Ronnie, Harry and Sylvia, and their daughter Caryn – at a public swimming pool in New Jersey. She wasn't an inhibited person. In the pool, she was all over me, rubbing against me, trying to fuck me through our bathing suits – right in front of my family.

They got this crazy idea that I was serious about her. Myra's own mother thought we were thinking of getting married. Where the fuck did they get that idea? I never gave marriage a thought. This was getting out of control!

Miklos warned me not to marry her. He told me she tried to come on to him, but I wouldn't believe him. I felt like my manhood was being challenged.

Then Mom warned me not to marry her, "Sollinue, she's not the girl for you."

Even Myra's mother tried to talk me out of it. She told me Myra was a compulsive liar, and cried crocodile tears to get what she wanted. She warned me not to believe anything Myra said. It was clear to me that Mrs. Finkel thought I was a nice boy, but below her daughter's class.

The more everyone said to stay away from her, the more determined I got. I'd show them I could make my own decisions. I was about to make the biggest mistake of my life, and with my eyes wide open I just let it happen. I fucked up. And suddenly, I was married. The truth is, I was an idiot.

Out of stubbornness, I stopped seeing Miklos. Like a fool, I got angry with him for trying to break up Myra and me. It was a sad time. I missed our friendship, and the great discussions we had. I still miss Miklos... if I had only listened to him.

When Myra and I got married, I stopped giving Mom my paycheck, and because of that, she took Harold back. My visits to The Bronx trickled down to a couple of days a month, and eventually disappeared.

HAVE BOARD
WILL TRAVEL

JOE SPOTTED ME walking into the office, "Sol! Thank God, you're here. We've got an unexpected problem. The Boys from Washington came up with a last minute correction."

I looked at Will, "I think these guys enjoy creating problems."

Joe interrupted, "We have no time for why they're doing it, Will's plane leaves in a couple of hours."

Will was frustrated, "Will you guys stop yapping, and get moving?"

I got myself together, but I seriously didn't think I could get the job done in time for Will's plane.

A short time later, Will rushed in with his finished sketches, "Here are the two spreads that have to change. If I need copies, I can get them in Washington."

"If I take the time to put it together for you here, you'll never make your plane."

Pete popped in, "I've got the cab waiting downstairs."

As Will was walking out, he looked back at me, "Oh, I forgot to tell you, you're going with me to the airport. And you're going to put the spreads together in the cab. Hurry, and get what you need! I'll be waiting for you in the cab." I went on automatic overdrive.

Freddy walked in, "Freddy, give me a hand. While I'm making stats, could you get an art board, razor blades, cement, and a T-square for me? Bring them down to Will's cab."

"What's happening?"

"Will's in a real rush. He has to catch a plane."

"Okay, it's done."

On our way to the airport, Will kept me company, talking to me like a kid brother, "Sol, you're an artist... how come I've never seen any of your work?"

"I'm not really that good. You have a different way of seeing things, but everything I do has been done already."

"Sol, nothing is new, it's always there, with or without you. You just have to open your eyes."

"Is that true? Nothing is new?"

Will thought about it, "No. I take that back, that's not completely true. Sol, here's how I see it. If you can take something simple that has been done a thousand times before, you can create with your own individual imagination – because no two minds are alike – something excitingly different, that has never been done before."

I had to race through the paste-ups in between bumps, and listen to Will at the same time. I was totally focused on re-doing the layouts with the new corrections: cutting, and rearranging the new copy, so it would fit around the art. Each time the cab stopped at a traffic light, I took advantage of the temporary lack of movement.

Just as we pulled up to the terminal, at Idlewild Airport, I finished the dummies. I don't know how I did it. Will grabbed the package, paid the cabby, and gave me money for my return trip. He slammed the door shut, and his voice trailed off... "Great job! See you in a couple of days."

Back at Will's, I walked into a discussion in the bullpen. Darwin was talking, "Having sex for a man is his primal right, his primal urge to get back into the womb. And the woman's primal urge is to have a man in her."

"What a crock of shit." I held up the legs of my pants, as I tiptoed past Darwin's desk, making sounds like I was squishing through a pile of shit.

Chuck opened the top drawer of my taboret, and mooched a cigarette. He was a nice guy, and easy to get along with, but he had a habit of bumming cigarettes from me. This time I was ready for him. He lit my cigarette at his art table, in the back of the room. "Ka-boom!" Strips of torn cigarette dangled from his mouth, and his face was white as ash. That was the last time he bummed a cigarette from me.

Chuck Kramer ghosted for Will. Some of the *PS* covers may have had Will's signature, but they were drawn, and inked by Chuck, who was a brilliant comic book artist himself. Chuck had graduated from SIA two years ahead of me. He looked like one of the kids in the neighborhood, and moved like he was unsure of himself. He wanted to be a part of the craziness at Will's, but didn't know how. But that crazy freedom was already in him, and erupted on the pages he drew.

With everyone so deep in the conversation, Dan didn't think anyone would notice him looking through his copy of *Playboy*. He caught me watching him, and embarrassed, he cleared his throat, "I only buy *Playboy* because it has interesting articles. And I use the pictures for anatomy studies."

All the guys heard him, and shouted with one voice, "Yeah, right."

The talk continued all afternoon, jumping from one subject to another.

Henry Lee said, "What are you saying, that there is nothing faster than the speed of light? I believe there is something faster – the imagination."

Darwin, who was so average that if he didn't make a sound, you wouldn't know he was there, answered, "Wait a minute, wait a minute... the imagination has no substance; it's not real."

Henry countered, "So, you're saying, our thoughts aren't real?"

Darwin continued the back and forth, "Come on, you know what I mean."

"No. What do you mean?"

"If you can't touch it, it's not real. It's ethereal. A wisp of thought is gone as fast as it came."

I joined in, "Didn't Einstein say that everything in nature is made of energy?"

Darwin looked puzzled, "Yeah? So?"

I continued, "So, when you use your imagination, you're creating energy that wasn't there before. It becomes something real, with substance. Einstein also said that energy never dies."

Darwin couldn't see the connection, "What has that got to do with the speed of light?"

I answered, "If energy is real and tangible, wouldn't it be possible for us to use our imaginations to penetrate time and space?"

"Sol... you're so full of shit, and you know it."

This interested George, "If that's true, with our imagination, we can travel back to the beginning of the universe."

Dan lifted his head up from his *Playboy*, "By using your imagination? Please!"

George answered, "I'm only asking if it's possible to penetrate time and space..."

"Come on, George, you're talking through your hat. Let's get real."

Joe's door was open, "Dan, let's accept it as being true, and have some fun with it."

Dan backed down. He was intimidated by Joe, and didn't want to tangle with him.

Then John Pomeroy got into the conversation, "Okay, let's accept it as true. That means we could see the Big Bang, and the beginning of our universe, just by using our imagination."

Pomeroy's mention of the Big Bang got me going. "Maybe there wasn't a Big Bang, but it was more like when you blow into a new balloon. You have to build up enough pressure inside it, for the balloon to finally expand. That sudden expansion of energy, with so much power... it could look like an explosion."

Freddy asked, "Where does the energy come from?"

"I've read that scientists have seen stars older than our Universe," said George.

Chuck stopped inking the cover art for *PS*, "Isn't it possible that they might be seeing stars from another Universe that's older than ours? Maybe, through some kind of portal that connects us?"

Darwin was frustrated, "But what has that got to do with the building up of energy, and where it comes from?"

I jumped in, "It's very possible there are many Universes, and they are separated by plasma membranes, and where they touch, if one Universe resonates with the other, they could easily exchange energies."

Freddy asked again, "I'd like to know, where did all this energy come from?"

Pomeroy took up the challenge, "What if there were two dimensions of nothing, an anti-nothing and a positive nothing, and just like matter and anti-matter, they could not exist in the same space. But whenever their edges touched, they created movement, and this movement pushed them away from each other, creating friction and light. And that could be the birth of energy."

Darwin said, "So, you're trying to tell me that you make up these assumptions, this complete guesswork, out of thin air, and just because you thought of them, that makes it a reality?"

I shot back, "Yes, before we thought of it, it didn't exist, did it? Now, it does."

Then, I decided to give Darwin the Thunderbird treatment: "Everything exists, but we can't see it until we invent a new point of reference, a form we can relate to. This way, we can make sense out of what we saw as chaos. That's what we're doing here, inventing something our senses can relate to."

Wait a minute... what I said made sense. I wasn't doing too good a job at imitating Thunderbird. That was enough for me. I was discussioned-out, and got back to work.

RECURRING THEME

BACK ON THE home front, Myra and I had a nice, sunny apartment on Beech Street, in Hackensack, New Jersey. When Larry was born, I named him after one of my favorite movie characters, Laurence Talbot *The Wolf Man*. My little Laurence was unbelievably cute, with blond, cherub curls, and huge, open blue eyes that loved me back. I would hold him in my lap by an open window for hours, imitating the sounds of cars, planes, and animals... whatever we saw and heard. I took care of him whenever Myra was away. I wanted him to like himself, and never have to go through the hell I grew up with.

But Myra demanded every ounce of my attention, and we fought over everything. We were from two different universes, matter and anti-matter, and each repelled the other. Even though we seemed to get by on my salary, it wasn't enough for Myra. She insisted that I find a job that paid more money. She was constantly at me about it, for weeks. The clincher came when she said, "You've got to face reality, Sol." I had faced reality all my life. Now, because of Larry, I thought again. Maybe she was right?

I gave Pete my notice.

As I walked to Will Eisner Productions, I passed the familiar landmarks for the last time. I felt numb, and tried to ignore the fact that this was my last day. I couldn't face Will to say goodbye... I felt like I was betraying him, and myself. Working for Will, and what I was able to accomplish there, showed me who I really was. I didn't know how to thank him.

My art table was covered in black paper, and a lonely lily lay in sharp contrast against the black. It was the work of Freddy Vales, who would replace me as Art Director of *PS Magazine*. Freddy was the only person who thought like me. If ever I could say I had a real friend, it would be Freddy. But after I left, I never saw him again.

There's a recurring theme here.

I never forgave myself for leaving Will's... another big decision I fucked up. The truth was, they could get along without me, but I couldn't get along without them. After Will's, every job I had was deadly, and piece-by-piece, started tearing away all the positive feelings I had built up for myself at Will's. I went from place to place, and ended up freelancing for my *PS* buddies, Pomeroy, Dave, and Joe, at their new jobs. But I was ashamed to go back to Will's.

I came home after work one night, and Myra was gone – taking my son with her. Myra was who she was, and I should have known better. Losing Larry devastated me. I was unconscious of the weeks that followed. My mom rescued me, and helped me break my lease. Being with her then, reminded me of how she always found the humor in hard times. Laughing with her woke me out of my stupor. She took charge and moved me back in with her, into my kid brother, Ronnie's room.

Harold was there to greet me. Right away, he started in on me, and ran at me screaming, "You Jew bastard!" He stopped just a few inches from my face. I wasn't that little, scrawny kid anymore. I stared back into his eyes, eyes filled with hate for me, and as he was cursing me, I bobbled my head derisively from side to side, shouting back into his face, "Blah! Blah! Blah! Blah!"

"I'll wipe up the floor with you!" And just like in the good old days, Harold punched me right on my jaw.

The old fuck was still pretty strong. I hauled off with a punch, knocking his ass clear across the room. He fell to the floor like a side of beef. The next thing he knew, I was on top of him. I hated him so much, instead of punching him, I pinched, and pulled at that hateful face, trying to tear away the nightmare that haunted me as a boy.

Vengeance wasn't as satisfying as I thought it would be. I got up, and called the cops. When they arrived, I imitated Harold and calmly greeted them like a perfect gentleman, leaning against the door jam with my arms folded. Quietly, I recounted how Harold had violently attacked me, for no reason at all.

Harold became enraged. He lost all control, and charged at me like a maniac. He was so strong it took both cops to hold him back. The calmer I became, the more violent he got.

I smiled, and pointed toward Harold, "See what I mean? The man is crazy." The cops cuffed him, and off to jail they went.

Now, *that* was satisfying.

During that time, I needed a complete change in my life and took up acting classes. At Actor's Mobile Theater, uptown, near where Lincoln Center was being built, we learned The Method. It took us beyond learning acting, and was more like therapy. The acting classes inspired me to open up and express myself through other creative arts – like sculpture.

When I finally got my first sculpture bronzed, I showed it to Pomeroy. He loved it, and asked if he could keep it for me in his loft. It found a home there. He held a cocktail party reception to introduce the new pieces he had collected, singling out my sculpture for acknowledgment by his professional, art-world friends.

A week later, John Pomeroy was murdered. The news from Joe came as a shock. John had been shot in Soho, the victim of a lover's triangle. To this day, I deeply regret I didn't go to his funeral and show him the respect he had always shown to me. I'd seen enough dead people in my life and I couldn't bear to face another. My life was going down the toilet, and now that Pomeroy was gone, I had no one to turn to. But I felt a strength inside me, and I was determined to turn my life around.

Even when I wasn't freelancing for Joe, I would drop into his office at *Women's Day Magazine*. He was teaching at School of Visual Arts and told me Will was also teaching there. I made a surprise visit to Will's class, and afterwards we went to lunch. We opened up our old friendship again, and I saw him often after that.

On one of my lunches with Will, he told me about trying to get his sequential art published as a book. "When the publisher asked me what kind of format my book is, I was stumped. I knew if I presented it as a comic book, he'd laugh me out of his office. I had to think quickly, and off the top of my head I came up with, "It's a Graphic Novel." That gave it the sound of respectability, and he loved the idea!"

I went with him to his afternoon class that day, and he noticed I had my portfolio with me, "Is that your work?"

"Yeah."

"You mean I'm finally getting to see your work?"

He looked through the photos of my sculptures, "I didn't know you're a sculptor." With excited short breaths, he pointed to each photo, "That's it! That's it! Wonderful! Your work is brilliant! That's what I've been trying to say... it's a marriage with fine art. Your sculptures say it all... this is saying it all."

I never saw him so excited. I didn't quite understand what he meant, but he made me feel good about myself again. This was the greatest compliment of my life.

Will and I lost touch when he moved to Florida. After he passed away, I took a walk to where it all began. There it was, still standing, the Little House on 32nd Street. Seeing the old building where I first met Will was like coming home again.

EPILOGUE

ALTHOUGH MY STORY of The Bronx ends with me leaving Will Eisner's, my time there had changed me forever.

Then I met Sharon, and learned what love was all about. She came for a job as fashion illustrator at a buying office on 31st Street where I was Art Director. I made her laugh so much she couldn't hold her brush steady. My plan for our first date was to see the premier of *Dr. No*. We went out for pizza and beer first, but got so engrossed in our conversation, and each other, that we forgot all about the movie. We haven't stopped talking since.

I went on to a career as a sculptor, showing at galleries and museums, and garnering commissions. For fun I created goofy little characters, which caught Jim Henson's eye. He really got into them and asked for the stories behind each one. That got me into his Studio doing freelance character development. Later on, I started writing sci-fi screenplays inspired by the movies I grew up with, and for a time I worked with producer Samuel Bronston.

But even after I stopped going back to The Bronx, its people and places remain with me wherever I am, and color everything I do. The Bronx is the blood that flows through my veins.

Author, Sol Rothman, was born in the South Bronx in 1936, to Russian-Bessarabian immigrants. After attending School of Industrial Arts, he went on to become an Art Director for the comic book legend, Will Eisner, where he discovered his comic-cosmic perspective. He has since created acclaimed sculptures, paintings, and drawings; co-founded an alternative school-without-walls; developed characters for Jim Henson; authored TV pilots and screenplays; and taken an active role in eco-political causes. Still a film buff, he resides in NJ with his wife of 56 years, Sharon, and has recently completed a series of abstract drawings, *Out of Chaos*.

"The cover title, SURVIVAL OF SPECIES, is filled with family photos of the real, main characters in my life, so you can sort them out as you read. Please check out my art archive at www.solrothman.com, and my book blog, www.solrothman.com/book-blog, where you're invited to leave an enthusiastic review!" – Sol

CPSIA information can be obtained
at www.ICGtesting.com
Printed in the USA
BVHW041139021020
590172BV00011B/209